Navigating Digital Communication and Challenges for Organizations

José Gabriel Andrade
University of Minho, Portugal

Teresa Ruão
University of Minho, Portugal

IGI Global
PUBLISHER of TIMELY KNOWLEDGE

A volume in the Advances in E-Business Research (AEBR) Book Series

Published in the United States of America by
IGI Global
Business Science Reference (an imprint of IGI Global)
701 E. Chocolate Avenue
Hershey PA, USA 17033
Tel: 717-533-8845
Fax: 717-533-8661
E-mail: cust@igi-global.com
Web site: http://www.igi-global.com

Library of Congress Cataloging-in-Publication Data

Names: Andrade, Jose Gabriel, 1983- editor. | Ruao, Teresa, 1969- editor.
Title: Navigating digital communication and challenges for organizations / Jose Gabriel Andrade, and Teresa Ruao, editors.
Description: Hershey, PA : Business Science Reference, [2022] | Includes bibliographical references and index. | Summary: "This book provides an in-depth review of research related to the concepts and theories around topics such as productivity, interactivity and participation in organizational communication settings, including, but not limited to conceptualizations, theoretical foundations, conceptual analysis, empirical studies, cases, applications, and interventions with an aim to contribute to an improvement in our understanding of digital communication in organizations"-- Provided by publisher.
Identifiers: LCCN 2021051913 (print) | LCCN 2021051914 (ebook) | ISBN 9781799897903 (hardcover) | ISBN 9781799897910 (paperback) | ISBN 9781799897927 (ebook)
Subjects: LCSH: Communication in organizations--Technological innovations. | Information technology--Management.
Classification: LCC HD30.3 .N378 2022 (print) | LCC HD30.3 (ebook) | DDC 658.4/5--dc23/eng/20211215
LC record available at https://lccn.loc.gov/2021051913
LC ebook record available at https://lccn.loc.gov/2021051914

This book is published in the IGI Global book series Advances in E-Business Research (AEBR) (ISSN: 1935-2700; eISSN: 1935-2719)

British Cataloguing in Publication Data
A Cataloguing in Publication record for this book is available from the British Library.

Advances in E-Business Research (AEBR) Book Series

In Lee
Western Illinois University, USA

ISSN:1935-2700
EISSN:1935-2719

Mission

Technology has played a vital role in the emergence of e-business and its applications incorporate strategies. These processes have aided in the use of electronic transactions via telecommunications networks for collaborating with business partners, buying and selling of goods and services, and customer service. Research in this field continues to develop into a wide range of topics, including marketing, psychology, information systems, accounting, economics, and computer science.

The **Advances in E-Business Research (AEBR) Book Series** provides multidisciplinary references for researchers and practitioners in this area. Instructors, researchers, and professionals interested in the most up-to-date research on the concepts, issues, applications, and trends in the e-business field will find this collection, or individual books, extremely useful. This collection contains the highest quality academic books that advance understanding of e-business and addresses the challenges faced by researchers and practitioners.

Coverage

- Sustainable E-business
- Electronic Supply Chain Management
- Intelligent Agent Technologies
- E-Business Management
- Web advertising
- E-Services
- Mobile Business Models
- Semantic Web
- Virtual Collaboration
- E-business models and architectures

IGI Global is currently accepting manuscripts for publication within this series. To submit a proposal for a volume in this series, please contact our Acquisition Editors at Acquisitions@igi-global.com or visit: http://www.igi-global.com/publish/.

The Advances in E-Business Research (AEBR) Book Series (ISSN 1935-2700) is published by IGI Global, 701 E. Chocolate Avenue, Hershey, PA 17033-1240, USA, www.igi-global.com. This series is composed of titles available for purchase individually; each title is edited to be contextually exclusive from any other title within the series. For pricing and ordering information please visit http://www.igi-global.com/book-series/advances-business-research/37144. Postmaster: Send all address changes to above address.

Titles in this Series

For a list of additional titles in this series, please visit: www.igi-global.com/book-series/advances-business-research/37144

Handbook of Research on Smart Management for Digital Transformation
Belem Barbosa (University of Porto, Portugal) Sandra Filipe (University of Aveiro, Portugal) and Claudia Amaral Santos (University of Aveiro, Portugal)
Business Science Reference • © 2022 • 614pp • H/C (ISBN: 9781799890089) • US $295.00

Handbook of Research on Digital Transformation, Industry Use Cases, and the Impact of Disruptive Technologies
Martin George Wynn (University of Gloucestershire, UK)
Business Science Reference • © 2022 • 487pp • H/C (ISBN: 9781799877127) • US $325.00

Handbook of Research on Pathways and Opportunities Into the Business of Esports
Sharon Andrews (University of Houston-Clear Lake, USA) and Caroline M. Crawford (University of Houston-Clear Lake, USA)
Business Science Reference • © 2021 • 473pp • H/C (ISBN: 9781799873006) • US $345.00

Complex Systems and Sustainability in the Global Auditing, Consulting, and Credit Rating Agency Industries
Michael I. C. Nwogugu (Independent Researcher, Nigeria)
Business Science Reference • © 2021 • 320pp • H/C (ISBN: 9781799874188) • US $195.00

Handbook of Research on Management and Strategies for Digital Enterprise Transformation
Kamaljeet Sandhu (University of New England, Australia)
Business Science Reference • © 2021 • 443pp • H/C (ISBN: 9781799850151) • US $275.00

Multidisciplinary Approaches to Crowdfunding Platforms
Carla Sofia Vicente Negrão (University of Coimbra, Portugal) and João António Furtado Brito (University of Cape Verde, Cape Verde)
Business Science Reference • © 2021 • 303pp • H/C (ISBN: 9781799832263) • US $205.00

Impact of Globalization and Advanced Technologies on Online Business Models
Ree C. Ho (Taylor's University, Malaysia) Alex Hou Hong Ng (INTI International University, Malaysia) and Mustafa Nourallah (Mid Sweden University, Sweden)
Business Science Reference • © 2021 • 399pp • H/C (ISBN: 9781799876038) • US $225.00

Rural Entrepreneurship and Innovation in the Digital Era
Sachithra Lokuge (RMIT University, Australia) and Darshana Sedera (Southern Cross University, Australia)
Business Science Reference • © 2021 • 337pp • H/C (ISBN: 9781799849421) • US $195.00

IGI Global
PUBLISHER of TIMELY KNOWLEDGE

701 East Chocolate Avenue, Hershey, PA 17033, USA
Tel: 717-533-8845 x100 • Fax: 717-533-8661
E-Mail: cust@igi-global.com • www.igi-global.com

List of Reviewers

Elmano Azevedo, *New University of Lisbon, Portugal*
Sara Balonas, *University of Minho, Portugal*
Margareth Boarini, *Catholic University of São Paulo, Brazil*
Daniel Brandão, *University of Minho, Portugal*
Nuno Brandão, *Catholic University of Portugal, Portugal*
Patrícia Dias, *Catholic University of Portugal, Portugal*
Ivana Domazet, *Institute of Economic Sciences, Serbia*
Alexandre Duarte, *University of Minho, Portugal*
Cristobal Fernández, *Complutense University of Madrid, Spain*
Manuel José Fonseca, *Polytechnic Institute of Viana do Castelo, Portugal*
Andreia Garcia, *School of Communication and Media Studies, Portugal*
Jorge Garcia, *Polytechnic Institute of Viana do Castelo, Portugal*
Maria Luisa Garcia, *Complutense University of Madrid, Spain*
Sofia Gomes, *University of Minho, Portugal*
Ana Teresa Machado, *School of Communication and Media Studies, Portugal*
Fernanda Magalhães, *University of Minho, Portugal*
Ana Melo, *University of Minho, Portugal*
Sandra Miranda, *School of Communication and Media Studies, Portugal*
Florin Nechita, *Universitatea Transilvania Brasov, Romania*
Sandra Pereira, *School of Communication and Media Studies, Portugal*
Clarisse Pessôa, *Catholic University of Portugal, Portugal*
Francisco Restivo, *Catholic University of Portugal, Portugal*
Sónia Sá, *University of Beira Interior, Portugal*
Adriano Sampaio, *Federal University of Bahia, Brazil*
Sónia Silva, *University of Trás-os-Montes e Alto Douro, Portugal*
Carolina Terra, *Cásper Líbero University, Brazil*
Mariana Victorino, *Catholic University of Portugal, Portugal*

Table of Contents

Detailed Table of Contents

Preface

THE IMPERATIVE OF DIGITAL COMMUNICATION IN CONTEMPORARY ORGANISATIONS

The driving force of digital communication in the universe of contemporary organisational communication is undeniable and its expression has increased exponentially in the context of the global pandemic that erupted in 2020. This scenario has given rise to significant changes in traditional communication players, circuits, networks, channels, and narratives produced inside and outside organisations, causing organisational communication professionals to face a moment of change in stakeholders' interaction management, regarding its forms and contents.

In truth, organisational digital communication is not developing a virtual world, but a real virtuality integrated with other forms of interaction in an increasingly "hybridised" organisational life. Relationships with the public can, potentially, be built around more symmetrical models, and citizens´ participation in communication processes must be welcomed, providing guidance to new business and institutional choices. The power of public involvement to promote an active circulation of digital media content may, therefore, generate economic and cultural value to organisations. Furthermore, public contact with organisational information in digital environments may be part of the way in which each individual experiences daily life.

But this scenario also includes challenges and risks. The current perspectives on the nature of interaction between audiences and organisations in the digital sphere reveal a new relational logic based on the attributes of online channels and the singularities of content production in these settings, but also on media features and new productivity drivers. In this sense, it is relevant to look at the rational of audience experience through the concepts of interactivity and participation. As it is pertinent to observe the frequent gap between the intentions of communication professionals and their organisations and the effective content circulation and retention rates among audiences of interest, as well as the distinctiveness between the processes of informing and communicating.

As we write this editorial, the coronavirus pandemic crisis continues to affect the world's population, impacting companies and institutions, with no clear end in sight. This context highlights the strong social impact of living in a more and more digitally connected world. But it also makes it more visible - for the effects are now on the surface of society - the advantages and costs of using digital platforms as primary organisational interaction devices. This scenario demanded the implementation of new communication models that operate without physical contact, to sell goods or services, but also to shape social beliefs, attitudes, and behaviours. Thus, to the extent in which social functioning, equality and democracy can be affected by the new communication models that are born and grow with the adoption of digital platforms, it is essential to promote a critical study and a permanent reflection on these matters.

In an attempt to respond to this need, the editors of this book have shared a set of research questions about the interception of Communication Sciences with Information Technology and Organizational Communication to a group of researchers that decided to participate in this edition. These authors have then studied the many challenges of analysing, prototyping, evaluating, and developing digital communication plans and services to deliver information and communication to corporate or institutional audiences in rapid and turbulent times.

The main conclusions of these studies are that, in view of current challenges, we need both communicational and technological approaches to build renewed organisational communication strategies. Thus, the book N*avigating Digital Communication and Challenges for Organizations* provides an in-depth review of research related to the concepts and theories around topics such as Communication and Publics, Interactivity and Participation, including different scientific exercises such as theoretical approaches, conceptual analyses, empirical readings and case studies. Through the enriching inputs of all the authors, we aim to contribute to improve the global understanding of Digital Communication in Organisations, in order to present new resources to companies and institutions that want to better navigate through the difficult moments that communication management is experiencing. This book presents a set of recent studies showing that digital technologies are a context and an interface that Organizational Communication must deal with. Fourteen original chapters highlight both multi- and interdisciplinary research findings.

The first chapter, "Internal Communication in Contemporary Organizations: The Digital Challenge in a Project Management Department," presents an action-research study on internal communication in the context of an innovation department of a multinational company. After a systematic assessment, which identified several communication problems, an intervention was carried out in the communication system through a digital approach, with the aim of improving team's performance. This chapter then presents and debates the pros and cons of this digital approach in a traditional environment.

The second chapter, "The Digital Influence Ecosystem and Its Relation to Organizational Communication: Characterizations, Possibilities, and Best Practices," discusses the ecosystem that constitutes digital organizational influence and its possibilities and shows its correlation with organizational communication. It compares organisational communication with Brazilian researcher Margarida Kunsch's integrated communication composite and explores how organisational influence fits into each of the diagram's communication pillars: internal, market and institutional.

Chapter 3, "Disruptive Communication: Challenges and Opportunities of the 21st Century," presents the complex challenges emerged for organisational communication since the dissemination and confluence of big data, artificial intelligence, and the internet of things. Ubiquitous and powerful, these technologies require specific knowledge, partnerships with different areas (data science), and learning to work with a new communicational agent, the non-human.

The chapter "Media Visibility in the Digital Context: Implications for Organizational Communication" promotes a reflection on the ways in which the media affect the communicative practices of organizations, especially in the construction of their visibility. It explores the concept of visibility and how this phenomenon has been changing with the development of media, especially with social media

Chapter 5, "How Small Companies Used Shopstreaming in Their Fight for Survival in a COVID-19 Scenario: Case Studies From Brazil and Portugal," presents the digital acceleration triggered by Covid-19 which provoked a disruptive transformation of society that was not prepared for such rapid changes in socialization, work, and consumption, among other activities. Stating that organisations were forced to reinvent themselves, this chapter looks at two examples: Mh2, a Brazilian fashion accessories company that used lives on Instagram to sell its products, and São Costureiras, a Portuguese clothing brand that did the same using Facebook.

Chapter 6, "COVID-19 Vaccination Campaigning: The Uruguayan Case, Contributions of Digital Communication," presents a case study of Uruguay's institutional communication. The study shows how communication played a key role in the implementation of the health strategy for the country and now in the vaccination plan. The credibility of the government has made it possible to move forward without harsh questioning. Throughout the process, digital communication enabled two-way communication flows, speed and reach in messaging.

"Health Communication on Social Media: Perceptions and Influences" is the seventh chapter. The authors set out to analyze how media users perceived health-related content disseminated on social media. They intend to verify how the dimensions "Entertainment", "Interaction", "Trend" and "Personalization" influenced the "Word of Mouth" that the user could give to other users regarding health-related contents.

The eighth chapter, "Beyond the Corporate Digital Newsroom 2.0," proposes a reflection on the strategic potential of corporate digital newsrooms. The central question lies in knowing whether it will be possible to identify an evolution in corporate digital newsrooms, with companies redefining their media relations strategies beyond a 2.0 model, to meet the so-called 3.0 newsrooms, typical of a cyber journalism scenario, which operates in the virtual environment.

Chapter 9, "Bridging Journalists and PR Practitioners in a Digital Context: A Good Practice Case Study," presents a project aiming at bridging journalists and PR practitioners in Romania, reflecting on the characteristics of the PR-journalism relationship in the historical context and analyses several digital challenges influencing the contemporary communication industry.

The next chapter, "Empathic Brands: Proposing a Model for Its Measurement and Evaluation," explores the world where brands are becoming increasingly ubiquitous, competition is increasing, and consumers are, every day, more demanding to create and maintain powerful, emotional and reciprocal relationships between brands and their parties. This can potentially be achieved by focusing on a brand purpose with which consumers identify and which can be stimulated by creating unique and distinctive experiences and by developing interpersonal feelings, such as empathy.

Chapter 11, "Place Branding, Digital Communication, and Citizenship," by reflecting on the existing tensions between digital communication strategies, focused on citizens and tourists in Brazil. This research tries to identify the approaches and distances in strategic communication developed by some Brazilian municipalities to animate public opinion in order to build public policies and, on the other hand, to position the cities as attractive tourist destinations for visitors.

Chapter 12 presents the study "Internet Marketing: Factor of Improving SME Business in Serbia" that analyses the presence of modern technological solutions in the business communication of small and medium enterprises (SMEs) in Serbia. The paper points out the role of information and communication technologies in improving business and identifies certain key issues faced by the SME sector in Serbia, which, among other things, hinder the implementation of modern forms of communication.

In Chapter 13, "The Use of CRM in Marketing and Communication Strategies in Portuguese Non-Profit Organizations," demonstrates the importance of CRM in relational marketing practices, particularly in non-profit organizations. The main result of this exploratory study seems to prove the importance of using CRM for the good practice of relational marketing strategies, in order to attract, retain and build trust with their stakeholders.

The last chapter, "Social Media Reputation, Corporate Reputation: Social Media Risks on Corporate Reputation and Precautions," aims to explain the role and risks of social media on corporate reputation through literature review. The results show that institutions need to know how to use social media adequately in order to create and protect their reputation.

In sum, this book joints different perspectives from researchers with several background approaches to organisational communication, marketing and information and communication technologies, systematising interdisciplinary knowledge on issues of Communication in the digital environment. Therefore, it may be an important source of information for researchers on those areas of expertise and a useful tool for a wide range of stakeholders—such as governments, public institutions, or companies, among others—that deal with the emergence of organisational communication in the digital context. Moreover, this is particularly relevant as the world experiences changes in communication projected in a global health emergency.

Throughout the 14 chapters, the book highlights the relevance of digital communication in organisations and institutions. Combining this with an in-depth reflection on devices, social media, digital services, their trends, characteristics, uses, ethical concerns, and awareness, this book covers the most significant items and threats of digital communication in contemporary organisations.

José Gabriel Andrade
University of Minho, Portugal

Teresa Ruão
University of Minho, Portugal

Acknowledgment

The editors would like to thank all the people involved in this project for their help, and more specifically the authors and reviewers who participated in the review process. Without their support, this book would not have become a reality.

First, the editors would like to thank each of the authors for their contributions. Our sincere gratitude goes to the chapter authors who contributed their time and expertise to this book.

Second, the editors wish to acknowledge the valuable contributions of the reviewers regarding the improvement of quality, coherence, and presentation of chapter content. Most of the authors also served as referees; we greatly appreciate their dual task.

José Gabriel Andrade
University of Minho, Portugal

Teresa Ruão
University of Minho, Portugal

Section 1

Chapter 1
Internal Communication in Contemporary Organizations:
Digital Challenge in a Project Management Department

Teresa Ruão
University of Minho, Portugal

Sandra Marinho
University of Minho, Portugal

Sónia Silva
University of Trás-os-Montes e Alto Douro, Portugal

ABSTRACT

This chapter reports an action-research study on internal communication in the context of an innovation project management department at a multinational company. An intervention was carried out in the communication system, with the purpose of improving team performance. The first action research cycle began with data collection through questionnaires, document analysis, direct observation, and focus groups. The sequent implementation stage was designed and carried out with a mid-term communication plan. After this, a new data collection process began. Results showed lack of communication skills, lack of information, and lack of involvement. This was the beginning of a second evaluation cycle, and a new communication plan was implemented. After this, another diagnosis emerged showing the persistence of some issues. These results are discussed, and the possibility of implementing a digital communication platform is addressed. This study seeks the development of knowledge on internal communication in the context of innovation projects.

INTRODUCTION

In the context of a European university-industry consortium, a study on internal corporate communication

DOI: 10.4018/978-1-7998-9790-3.ch001

was developed in a project management department of a multinational company, dealing with innovation processes inherent to industrialization. These processes begin in the project management department, where project managers (PjM) are accountable for coordinating all innovation projects, from the ordering phase to completion, which happens when the product goes into mass production. It is up to each project manager to select and lead the team responsible for fulfilling all tasks associated with developing new production lines. According to Qusef and Ismail (2016), this manager must be a qualified specialist, as he is responsible for defining a plan and assigning tasks appropriately to each member of his team, depending on information quality and motivation to carry on the entire process.

PjMs spent about 75% of their time interacting and exchanging information and, for this reason, communication is a fundamental part of project management and innovation processes, supporting each of its phases. According to Zerfass and Huck (2007), project management must be understood as an integrated system of cooperation and interaction, which needs to be strategically planned and supported by communication.

Aiming to contribute to the development of theoretical and practical knowledge on internal corporate communication in the context of innovation projects, this study sought to analyse and intervene in the communication system of the aforementioned project management department, namely through a digital communication approach. To this end, and using action research as a methodology, it started with a diagnosis that identified the communication barriers existing in industrialization projects and proceeded with the implementation of tailored measures to promote a more efficient project management environment. The consequences of those measures were afterwards assessed and discussed in order to prepare a second intervention cycle.

LITERATURE REVIEW

Internal Communication and Innovation Processes

Innovation projects concern temporary efforts with the objective of creating a unique product or service with limited human, financial, and material resources (Bosch, 2017). Thus, these projects are constituted as temporary organizations (Turner and Müller, 2003) that can integrate a large number of collaborators, often geographically distant and culturally diverse (Ruão et al., 2018). In this context, communication processes are particularly relevant and complex.

Innovation Communication is actually a subdiscipline of Organizational Communication that began to stand out in 2004 (Gerhard et al., 2001). According to Mast et al. (2005), this field of study focuses on the analysis of symbolic interactions between an organization and its audiences, as they deal with the development of new products or services. And innovation communication seems indispensable today, in times of rapid technological change, intense competition, and global economic markets, as innovation enhances performance and revenues. "Yet, this innovation is no longer created in isolated labs or by a single innovation leader (Schumpeter, 2006), but through processes of Open Innovation" (Linke & Zerfass, 2011, p. 334). In fact, many stakeholders can be involved in the innovation process, from idea generation through implementation. Innovation is therefore a result of a collaborative cooperation between different groups (Gutiérrez-García et al., 2020).

Innovation is commonly pursued through project management approaches (Kapsali, 2011). Project management can be defined as the application of knowledge, skills, tools and techniques to design activities that make it possible to respond to project requirements. This profession was, in fact, being practiced ad hoc until the middle of the 20th century (Munns and Bjeirmi, 1996), but today it is a professional area rooted in organizations and taught at universities. This area of studies and professionalization has been feeling the need to reinvent itself in order to be able to respond to the demands that organizations and businesses currently face.

Thus, the knowledge developed in the field of internal corporate communication has been used to reproach project management practices (Ruão, at al., 2020). According to Welch and Jackson (2007), internal communication is the "strategic management of interactions and relationships between stakeholders at all levels within organizations" (p. 183) and it is "crucial for successful organizations as it affects the ability of strategic managers to engage employees and achieve objectives" (p. 177). Internal communication may mean either the formal communicative activities carried on between employee groups or departments (e.g. meetings and other formal information flows), or can be the processes where two or more groups work together, have a mutual understanding and a common vision, share resources, and achieve collective goals. In fact, empirical findings suggest that a certain amount of interaction is necessary in innovation processes, but also shows that it predicts innovativeness less strongly than collaboration (Kivimäki et al., 2000). In project management, likewise, internal communication requirements are huge and include the need to develop quality interactions, but also collaborative relationships between team members throughout all phases of the project (Remidez and Jones, 2012). Therefore, internal communication can be used to promote information flows, but also to supplement internal climate with participatory practices.

Moreover internal communication does not only allow to stimulate active employees, it can also create ideas. A crucial task is to enhance employees' potential and make them use it effectively. Internal communication therefore plays a central role in creative environments, because innovation requires informed and motivated individuals. Organizational members must be willing to contribute with time and effort to the development of innovative ideas (Linke & Zerfass, 2011; Gode et al., 2020).

The present study combines existing knowledge in the field of internal communication with innovation communication research and project management knowledge. Existing research has identified communication as a critical factor for business success (Kivimäki et al., 2000). A variety of communication instruments exist inside companies and help to inform organizational members, to communicate with them, to persuade them, to promote loyalty, and to improve job satisfaction. This chapter explores this increased perception on the relevance of communication and presents questions about its interplay with innovation and project management.

Project Manager as a Communication Leader

In project management, each innovation team has a manager. The core function of the innovation project´s manager is to coordinate the tasks and expectations of all individuals who make up these temporary organizations, which, as indicated by Rutten (2016), are constituted with the mission of accomplishing a certain task, in a certain period of time, after which they dismantle. Thus, communication, as the element responsible for creating and maintaining relationships in organizational contexts, takes on relevance (Shenhar and Dvir, 1996).

In fact, an analysis of internal project management documents (PMBok) has allowed us to realize that project managers' functions are described in a way that emphasizes their role as leaders and as communicators. They are anchors that coordinate teams involved in developing new products, services or processes, whereby they are challenged to reveal leadership and interaction skills. These are, moreover, functions traditionally attributed to internal communication, which is fundamental in the processes of planning and controlling information flows and in aligning and motivating stakeholders (Welch and Jackson, 2007). Thus, a project manager is a leader who must be able to coordinate team work through communication:

a. Ensuring the integration of all innovation activities, as an intermediary between team members;
b. Creating, supplying, sharing and keeping updated all the project's documents, in all phases;
c. Monitoring all tasks, to ensure that the goals are met according to deadline, budget and stipulated quality;
d. Motivating, supporting and informing team members throughout the project, managing their needs and expectations; by keeping the entire team informed on the status of tasks and by involving them, whenever possible, in decisions (Bosch, 2017; PMI, 2017).

In order to successfully develop these roles, some skills are described as important, namely: (a) to choose the appropriate communication channels and contents for different stakeholders; (b) to ensure that the receiver understands the message as intended; (c) to accept the opinions of team members on relevant issues; (d) to listen others patiently; (e) to give and ask for feedback; (f) to create team spirit by developing group identity; (g) to lead with motivation, commitment and enthusiasm, always showing a positive attitude; (h) to develop relationships of trust, transparency and honesty with the entire team; (i) to provide and receive guidance to improve individual and team performance; (j) to use influence to ensure the fulfilment of the tasks of each team member and; (k) to know theirs and the team's needs, strengths and weaknesses, and manage them in the best possible way (Bosch, 2017; PMI, 2017).

In short, a project manager is, above all, a communication manager. In this sense, he is expected to be able to plan, manage and monitor all the project's communications, while maintaining reciprocal interaction between all members, in which information, decisions, ideas and doubts are transmitted and shared. In fact, the success of the project seems to depend a lot on the way the manager relates to the project team, handling expectations and guaranteeing everyone's commitment during the new product/production development cycle (Hamdi and Rajablu, 2012; Ozaeta and An, 2014).

Reminding the CCO Principle – or the proposition that advocates the "communicative constitution of organizations", supported by Organizational Communication authors (as Weick, 1979) -, all the above ideas on the communicative axis of project management become intelligible, as communication is central to every organization. It represents the mechanism through which human beings produce and reproduce reality, giving meaning and direction to their practices. Organizations exist because there are people inside who communicate and "organize" (Vuuren et al., 2006). Within project management temporary organizations, the same logic can be found: people are the central factor for the development or manufacturing of any product or service, dictating its success or failure. The main challenge for the project manager is, then, to create collaborative work within teams that share feelings of belonging, able to develop cohesive, motivated, involved and committed work to the achievement of a common goal that is, in this study, the result of the innovation process. To this end, PjM's leadership skills are essential (Hamdi and Rajablu, 2012; McCartney and Campbell, 2006; Zerfass and Huck, 2007).

In general terms, leadership can be defined as the process that is carried out to influence others to pursue a certain result or objective (Hamdi and Rajablu, 2012). According to several theorists, communication is closely related to leadership ability and is central to its good execution (Hamdi and Rajablu,

2012; Vries et al., 2009). In turn, leadership is described as a decisive procedure for organizational commitment (Shirbagi, 2007; Zerfass and Huck, 2007). In order to explain this relationship, Hamdi and Rajablu (2012) stated that when organizational communication is clear and precise, it is more likely to generate interaction between employees and managers, thus facilitating the creation of feelings of belonging and commitment and, consequently, it has positive effects on productivity and efficiency. Good communicative skills seem, in fact, to portray a good leader and, therefore, the development of strong organizational commitment is directly related to the quality of the interaction between managers and their employees.

In terms of communication quality, the responsiveness of the organizational leader represents a decisive variable for the creation and maintenance of good relationships. According to Lipäinen, Karjaluoto, and Nevalainen (2014) and Men (2015), when leaders use two-way communication strategies that privilege behaviours of honesty and real listening, empathy, understanding, sincerity, kindness, compassion and feedback, they are able to generate positive feelings within the team and promote motivated attitudes, committed to success. This environment of motivation and commitment is likely to be reinforced when the ability to respond coexists with the possibility of real participation. This happens in leadership contexts in which opinions and ideas of employees are considered in the process of organizational decision making. As important members of a common project, employees' thoughts can be quite valid to decide future directions (Hamdi and Rajablu, 2012). Thus, legitimizing belonging reinforces team commitment.

These considerations can, moreover, be applied to project management. As stated by Vuuren et al. (2006), a successful project is always strongly dependent on the leadership communication skills of its manager and its ability to motivate and cooperate with its team members. In the context of this study, leadership becomes more complex because it involves multicultural and geographically distant teams, who have no exclusive ties to the project. In addition, the fact that these teams carry out tasks with the notion that their collaboration is temporary and transient, hinders the ability to generate feelings of belonging, involvement and motivation that are necessary for the good performance of the project (Ruão et al., 2018). This is a great challenge for the project manager, who is expected to have a leadership profile based on good communication skills.

Communication Systems in Project Management and the Digital Challenge

To comprehend and intervene in the project management communication process, it is important to analyse, not only the role of the PjM, but also the communication flows and channels in use in project management environment, as structures of the internal communication system. This system aggregates informal chats on the "grapevine", as well as our core subject: managed communication.

In order to coordinate team work, PjMs then need to manage internal communication: keeping open vertical communication flows (ascending and descending) - to assign tasks and to receive feedback on the status of the project -, and horizontal and diagonal flows - to allow the interaction between project members, who, in some cases, belong to different departments and are in different facilities or countries (Remidez and Jones, 2012). In this context, the communication skills of the project managers, as well as the development of communication strategies are fundamental.

These concerns were also stressed by the document analysis applied to the company under study. This research showed that the careful definition of means to send and receive information is important to a successful project management. To this end, one of the documents the project manager is accountable for is, precisely, the Communication Plan, whose objective is to identify the communication stages and channels for information exchange and interaction between all project stakeholders (internal and external), following the PMBok recommendations. Thus, this document regulates all communication actions for the entire project team, including the production of weekly status reports and the scheduling of meetings.

However, this plan covers only a small part of what makes up the internal communication of project management departments. Other very important communication abilities - such as guidelines for adapting the communication channels to a dynamic reality or the definition of strategies to guarantee the involvement, commitment and motivation of the team members (Verčič et al., 2012) - are not considered. In addition, this plan does not mention the communicative skills that can be useful for project manager to solve some of the problems they face in their day-to-day.

Furthermore, the communication plan model in use is very traditional and does not favour new trends, such as the use of social media channels. According to several studies (Baltatzis, Ormrod and Grainger, 2008; Men, 2015; Ingelmo Palomares et al., 2018), technological development has transformed the global communication landscape as well as the internal communication formula for companies (above all multinational ones). In this context, easy access to countless social media (as Facebook, Twitter, instant messaging systems, Skype, LinkedIn, YouTube, among others) has changed the way organizations communicate in all hierarchical levels. In general, these new communication tools have been welcomed by employees, who seem to accept their growing inclusion, although some cases of resistance are reported. The lack of skills in the usage of communication technologies, the time spent updating information and publishing on platforms or the complexity in the management of these digital technologies make some employees favour traditional channels such as phone calls or face-to-face interaction (Baltazis et al., 2008; Men, 2014, 2015; Zyl, 2009).

However, these social platforms can be very useful for corporate internal communication. Social media facilitate the distribution of information and promote permanent interaction between all hierarchical levels, softening the boundaries between managers and employees. In a way, social media can encourage the democratization of the organizational environment because they promote upward communication through dialogue between employees and managers, thus simplifying the exchange of ideas, the sharing of opinions and feedback regarding the status of tasks (Baltatzis et al., 2008; Ewing at al., 2019; Men, 2014, 2015; Men and Bowen, 2017; Zyl, 2009).

Some of the most common platforms in use are, according to Lipäinen et al. (2014), Qusef and Ismail (2016) and Zyl (2009):

Wikis: a website that allows online collaboration in which individuals can create and modify content simultaneously; Wikipedia is an example;

Blogs: a communication tool that resembles an online newspaper and allows its owner to publish periodic messages; in which readers can follow, share, and comment on these messages;

Intranet: an internal network that, ideally, contains all the information needed and facilitates the contacts that are essential for all employees to be able to carry out their tasks; besides access can be given to other sites relevant to the work context;

Email: a platform that allows the exchange of messages quickly and simply, for several recipients at the same time;

Instant messaging systems: a platform that enables the rapid exchange of messages, in real time, with one or more individuals at the same time; Skype, WhatsApp are instant messaging systems and Instagram, Snapchat, LinkedIn and Facebook also allow this type of interaction;

Collaborative real time editor: a type of software or application that allows simultaneous real-time editing of the same document or other digitally stored content; Google Docs is an example;

Social bookmarking: an online service that allows users to create, annotate, edit, and share their list of favourite websites with other individuals;

Social networks: platforms that allow the creation of personal profiles and interaction with various individuals or groups through the sharing of content, comments or instant messages; Instagram, Snapchat, LinkedIn, Facebook and YouTube are the best known.

From the platforms presented, email seems to be the one preferred by organizations. Its speed and ease of use makes it a widely chosen internal communication tool. However, the trivialization of its use has brought problems, namely, it produces information overload and a consequent decrease in its relevance that leads to growth in response times (Lipäinen et al., 2014).

Considering the potential of digital communication and social media to simplify information flows, to encourage relationships and to promote a sense of community, in 2008, the concept of Social Project Management (SPM) emerged. Such an approach arose because social media has become an accessible alternative to traditional communication channels, namely in project management. These tools have increased the volume and speed of communication and information exchange. Further, they have the potential to stimulate sharing, co-creation, interaction and debate, bringing the project manager closer to the team, significantly improving communication outcomes (Fernandes et al., 2018; Silvius, 2016).

This approach has been discussed and introduced in the project management department of the company under study. However, some resistance was encountered as a result of the dispersion of content in different sites and the need to update multiple channels, giving PjMs the feeling of being wasting time with these platforms. In fact, without a holistic approach, the potential of these channels is likely to be lost.

So, do the existing communication systems in this project management department facilitate the efficiency of the innovation process? Do the installed communication models promote team performance? Can digital communication enhance organizational innovation processes? What improvements should be made in the communication system of this department? These were the questions that we looked to answer, using a qualitative methodology, through action research.

METHODOLOGY: ACTION RESEARCH AS A FORM OF INTERVENTION

Considering this theoretical framework and the research questions, an action research intervention study was developed at the project management department of a multinational in Portugal. This automotive industry factory has around 3500 employees, of which 101 belong to the innovation projects' department, being responsible for coordinating the company's innovation processes.

Implementing sequential action research cycles was identified as the best methodology to promote in depth changes in the project management communication system of the company. The first cycle included a communication audit, followed by an action plan. At the end of the implementation phase, a new diagnosis was carried out, giving rise to a new intervention cycle to improve the communication system of the project management department.

As an ongoing, systematic and empirically grounded attempt to improve practice (Baum et al., 2006; Coghlan, 2019; Tripp, 2005), action research is an interactive method that involves the collaborative participation of researchers and professionals who seek to solve a problem through diagnosis, planning and implementation of appropriate actions (Avison et al., 1999). Improving practices is, therefore, the purpose of action research and, as such, its emphasis is on the actions taken and its ability to solve problems.

Figure 1. Action-research process, Lewin's 1946 cited by Dickens e Watkins, 1999

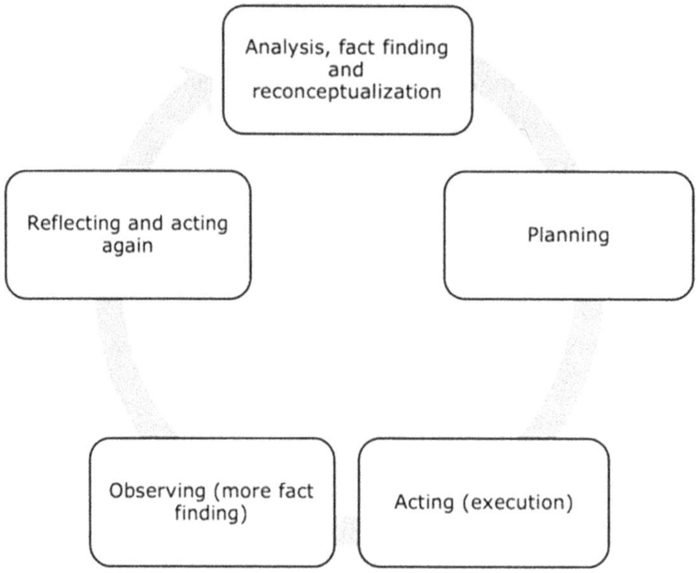

Within the scope of this commitment to improvement, the team of professionals and researchers goes through a spiral of steps - which include analysis, planning, action, evaluation and readjustment of the action – that are monitored and adjusted as needed. Thus, the cyclical nature of this methodology recognizes the importance of designing flexible action plans and responding to the needs of the context in which it is applied (Dickens and Watkins, 1999). In addition, action research enthusiasts argue that complex social processes can be better studied by introducing changes and observing their effects (Baskerville, 1999).

The development of action research begins with the identification of a problem in its context (Figure 4). The team of researchers then collects the relevant data using appropriate methods that may include interviews, observation, document analysis or other social sciences techniques. This collection and subsequent analysis of data is carried out with the aim of proposing possible solutions to the identified problem, facilitating the appropriate change in the context under study. The next step is to implement the actions in the real environment, which can be an organization. Then, researchers analyse the effects of the changes implemented through the collection of new data that allows the evaluation of the results, according to which the problem is reformulated and, consequently, new ways of action are considered. Researchers structure their activity around this cycle until the problem initially identified is solved. It is likely, in fact, that the research team will go through several cycles of revaluation and implementation until the problem is fully resolved (Dickens and Watkins, 1999).

This is, moreover, a method widely used in organizational environments since it can be applied to intervene and improve their different contexts. In addition, as Dickens and Watkins (1999) point out, action research has already been used in studies developed in multinational technology companies, because it presents itself as a good strategy to intervene in the practical solution of certain problems. This is the environment of our study that aimed at auditing innovation project management communication practices and proposing a taylormade plan of improvement. The study looked at three key points: (1) the

Table 1. Communication barriers in project management

Lack of communication skills	PjMs reported difficulties in communicating with their teams. Although there is an understanding of the importance of communication for the performance of the project, managers consider they have no adequate communication skills to manage team work effectively.
Lack of information	The innovation process was not clear to all parties involved.
Scattering of channels	The existence of many communication channels and the fact that they are not used regularly causes information dispersion and duality.
Lack of team involvement	PjMs call all team members to periodic meetings, but most members are not actively involved in the debate, as its subjects are not of interest to all participants. Instead, team members prefer to use this time to carry out other tasks.
Lack of communication strategy	The communication plan is an administrative document that serves the PjM exclusively, but would be a useful tool to guide communication interaction for all team members.

internal communication flows in the project management department; (2) the communication planning model in use; and (3) the communication and leadership skills of project managers.

As mentioned, this paper describes the entire action research process, but focuses on discussing the second evaluation phase that assessed the actions taken in the first implementation cycle. Results of the first cycle are summarized, including the list of the communication barriers identified and the solutions implemented. Thereafter, the techniques adopted to evaluate the implemented actions are described and the results presented, highlighting the persisting communication problems.

RESULTS

The First Cycle: Communication Barriers and Solutions

In the first cycle of action research, methodological triangulation was used, including document analysis of the company and its procedures, non-participant observation of the work environment and meetings of the project teams, a survey to project managers, and focus groups with members of the department. The following communication problems (table 1) were, then, found:

To solve these problems, an action plan then was designed (table 2), including:

Table 2. Communication intervention plan in project management

1. Communication Skills Training in Workplace	Workshops on topics such as human, organizational, intercultural and non-verbal communication, and leadership.
2. Communication taylormade guide	Tips and Tricks guidebook on the best practices of communication in industrialization project management at that company.
3. Communication planning guidelines	Review of the communication plan template in use.
4. SPM approach testing	Establishment of a PjM community on the internal social network

The Second Cycle: Reassessment and Discussion

After the implementation of this action plan, a new cycle of action research was initiated with the evaluation phase of the communication system of the project management department, considering the actions carried out previously. To make this diagnosis, data collection privileged: a new survey applied to project managers, which aimed to assess the effectiveness of the workshops held; document analysis on the progress of project management procedures and functions in that department; and unsystematic non-participant observation of the project management work environment and team meetings, for three months. .

Based on collected data, a model was built (table 4) in order to validate communication problems encountered. To this end, communication barriers were listed and a small team (with the head of PjMs and two other PjM) was asked to validate these problems using two scales: agreement and importance. These levels of agreement and importance were measured on a scale of 1 to 5, as explained in table 3.

Table 3. Scales of agreement and importance

Level of agreement	Level of importance
1 – Completely disagree	1 – Very low
2 – Disagree	2 – Low
3 – Neither agree nor disagree	3 – Average
4 – Agree	4 – High
5 – Completely agree	5 – Very High

To simplify the presentation of results, sentences from the validation model will be identified with an S, followed by their respective number. Through data analysis, the following main communication problems were identified, some of which persist since the first implementation cycle:

Table 4. Results of the validation process

Communication Barrier types		Level of agreement	Level of importance
Communication channels and flows	1. I get a lot of emails per day, many of which not relevant	Completely agree	Very High
	2. Some of the issues solved through email can be worked out through live conversation	Completely agree	High
	3. There are platforms that allow the updating of information still debated by email	Agree	Average
	4. Email management takes up a considerable portion of my day	Completely agree	Very High
	5. There are too many communication tools	Agree	High
	6. The communication tools cause dispersion of information	Neither agree nor disagree	Average
	7. The communication tools generate task replication	Completely agree	Very High
	8. The communication tools do not allow the feedback and follow-up needed in each phase of project management	Neither agree nor disagree	High
	9. Team members do not update task status in the tools	Agree	High
	10. Communication tools are not used with due frequency	Disagree	Average
	11. Team members do not frequently check project related documents	Completely agree	Very High
	12. Team members do not frequently consult shared documents	Agree	High
	13. In general, team members do not efficiently and effectively use the communication tools	Agree	Very High
	14. The existing communication tools do not reach the pretended results	Agree	High
	15. There is not an adequate platform for the management of information regarding all the phases of the project	Agree	High

Inadequacy of Existing Communication Channels

The existence of many communication channels gives rise to serious problems: the replication of tasks (S7); the lack of information updating by team members, regarding the status of the project (S9); the absence of project documents consultation (S11 and S12); and the trivialization of the use of email as a means to make any type of interaction or to clarify any subject, even when the answer is available by searching documents on the platforms (for example, task completion dates) (S1 and S4) . In fact, email overload seems to be one of the main problems that PjMs deal within their daily lives.

Bearing in mind these difficulties, which were classified with high or very high levels of importance, it became clear that respondents agreed with statements S13, S14 and S15, which confirm that project

Table 5. (continued)

	16. Meetings are useful	Completely agree	Very High
	17. Meetings enable the solving of problems found in the execution of tasks	Agree	High
	18. Team members value face-to-face meetings	Neither agree nor disagree	High
	19. Most team members attend to meetings they are summoned to	Disagree	High
	20. Team members do not always attend to meetings	Agree	High
	21. The number of meetings between teams is excessive	Neither agree nor disagree	High
	22. Face-to-face contact between all members involved in the project is sufficient	Neither agree nor disagree	Average
	23. Team members are not usually aware of the project schedule	Neither agree nor disagree	Very High
Communication planning	24. The current communication plan template is useful for planning communication at all stages of the project	Disagree	Very High
	25. Existing standards and communication channels facilitate the work of project manager	Disagree	Very High
	26. It would be useful if there were communication procedures (rules and templates) to accomplish tasks and solve problems	Completely agree	Very High
Project manager leadership and communication skills	27. Team members are unaware of the role of project manager	Agree	High
	28. The industrialization project process is not clear to all parties involved in the projects	Neither agree nor disagree	Average
	29. Team members are motivated to perform tasks	Neither agree nor disagree	High
	30. As a project manager, I feel that I can promote good interaction and communication between all members of the team	Agree	Very High

members do not use communication tools efficiently and effectively, and that there is still no adequate platform for the management of information and interaction in all stages of the project. This reinforces the need to implement a software solution to aggregate all PjM procedures, information and communication channels. As we can see in Table 4, most sentences related to communication tools (S1 to S15 and S25), except for S6 and S10, reached levels of agreement or total agreement and these subjects were classified with levels of high or very high importance.

Table 6. (continued)

	31. The communication skills of project manager are adequate to solve the problems that arise day-to-day	Agree	High
	32. The exchange of experiences and tactics between project managers is common	Agree	High
	33. Project manager has the habit of talking to colleagues whenever a problem arises that they do not know how to solve	Completely agree	Very High
	34. Interaction between the different PjM teams is frequent	Disagree	Average

Lack of Communication Planning

The current communication plan, as already mentioned, has the main function of scheduling project meetings, and serves, mainly, for the use of PjM. Thus, the lack of an adequate communication plan was identified as a communication failure (S24, S25 and S26). The validation model proved that, despite the intervention carried out in phase one, the still existing communication form plan is not useful to help PjM structure the information and interaction activities in all phases of the project (S24 and S25) and, therefore, the respondents considered that the level of importance of this subject is very high and, in this sense, they totally agree with deepening the changes on communication procedures (rules and templates) to accomplish tasks and solve problems (S26).

Lack of Team Involvement and Motivation

This diagnostic phase allowed us to perceive that PjMs have serious problems in promoting feelings of belonging within their teams, so that they all are committed to the project's mission. As it can be seen in table 4, although team meetings are evaluated as important communication tools for the good performance of the project (S16 and S17), the degree of attendance of team members to those meetings is low (S19 and S20). The employees assigned to the project teams are responsible for other tasks and tend to attribute little relevance to these face-to-face contacts.

One of the reasons for this lack of team involvement and commitment may be related to the lack of recognition of the PjM functions (S27). But, in addition, and although respondents agree that project manager's communication skills are adequate to promote good interaction between the team and to solve the problems that arise in daily life (S30 and S31), it is also true that they are unable to form an opinion as to the degree of motivation of the project members regarding the execution of their tasks (S29). Thus, the deepening of the feelings of belonging and commitment in project teams may come from the improvement of the communication and leadership skills of PjMs. This vision is shared by the project managers themselves, who positively evaluated the communication workshops and confirmed their interest in maintaining regular training.

Introduction of a New Digital Platform

Given the results presented above, it was then possible to think about the next step of a third intervention program. Data gathered gave us some clues about the team perception on the introduction of a new digital platform aiming to store and share all the information and communication about current and past projects – in line with the *social project management perspective*. This platform would replace all the dispersed systems already in use.

Regarding this issue, PjMs agreed that implementing an integrated platform to support project management and tailored to the company was a good internal measure (S3 and S15). This digital system should have the ability to concentrate information, to enable monitoring the status of each project, and to be used in the teleworking mode or through a mobile application These two last suggestions can be justified by the context of the global pandemic, caused by COVID-19, in which this study was conducted.

Altogether, results show that the innovative project management platform should favor the development of an easy-to-use digital interface that facilitates information and communication flows. Although, attitudes of distrust and resistance towards the emergence of "another communication platform" were also noticed. There is some fear that the introduction of this information repository and communication channel will further accentuate information dispersion and task duplication. These attitudes of mistrust seem to be related to the lack of knowledge about the features and potential of the new system. To be introduced, this new software should be presented to and discussed with all team members. As already mentioned and according to the principles of Innovation Communication, individuals who will be "affected" by innovation must be motivated to participate in the development process and to share ideas and prospects, to establish a position of commitment and trust. As so, this procedure of sharing the software status regularly should be a communication action considered by the company, as the best way to develop an internal digital communication system that corresponds to the needs and welcomes the interest of all members who make up project management.

CONCLUSION

Organizations have been facing quite challenging contexts with increased competition, strong market demands and growing requirements for product, service and process innovation. In order to respond to these challenges, companies develop new and more flexible organizational forms in which projects are strategically important. In fact, innovation seems to be highly enhanced through project management, as a set of rules, processes and structures with viable application in organizations and able to create product and process innovation (Hobbs et al., 2008).

But innovation is also a social concept, as it affects society and organizational environments and is affected by them. In that sense, it crosses communication sciences concerns. As showed in the analysis presented here, fluent internal corporate communication may facilitate innovation: it increases the diversity and amount of ideas within an organization, which may enhance new and valid solutions. In line with other empirical studies (Kivimäki et al., 2000), this research shows that a communication culture favors innovation, that can only be reached through high participation and interaction in task performance, but also through motivation and commitment.

It became clear in our research that the traditional one-way model of information transmission (Shannon and Weaver, 1949) can create issue awareness (as already stated by Linke & Zerfass, 2011; Malte,

2013), but it does not promote team interaction and does not apply for all project phases, as audiences, goals and context need to be considered in order to define the appropriate communication program. Pushing stakeholders from issue attention (awareness) to interest (understanding), through desire (acceptance) to action (as described in the AIDA model, from Elias St. Elmo Lewis, 1925), requires the use of the right tools, in order to allow information absorption, but also team interaction, commitment and collaboration. For example, staff meetings, which showed high relevance for action in this study, can be used in a communication mix with social media, more useful to create attention and interest, also highly valued by PjMs. Thus, a project management internal communication plan for innovation should include different means of communication and, to be effective, it must respond to project objectives and the team's expectations. Besides, it must also consider information overburden effects. As mention in the interviews, having to attend too many meetings or receiving loads of emails can overload employees with information, which, in turn, hinders innovative activities.

In sum, in order to enhance innovation practices in project management, internal communication should aim to inform, but most also to lead, motivate and acknowledge employees' participation through the different phases of the process. This seems to increase work satisfaction, performance and productivity. And moving from analog communication to an integrated digital communication solution may be a good path to explore.

ACKNOWLEDGMENT

This work is financed by national funds through FCT – Fundação para a Ciência e a Tecnologia, I.P., under the project UIDB/00736/2020 (base funding) and UIDP/00736/2020 (programmatic funding).

REFERENCES

Avison, D., Lau, F., Myers, M., & Nielsen, P. A. (1999). Action Research. *Communications of the ACM*, *42*(1), 94–97. doi:10.1145/291469.291479

Baltatzis, G., Ormrod, D. G., & Grainger, N. (2008). *Social Networking Tools for Internal Communication in Large Organizations: Benefits and Barriers*. Paper presented at the 19th Australasian Conference on Software solutions, Australia.

Baskerville, R. L. (1999). Investigating Software solutions with Action Research. *Communications of the Association for Software Solutions, 2,* 1-32. doi:10.17705/1CAIS.00219

Baum, F., MacDougall, C., & Smith, D. (2006). Participatory action research. *Journal of Epidemiology and Community Health*, *60*(10), 854–857. doi:10.1136/jech.2004.028662 PMID:16973531

Bosch. (2017). *Guiding You Through Industrialization Projects Management: the workbook*. Bosch Car Multimedia.

Coghlan, D. (2019). *Doing action research in your own organization*. Sage.

Dickens, L., & Watkins, K. (1999). Action Research: Rethinking Lewin. *Management Learning*, *30*(2), 127–140. doi:10.1177/1350507699302002

Ewing, M., Men, L. R., & O'Neill, J. (2019). Using social media to engage employees: Insights from internal communication managers. *International Journal of Strategic Communication, 13*(2), 532–550. doi:10.1080/1553118X.2019.1575830

Fernandes, G., Pessôa, C., Martins, A. R., Pinto, E. B., Ruão, T., Araújo, M., Pontes, J. P., & Machado, R. J. (2018). *A Conceptual Social Media Tool for Supporting Collaborative University-Industry R&D Programs.* Paper presented at the 2018 IEEE International Conference on Engineering, Technology and Innovation (ICE/ITMC), Stuttgart, Germany. 10.1109/ICE.2018.8436297

Gode, H. E., Johansen, W., & Thomsen, C. (2020). Employee engagement in generating ideas on internal social media: A matter of meaningfulness, safety and availability. *Corporate Communications, 25*(2), 263–280. doi:10.1108/CCIJ-03-2019-0024

Gutiérrez-García, E., Recalde, E., & Alfaro, J. (2020). Corporate communication in open innovation: A case-study of three multinationals. *Corporate Communications, 26*(2), 348–364. Advance online publication. doi:10.1108/CCIJ-02-2020-0048

Hamdi, S., & Rajablu, M. (2012). Effect of Supervisor-Subordinate Communication and Leadership Style on Organizational Commitment of Nurses in Health Care Setting. *International Journal of Business and Management, 7*(23), 7–18. doi:10.5539/ijbm.v7n23p7

Hobbs, B., Aubry, M., & Thuillier, D. (2008). The project management office as an organisational innovation. *International Journal of Project Management, 26*(5), 547–555. doi:10.1016/j.ijproman.2008.05.008

Ingelmo Palomares, M., Navarro, C., & Sanz Lara, J. Á. (2018). Determining factors of success in internal communication management in Spanish companies: The influence of social media. *Corporate Communications, 23*(3), 405–422. doi:10.1108/CCIJ-03-2017-0021

Kapsali, M. (2011). Systems thinking in innovation project management: A match that works. *International Journal of Project Management, 29*(4), 396–407. doi:10.1016/j.ijproman.2011.01.003

Kivimaki, M., Länsisalmi, H., Elovainio, M., Heikkilä, A., Lindström, K., Harisalo, R., Sipilä, K., & Puolimatka, L. (2000). Communication as a determinant of organizational innovation. *R & D Management, 30*(1), 33–42. doi:10.1111/1467-9310.00155

Linke, A., & Zerfass, A. (2011). Internal communication and innovation culture: Developing a change framework. *Journal of Communication Management (London), 15*(4), 332–348. doi:10.1108/13632541111183361

Lipäinen, H. S. M., Karjaluoto, H. E., & Nevalainen, M. (2014). Digital channels in the internal communication of a multinational corporation. *Corporate Communications: An International Journal of Business and Management, 19*(3), 275–286. doi:10.1108/CCIJ-07-2012-0050

Malte, A. (2013). The communication of innovation: an empirical analysis of the advancement of innovation. *Discussion Papers on Strategy and Innovation*, 1-29.

McCartney, W. W., & Campbell, C. R. (2006). Leadership, management, and derailment. *Leadership and Organization Development Journal, 27*(3), 190–202. doi:10.1108/01437730610657712

Men, L. R. (2014). Strategic Internal Communication: Transformational Leadership, Communication Channels, and Employee Satisfaction. *Management Communication Quarterly, 28*(2), 264–284. doi:10.1177/0893318914524536

Men, L. R. (2015). The internal communication role of the chief executive officer: Communication channels, style, and effectiveness. *Public Relations Review, 41*(4), 461–471. doi:10.1016/j.pubrev.2015.06.021

Men, L. R., & Bowen, S. A. (2017). *Excellence in internal communication management.* Business Expert Press.

Munns, A. K., & Bjeirmi, B. F. (1996). The role of project management in achieving project success. *International Journal of Project Management, 14*(2), 81–88. doi:10.1016/0263-7863(95)00057-7

Ozaeta, D. E. L., & An, I. L. (2014). Use of Internal Communication Tools among AG&P Employees. *Journal of Education and Literature, 1*(1), 20–30.

PMI. (2017). *A guide to the project management body of knowledge: (PMBOK® guide).* Project Management Institute.

Qusef, A., & Ismail, K. (2016). *Social Media in Project Communications Management.* Paper presented at the 7th International Conference on Computer Science and Information Technology (CSTT), Amman, Jordan.

Remidez, H., & Jones, N. B. (2012). Developing a Model for Social Media in Project Management Communications. *International Journal of Business and Social Science, 3*(3), 33–36.

Ruão, T., Lopes, A., & Pessôa, C. (2018). Gerir identidades e culturas em organizações temporárias: o papel da comunicação [Managing identities and cultures in temporary organizations: the role of communication]. In J. Ferreira & A. T. Peixinho (Eds.), *Narrativas mediáticas e comunicação: construção da memória como processo de identidade organizacional* (pp. 1–19). Imprensa da Universidade de Coimbra.

Ruão, T., Marinho, S. & Silva, S. (2020). Scientific report E1.2.1 Software solution requirements for supporting project management processes. *Factory of Future Project.*

Rutten, R. (2016). Knowledge Creation in Temporary Organizations. In M. Peris-Ortiz & J. Ferreira (Eds.), *Cooperative and Networking Strategies in Small Business, Innovation, Technology and Knowledge Management.* Springer International Publishing.

Shenhar, A. J., & Dvir, D. (1996). Toward a typological theory of project management. *Research Policy, 25*(4), 607–632. doi:10.1016/0048-7333(95)00877-2

Shirbagi, N. (2007). Exploring Organizational Commitment and Leadership Frames within Indian and Iranian Higher Education Institutions. *Bulletin of Education & Research, 29*(1), 17–32.

Silvius, G. (2016). Social Project Management? In G. Silvius (Ed.), *Strategic Integration of Social Media into Project Management Practice* (pp. 207–293). IGI Global. doi:10.4018/978-1-4666-9867-3.ch017

Tripp, D. (2005). Pesquisa-ação: Uma introdução metodológica [Action research: a methodological introduction]. *Educação e Pesquisa, 31*(3), 443–466. doi:10.1590/S1517-97022005000300009

Turner, J. R., & Müller, R. (2003). On the nature of the project as a temporary organization. *International Journal of Project Management, 21*(1), 1–8. doi:10.1016/S0263-7863(02)00020-0

Verčič, A. T., Verčič, D., & Sriramesh, K. (2012). Internal communication: Definition, parameters, and the future. *Public Relations Review, 38*(2), 223–230. doi:10.1016/j.pubrev.2011.12.019

Vries, R. E., Bakker-Pieper, A., & Ostenveld, W. (2010). Leadership = Communication? The Relations of Leaders' Communication Styles with Leadership Styles, Knowledge Sharing and Leadership Outcomes. *Journal of Business and Psychology, 25*(3), 367–380. doi:10.100710869-009-9140-2 PMID:20700375

Vries, R. E., Bakker-Pieper, A., Siberg, R. A., Gameren, K., & Vlug, M. (2009). The Content and Dimensionality of Communication Styles. *Communication Research, 36*(2), 178–206. doi:10.1177/0093650208330250

Vuuren, M., Jong, M., & Seydel, E. R. (2006). Direct and indirect effects of supervisor communication on organizational commitment. *Corporate Communications: An International Journal of Business and Management, 12*(2), 116–128. doi:10.1108/13563280710744801

Weick, K. E. (1979). *The Social Psychology of Organizing*. Random House.

Zerfass, A., & Huck, S. (2007). Innovation, Communication, and Leadership: New Developments in Strategic Communication. *International Journal of Strategic Communication, 1*(2), 107–122. doi:10.1080/15531180701298908

Zyl, A. S. (2009). The impact of Social Networking 2.0 on organisations. *The Electronic Library, 27*(6), 906–918. doi:10.1108/02640470911004020

KEY TERMS AND DEFINITIONS

Communication Plan: The strategic design of the interaction moments that should happen between the organization and its internal and external publics, including the definition of channels and key messages.

Communication System: The architecture of the information flows that take place in an organization, involving vertical and horizontal levels.

Internal Communication: It concerns all the interactions and relationships between stakeholders at all levels within organizations and it is crucial to engage employees and achieve the organizational mission.

Innovation Communication: Is a field of study that focuses on the analysis of the symbolic interactions between an organization and its stakeholders as they deal with the development of new products or services.

Leadership: Can be defined as the process that is carried out to influence others to pursue a certain result or objective.

Project Management: It can be defined as the application of knowledge, skills, tools and techniques to design activities that make it possible to respond to project requirements.

Project Manager: The person that coordinates the tasks and expectations of all individuals within a project and whose function involves primary communication management.

Social Project Management: An approach that advocates the use of social media as an accessible and successful alternative to traditional communication channels in project management, as they increase the volume and speed of communication and information exchange and stimulate sharing, co-creation, interaction, and debate, bringing the project manager closer to the team, significantly improving communication outcomes.

Chapter 2
The Digital Influence Ecosystem and Its Relation to Organizational Communication:
Characterizations, Possibilities, and Best Practices

Carolina Frazon Terra
Cásper Líbero University, Brazil

ABSTRACT

The digital influencer market has been growing by significant numbers year after year (data from the Influencer Marketing Hub predicts USD $16.4 billion by the end of 2022). In a post-coronavirus pandemic landscape, organizations have relied more on digital influencers to reach their audiences on digital social platforms, as shown by the results of the ROI & Influence 2021 Survey by YouPix (71% of companies consider influencer marketing important in their communication strategies and intend to increase investment in that area). This chapter discusses the ecosystem that makes up digital organizational influence and its possibilities and shows its correlation with organizational communication. It compares the organizational communication with the integrated communication composite by the Brazilian researcher Margarida Kunsch and explores how organization influence fits into each of the diagram's communication pillars: internal, market, and institutional.

INTRODUCTION

The digitalization of individuals, organizations, and processes tied to mediatization and a dependence on online social platforms reveals a patchwork of actors and agents in communication environments. Saad (2021 as cited in Terra, 2021, p. 13) highlights how much this alters the communicational act: "Audience, media, brands, characters and, mainly, algorithms and bots that constitute a *habitus* very particular to our time reframe and impact the communicative praxis" (p. 13).

DOI: 10.4018/978-1-7998-9790-3.ch002

Saad (Saad, as cited in Terra, 2021) points to the world of communication as the center of this reframing "whether by their direct connection to digital acts, or by their permeability in the social fabric" (p. 13).

For Han (2018, p. 13), digital communication and social networks are shown as spaces for exposing the private. There is, then, what the author points out as the privatization of communication by digital media, since it shifts the production of information from the public to the private (as the modus operandi of the social media platforms). This is the context in which people relate, expose themselves, dialogue and are influenced.

In this article, I will discuss one of the aspects that was remodeled by online social platforms: the universe of digital influence and its correlations with and impacts on organizational communication. This theme has been a topic of interest both in the market (Youpix, Influencer Marketing Hub, Zeeng, Instituto Qualibest, among others) and in academia (Karhawi, 2017, 2020; Terra, 2017, 2021).

For Borchers (2019, p.255) organizations can cooperate with digital influencers, whom the author calls SMI, Social Media Influencers, to achieve PR and Marketing goals, as follows: for commercial partnerships, integration of commercial content in organic narratives or as independent critics. It adds that digital influencers can have roles as intermediaries, content distributors, creative content producers, community managers, issuing testimonials, strategic advisors or even event hosts. This myriad of roles opens up new opportunities for strategic communication and is capable of producing synergies for both sides (organizations and influencers).

Still on the importance of digital influence for the communication of organizations, it is possible to bring Enke and Borchers (2019):

Strategic influencer communication has become a major topic in strategic communication. Many organizations have identified social media influencers (SMIs) as relevant intermediaries, most notably because they provide access to and might even influence hard-to-reach stakeholders, e.g., teenage and young adult consumers or special interest groups. (p. 261)

A study by the Statista Global Consumer Survey (2021) conducted in 56 countries with over 1 million respondents between the ages of 18 and 64, from February 2020 to March 2021, showed that Brazil is the country that buys the most products motivated by digital influencers, followed by China and India. The State of Influencer Marketing 2021: Benchmark Report (Influencer Marketing Hub, 2021) predicts that the influencer marketing market will reach USD $13.8 billion by the end of 2021. The report also shows that "90% of our survey respondents believe influencer marketing to be an effective form of marketing".

Other data that proves the importance of individuals as a source of information and influence is the Edelman Trust Barometer (2021) that for years has placed ordinary people at the top of the trust ranking. Digital influencers have come to occupy this place of impact on people's decision-making.

The study ROI and Influence (2021) by YouPix, conducted in 2017, 2019, and more recently in 2021, shows that in Brazil the strategic relevance of the use of influencer marketing by organizations grew from 67% in 2017, to 68% in 2019, and to 71% in the latest survey.

However, this is a new field for communications studies and practices. Enke & Borchers (2019, p. 261) indicate that given the recent field, conceptual and theoretical approaches to the subject are still scarce, especially in relation to strategic communication.

Although organizational communication finds itself on shifting sands due to its state of impermanence, ephemerality, speed, and dynamism, it is necessary to take a theoretical and scientific look at the relations between communication, media, and society.

The area of organizational communication, thus, takes on another role in the list of activities it already has. The use of digital influencers as a strategy, or even becoming an influencer organization in its own right, is what drives the brand's relationship, exposure, and visibility with its target audience.

Therefore, the purpose of this chapter is: 1) to discuss the ecosystem that involves digital influence, 2) to show the opportunities to use each one of the categories with examples, and 3) to correlate it with Kunsch's integrated communication framework (2003, p. 151).

BACKGROUND

The background for this article revolves around the digitalization of life (both individual and corporate), digital influence, and the resulting relations with organizational communication.

As a starting point, digitalization is considered inseparable from the contemporary field of communication, which consequently causes significant impacts in the relations of consumption, sociability, influence, business, entertainment, education, religion, politics, etc. The effects of the digital transformation can be seen in the way that recurring communication activities in the organizational context are studied, thought of, planned, and executed. Regarding the digitization process being compulsory and irreversible, Han (2017) states:

Indeed, today we make ourselves important on social networks, on Facebook. We produce information and accelerate communication, as long as we are "producing", we make ourselves important. We gain visibility, we display ourselves like merchandise. We produce ourselves for production, for the accelerated circulation of information and communication. (p. 126)

Karhawi and Schmitz (2021, p. 107) show that the first studies about what is understood today as digital influence were carried out at the end of the 1990s and the beginning of the 2000s. At the time, the term "digital influencer" did not refer to the individuals who were seen as online opinion makers.

Terra (2021) understands influence to be "the capacity that an agent has to convince, impact or have power over, even if it is just to influence a decision, to have authority" (p. 27). For Henriques and Silva (2021), the idea of influence carries a "notable approximation to thoughtful movements that have taken shape on distinct fronts in the social sciences in recent decades by emphasizing, from multiple dimensions, the complexity that characterizes the construction and circulation of meanings in our society" (pp. 2-3).

The influencer agents in the digital environment are the new opinion makers. An endorsement by a digital influencer, journalist, media outlet, complaint site or any other entity impacts people's perception of brands, products, services, and individuals. Hence, mapping who is a part of the digital organizational influence ecosystem helps to choose which strategy is best for each moment and who to use.

For Abidin (2021), there are a variety of influencers:

(...) it is really difficult to generalize, because influencer refers to a type of occupation, a type of practice, a model of online communication. But just as there are many varieties of followers and subjects in the world, there is also a wide range of influencers.

This multiplicity of subjects and agents is what is explored here in the article, however, with a focus on the possibilities of digital corporate influence to which an organization could have.

Figure 1. The digital influence ecosystem (Terra, 2021)

Organizational communication serves as a stage for all of this, with its fundamental, leading role not only in quotidian organizational routines but also in the daily life of individuals. Within the scope of organizational relationships with the target audiences, there is also the need to incorporate the digital environment and its characters into strategy, and influence is part of this new demand. To better understand the context, I propose a map of digital corporate influence: what characters participate and how they do so.

THE DIGITAL CORPORATE INFLUENCE ECOSYSTEM

Through studies, observations, and theoretical and practical research, the relational possibilities between an organization and the universe of digital influence were mapped. Thus, some possibilities (referred to as the digital organizational influence ecosystem) are shown.

Before presenting the ecosystem itself, it is necessary to define what this concept means. Ecosystem is the term used to refer to a set of communities that exist in a determined location and interact amongst themselves and with the environment, forming a system. The word was coined by Arthur George Tansley, an ecologist who used it for the first time in 1935. In this text, the digital corporate influence ecosystem means the set of agents, groups, and individuals that influence and impact the relationships, perceptions, opinions, and decisions of an organization with its diverse public, communities, and audiences.

We will now discuss an ecosystem of organizations' influence in the digital environment.

Digital influence can happen through:

1. Internal influencers: employees of the organization with potential content outlets. They can be:
    a. Leadership as digital influencers (C-level in general or other management)
    b. Employees as digital influencers

2. Exclusive influencers: when the organization has an exclusive social actor as a personality or persona that represents the brand on digital social platforms. They can be:
    a. Virtual influencers: avatars designed for the role
    b. Exclusive influencers: a representative figure of the brand who works exclusively for that organization
3. Digital Influencer Brands: when the organization systematically and strategically produces content, is relatable, opens itself up, and has visibility to convince, persuade and act as an influencer agent.
4. Influencers, who are:
    a. Brand owners
    b. Brand partners
    c. Or in other corporate roles inside the organizations, taking on a management or executive position.
5. External influencers of any size (nano, micro, medium, macro or celebrity) and the various possibilities of paid, exchanged or co-created posts, organic relationships, etc.
6. Content producer user[1] (TERRA, 2018, p. 128): an active user of digital social platforms who produces, shares, and spreads content that is their own, that of their peers or from other information sources, as well as endorsing it to their audiences on social network sites, blogs, microblogs, online discussion forums, and news sites, among others.
7. Brand communities created by both the organizations and the target audiences.
8. Brand ambassadors: people who like and/or defend an organization or its products and services in a way that is spontaneous and deliberate on social media.
9. Affiliate and partnership program: solutions created by companies so that more individuals or representatives can sell their products and services.
10. Journalists and the press/media: they have generally always maintained their relevance, importance, and credibility with society and public opinion.
11. Ranking, opinion, and complaint sites: resources used by users to display their dissatisfaction, opinions, and so forth.

We will now show the uses of each category with real-world examples that are considered best practices.

Employees

They are called internal influencers or employees of the organizations who are selected to integrate the brand's promotion teams both internally and externally. According to Santora (2021):

An influencer marketing trend for 2021 that stems from the demand for more authentic content is that the desire to see employee-driven or employee-based content will increase. We've already seen how user-generated content can have a huge impact on sales and how brands are perceived; it only makes sense for brands to begin treating their own employees as influencers through employee advocacy programs. (para. 24)

The employees are on the front lines of consumer contact and promoting a brand. Audiences like to see behind-the-scenes information, how an organization works, what it is like to work there, etc.

The Dutch airline KLM (Klm, 2021) chose four of its employees to be representatives of the company on its social media profile. The idea is to use the four employees, from different areas of the company, as spokespeople for the brand on the official Instagram profile, but they would also produce content on their personal profiles and help create buzz about the company in their contact networks.

The food and beverage company Pepsico (Andrade, 2021) has a program called Pepfluencers where preselected, trained employees organize events, receive information and products first-hand, and spread information about the company on their personal social networks.

Leadership is a source of influencers. Some managers, like the Chief Marketing Officer of McDonald's Brazil João Branco (2021), or the Chief Marketing Officer of Pepsico Brazil Daniela Cachich (2021), use their social media profiles, especially LinkedIn, to share projects, actions, numbers, and campaigns from the brands they represent. Organizations would ideally have structured and systematic programs (with training and materials) for this to happen, recognizing and, in many times, remunerating employees who help bring more visibility to the company.

Next, the exclusive influencer is proposed, also considering the internal environment of organizations.

Exclusive influencers

Organizations can also create or develop their own digital influencers. It is a way to control the narrative and bring visibility to the brand's attributes and values using a persona that was planned, thought out, and designed to fulfill that role. When dealing with virtual influencers, i.e. avatars created specifically for that function, Brazil has dozens of examples of brands that use this strategy, such as: Lu (Magazine Luiza, 2021) from the retailer Magazine Luiza; CB (Casas Bahia, 2021) from the competition Casas Bahia; Carina, from Carrefour Brazil (2019); Rennata from Renner (2021); Mara from the clothing brand Amaro (2021); and Rê from Unilever's brand Rexona Brazil (2021), among others. Some prefer having a real person, like in the case of the influence marketing company Influencer Marketing Hub, with their brand representative (Influencermh, 2021) who is tasked with being the face in the videos shown on the organization's social media profiles. It is, literally, the face and voice of the brand on social media. In addition to trained or selected employees or avatars created for the role of representatives of brands, the organization itself can become a digital influencer, as explained below.

Digital influencer brands

Many organizations understand that they can produce their own content and have exposure, relationship, and visibility strategies on social media platforms. They are assuming the role of media and publishers (Terra, 2021, p. 70), creating their own communication outlets with the potential to directly reach their target audiences and, as a consequence, influence them. At Terra (2021) there is a methodology—referred to by the acronym REATIVA[2]—that helps transform brands into digital influencers step by step. A digital influencer brand is, thus, an organization that: produces relevant, convincing, evolving, and impactful content; is fluent in digital language; knows digital social platforms; brings together people, users, other brands, influencers, and etc.; has a purpose; supports social topics; defines its metrics and KPIs; and is, above all, a digital strategist. Oreo Spain created an initiative called Oreo Academy (2021), a website that also has an Instagram profile. With the initiative, the brand teaches recipes using the cookie, invites famous chefs to create new recipes, and even incentivizes consumers to not only make the recipes but also to publish and reference the brand. It is a way to generate their own content that influences purchasing, but it also works on the relationship with users and recognizes them. The organization positions itself as a reference source in recipe content and brings together influencers, chefs, consumers, and interested parties. With this action, the brand saw a 35% increase in cookie sales in Spain. Another possibility for the brand to become influential is using digital influencers in corporate functions, as is possible to see below.

Influencers in Executive Roles

Some digital influencers reach a successful size, visibility, and relevance that they are invited (or decide) to create their own brands or product lines. In Brazil, the beauty and makeup influencer Bianca Andrade launched a product line called Boca Rosa Beauty with the brand Payot (Payot, 2021). The singer Anitta was invited by the beer brand Skol to be the head of creativity and innovation for the product Beats (Anitta, 2021), and more recently she was invited to join the administrative board of the Brazilian digital bank Nubank (Redação Nubank, 2021). Many other influencers have caught the attention of companies and have taken on corporate roles or functions, contributing by bringing greater visibility to the brand and offering their expertise and knowledge of the digital world and networks. The most common or conventional use for the partnership between brands and influencers is the hiring of external influencers, as it is possible to see in the next topic.

External influencers

The most well-known and used category in influence marketing, these digital influencers can be categorized by their nature, origin and/or number of followers. There are micro-influencers (small-sized influencers or those dedicated to a specific topic); influencers (originated on social media platforms, became professionalized and rose to become experts on some topics, and have significant audiences); and digital celebrities (those who didn't necessarily originate on digital social platforms, but understand that digital platforms can be important to disseminate their programs, shows, events, partnerships, etc. They are actors, singers, artists, presenters, athletes, musicians, etc.).

The actions with these groups can be:

1. Paid partnership: When the organization and/or agency pays the influencer to make a post.
2. Relationship: must be organic. The organizations send information or products and services to be tested by the influencer, but there is no obligation or promise from the influencer to publish reviews.
3. Co-creation: when the brand and influencer reach an agreement about how, where, and in what way the content will reach the desired audiences and create this action together.
4. Take over: when the influencer takes control of the brand's profile for a predetermined period. It could be to cover an event, launch or situation.
5. Exchange: when the organization offers a product, service or benefit in exchange for the influencer sharing content.

It is considered that an ordinary and connected user of online social networks, can also be an influencing agent. It was conventionally called as a content producer user (as can be seen in the next item), as it behaves as a vehicle that produces, shares or diffuses content that mentions the brands.

Content producer user

Content producer users (Terra, 2011, p. 68) are common people that are on social media producing content about experiences they have had with brands, products or services. They comment on purchases, post-sales, and conversations with organizations and customer service or even show the products or services they acquired, with the intention to offer services to their partners or simply express good or bad experiences on social media. The organizations can have a relation with this type of influencer by stimulating them to produce spontaneous content about their products and services.

That is what M&M chocolate and the makeup brand Quem Disse Berenice did in Brazil: they asked consumers to produce makeup looks according to the color of M&M that came out of the package. The brands captured the results using the hashtag #MMsEscolheMinhaMaquiagem[3] (2021). Both brands made the user-generated content available to be replicated on both profiles. They also created together lists of people who admire and/or consume the brands and, later, they could do relationship sales and other actions, obviously remaining in compliance with the general data protection laws.

The Brazilian soft drink company Guaraná Antarctica celebrated 100 years in 2021 and created a hotsite to invite fans to produce content, vote on campaigns, and actively participate in the brand's strategy. The campaign "Be a 100-year partner" (Guaraná Antarctica, 2021) solicits participants to register in order to win cash prizes, choose the best ads, get a VIP discount on the drink delivery app Zé Delivery, which is owned by the brand, and choose the new tagline for the brand's Youtube channel. Content producer users can also be professional consumers who buy and test products or are invited by organizations to perform this role.

A study conducted by Stackla and published by Kiso (2021) shows that 59% of those interviewed agree that content created by other consumers (user-generated content) is the most authentic type of content. Using content producer users is a way to spread and share brand content on the social media profiles and contact networks of regular people who have some relation to the organization and its products and services, whether they are already clients, admirers or interested in it, or because they want to share their experiences and opinions with their audiences and networks.

Users interested in or loyal to a brand can be gathered in brand communities, managed by the organization itself. That is the focus of the next item.

Brand communities

Brand communities can be created by both the organizations themselves and by their consumers and/or fans. The company Canon has a community to share information and tips and tricks about photography and filming with their customers and fans. In the words of the brand itself (Canon Connected, 2021): "Join our Canon Ambassadors, community, and experts as they challenge their own creativity to adapt to the ever-changing world, to develop, inform and entertain our Canon Connected community."

The GoPro company also has a community of fans and followers, and even created a prize for the best images and videos produced by users: the #GoProAwards (GoPro, 2021), with the motto, "Get the shot. Get featured. Get paid."

The toy company Lego has various communities created and maintained by fans across the globe, as is the case of LUG (Lego Users Group) Brazil (2021): "[a nonprofit club that] unites people in order to swap experiences about the LEGO® toy hobby, through their various possibilities and topics." Communities like Brick Fanatics (2021) or AFOLs (LEGOMBRINQ, 2021), Adult Fans of Lego, are present around the world and are organized and managed by devoted fans of the brand. In the cases of Canon and GoPro, the organizations are concerned about forming communities of people interested in their brands, products, and services, supplying them with information, tips, training, and even financial recognition. In the case of Lego fans, communities form more spontaneously. There is a possibility that a user is a fan of a brand for a variety of reasons. By appreciating the organization, its products or services, can become a brand ambassador. It is about these subjects that is discussed below.

Brand ambassadors

These are users who like a brand, product, and service and support it spontaneously without expecting anything in return, within their contact network, on social media, and in reviews, etc. Fans of Netflix (#Netflixlovers, 2021), Apple (#Applemaniac) or the singer Lady Gaga (Little Monsters, 2021) fall into this group.

The department store Macy's created an ambassador program that also included its employees: Macy's Style Crew (2021). Through the hashtag #MacysStyleCrew it is possible to find the items suggested by the brand's ambassador team in a wide range of sectors.

The brand Victoria's Secret launched the VS Collective (2021) with female representatives from society, substituting the team of models formerly called Angels. The brand announced the collective as a partnership platform:

We are proud to announce an exciting new partnership platform, #TheVSCollective, designed to shape the future of Victoria's Secret. These extraordinary partners, with their unique backgrounds, interests and passions will collaborate with us to create revolutionary product collections, compelling and inspiring content, new internal associate programs and rally support for causes vital to women.

Today we welcome:

@adutakech

@amandadecadenet

*@eileen_gu_*

@mrapinoe

@palomija

@priyankachopra

@valentts (Victoria's Secret, 2021)

El Qudsi (2020) points out that many organizations prefer to engage influencer communities and ambassador programs instead of doing one-off actions with digital influencers: "In an effort to maintain genuine influencer partnerships and keep those loyal, high-performing influencers in their inner circles, many brands are switching from one-off campaigns to the creation of influencer communities and ambassador programs" (para. 12).

Users who want to earn some money from the sale of products and services on their personal social media profiles can apply for affiliate programs, especially retailers that nurture such type of initiative. Competing for such users to influence other consumers is the objective of the affiliate and partner programs discussed below.

Affiliate and Partnership Programs

Affiliate programs are mechanisms created by brands so that influencers and average people become a display window for their products and services, paying them with a percentage of the sales they generate on their social media profiles and/or sites and blogs.

Affiliate programs reward individuals who help promote and sell products and services through a commission on the sales of what they helped promote.

Amazon, for example, has a program for sellers to market their items on the platform and for affiliates, those who want to display items from the retailer in their own digital environments like sites, blogs, and social media profiles. Amazon Associates is divided into the Amazon Influencer Program (2021a) and Amazon's Affiliate Marketing Program (2021b).

A public that has always been considered an influencer and opinion maker are journalists and media outlets. With the communication based on platforms and the inclination to the digital, these agents started to produce content on this environment as well. The following explains why they are considered digital influencers.

Journalists and the Press/Media

Independent of being individuals on social media, journalists and publishers, in general, influence, impact, and generate perceptions about organizations, their executives and employees, and their products and services. What these figures and institutions publish has a high chance of gaining visibility and generating repercussions. It is not without reason that many media outlets are creating profiles on TikTok, using formats and languages that are very distinct from traditional journalism. It is a means to impact audiences on this platform, influencing, convincing, and bringing in more readers/viewers to the press. As examples, we can cite the French newspaper Le Monde (2021), the Argentine paper La Nación (2021), and the Brazilian news program Jornal da Record (2021).

However, it is not only adopting new formats or languages that make journalists or the outlets they represent gain notoriety and influence. The fact they are a part of the media makes their content expressive, visible, and credible. This is why they can be considered influencers.

Sites that gather complaints and user experiences, commercially or not, are an important source for other consumers, for the press and for public opinion in general. For these reasons, it is explained below why they are considered agents that exert influence and impact on organizations.

Complaint, Opinion, and Ranking Sites

These are environments where people search and do research. How organizations deal with complaints, buyers' reviews, and negative transaction experiences, etc., is of interest to users before making a purchase or commercial transaction. The concern that companies have towards client servicing and post-sales interferes in many purchasing decisions.

The Brazilian complaint site Reclame Aqui is one such site. Reviews about products and services can also be obtained on sites like eBay, MercadoLivre, Amazon, and AliExpress, among others.

There are also sites like Glassdoor, a site where employees and former employees of companies can give their opinions about the work and organizational environment, salary policies, leadership, and possibilities for development and recognition, among other items, and influence whoever is in search of a job or wants to know more about a determined company. In the company description on its website, they state:

Built on the foundation of increasing workplace transparency, Glassdoor combines the latest jobs with millions of company ratings and reviews, CEO approval ratings, salary reports, interview reviews and questions, benefits reviews, office photos, and more. Unlike other job sites, all of this information is shared by those who know a company best — the employees. In turn, job seekers on Glassdoor are well-researched and more informed about the jobs and companies they apply to and consider joining. This is why thousands of employers across all industries and sizes turn to Glassdoor to help them recruit and hire quality candidates at scale who stay longer. Glassdoor is available anywhere via its mobile apps. (GLASSDOOR, 2021)

The organization Sleeping Giants and its branches around the world also work as a tool to put pressure on and influence organizations. They leading global movements: in Brazil in June 2021, they were able to convince various brands to break partnerships and stop advertising on Sikêra Jr.'s television program after the presenter made homophobic, aggressive comments about a Burger King campaign on how to approach the topic of same-sex unions with children. Called #DesmonetizaSikera* (Sleeping Giants Brasil, 2021), the movement gained the attention of the media and forced the TV network to rethink its program.

Other movements like #StopHateForProfit or the petitions produced by GreenPeace also serve as a tool to put pressure on and influence brands, obligating them to take a stance.

Next, we will relate all the above possibilities to organizational communication.

THE INTEGRATED ORGANIZATIONAL COMMUNICATION COMPOSITE AND DIGITAL CORPORATE INFLUENCE

Integrated communication presupposes a combination of institutional communication, marketing communication, internal communication, and administrative communication, forming a mix, a composite of organizational communication. The author of this framework adds that these forms allow the organization to relate to their audiences' universe and to society in general (Kunsch, 2003, p. 150).

Kunsch (2016, p. 9) highlights that organizational communication must be understood as a phenomenon and a communicative process in constant interaction between the organization and its various interlocutors, in a way that is dialectic and seeking to find consensus through negotiation. She also shows that all the actors involved in this context confront challenges in a society that is under frequent transformation, turbulence and adversity, and that organizations' communication plays a fundamental role in such situations. Contemporary organizational communication shifts from a tactical role to a strategic one, considering the human factor and adding value to the organizations (Kunsch, 2016, p. 45).

Figure 2. Integrated communications framework
Source: Kunsch, 2003, p. 151.

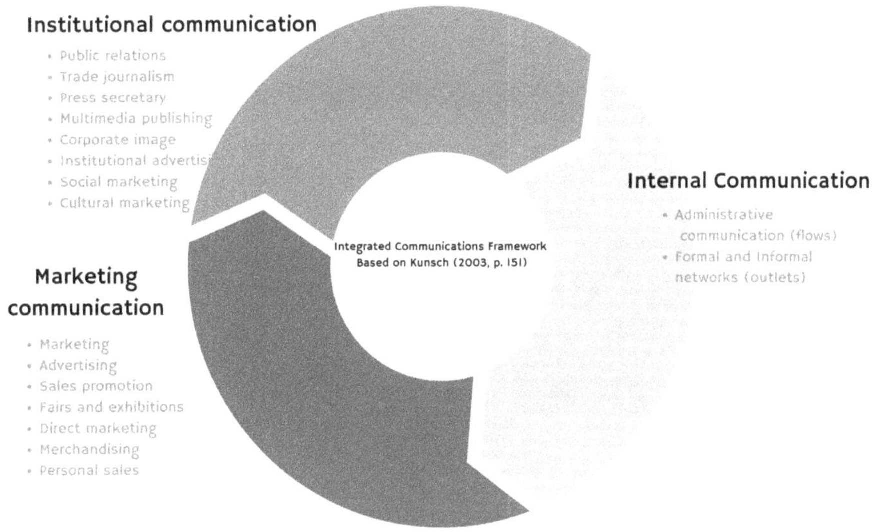

Communicational organization, using Kunsch's diagram of integrated communication (2003, p. 151) as a base, is divided into internal communication, institutional communication and marketing communication, as reproduced below.

Internal communication, according to Kunsch (2003, pp. 153-154), is characterized by administrative communication, its flows, levels, and formal and informal networks, and by planned communication to enable possible interactions between organizations and employees, their instruments and tools.

Marketing communication, in turn, is linked to marketing and has the purpose of disseminating advertising.

Institutional communication, according to Kunsch (2003), "is directly responsible, through the strategic management of public relations, for the construction and editing of a strong, positive corporate image and identity of an organization" (p. 164).

Now that we have an understanding of the integrated communication framework, we will apply the diagram to the universe of digital influence.

SOLUTIONS AND RECOMMENDATIONS

The ecosystem of digital influence, proposed here, fits into Kunsch's three pillars in various ways. We will discuss the possibilities now.

Under **internal communication**, actions of relationship, visibility, and exposure with internal and/or exclusive influencers can be used with the goal of acting as internal agents of persuasion and impact, together with the company's other internal public. They are chosen, trained, and capable of promoting content and key messages, and they bring visibility to the organization's topics of interest, among other possibilities. They can be employees, leaders, managers or another person specially chosen for the role.

Figure 3. Integrated communications framework adapted to influencer communications context
Source: Carolina Terra based on Kunsch's (2003, p. 151) original framework.

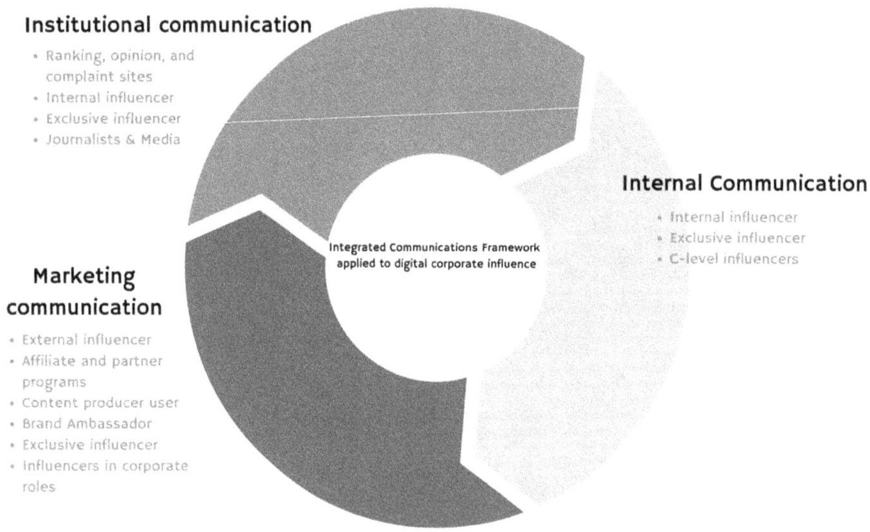

Under **institutional communication** there are possibilities for building relationships and the brand through the actions of internal influencers, who can act both as internal agents, as discussed above, and also contribute to giving more personalization and humanization to the organization externally; with exclusive influencers, creating personas that represent the brand and speak in its name; with journalists and communication outlets, in the sense of selling agendas, ideas, and content; and finally, working to improve the corporate image and reputation on complaint, opinion, and review sites by monitoring and responding to the needs that appear.

Lastly, under **marketing communication** the myriad of possibilities is broader: paid and organic actions can be created with external influencers; influencers can be hired by brands to fill corporate, management, consultant or creative roles; virtual or exclusive influencers can help with sales and commercial talking points; business partners and affiliates can be used and compensated for visibility and sales; and relationship and recognition programs with content producer users and brand ambassadors can be designed.

With this, we conclude our rereading of the classic concept of Kunsch's integrated communication and its possible correlation with the context of digital corporate influence.

FUTURE RESEARCH DIRECTIONS

The digital influence ecosystem can be tested in practice, in the market, and other agents can be added to this composite, depending on the type of organization, negotiation, sector, and specificity. Mapping the agents and influencer groups that each organization has, according to *Figure 1* (The Digital Corporate Influence Ecosystem) is recommended. It is also suggested that the organizational communication be planned and executed in a holistic and integrated way. Thus, depending on the desired communication goals, the best strategy within the integrated communication composite adapted for digital influence (as seen in *Figure 3*) can be used.

CONCLUSION

This article approached the triad:

- **the digitalization** (of individuals and corporations) on account of the need for presence, exposure and engagement in the digital realm, and especially on digital social platforms;
- **the influence**, as a factor of attention for organizations that want to stand out, building image and reputation and even impacting sales; and finally,
- **the communication** in the context of the organizations that has not only gained more visibility and relevance, but has also come to play a fundamental role in building relationships and strategies that help to sell and build a good image and reputation in volatile times of hyperconnection and extreme concern with media visibility.

The tripod explained above is in the context of a platform society (van Djick, 2019, 2013) and datafication scenario (Mayer-Schoenberger and Cukier, 2013; van Djick, 2014). The digital influence has, in this context, an impact factor in corporate communications. The platformization concerns about the dependence of individuals and organizations on social and digital media platforms. Datafication, in turn, is anchored in the collection of data generated by individuals and institutions in the environment of digital social platforms. Finally, the influence happens due to these two scenarios: people and brands in digital environments interacting, exposing themselves and consequently generating data.

The other objective of this article was to introduce a system of mapping digital influencer agents that impact organizations. The digital organizational influence ecosystem was created, and it can be applied to companies of any sector, segment or size with the goal of identifying opportunities for relationships, exposure, and visibility.

The ecosystem, as highlighted throughout the paper, can be contained within the integrated communication framework and seen through this lens. Depending on the organization's communication objective, approaching an agent of influence or becoming a digital influencer brand is suggested.

The integrated communication composite allows digital influence to be applied to internal, institutional and/or marketing communication through the actions and activities with influencers of various types, roles, and objectives.

Finally, it can be said that through a digital influence strategy, organizations are able to construct narratives in the digital environment, especially on social media platforms, that combine content, exposure, visibility, and relationship and, therefore, contribute to building the brand, image, and reputation both for themselves and the institutions involved.

REFERENCES

Abidin, C. (2021, March) Digital influencers, internet celebrities and bloggers: an interview with Crystal Abidin. Interviewed by Issaaf Karhawi. *Intercom, Brazilian Journal of Communication Sciences, 44*(1). https://www.scielo.br/scielo.php?script=sci_arttext&pid=S1809-58442021000100289&lng=pt&nrm=iso&tlng=pt

Amaro. (2021). *Hi, I am Mara*. https://amaro.com/br/pt/mara-influencer-virtual-3d

Amazon. (2021a). *Amazon Influencer Program*. Retrieved from https://www.amazon.com/shop/info

Amazon. (2021b). *Amazon Associates - Amazon's affiliate marketing program*. Retrieved from https://affiliate-program.amazon.com/

Andrade, T. (2021). *Pepfluencer*. Instagram. Retrieved from https://www.instagram.com/p/COQnGer-romM/

Anitta [@anitta]. (2021, September 30). *Skol Beats*. Instagram. Retrieved from https://www.instagram.com/p/B3DUlDonudG/

#Applemaniac. (2021). *#AppleManiac*. Instagram. https://www.instagram.com/explore/tags/applemaniac/

Branco, J. (2021). *João Branco from Méqui*. LinkedIn. Retrieved from https://www.linkedin.com/in/falajoaobranco/

Brasil, L. U. G. (2021). *Who we are*. Retrieved from https://lugbrasil.com/quem-somos/

Brick Fanatics. (2021). *About*. Retrieved from https://www.brickfanatics.com/about/

Cachich, D. (2021). *Daniela Cachich, Pepsico's CMO*. LinkedIn. Retrieved from https://www.linkedin.com/in/daniela-cachich/

Canon website. (2021). *Canon Connected*. Retrieved from https://www.canon-europe.com/pro/canon-connected/

Carrefour Brasil. (2019, October 16). *Carina, elected Carrefour's new virtual assistant* [video]. Youtube. Retrieved from https://www.youtube.com/watch?v=0EC6WW9Pr_0

CB [@casasbahia]. (2020, October 16). *Casas Bahia store*. Instagram. Retrieved from https://www.instagram.com/p/CGZ8MX3gG1X/

Edelman. (2021) *Edelman Trust Barometer 2021*. Retrieved from https://www.edelman.com.br/sites/g/files/aatuss291/files/2021-03/2021%20Edelman%20Trust%20Barometer_Brazil%20%2B%20Global_POR_Imprensa_1.pdf

El Qudsi, I. (2020, December 21). The state of influencer marketing: top insights for 2021. *Forbes*. https://www.forbes.com/sites/forbesagencycouncil/2020/12/21/the-state-of-influencer-marketing-top-insights-for-2021/?sh=6681a177ddcd

Enke, N., & Borchers, N. S. (2019). Social Media Influencers in Strategic Communication: A Conceptual Framework for Strategic Social Media Influencer Communication. *International Journal of Strategic Communication, 13*(4), 261–277. doi:10.1080/1553118X.2019.1620234

Glassdoor. (2021). *About us*. Retrieved from https://www.glassdoor.com/about-us/?_gl=1%2Ap63aiu%2A_ga%2AMTM5MzY3OTE2OC4xNjI0ODg5NjEw%2A_ga_RC95PMVB3H%2AMTYyNDg4OTYwOS4xLjAuMTYyNDg4OTYxNC41NQ

GoPro. (2021). *The GoPro Awards recognizes you*. Retrieved from https://gopro.com/pt/br/awards

Guaraná Antartica. (2021). *Become a member of the 100 years*. Retrieved from https://www.guaranaantarctica.com.br/100anos/promocoes

Han, B.-C. (2017). *The burnout society*. Vozes Publishing House.

Han, B.-C. (2018). *In the Swarm: Digital Prospects*. Vozes Publishing House.

Henriques, M. S., & Silva, D. R. (2021, July). *Indirect influence and strategy: notes on the inter-influence system and its possibilities for organizational communication* [Paper presentation]. 30th Annual Meeting of Compós 2021, São Paulo. https://proceedings.science/compos-2021/trabalhos/influencia-indireta-e-estrategia--notas-sobre-o-sistema-de-interinfluencias-e-suas-possibilidades-para-a-comunicacao-org

Influencer Marketing Hub. (2022). *The State of Influencer Marketing 2022: Benchmark Report*. Retrieved from https://influencermarketinghub.com/influencer-marketing-benchmark-report/

Influencermh [@influencermh]. (2020, June 28). *What is an influencer.* Instagram. Retrieved from https://www.instagram.com/p/CCByOaRjijq/

Jornal da Record [@jornaldarecord]. (2021). *Daily News from Record*. TikTok. Retrieved from https://www.tiktok.com/@jornaldarecord

Karhawi, I. (2017, May). *Digital influencers: concepts and practices under discussion* [Paper presentation]. XI Brazilian Scientific Congress of Organizational Communication and Public Relations Researchers – Abrapcorp 2017, Belo Horizonte, Brazil. https://www.abrapcorp.org.br/portal/index.php/2011/10/anais-online/

Karhawi, I. (2020). *From blogger to influencer: Stages of professionalization of the Brazilian fashion blogosphere*. Sulina Publishing House.

Karhawi, I., & Schmitz, D. (2021). Will there be a new post-pandemic digital influence? Four questions for debate. In R. C. Oliveira, D. Christino, & E. V. Machado Jr., (Eds.), *Covid -19 and the communication*. Cegraf UFG.

Kiso, R. [@rkiso]. (2021, August 19). *What kind of content is most authentic?* Instagram. Retrieved from https://www.instagram.com/p/CSwMlSbrJhQ/?utm_medium=share_sheet

KLM [@klm]. (2021, February 24). *Blue Crew* [video]. Instagram. Retrieved from https://www.instagram.com/p/CLq1fYpFz6g/

Kunsch, M. M. K. (2003). *Public relations planning in integrated communications*. Summus Publishing House.

Kunsch, M. M. K. (2016). *Strategic organizational communication: conceptual and applied contributions*. Summus Publishing House.

La Nación [@lanacioncom]. (2021). *La Nación*. TikTok. Retrieved from https://www.tiktok.com/@lanacioncom?lang=pt-BR

Le Monde [@lemondefr]. (2021). *Le Monde*. TikTok. Retrieved from https://www.tiktok.com/@lemondefr?lang=pt-BR

LegoMBrinq. (2021). *Fãs da marca Lego* Retrieved from https://www.legombrinq.com.br/fas

#LittleMonsters. (2021). *#LittleMonsters*. Instagram. https://www.instagram.com/explore/tags/littlemonsters/

Macy's. (2021). *Macy's Style Crew*. Retrieved from https://www.macys.com/style-crew/

Magazine Luiza [@magazineluiza]. (2021). *Magazine Luiza Store*. Instagram. Retrieved from https://www.instagram.com/magazineluiza/

Mayer-Schoenberger, V., & Cukier, K. (2013). *Big data*. Campus Publishing House.

#M&MChooseMyMakeup. (2021). *#M&MChooseMyMakeup*. Instagram. https://www.instagram.com/explore/tags/mmsescolheminhamaquiagem/

#NetflixLovers. (2021). *#Netflixlovers*. Instagram. https://www.instagram.com/explore/tags/netflixlovers/

Oreo Academy. (2021). *What is the Oreo Academy?* Retrieved from https://www.oreoacademy.es/oreo-academy.php

Payot. (2021). *Boca Rosa by Payot*. Retrieved from https://www.lojapayot.com.br/bia%20todo%20dia?utm_source=Google&utm_medium=cpc&utm_campaign=lancamento-bia-todo-dia

Redação Nubank. (2021, June 21). *Anitta is the new board member*. Retrieved from https://blog.nubank.com.br/anitta-nubank-membro-conselho/

Renner. (2021). *Meet Rennata*. Retrieved from https://www.lojasrenner.com.br/lp/conheca-rennata

Rexona Brasil [@rexonabrasil]. (2021, March 22). *Should I turn off the faucet when soaping my hands?* Instagram. Retrieved from https://www.instagram.com/p/CMvCXs9jViS/

Santora, J. (2021). *13 Influencer Marketing Trends to Watch in 2021*. Influencer Marketing Hub. Retrieved from https://influencermarketinghub.com/influencer-marketing-trends/

Sleeping Giants Brasil. (2021, June 28). *#desmonetizasikera*. Twitter. Retrieved from https://twitter.com/slpng_giants_pt/status/1409529130195038209

Statista Global Consumer Survey. (2021). *The influence of influencers*. Instagram. Retrieved from https://www.instagram.com/p/CPa8AahLuJV/

Tansley, A. G. (1935). The use and abuse of vegetational concepts and terms. *Ecology*, *16*, 284–307.

Terra, C. F. (2011). *Social Media...Now What? What you need to know to implement a social media project*. Difusão Publishing House.

Terra, C. F. (2017). From broadcast to socialcast: notes on the long tail of digital influence. Communicare Magazine, 17, 80-95.

Terra, C. F. (2018). Content producer user. In D. Scheid, J. Machado, & P. M. Pérsigo (Eds.), *Strata of entries: dictionary of organizational communication* (p. 128). FACOS-UFSM.

Terra, C. F. (2021). *Digital influencer brands: How to transform organizations into digital content producers*. Difusão Publishing House.

Van Djick, J. (2013). Facebook and the engineering of connectivity: a multi-layered approach to social media platforms. *Convergence: The International Journal of Research into New Media Technologies*. https://journals.sagepub.com/doi/abs/10.1177/1354856512457548

Van Djick, J. (2019). *The platform society: An interview with José van Dijck*. DigiLabour Research Group. https://digilabour.com.br/2019/03/06/a-sociedade-da-plataforma-entrevista-com-jose-van-dijck/

Victoria's Secret [@victoriassecret]. (2021, June 16). *VS Collective*. Instagram. Retrieved from https://www.instagram.com/p/CQMruB5n9jx/

Youpix. (2021). *ROI and Influence 2021*. Retrieved from https://drive.google.com/file/d/1qbOuD6mJvBhPoFDv0LyNnDYUpPBwP8ko/view

KEY TERMS AND DEFINITIONS

Brand Ambassadors: Individuals or communities that love a brand, service and/or product and voluntarily and deliberately produce content about an organization.

Content Producer User: A connected user, producer and/or curator of active content that produces, shares, and spreads their own content, that of their peers, and content from other sources of information, as well as endorsing it to their audiences on social media platforms.

Digital Influence: The capacity to impact and motivate actions regarding decisions, ideas, and ideologies using social media platforms.

Digital Influencer Brands: Organizations that produce content and become a reference point in their segments or sectors and have defined strategies for relationships, exposure, and visibility in digital media. Due to their relevance and engagement capacity, they are usually content publishers in their areas of specialization.

Digital Influencers: Agents who produce or curate content on digital social platforms and have a captive audience on social media.

Digital Organizational Influence Ecosystem: Proposed mapping of influencer agents that impact the perceptions, decisions, and actions of the public and audiences in relation to an organization.

(Integrated) Organizational Communication: Communication composite within the context of organizations that includes internal communication, institutional communication, and marketing communication.

Internal Influencers: Employees and/or leaders and managers who are reference sources and considered influential both within the organizations they are a part of and by external audiences. They can be part of a systematized program or only figures who play this role within their companies.

Virtual Influencers: Avatars designed with the purpose of engaging, interacting, and being spokespeople of the organizations they represent.

ENDNOTES

[*] Translator's note: #DefundSikera.

[1] The original term, in Brazilian Portuguese, is *Usuário-Mídia*. Therefore, the most reasonable translated version of that expression is "Content Producer User".

[2] In Brazilian Portuguese, REATIVA means reactive. The acronym, in its original language, is a perfect match to every letter on it: R (relationship and recognition); E (entertainment and engagement); A (action and authenticity); T (transparency); I (interaction); V (visibility); and A (in Portuguese, evaluation is *avaliação*).

[3] Translator's note: #MMsChoosesMyMakeup.

Chapter 3
Disruptive Communication: Challenges and Opportunities of the 21st Century

Margareth Boarini
Pontifícia Universidade Católica de São Paulo, Brazil

ABSTRACT

Challenges became more complex to organizational communication since the dissemination and the confluence of big data, artificial intelligence, and internet of things. Ubiquitous and powerful, these technologies require a specific knowledge, partnerships with different areas (data sciences), and learning how to work with a new communicational agent, the non-human. Bots should produce content e become popular as brand virtual influencer among other things. There are many and good opportunities to create and implement more assertive strategies by using data-driven and IA tools. The purpose of this chapter is to contextualize digital transformations and to highlight challenges and opportunities on what the author has defined as second disruptive wave to organizational communication. The first one happened when social media emerged as the main social arena on the contemporary society. The research was supported by a qualitative methodology with a theoretical framework and documentary research from various fields of knowledge.

INTRODUCTION

The confluence of big data, artificial intelligence and internet of things technologies should inaugurate a new phase of reconfiguration in the communication field, demanding an inter- and multidisciplinary look from industry professionals to explore opportunities and overcome challenges.

Ubiquitous, the three technologies, when combined, have their power enhanced. As explained by Gabriel (2019, p. 28): "big data without artificial intelligence is like a brain that only has memory but cannot process. Artificial intelligence without big data is like a brain that only has processing capacity, but nothing to process". The internet of things, when it joins the two, creates a driving force whose power allows it to structure semantic systems.

DOI: 10.4018/978-1-7998-9790-3.ch003

Simultaneously with the advent of technologies with such characteristics, the current context experienced by humanity and defended by Schwab (2016) as the Fourth Industrial Revolution has been marked by phenomena with important impacts on organizational communication, such as misinformation and fake news, digital influencers, and activism. The arrival of bots, as has already happened in the disciplines of journalism, law, or advertising, for example, also requires constant observation. In the same way that there are situations to explore a differentiated communication strategy, using a non-human digital influencer, such as those already present on the Instagram social network, possibilities may arise to replace human labor with robots to perform repetitive tasks.

As Kunsch (2016, p. 39) states, the contemporary world leaves no doubt about the relevance of communication, mainly due to its ability to cross the entire global social system, and, for this reason, in his understanding, the quality of contextual analysis, reflections and work planning are linked to the communicator's ability to know how to situate society.

Supported by a qualitative, exploratory methodology with a theoretical framework and documentary research from various fields of knowledge, this chapter presents a reflection on what the author calls the second disruptive wave in organizational communication, formed by the effects of big data (BD), artificial intelligence (AI) and internet of things (IoT) technologies within the sector.

In the author's assessment, the first wave took shape from the 2000s onwards, a period in which digital social networks and media emerged as the main social arena. The dynamics of this type of environment and the strong characteristics of scalability and immediacy forced a series of reconfigurations in narratives, relationships with audiences, in addition to contributing to the approach of marketing and public relations disciplines (Scott, 2017).

The reason for timing the first and second wave, respectively, beginning with the consolidation of digital social networks and media and the dissemination of BD, AI and IoT technologies, is justified by the strongly disruptive nature of these two moments, with deep implications for the entire life of society and, consequently, also for the profession of communicator is exercised.

The focus is on the universe of communication agencies because this kind of company operates as a hub, having clients of all profiles on one side, the most diverse audiences on the other, and characterized as a service provider which operates in all areas of communication. For these reasons, an agency can be recognized as an important thermometer of the movements experienced by the organizational communication field.

The discussion highlighted in this chapter becomes relevant to the organizational communication field by contributing to the promotion of reflections on contemporary demands and how to meet them, to ensure that the sector maintains its strategic and relevant image.

CONTEXTUALIZING THEORY INTO FACTS

The presentation of disruptive waves in communication requires a contextualized observation of the facts to translate the challenges, reveal the opportunities and the paths to follow. In the dictionary, the world "context" expresses the meaning of the interrelationship of circumstances of an act or event (Houaiss, 2009, Webster's 2003), and, in an era in which inter- and multidisciplinary has become imperative, the ability to be transversal emerges increasingly as a determining factor for the achievement of goals.

Revisiting past facts contributes to the reconstruction of structural changes that were already taking place at a certain time, but, due to the dynamics of everyday life, were not evident in such a transparent way. Three facts portrayed bellow illustrate the complexity of the transformations that took place within the scope that covers the same period of the research: from the beginning of the 2000s, when digital social networks and digital media began their consolidation, to the current moment, marked by network life and ubiquitous technologies.

Although the episodes are presented briefly, they illustrate some of the phenomena theorized by those who study communication. Cases show theory in practice. Among these phenomena, the following stand out: the rise of the prosumer (Toffler, 2014), which combines production and circulation of its own content, the prevalence of trust among peers and no longer exclusively in institutions, the multidirectional flow of information and communication and the relevance of the rise of the network society (Castells, 2003).

The effect of information contagion (Berger, 2014) can be detected in all the cases below and reflects the context in which the event is inserted. In the first example presented, the force of propagation was concentrated in the traditional press, in the information flow based on the vertical transmitter-receiver dynamic, and by word of mouth. In the second and third events, the contagion process relied on the scalability and immediacy of the networks, on the influence of ordinary people, on post-to-post, on the horizontality of the information flow.

In the wake of this phenomena, it is possible to observe between the lines the effects of the intersection between communication and technology, through how the cell phone has progressively gained prominence and how the ubiquitous technologies of contemporaneity began to spread, such as big data and artificial intelligence.

2001 – On the morning of September 11, 2001, the United States suffered a series of terrorist attacks, when commercial aircrafts were used as weapons. In New York City, the targets were the buildings of the Twin Towers complex, two architectural icons located in a busy and important area of the city, which have always been part of the scene of photos and videos of tourists, media and people in general. This, plus the characteristics of the attack contribute to the information about tragedy being quickly documented, publicized, and spread.

The world watched the live broadcast on TV. Traditional media show images of the attacks. Press media also did its coverage on internet, but unlike what happens today, the prevalence was long texts and not so many images. Salaverría (2005) observes that 9/11 event revealed some weaknesses in the coverage of press media on the internet: lack of technological foresight, lack of editorial prudence, lack of own identity. Digital social networks were not yet so present and popular. Facebook, for instance, was created in 2004. Twitter, in 2006.

At the time of the attack, people faced serious communication problems because the terrorist attack. Telecommunication was seriously compromised in the New York City region by the destruction of several cell towers, affecting the wireless network and interrupting the signal of the lines of many people near the Twin Towers. Reports from relatives and survivors showed that many people who were inside the buildings at the time of the accidents contacted their relatives through phone calls (desk phone). In calls made from inside planes, in most cases, people used airphones, available on planes, whose radiotelephonic technology made it possible to make up eight calls at the same time (Zuckoff, 2019).

Cell phones were already widely used, and SMS (short message service) was the predominant type of the text message. In fact, SMS is largely used in US even today differently from other countries as Brazil where WhatsApp is the more downloaded app. In the beginning of 2000s, smartphones, cameras, and Bluetooth technology (Ericsson) were the innovations in cellphone market. In 2001, there were between 118 million and 128 million wireless network subscribers for mobile phones, according to data released from the CTA Wireless Association (Reardon, 2011).

From an organizational communication perspective, the tragic episode became a classic case of crisis management. Argenti (2002) notes how difficult the details of the event were: "Many companies have crisis contingency and disaster recovery plans but only few had been rigorously tested as they were on September 11".

According to professor and consultant, some companies lost scores of employees, many others saw key components of their infrastructure destroyed, many other companies had to face secondary effects (customers and suppliers) but every company in the US had to deal with traumatized workers. "Suddenly, crisis management was every executive's job" (Argenti, 2002).

2009 – On the morning of January 15, 2009, the pilot of U.S. Airways flight 1549 landed the Airbus 320 on the Hudson River (New York) after detecting a serious technical problem that made impossible to reach the nearest airport safely.

The whole world, including the traditional media, only were informed about the fact from a post published, and quickly shared, on the social network Twitter. Janis Krums, author of the post, is a businessman who was coincidentally on a ferry headed for New Jersey. Surprised by a plane landing there, Krums quickly took his iPhone, took a photo, accessed his Twitter account (TwitPic), wrote a post and published it along with the photo: "There's a plane in the Hudson. I'm on the ferry going to pick up the people. Crazy".

The episode illustrates the strong presence of digital social networks at the time and its impact on the dynamics of the press. It also highlights the power of the empowered user to produce and share his own content. Provided with a smart mobile device with internet access and present on social network, Krums produced and shared (posted), in matter of minutes, content with photo and text. Shared on networks, the post attracted attention around the world, including the mainstream media world. 34 minutes was the time between Krums posted on Twitter and its first interview to mainstream media (MSNBC TV) about the event (Kullin, 2009).

Not only Krums was famous, but the event made a revolution for Twitter and became emblematic in the history of social media. It showed in practice the theory of the prosumer (Toffler, 2014), of media convergence (Jenkins, 2015), of the strong presence of digital social networks in the life of society. Besides all this, the tweet posted by Krums about the landing of flight 1549 on the Hudson River became internationally recognized as "Twitter's defining moment". Twitter co-founder Jack Dorsey said in an interview to CNBC in 2013 that the episode changed everything (Langer, 2014): "Suddenly the world turned its attention because we were the source of news - and it wasn't us, it was this person in the boat using the service, which is even more amazing."

Poynter Institute also highlighted how relevant was this tweet, replying to an excerpt from the newspaper The Telegraph (Shedden, 2015):

The incident also provided some interesting insights into new media versus old new media. As Twitter user hrhmedia pointed out, the FlightStats information website was showing the downed flight as 26 minutes late, but still 'en route' to its destination of Charlotte in North Carolina. And while Twitter's trends page, which identifies the hot keywords used in tweets, was flagging up terms such as 'US Airways', 'Hudson', 'plane' and 'crash', Google's similar trending service showed no signs of those keywords an hour and more after the incident occurred.

Wikipedia, though, was almost instantly updated following the plane crash, both to add a whole page about flight 1549, and also to amend an entry about water landings, and the survival rate of those involved.

As in countless previous disasters, from the China earthquakes to the Mumbai terrorist attacks, the social media has been at the forefront of breaking and disseminating news. It provides an invaluable real-time running commentary on events, which, when taken together with the factual accuracy, analysis and commentary of the mainstream media, provides a fascinating and rich account of major incidents.

As the iPhone blog puts it: 'Paradigms shift. It happened with telegraph, with radio, with television, with satellite… is it happening again with the iPhone and Twitter?

Twitter has become over time a powerful platform for telling stories, expressing opinions, advocating causes. Born in 2006, the network strengthened its projection in 2009, when it added its retweet button and began to be recognized as a journalistic broadcasting platform. Besides the Hudson River episode, Michael Jackson's death and the elections in Iran were some of the most commented news on the network that year (Jesus, 2019).

2020 – On March 11, 2020, the World Health Organization (WHO) declared the Covid-19 pandemic. By then, the world had already been following the cases of the disease spreading around the world, which had started in China. The world also followed attentively any news about the unknown virus, its possible origin, what the symptoms were like, how the disease was transmitted. Attention was also focused on the beginning of research and partnerships between universities and industry in the search for vaccines, medicines, cures.

In the year 2020, life already had a preponderant digital dynamic. In additional to digital social networks, instant messages apps also became an important channel to flow information about the pandemic scenario. The pandemic scenario has shortened society's most radical digitalization process, transposing to the virtual ambience family and professional meetings, religious or entertainment events, as well as medical, psychological consultations, and even wake ceremonies.

The annual We are social 2021 study (Hootsuite) revealed, among many other findings, the growth in the relevance of online life, which takes up 40 percent of our time. Of a world population estimated at 7.7 billion by the United Nations Organizations (2021), 4.66 billion people are internet users total, who record an average navigation time of the order of 6h54m (from any type of device). Access to the internet exclusively through cell phones is provided by 4,38 billion people. According to Statista (2021), the number of mobile devices operating worldwide is almost 15 billion. By 2025 almost 19 billion are expected. Regarding digital social networks, the study showed that 4.20 billion people are regularly active in this kind of environment.

It is relevant to observe that the number of unconnected people in the world is equally big: more than three billion. For this reason, they are not included in a series of important government action that plan professional and educational development programs, health programs or even communication initiatives.

During the pandemic, people showed strong preference for audio and video tools on social media and TikTok, Instagram (Reels) or ClubHouse are examples of that.

The impact of the pandemic on digital transformation of society was not only on social media.

Other technologies market had registered expressive and exponential growth. The 2021 edition of the Worldwide Big Data and Analytics Spending Guide study, conducted by the International Data Corporation (IDC), pointed to a 10 percent increase in worldwide investments related to big data and analytics solutions, totaling just over UD$ 215 billion. Within the pandemic scenario, big data showed its strategic importance by revealing patterns to support the understanding of the disease, treatments, initiatives in general.

"Big data is not about trying to 'teach' a computer to 'think' like a human being. Rather, it is about applying mathematics to huge amounts of data to predict probabilities [...]", state the authors Mayer-Schoenberger & Cukier (2013, p. 8).

The development of big data, the crucial 'feeder' of artificial intelligence, has great impact in all areas of society. From data it is possible to get a strategic information that allows to draw a prediction. Siegel (2017) considers prediction the true gold of contemporary society because of its characteristics to reinvent sectors and to refine offers of products and services, for example.

Apart from advantages in use big data and prediction in many situations, it is important to know all the risks brought by them too. The dynamics of filter bubbles (Pariser, 2011) has strong effects and synthesizes this complex process of data flow. "Customization is based on bargain. In exchange for the filtering service, we give large companies a huge amount of data about our daily lives" (Pariser, 2011, p. 224). The concept of filter bubbles (Pariser, 2011) shows how the algorithms isolate people in their own bubble, avoiding another perspective from any fact.

As in technology, good and bad are always close, every communicator must be careful not to cross the thin frontier between what can harm the audience's right to privacy and what can generate communication opportunities without harm in this regard.

Many phenomena that existed before digital transformation of society became stronger and more frequent by the use and features of new technologies, bringing effects in the communication sphere of organization, brands, and citizens.

In 2016, the term fake news still seemed to be able to synthesize the process of dissemination of rumors or lies, with or without intention to cause harm. Not anymore. "The weaponization of context", as defined by Wardle (2019), demonstrates how this kind of market of lies has become more and more robust and improved by the features of new technologies. The term information disorder was chosen by her because it expresses a complex process formed by misinformation, disinformation e malinformation, three categories that specify different kinds of lies (intention or not to harm).

During the pandemic, the flow of misinformation about the Covid-19 was so strong e brought so many negative effects to citizens, governments worried about treatments approved by scientists, that WHO created a new term, disinfodemic, to express wrong and false information can cause death. According to the study "Disinfodemic: deciphering Covid-19 disinformation", produced by Julie Posetti & Kalina Bontcheva (2020), and released by WHO in 2020:

Disinformation long predates COVID-19. Falsehoods designed to undermine the validity of science extend from the resurgence of the 'flat earth movement' to those that dispute scientific consensus on climate change, usually for narrow political or economic gain. The fabrications that contaminate public health information today rely on the same dissemination tools traditionally used to distribute disinformation. What's novel are the themes and the very direct impacts. COVID-19 disinformation creates confusion about medical science with immediate impact on every person on the planet, and upon whole societies. It is more toxic and more deadly than disinformation about other subjects. That is why this policy brief coins the term disinfodemic.

TECHNOLOGIES AND NEW AGENTS

Historically, communication has taken advantage of the benefits brought by technological advances, but challenges and opportunities can be highlighted by the context: consumer and citizen behavior, brands influence, and so strategies can be better designed.

The contemporary world leaves no doubt about the relevance of communication and the role of its professionals, mainly due to its ability to cross the entire global social system, understanding and contextualizing events (Kunsch, 2016, p. 39).

The identification of the two disruptive waves in organizational communication results from a process of analysis of the social context since the maturity of social media until the complexities faced by professional during the recent years. This does not mean that there were no other challenges periods. The option to delimitate from the beginning of 2000s until now is base fundamentally on two factors. The first concerns the social structural impacts (behavior and way of living) from relevant technological advances and the second refers to the emergence of new communication agents.

The first disruptive wave contemplates the consolidation of digital social networks, the way they established a new dimension of life, an online life, media convergence (Jenkins, 2015) and the prosumer important role (Toffler, 2014).

The second wave is based on the popularization of three technologies: big data, artificial intelligence and internet of things and the way they already impact and the potential to create more impacts during the next years. This wave is also affected by the arrival of the non-human (Latour, 2012) to the organizational communication universe as a powerful communicational agent. Technologies are characterized by ubiquity, something present simultaneously everywhere, surpassing space and physical time (Santaella, 2013).

THE FIRST DISRUPTIVE WAVE

The first disruptive wave happened with the consolidation of social networks and some socio-economic phenomena instituted new paradigms in relationships. The exclusively unidirectional and verticalized strategy until then was replaces by a multidirectional conversation, supported not only by technological tools and media convergence (Jenkins, 2015), but by the user's empowerment through the ability to produce and share their own content at a low cost, immediately and in a capillary way.

Jenkins (2015) defines as convergence "the flow of content across multiple media platforms, the cooperation between multiple media industries, and the migratory behavior of media audiences who will go anywhere in search of the kinds of entertainment experiences they want".

The emergence of the prosumer (Toffler, 2014) redesigned the flow of information by overthrowing the hierarchical order between sender and receiver. The benefits of an organization by participating in social media were soon perceived as they emphatically contribute to generate reputation, sales, prospect opportunities and capture new audiences within an environment of authentic interaction (Mesquista, Ruão & Andrade, 2020). The authors alert organizations that the relationship with audiences can transform customers in brand ambassador by a good communication work.

The user empowerment process started to set the tone in the relationship between organizations and their audiences and reconfigured the way how brands became trustful to the customers. Instead of 'buying' the official message about the qualities of a brand, the empowerment user decided to 'listen' to other users to believe or not in any brand. Trust was built by the peers and "companies are naked on the web" (Brogan & Smith, 2020, p. 14).

"We read product reviews on websites, believing that they are a reflection of what the reviewers think of the product—only to find out that products returning a higher cut of the profits are always rated higher than products that may be superior in quality", say Brogan & Smith (2020, p. 8). The authors explored 'trust agents' term to express that people nor oriented to sale.

The social media user provoked crucial changes to communication. Previously based on influencing and convincing media and their audiences, organizations had to shift the focus of their relationships programs to identify users and develop initiatives to generate trust and credibility (Terra, 2016, p. 259).

Much of the commercial success of companies such as Amazon, TripAdvisor and Netflix was obtained through the dynamics of collaborative reviews and a particular style of conversation between brand and their users, appropriate to new environments, well perceived and responsible for more engagement (Boarini, 2015).

Empowerment users and their peers are responsible for business, trust, reputation and for more data collected.

THE SECOND DISRUPTIVE WAVE

After two decades, it is possible to observe that organizational communication overcome the challenges emerged during the first disruptive wave. There are other challenges now, another moment of disruption, designed by another social and technological context. Ubiquitous and powerful technologies require specific understanding and the exercise of multidisciplinarity between different disciplines, as data sciences or mathematics, for example. Multidisciplinarity will also be mandatory to create teams (employee or by external suppliers) with people from multiple skills and different backgrounds to think and deliver the best communication plan of this era of big data, artificial intelligence, and internet of things.

This will be one of the major challenges for the communication leaders. "The market does not expect the professional of communication to become a big data specialist, but someone with the capacity to dialogue with those who understand and work with the topic and who is not afraid of mathematics" (Boarini, 2020).

The use of data has been more common in the marketing area, but progressively it can become a reality in organizational communication as well, in principle in large agencies until it becomes popular and accessible to companies of all sizes.

Large communication groups have been investing in data and analytics units in recent years. Although the marketing area may have been the initial concern, companies have signaled the relevance of data for the development of products, services, and for decision making in all communicational fields.

IPG Group announced the acquisition of Acxiom in October 2018. A year after acquiring the company (2019), the group was satisfied with the operation, attributing to it the achievement of several business deals (Monllos, 2019).

The Edelman group has also expanded investments in the area. In an interview for the portal ResearchLive (2020), chief executive Richard Edelman said that the decision to bring together the "research, analytics, performance and paid marketing times, and increase our investment in technology, we have removed the silos and built systems that are enabling real innovation."

Data highlights opportunities and risks. As opportunities: new ways of interaction, new audiences to be reached, the development of new products and services or even the creation of a new business unit. Data can also identify possible image crisis hotspots. The important thing is to know how to transform date into information and then create a communication strategy appropriate for each moment. The communication professional will need the partnership of data scientists (Boarini, 2019).

Many organizations (from various sectors) have even welcomed data scientists on its boards of directors (Davenport, 2017).

Since the consolidation of digital social networks, Scott (2017) draws attention to the proximity of the marketing and PR (Public Relations) disciplines. Digital technology tools have blurred the boundaries between them and made marketing less seen as advertising while PR became less focused on the media (Scott, 2017). This scenario must be kept.

The arrival of the non-human will open new perspectives. Bots can be used to produce content in general, monitoring crisis and relationship programs, summarize information for employee or even to 'give life' to virtual influencers. In the same way, digital influencers (humans) participate of special campaigns created by organizational communication teams, virtual influencers (non-humans) can be part of it.

Journalism experienced similar situation almost ten years ago when many media companies introduced bots to produce content.

In the competitive financial information market, Cyborg is the bot with a mission to put Bloomberg ahead of Reuters, for example. Heliograf works for The Post and, in 2018, won the Global BIGGIES Award in the category "Excellence in Use of Bots", a recognition of the use of good practices in products and strategies in big data and artificial intelligence in the media market (Peiser, 2019).

Born as bot and engaged in human causes (against racism and in favor of the feminism), Lil Miquela is a 19-year-old 'girl', who has three million followers on her Instagram page (2021), where she introduces herself as a 'robot' living in Los Angeles (United States). The life of this bot is managed in such way that there is no rupture between the online and offline dimensions for the followers' eyes. Lil Miquela appears naturally in photos interacting with humans, participating in brand campaigns, and embracing causes.

Not so famous, Noonoouri, a 19 years old 'girl' and about 400,000 followers, is also a bot and present herself as a digital character and vegan activists on her Instagram page (2021).

Karhawi (2021, p. 142) states that digital influencers exploit their own reputation, built together their universe of followers to contribute to the reputation of brands. In this case, there would be no difference between associating the brand with human and non-human influencers since they have a good reputation.

The second disruptive wave, however, does not only bring opportunities to the professional of organizational communication. Among the issues, information disorder is a topic to be observed daily. It is a phenomenon not born nowadays but which gained a great power of dissemination and destruction during the recent years. Amplified by powerful technological tools, it has been exploited by groups that want to cause social instability or by totalitarian governments.

Ferrari (2021) defines misinformation as the great parasite of the 21st century. The damage caused is immense in all types of institutions (governments, media, organizations, science, etc) and in all the roles of a person (citizen, consumer, professional, etc). "The battle of fact-checking is relevant for a world where critical thinking prevails, where citizens can evaluate and decide better. A world where people are less manipulating" (Ferrari, 2021).

An efficient battle against misinformation requires vision and transversal initiatives from communication. For this, it will be necessary to approach areas beyond communication, such as psychology, for example. To create narratives that rebut a lie it may be relevant to understand what makes a person share it.

The article "Psychology of fake news", written by Pennycook & Rand (2021) states that "the spread of misinformation online presents both a scientific puzzle and a practical challenge" and digital literacy can be one of the strategies to help.

Brogan & Smith (2020, p. 16) observe that "this is the era of "fake news. Fewer people than ever before can easily discern between a credible news source and fabricated news. We need trust agents in companies. In fact, businesses cannot exist without them anymore".

The volatility of public opinion is another constant issue which requires a frequent contextualizing monitoring. Farias (2019, p. 136) analyzes public opinion as something that changes very quickly in the social ecosystem:

Mutatis mutandis, the opinion is really a system under permanent construction, absolutely fluid. The result of information facing the consequences originated in the filters to which they are submitted, generating perceptions thar go beyond place and time, as they result from elements impregnated to the thought that comes from outside, from the experience and the report of others.

Education to promote critical thinking is part of the same strategy to combat misinformation and any type of manipulation that one intends to address to public opinion. Farias (2019, p. 136) argues that opinion is born from a process of construction, debate, and dialogue, and reinforce that man and society evolve free thought, free will and free expression.

The frenetic pace of changes and the confluence of important innovations on several fronts led Schwab (2016) to define the moment as the Fourth Industrial Revolution, a period formed by interaction and fusion of technologies such as quantum computing, gene sequencing and renewable energies, in addition to the interaction between the physical, digital, and biological domains. It is a term to describe a set of ongoing and impeding transformations in the systems that surround us (Schwab, 2016).

According to the author, in the three previous industrial revolutions, changes did not happen at such an exponential pace and took place in a more linear way, compared to contemporary transformations. "The revolution is not just modifying 'what' and 'how', but also 'who' we are (Schwab, 2016, p. 13).

The second disruptive wave requires a multidisciplinary look and attitude, partnerships with companies and professionals from different areas, such as data scientists, and investment to improve knowledge to ensure opportunities for the business, for the career and to face competitiveness with the non-human "colleague".

BIG DATA, ARTIFICIAL INTELLIGENCE, INTERNET OF THINGS

In early 2018, when the author started this present research, big data and artificial intelligence were still a promising trend for the organizational communication. However, despite of while slow the popularity of internet of things (IoT) technology and its association with two others, it should accentuate a trend of using these technologies in communication business and relationship opportunities.

Below there is a brief explanation of each technology.

Big data has become traditionally known for being based on "Vs": volume, variety, velocity, and value. Mayer-Schoenberger & Cukier (2013) explain that the advent of digitalization has facilitated and made the entire process of capture and analyze, storage and processing easier, shortening the period from years to days. In Amaral's definition (2016, p. 5), data refers to facts collected and generally stored, while information is analyzed data, which already carries some meaning.

"In data analysis, information is what emerges from a set of aggregate data, giving meaning [...]. Knowledge is the articulation of this information with another information (Lemos, 2021, p. 272-273).

Big data should be used as a relevant tool in various organizational communication process, such as reputation management process, identifying risks, to improve decision-making related to relationship programs, prospecting business opportunities (Wiencierz and Roettger, 2019, Riel, 2014). Wiencierz and Roettger (2019, p. 12), states:

Our study shows that big data makes it easier to identify correlations between practitioner communication actions and the behavioral actions of stakeholders or organizational outcomes. With the big data application tools, existing analyses can be optimized by conducting them with a much broader database. For example, the optimized analysis of the share of voice was mentioned in order to gain detailed insights in real time about the public attention to the brand, the products or the company compared to the competitors. Issues management can also be extended to automated, permanent real-time crisis monitoring. As our model illustrates, it is crucial that big data measures such as real-time crisis monitoring are integrated into the communication process. In this case, an internal crisis plan must contain information on who receives which automatic messages from the system in a crisis situation and how to proceed in this situation.

Artificial intelligence, according to Kaufman (2019, p. 178-181), expresses the "symbiosis between human and machine by coupling artificial intelligence systems to the human body and the interaction between human and machine a two distinct species connected". It is a field linked to intelligence and learning problem solving.

AI is like a big umbrella that houses subfields as machine learning and deep learning and relates to countless others. Machine learning refers to the process in which computers are given the ability to learn without being programmed, making use of algorithms and methodologies that will take care of improving learning (performance) from data collection (Gabriel, 2018). From the large volume of data and the mining process, machine learning systems will gain experience and perform better.

"Deep learning employs artificial neural network algorithms, deepening the processing in layers of artificial neurons to solve more complex problems. [...] Deep learning is paving the way for an AI future closer to what we see in fiction, to reach the human level of intelligence" (Gabriel, 2018)

"Since the goal of IA is the development of intelligence, it relates to all areas of knowledge that are used in the study of intelligence, as well as methods, algorithms, and techniques that can make software/ hardware intelligent in the human sense of the word", states Gabriel (2018, p. 188)

It has stopped being science fiction and has become reality. Like so many other technologies, it has ubiquitous and pervasive characteristics, and that is why we do not always realize that we are using it. The searches we do on Google, the routes we take on Waze, the interactions with Siri are all examples of how artificial intelligence has been embedded in our society for some time now.

In the opinion of futurist Amy Webb (2019, p. 9), "it is the third era of computing. We are in the midst of significant transformation, not unlike the generation who lived through the Industrial Revolution".

The concept behind the internet of things is one that connects almost everything to the internet. Internet of things is the expression that seeks to designate the whole set of new services and devices that bring together at least three elementary points: connectivity, use of sensors and computational capacity for processing and storing data (Magrani, 2019, p. 22).

Gabriel (2018, p. 28) neatly summarizes the dynamics of the confluence of big data, artificial intelligence, and the internet of things: "big data without artificial intelligence is like a brain that only has a memory but cannot process. Artificial intelligence without big data is like a brain that only has processing capacity but nothing to process". The internet of things joins the two and establishes a driving force, whose power allows it to structure semantic systems.

The algorithm is a relevant element in this dynamic. It is a kind of a guide containing a series of instructions to reach a task. Lemos (2021, p. 426) defines algorithm as the new media, since "they are ways of shaping reality, being at the same time a message, a channel, a sender and a receiver, they not only process information and perform tasks, but those tasks compel us to do something". And, in his opinion, "the culture of algorithms is now the basis of digital culture".

Would it be possible to make this gear more powerful? Yes, through the prediction process. According to the authors Agrawal, Gans and Goldfarb (2018, p. 385), the prediction process uses information that already exists to generate information that does not exist. It is considered important to analyzing and drawing correlations, either with data on consumptions preferences, or interactions with friends, or humor status in posts, for example.

This mapping process is already a reality. Marketing already exploits this.

All these technologies bring many good opportunities. However, communication professionals and companies must be aware of the specific legislations that guide the use of data and ethical aspects. European Union has the General Data Protection Regulation (GDPR) since 2016. Brazil has its General Personal Data Protection Law (LGPD) since 2020. China announced Personal Information Protection Law (PIPL) to the end of 2021.

FROM THE DREAM OF COLLABORATION TO TOTAL CONTROL

The communicational challenges are not only concentrated in the use of technologies but are enhanced by a series of phenomena that have arisen in the context of disruptions promoted by them.

When social networks became widespread and established themselves as the great arena of contemporary society, the predominant feeling was that the possibility of free access, connection and collaboration between people, production of own content, among other examples, would contribute to a more plural world. Over the last few years, however, the reality that has been unfolding also shows the other side of life on the net: misinformation, propagation of hate speech, authoritarianism, end of privacy.

In the book The Hype Machine, Sinan Aran (2020), director of the MIT Initiative on the Digital Economy, highlighted how important networks (Facebook, Twitter, WhatsApp, and Instagram) were during pandemic 2020 in the process of global collaboration, spread of good information on care to avoid the disease and the spread of the virus, and to keep the professional life active. "They became indispensable sources of human connection, timely medical information, social support, outreach, pandemic fundraising, free impromptu concerts, collaborative art projects, and real-time updates about the spread of the virus" (Aran, 2020, p. 9). On the other hand, the author also highlighted the perils of network life.

The author coined the term "the Hype Machine" to express real-time communications ecosystem created by social media. According to him (2020, p. 16):

We've constructed an expansive, multifaceted machine that spans the globe and conducts the flow of information, opinions, and behaviors through society. This Hype Machine connects us in a worldwide communication network, exchanging trillions of messages a day, guided by algorithms, designed to inform, persuade, entertain, and manipulate us. The object of this machine is the human psyche. It was designed to stimulate our neurological impulses, to draw us in and persuade us to change how we shop, vote, and exercise, and even who we love. It analyzes us to give us options for what to read, buy, and believe. It then learns from our choices and iteratively optimizes its offerings. As it operates, it generates a data exhaust that traces each of our preferences, desires, interests, and time-stamped, geolocated activities around the world. It then feeds on its own data exhaust, refining its process, perfecting its analysis, and improving its persuasive leverage. Its motivation is money, which it maximizes by engaging us. The more precise it gets, the more engaging and persuasive it becomes. The more persuasive it becomes, the more revenue it generates and the bigger it grows. This is the story of the Hype Machine — the social media industrial complex: how it was designed, how it works, how it affects us, and how we can adapt to it.

Lemos (2021, p. 246) states that "our lives are being turned into data. And that's not a metaphor. Everything you do with your smartphone is turned into digital data that is captured, analyzed, and turned into inputs".

"Surveillance capitalism unilaterally claims human experience as free raw material for translation into behavioral data", says Zuboff (2019, p. 8).

Magrani (2019, p.12) argues that the internet of things promotes a strong process of connection and exchange information about collected personal data. For this reason, the author advocates a regulation of the "use of technology to prevent it from being used as a tool to violate fundamental rights such as the right to privacy and the right to identity".

Much of contemporary life is ruled by large technology companies, whether through networks, search engines, artificial intelligence, the dynamics created by the internet of things, and always by the capture and use of data. When discussing competitiveness in the field of artificial intelligence, Webb (2019) classifies the group of these big companies (originated in the United States and China) as the Big Nine: Google, Microsoft, Amazon, Facebook, IBM, and Apple (US), and Baidu, Alibaba, and Tencent (China).

ON THE RADAR

This study about the impact of big data, artificial intelligence, and internet of things on organizational communication is not complete. It intends to be a contribution to highlight challenges, issues and opportunities created by new technologies and phenomena in contemporary society. Communication context is very complex, there are many intersections to reveal and many topics for research should emerge from the daily routine experience with multidisciplinary disciplines.

CONCLUSIONS

The chapter had the purpose to contextualize the scenario of the formation of the second disruptive wave in organizational communication and to highlight challenges, issues, and opportunities of the confluence of big data, artificial intelligence, internet of things and phenomena that impact communication. The second wave requires a contextualized look at the transformations to promote inter and multidisciplinary efficient initiatives.

Technological advances present in the first disruptive wave brought numerous challenges but, in a way, closer to communicational universe, such the emergence of prosumer, the media convergence, narratives in a new environment, management and maintenance of relationships with different kind of audiences, exploration of audiovisual resources, among many other elements.

The second wave includes more complex challenges, because they demand help and joint work with professionals from other disciplines, with specific knowledge about BD, AI and IoT technologies, besides many others that orbit them. Identifying business and career opportunities will depend on how companies and professionals are prepared for.

The arrival of non-human as new communication agent can be face as a good opportunity to improve communication and to optimize work at the same time it can reshape the tasks. Given the complexity of the context, the author suggests that organizational communication professionals invest in multidisciplinary knowledge to develop business and career strategies consistent with the demands of the market and competition with the non-human, and to be attentive to partnerships with companies specialized in the technologies presented.

REFERENCES

Agrawal, A., Gams, J., & Goldfarb, A. (2018). *Prediction machines*. Harvard Business Review Press.

Amaral, F. (2016). *Introdução à ciência de dados* [Introduction to data science]. Editora Alta Books.

Aral, S. (2020). *The Hype Machine*. Random House.

Argenti, P. (2006, July). How technology has influenced the field of corporate communication. *Journal of Business and Technical Communication, 20*(3), 357-370. Retrieved 10 August, 2021, from https://web.archive.org/web/20200320012849id_/https://study.sagepub.com/sites/default/files/2%20Argenti%202006.pdf doi:10.1177/1050651906287260

Argenti, P. A. (2002, December). Crisis communication: Lessons from 9/11. *Harvard Business Review*. https://hbr.org/2002/12/crisis-communication-lessons-from-911

Aronoff, C. (2012). *Acidente na Pennsylvania Road, 1908. In: Relações públicas: profissão e prática. 3a. edição* [Accident on Pennsylvania Road, 1908. In: Public relations: profession and practice. 3rd edition]. AMGH Editora. Retrieved 10 August, 2021, from https://bit.ly/3Lssw8F

Basu, T. (2021, January 25). The future of social networks might be audio. *MIT Technology Review*. Retrieved 10 August, 2021, from https://www.technologyreview.com/2021/01/25/1016723/the-future-of-social-networks-might-be-audio-clubhouse-twitter-spaces/

Berger, J. (2014). *Contágio* [Contagion]. Texto Editores Ltda.

Boarini, M. (2018). *Big data e inteligência artificial são a nova onda disruptiva a desafiar os profissionais* [Big data and artificial intelligence are the new disruptive wave to challenge professionals] [Paper presentation]. The meeting of Abrapcorp 2018, Goiânia-GO, Brazil. Retrieved 10 August, 2021, from https://abrapcorp.org.br/

Boarini, M. (2019). *Big data e inteligência artificial: aliados na detecção de oportunidades e crises* [Big data and artificial intelligence: allies in detecting opportunities and crises] [Paper presentation]. The meeting of Abrapcorp 2019, São Paulo-SP, Brazil. Retrieved 05 November, 2021, from https://abrapcorp.org.br/

Boarini, M. (2020). *A comunicação disruptiva do século XXI* [The disruptive communication of the 21st century XXI] (Unpublished Doctoral's thesis). Pontifícia Universidade Católica de São Paulo (PUC-SP), São Paulo-SP, Brasil.

Boarini, M. (2021). A audiência revelada: o big data acentua os desafios profissionais [The audience revealed: big data accentuates professional challenges]. In C. Terra, B. M. Dreyer, & J. F. Raposo (Eds.), *Comunicação organizacional: práticas, desafios e perspectivas digitais* (pp. 126–137). Summus Editorial.

Brogan, C., & Smith, J. (2020). *Trust agents*. Wiley.

Castells, M. (2003). *Sociedade em rede* [Networked Society]. Paz e Terra.

Davenport, T. H. (2017). *Big data no trabalho* [Big Data at Work]. Editora Alta Books.

Ferrari, P. (2021). *Como sair das bolhas* [How to get out of bubbles] (2a. ed. rev.). Educ São Paulo.

Gabriel, M. (2018). *Você, eu e os robôs* [You, me and the robots.]. Editora Atlas.

Jenkins, H. (2015). *A cultura da convergência* [The culture of convergence]. Ed. Aleph.

Jesus, A. (2019, March 21). A evolução da Plataforma Twitter em imagens e vídeos [The evolution of the Twitter Platform in images and videos]. *Techtudo*. Retrieved 05 November 2021, from https://www.techtudo.com.br/noticias/2012/03/evolucao-da-plataforma-do-twitter-em-imagens-e-videos.ghtml

Karhawi, I. (2021). Comunicação organizacional e influenciadores digitais: aproximações e conflitos [Organizational communication and digital influencers: approximations and conflicts]. In Comunicação organizacional: práticas, desafios e perspectivas digitais (pp. 141-153). Summus Editorial.

Kaufman, D. (2019). *A inteligência artificial irá suplantar a inteligência humana? (Coleção Interrogações)* [Will artificial intelligence supplant human intelligence? (Question Marks Collection)] (Locais do Kindle 178-181). Estação das Letras e Cores. Kindle.

Krums, J. (2001, September 11). *Post on TwitPic*. Retrieved 10 August, 2021, from https://twitpic.com/135xa

Kullin, H. (2009, January 16). *Social media in the Hudson River plane crash*. Retrieved 10 August, 2021, from https://www.socialmediatoday.com/content/social-media-hudson-river-plane-crash

Kunsch, M. M. K. (2016). Prefácio. In M. M. K. Kunsch (Ed.), *Comunicação organizacional estratégica: aportes, conceitos e aplicados* [Strategic organizational communication: contributions, concepts and applied] (pp. 9–13). Summus Editorial.

Langer, E. (2014, January 15). *The five-year anniversary of Twitter's defining moment.* CNBC. Retrieved 10 August, 2021, from https://www.cnbc.com/2014/01/15/the-five-year-anniversary-of-twitters-defining-moment.html

Latour, B. (2012). *Reagregando o social. Uma introdução à teoria do ator-rede* [Reaggregating the social. An introduction to actor-network theory]. Edufba.

Lemos, A. (2021). *A tecnologia é um virus* [Technology is a Virus]. Editora Sulina.

Lil Miquela [@lilmiquela]. (2021, October 9). *Instagram.* Retrieved 09 October, 2021, from https://www.instagram.com/lilmiquela/?hl=pt-br

Magrani, E. (2019). *Entre dados e robôs* [Between data and robots]. Arquipelago Editorial Ltda.

Maia, B. (2021, June 9). A importância do analytics na crise da Covid-19. [The importance of analytics in the Covid-19 crisis]. *MIT Sloan Management Review.* Retrieved 10 August, 2021, from https://www.mitsloanreview.com.br/post/a-importancia-do-analytics-na-crise-da-covid-19

Mayer-Schoenberger, V., & Cukier, K. (2013). *Big data: como extrair volume, variedade, velocidade e valor da avalanche da informação cotidiana* [Big data: how to extract volume, variety, speed and value from the avalanche of everyday information]. Editora Campus.

Mesquita, K., Ruão, T., & Andrade, J. G. (2020, December). Transformações da comunicação organizacional: novas práticas e desafios nas mídias sociais. Dinâmicas comunicativas e transformações sociais [Transformations of organizational communication: new practices and challenges in social media. Communicative dynamics and social transformations]. In *Atas das VII Jornadas Doutorais em Comunicação & Estudos Culturais.* CECS – Centro de Estudos de Comunicação e Sociedade Universidade do Minho Braga. Retrieved 10 August, 2021, from http://www.lasics.uminho.pt/ojs/index.php/cecs_ebooks/article/view/3301/3190

Monllos, K. (2019, August 5). 1 year in, IPG attributes growth and new business wins to Acxiom acquisition. *Digiday.* Retrieved 05 November 2021, from https://digiday.com/marketing/one-year-ipg-attributes-growth-new-business-wins-acxiom-acquisition/

Noonoouri [@noonoouri]. (2021, October 9). *Instagram.* https://www.instagram.com/noonoouri/?hl=pt-br

Pardes, A. (2020, December 16). The future of social media is all talk. *Wired.* Retrieved 10 August, 2021, from https://www.wired.com/story/the-future-of-social-media-is-all-talk/

Pariser, E. (2011). *O filtro invisível* [The invisible filter]. Jorge Zahar Editor. Kindle.

Peiser, J. (2019, February 5). The rise of the robot reporter. *The New York Times.* Retrieved 10 August, 2021, from https://www.nytimes.com/2019/02/05/business/media/artificial-intelligence-journalism-robots.html

Pennycook, G., & Rand, D. G. (2021, May). The Psychology of Fake News. *Trends in Cognitive Sciences*, *25*(5), 388–402. doi:10.1016/j.tics.2021.02.007 PMID:33736957

Reardon, M. (2011, September 7). Post 9/11: Can we count on cell networks. *CBS News*. Retrieved 10 August, 2021, from https://www.cbsnews.com/news/post-9-11-can-we-count-on-cell-networks/

ResearchLive. (2020, October 21). *Edelman relaunches intelligence unit*. Retrieved 05 November, 2021, from https://www.research-live.com/article/news/edelman-relaunches-intelligence-unit/id/5075542

Riel, C. B. N. (2014). *Reputação* [Reputation]. Editora Campus.

Salaverría, R. (2005). An immature medium. *Gazette The International Journal for Communication Studies*, *67*(1), 69–86. Retrieved 10 August, 2021, from https://dadun.unav.edu/bitstream/10171/5076/1/gazette67_salaverria.pdf doi:10.1177/0016549205049179

Santaella, L. (2013). *Comunicação ubíqua* [Ubiquitous Communication]. Editora Paulus.

Schwab, K. (2016). *A quarta revolução industrial* [The fourth industrial revolution]. Edipro.

Scott, D. M. (2017). The new rules of marketing and PR (6a. ed.). Wiley. Kindle.

Shedden, D. (2015, January 15). *Today in media history: 2009 Hudson River crash-landing photo sent with Twitter.* Poynter Institute. Retrieved 10 August, 2021, from https://www.poynter.org/reporting-editing/2015/today-in-media-history-2009-hudson-river-crash-landing-photo-sent-with-twitter/

Siegel, E. (2017). *Análise preditiva* [Predictive analysis]. Editora Alta Books.

Silva, S. T. M. (2010). *Relações públicas: história e contextualizações* [Public relations: history and contextualizations]. Interprogramas de Mestrado das Faculdades Cásper Líbero. Retrieved 10 August, 2021, from https://casperlibero.edu.br/wp-content/uploads/2014/04/Sandro-Takeshi-Munakata-da-Silva.pdf

Statista. (2021, September 24). *Forecast number of mobile devices worldwide from to 2020 to 2025*. Retrieved 05 November, 2021, from https://www.statista.com/statistics/245501/multiple-mobile-device-ownership-worldwide/#:~:text=In%202021%2C%20the%20number%20of,devices%20compared%20to%202020%20levels

Terra, C. F. (2009, September 4-7). A comunicação organizacional em tempos de redes sociais on-line e de usuários-mídia [Organizational communication in times of online social networks and users-media]. *Intercom IX Encontro dos Grupos/Núcleos de Pesquisa em Comunicação, evento componente do XXXII Congresso Brasileiro de Ciências da Comunicação*. Retrieved 10 August, 2021, from http://www.carolterra.com.br/wp-content/uploads/2015/06/Artigo_Intercom2009.pdf

Terra, C. F. (2011). *O que as organizações precisam fazer para serem bem vistas nas mídias sociais sob a ótica da Comunicação Organizacional e das Relações Públicas* [What organizations need to do to be well-viewed on social media from the perspective of Organizational Communication and Public Relations]. The meeting of Abrapcorp 2011, Brazil. Retrieved 10 August, 2021, from http://www.carolterra.com.br/wp-content/uploads/2015/06/Abrapcorp-2011.pdf

Toffler, A. (2014). *A terceira onda* [The third wave]. Editora Record.

Wardle, C. (2019, October 21). Information disorder: "The techniques we saw in 2016 have evolved". *First Draft*. Retrieved 10 August, 2021, from https://firstdraftnews.org/articles/information-disorder-the-techniques-we-saw-in-2016-have-evolved/

We are social. (2021). *Digital 2021 Global overview report*. Retrieved 10 August, 2021, from https://wearesocial-cn.s3.cn-north-1.amazonaws.com.cn/common/digital2021/digital-2021-global.pdf

Webb, A. (2019). *The big nine*. Hachette Book Group.

Wiencierz, C., & Roetgger, U. (2019, May). Big data in Public Relations: A Conceptual Framework. *The Public Relations Journal*, *12*(3). Retrieved August 10, 2021, from https://prjournal.instituteforpr.org/wp-content/uploads/Wiencierz-Roettger_Big-Data-in-Public-Relations-A-Conceptual-Framework_PR-Journal.pdf

Zuboff, S. (2019). *The age of surveillance capitalism*. PublicAffairs Hachette Book Group.

Zuckoff, M. (2019). *Fall and rise: The story of 9/11*. Harper.

KEY TERMS AND DEFINITIONS

Artificial Intelligence (AI): It's a complex field of study launched as a term and as a discipline at Dortmouth Summer Research Project on Artificial Intelligence in 1956 (United States). AI involves various disciplines, such as philosophy, biology, psychology, and computer science among others. John McCarthy, considered one of the 'fathers' of AI, defined it as "science and engineering of making intelligent machines".

Big Data (BD): Big data is a complex system for collecting, storing and parametrizing data, possible by advances on digital technology (as cloud, e.g.). BD is popularly known by its "Vs": volume, variety, velocity, and value. Impacts brought by big data are immense because of data and information generated from it allow a better knowledge of everything and everybody.

Bots: It's a short for robot, it is linked to artificial intelligence field and operates as a computer program. Bots do not have a physical body but can be represented by avatars.

First Disruptive Wave: It is a movement started with social media consolidation as the main social arena of contemporary society. The emergence of prosumer (producer and releaser of own content) and convergence of media were two big challenges brought by this wave, forcing a reconfiguration of informational and communicational flow.

Information Disorder: Information disorder is a term studied and presented by Claire Wardle and Hossein Derakhshan in 2017: Information Disorder: toward a multidisciplinary framework for research and policy making. The term understands all phenomena that happen to information universe divided into three categories: misinformation, disinformation, malinformation.

Internet of Things: In a very simplistic way, internet of things synthesizes the connectivity, provided by internet, of all kinds of objects.

Second Disruptive Wave: It is a movement caused by confluence of ubiquitous technologies (big data, artificial intelligence, internet of things) and phenomena that impact organizational communication. The second disruptive wave brings as complex challenges for communication professionals: the need to work with different areas, the need to seek knowledge about new technologies and ways of working with a new communicational agent, the non-human.

Chapter 4
Media Visibility in the Digital Context:
Implications for Organizational Communication

Daiane Scheid
Federal University of Santa Maria, Brazil

ABSTRACT

This chapter promotes a reflection on the ways in which the media affect communicative practices of organizations, especially in the construction of their visibility. It explores the concept of visibility and how this phenomenon has been changing with the development of the media, especially with social media. The theoretical framework covers the mediatic and digital context, including other concepts: organizational communication, strategic communication, mass media, and social media. Following this, the main focus is on visibility, by considering visibility as a social and media phenomenon and its particularities in social media. Implications of these issues for organizations and their communicative practices are reported, and some solutions and recommendations focused on a strategic and responsible performance by organizations in managing their (in)visibility. Some directions for future research are listed and then the conlusion returns to some central ideas.

INTRODUCTION

There is a wide development of investigations that seek to follow the digital phenomena that have changed communicational practices in several domains, including the organizational one. Based on this, this chapter promotes a reflection on the ways in which the media have affected communicative practices of organizations, especially in the construction of their visibility.

It is understood that the current visibility regime is complex and peculiar, especially with regard to social media, which results in an abundance of information for investigation. Such a phenomenon is

DOI: 10.4018/978-1-7998-9790-3.ch004

of interest to organizations as part of their effort to achieve recognition among the public and society. Therefore, the choice for the present topic is justified.

This chapter explores the concept of visibility and how this phenomenon has been changing with the development of the media, thus presenting new logic and alternation in power relations. Firstly, the mediatic and digital context is approached as a background for reflection. Then, the classical notion of visibility is characterized, advancing to media visibility and on social media. During this journey, the author reflects on implications – of the scenarios and phenomena reported – for organizations and their communicative practices. Finally, the author highlights the relevance of a strategic and responsible performance by organizations in managing their visibility, which is paradoxical in this context.

BACKGROUND

The current social configuration places the media as part of the functioning of other institutions, a phenomenon recognized as mediatization (Hjarvard, 2013/2014). "The growing integration of various media into ever-more institutional contexts and into the situated interaction

of daily life reflects an intensified form of mediatization" (Hjarvard, 2019, p. 259). Such a phenomenon is considered essential for the interpretation of the communicational reality experienced by organizations because it favors the understanding of the relationship between media and society at a time when "media logic" becomes the basis of social relations (Barichello, 2014).

To enable a full understanding of this process of change (Heep, 2014), the notions of medium/media, mediation, interaction and their relationship with mediatization are detailed. By exemplifying uses of the terms "mediation" and "mediatization" according to different theorists, Heep explains that "... 'mediation' is a concept to theorise the process of communication process in total; 'mediatization', in contrast, is a more specific term to theorise media related change" (2014, p. 47).

In other words, "mediation" refers to all communication between two parties through a medium, which implies interaction (Hjarvard, 2013/2014; Sodré, 2013). "Mediatization" refers to mediation performed through a particular type of interaction, but "technointeraction" is characterized by "... a technological and marketing prosthesis of a sensible reality", i.e. the medium (Sodré, 2013). Hence, unlike mediations, mediatization does not cover the entire social field, but is the combination of multiple institutions with the media.

According to Sodré (2013, p. 20), "...medium is the communicational flow, coupled with a technical device...". This understanding is in line with the one proposed by Verón (1997), who understands communication medium as a technological device added to specific conditions of production and reception practices of the messages that this device allows to produce and circulate. In addition, Hjarvard (2013/2014) highlights that the media do not only include technologies, but also the social and aesthetic forms that interfere in the way they are used.

Based on the researchers' considerations, it is understood that the media (media or medium) are more than just a channel designed for interaction, as they constitute a type of ambience structured with their own codes, as pointed out by Sodré (2013). The term "media" is used, according to Heep (2014), to refer to the various types of media that we use to enhance communication, such as television, newspapers and digital social networks.

In addition, the change accelerated at the end of the 20th century towards "...a given phase or situation in the overall development of society and culture in which the logic of the media exerts a particularly predominant influence on other social institutions" (Hjarvard, 2013/2014, p. 31) configures the phenomenon reported here as mediatization.

As a general definition, it is possible to understand mediatization "... as the concept used to analyze the long-term processes of the interrelation between media change on the one hand and social and cultural change on the other in a critical way" (Heep, 2014, p. 51). This definition expresses a duality, which is also present in the portrait of the mediatization process made by Hjarvard (2013/2014). That is, on the one hand, the media become more integrated into practices of other institutions and, on the other hand, they also acquire the status of institutions. Thus, one sees the potential of mediatization to affect social practices, including those of organizations.

Barichello (2014) also recognizes the ongoing mediatization process, with media logic exerting influence and/or being appropriated in the practices of other social fields, and also the organizational communication by using strategies from the media field. It is understood that the mediatization process is related to the expansion of opportunities for interaction in virtual spaces. Therefore, organizations are affected by media logic and by technologies.

According the Digital 2021 (Hootsuite & We Are Social, 2021), the global internet penetration now stands at 59.5 percent and the total of social media users is now more than 53 percent of the world's population. This shows how communication technologies are increasingly part of the social context.

Institutions were once more related to specific places. Nowadays, individuals participate and partake in various social institutions regardless of their physical location, therefore, configuring the phenomenon of virtualization of institutions. The bond is diluted in different spaces and moments from our home or anywhere else by using, for example, a smartphone. With this experience, the idea proposed by Hjarvard (2014) is revealed, i.e. the relationship between institutions and individuals takes place in an increasingly individual scope and, therefore, in terms of choice.

As one can see, most organizations maintain physical and geographical bases as important structures for their practice. However, these spaces start to interact with virtual spaces, which has consequences on actions in face-to-face spaces (Hjarvard, 2014). In other words, acting in virtual spaces constitutes a new space for action, but it also interferes with the functioning of institutions outside the digital environment. In the author words: "... the presence of online media creates a new social geography by which the boundaries of the institution become permeable and less tied to physical space" (Hjarvard, 2019, p. 251) and "[t]he virtualization of institutions and social interaction does not render physical space superfluous. Instead, a blending of physical and virtual spaces is taking place (Hjarvard, 2019, p 252).

With the virtualization of social institutions (Hjarvard, 2013/2014; 2019) and the conception of a new qualification of life – a virtual bios (Sodré, 2013), there is an expansion of opportunities for interaction in virtual spaces, interfering in the performance of organizations even outside the digital environment. It is understood that each medium constitutes an ambience with its own logic, which makes up an ecosystem (media ecology – Scolari, 2013).

From the perspective of media ecology, the author is particularly interested in the idea that these media coexist in a system that adapts itself based on technological changes.

In a context where new media species proliferate (every week a new medium appears that threatens to extinguish the others), interfaces are born that increasingly extend our cognitive system and the communication system exists in a permanent state of tension... (Scolari, 2013, p. 34)

As an example, it is observed that communication systems such as the press still occupy an important place in this ecosystem and start to coexist with social media, which are more recent. The complexity of the current media ecosystem stands out, in which communication systems with very different logic coexist and interact.

There are mass media or traditional media (such as print media, radio and TV) that have, in their origin, a logic that differs from more recent media (such as social media), which are still present in a digital environment.

In these so-called mass or traditional media, there is a greater separation between the contexts of production and reception and the control of the broadcasters over the contents that circulate in these media. In comparison, social media (especially social networks) emphasize the active role of interactors in the communication process and promote more power symmetry when putting content into circulation in the medium. "Currently, many users have the opportunity, through social media tools, to express themselves and engage in dialogues in the so-called socialcast process" (Terra, 2019, p. 22), diverging from the broadcast format, which was more present in the pre-internet era.

Such a potential for action of users of these media is also expressed by Hjarvard (2014, p.50), who points out that: "With the media – especially digital – integrating into the everyday world of other institutions, users also start to produce media content" (Hjarvard, 2014, p. 50). More than producing content, it can be said that these users start to constitute media, as Terra (2011) explains:

We are in the age of mediatization of individuals, of the possibility of using digital media as an instrument for dissemination, exposure and personal expression; hence, the term media user. Each one of us can be a channel of this media: a producer, creator, composer, editor, presenter, remixer or just a diffuser of the content itself. (p. 67)

However, it is necessary to be aware that not every user, as well as not every organization, explores the media potentialities to the fullest. There are those who "...just consume content and replicate it; those who only participate with comments in third-party online initiatives; and those that actually produce content actively" (Terra, 2011, p. 68). In addition to this, Terra (2020, p. 105) addresses the tendency of brands to become digital influencers/publishers themselves and highlights that for them to stand out in this context "... the communication of organizations needs to be legitimate, influential, interactive, captivating and visible."

Even without detailing the characteristics of all currently available media – whether online or not – it is noticeable that the media ecosystem gains new contours with the digital media. However, it is important to consider that this environment is not only created by information and communication technologies, but by the relationships among their social actors (Vizer & Carvalho, 2013). And it is in this environment – with diverse media systems – that organizations create their communicative strategies and actions.

Therefore, it is understood that the media logic is increasingly reflected in organizations, and can be observed both in the concern with the relationship with traditional media and in the large number of media that organizations themselves establish and manage, enhanced by digital media.

In this context, organizations are encouraged to take ownership of social media as a means to establish relationships with their interlocutors even if not always in a strategic way. The need for interaction between the organization and the public is even more explicit with digital media, as they expand the possibilities of dialogue based on technologies.

According to the results of the Latin American Communication Monitor 2020-2021 (Álvarez-Nobell et al., 2021), in the view of professionals in the field, some topics will be the most important for the management of communication/public relations in the next three years. The main ones are: Facing digital evolution and the social web; using big data and/or algorithms for communication; exploring new forms of creating and distributing content. The same report shows the importance of communication channels and instruments today and in the future. Social media and social networks (Blogs, Twitter, Facebook, Linkedin, Instagram, among others) are in first place. Second is mobile communication (aap, websites for mobiles/tablets) and finally, online communication via web, email and intranets.

This demonstrates the insufficiency of the classical informational paradigm to meet the complexity of communication and relationship flows that are part of the organizational reality, as suggested by Oliveira and Paula (2007). This idea can be associated with the view that communication processes take place through both informational and relational flows (Oliveira & Paula, 2007) established between the organization and the social actors with which it interacts. Informational flows are formed by the actions and instruments used to convey information, while relational flows are created by actions that enable the "encounter", that is, the dialogue between the organization and the public. It is understood that, the more the organization focuses on conveying informational content, the closer it gets to a traditional communication model, while the more the organization promotes relational flows, the closer it gets to a dialogic model.

Therefore, attention is paid to the concept of strategic communication – as a practice that seeks to project the identity of organizations in a reliable image before society and the adhesion of their audiences (Tironi and Cavallo, 2006) – and to the management of relationships as one of its main components. The management of relationships "... is a strategic component, as it emphasizes opportunities for interaction and dialogue between the organization and the social actors, which are planned and conducted in a systematized and monitored way" (Oliveira and Paula, 2007, p. 47). In regard to this aspect, it is perceived that social media increase the chances of dialogue between the organization and its audiences in media spaces, which can be proposed by the organization itself, according to its own objectives. In addition, these media make it possible to monitor exchanges between the organization and the public, which are recorded in computer-mediated communication and, therefore, can be measured and assessed by the organization.

Terra (2011) states that organizations need to develop a strategic communication positioning that considers this scenario, in which users gain expression and mobilization power. Yet it is still possible to observe the difficulties faced by organizations to use social media as a means to build a relationship with their interlocutors in an effective way. The author considers dialogue to be the main purpose of social media as well as the greatest challenge for organizations because these media should not be used only as spaces to reproduce the messages of the organization, but also to listen to what is said by other users in order to take action. Terra (2011) emphasizes that organizational communication does not only imply establishing relationships, but strategically managing communication with audiences aiming to maximize exchanges between them and the organization itself.

Social media is, nowadays, part of this process. It provides opportunities for practices aimed at expanding the dialogue between the organization and its interlocutors, getting to know the audiences, as well as monitoring and evaluating exchanges between the organization and other social actors. In the area of digital organizational communication, the understanding that the public participates in communication is reinforced, whose control is not only in the organizations, but also in the media users who interfere in the communication strategies of the organizations (Terra, 2011). All of this makes the strategic role of communication emerge in the digital context as a condition to transform the potential for visibility and interaction into reality.

The interaction and visibility between organizations and audiences in social media has potential to increase in the coming years. For example, roughly 45 percent of global internet users say that they turn to social networks at least once per month when looking for information about products or services that they are thinking of buying. That figure is considerably higher amongst younger age groups, that is, Gen Z internet users (Hootsuite & We Are Social, 2021). Another point is, at least 98 percent of users on any social media platform use at least one other social platform (Hootsuite & We Are Social, 2021). This data suggests the importance of a planned visibility on one or two platforms rather than being visible everywhere.

The concept of visibility, as explored in this chapter, is based on the propositions of Foucault (1975/2014). The following topic focuses on the discussion about this phenomenon and, based on different authors, reveals how it is related to media development and organizational communication.

VISIBILITY AND THE MEDIA

Visibility as a Social and Mediatic Phenomenon

Foucault (1975/2014) approaches surveillance and visibility issues as part of what can be called "disciplinary technology". He explains that, traditionally, power is what you see, the light is more on who exercises power and less on who power is exercised over. On the other hand, disciplinary power becomes invisible and imposes constant visibility on those it focuses on, as explained by the panoptic model.

Foucault (1975/2014) shows this inversion of visibility, which is found in the Panopticon, taken as a surveillance and visibility system. The design is surrounded by a ring-shaped building and in the center a tower with windows on all sides. This ring-shaped building is divided into cells separated laterally from each other. Whoever stays in the tower can observe who is in the cells by virtue of lights from the tower which then shine into the cells. However, the architecture contains details that make whoever is in the cell unable to see the observer, who may or may not be in the tower. Hence the inversion of visibility, which starts to focus on those who occupy the cells (inmates, workers, etc.), makes those who observe the cells invisible. This architectural system allows "… a state of conscious and permanent visibility that assures the automatic functioning of power" (Foucault, 1975/2014, p. 195), which becomes automatic and is no longer focused on one subject, for example, a sovereign.

In other words, the Panopticon constitutes a visibility means not by chance, but by the way it is structured. Therefore, the phenomenon implies not just being visible or not, but also the logic that permeates this play of light and it has particular contours throughout history. Visibility assumes different forms at each time, but every society considers "[...] self-representative regimes or regimes of public visibility [...]" (Sodré, 2013, p.16). Thus, visibility is related to the communication technologies available at different time periods which help build architectures of visible spaces, and the media are seen as visibility devices.

Thus, Thompson's study (2008a, 2008b, 2020) is used to understand the changes in the nature of visibility (and related power relations) as a result of the media development. Based on this approach, the impact of the development of communication media on visibility is analysed from the press to social media as well as their importance in sociopolitical life and, consequently, in organizations.

"Increasingly, individuals are caught up in a new system of power in which visibility is a means of control" (Thompson, 2008a, p.121). Similarly to this understanding, Bruno (2013) recognizes that modern society has encouraged individuals, who are understood as spectators, towards a visual culture through the advent of new image technologies, such as photography and cinema. Following that, mass communication technologies start to integrate the visibility regime, therefore, bringing new configurations to the practices of seeing and being seen.

Thompson (2008a) states that communication media comprise of a relationship of power and visibility that is different from what happens in the panoptic model. According to the author,

... the development of mediated communication has provided the means by which many people can gather information about few people and, at the same time, a few can appear in front of many; thanks to the media, it is primarily those who exercise power, rather than those over whom power is exercised, who are subject to a certain kind of visibility. (p. 121)

In addition to focusing on visibility on those who exercise power, this new type of visibility is characterized by no longer depending on sharing a common place; it no longer depends on face-to-face interaction. Thompson (2008a) discusses these transformations in the nature of visibility and in its relationship with power from communication media.

The author explores the impact of media development on these issues, starting with the press. He explains that "...while the relationships between the authors/producers of written pieces and their recipients did not have a dialogic nature, the reception process was closely linked to the various forms of dialogic communication" (Thompson, 2008a, p.113). This argument is based on a past habit of reading books and pamphlets aloud, thus providing access to those who did not know how to read. As a result, the advertising created by the press became accessible in co-presence contexts. However, little by little, the silent and individual reading of newspapers began to grow, distancing itself from interactions through dialogue that initially characterized the reception contexts (Thompson, 2008a).

Therefore, one can observe that the development of traditional media created a new space defined as "... a non-localised, non-dialogical and open-ended space of the visible, in which mediated symbolic forms can be produced and received by a plurality of non-present others" (Thompson, 2008a, p. 213). As the author explains, it is a space in the sense that it consists of a sphere of possibilities in which symbolic forms appear, but it is a non-localised space as it is not linked to specific spatial or temporal locations. It is non-dialogical because, in general, it does not enable dialogue between producers and recipients of mediated contents. As is known, in the mass communication model, the relationship between producers and recipients is asymmetric, and it is an open space in the sense that this advertising is creative, uncontrollable and its consequences cannot be prevented or controlled.

Based on his notion of mediated advertising, which configures the visibility area, with the advent of the press and especially the electronic media, the author recognizes "... the importance that *the struggle for visibility* has acquired in the sociopolitical life of societies" (Thompson, 2008a, p. 214). Thus, the strategic role of visibility becomes evident.

It is understood that the construction of media visibility, nowadays, implies strategies on the part of: social actors (individuals, groups and organizations) in different environments, considering a mass public scene (newspapers, magazines, television, etc), interactive public scene (websites, blogs, social media, etc.) and hybrid public scene (Web radio, YouTube, etc.) (Trivinho, 2011). This idea is presented in Figure 1.

Figure 1. Media Visibility in the digital context. (Adapted from [Trivinho, 2011]).

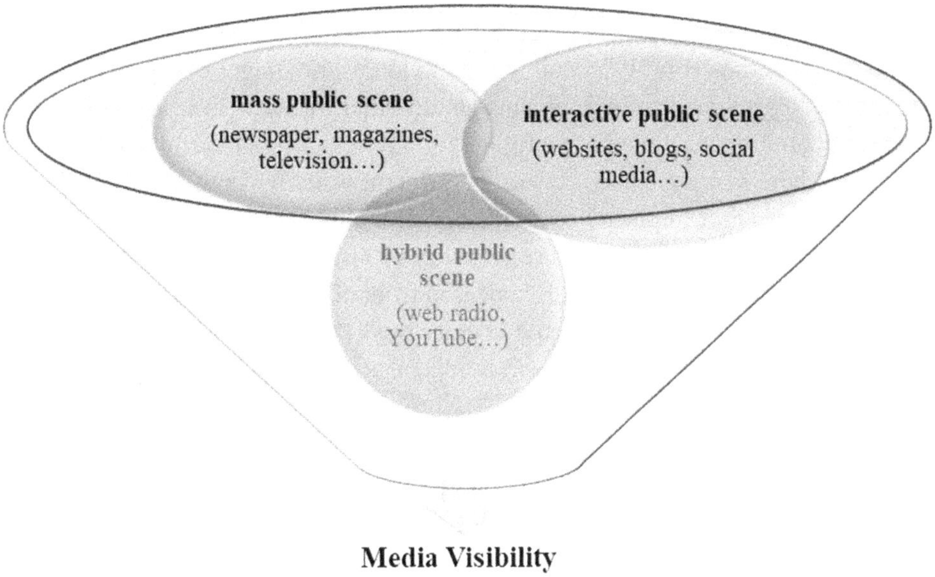

It is observed that social media are now part of the media ecosystem, thus enabling new visibility practices. Therefore, it shows the multiplicity of the current regime of visibility that includes several devices that affect each other and makes it possible to understand media visibility as a result of these communication flows and the strategies of the social actors involved.

Visibility in Social Media

As already shown, communication technologies have made possible new forms of visibility in the digital context:

They have greatly increased the flow of audio-visual content into the networks of communication and enabled a much wider range of individuals to create and disseminate this content. Moreover, given the nature of the Internet, it is much more difficult to control the flow of symbolic content within it, and hence much more difficult for those in power to ensure that the images made available to individuals are those they would wish to see circulated. (Thompson, 2008b, p. 23, 24)

It is possible to see a shift in power in the visibility process, as now almost anyone can make issues that are important to them visible.

On the Internet, the technologies of seeing and being seen were further expanded, making individuals ... relatively more autonomous in the production of their own visibility, given that, in this case, the exposure of the self is not subject to the authorization and intervention of a third party. (Bruno, 2013, p. 58,59)

Based on studies developed by Foucault (1975/2014), it is known that in disciplinary societies the focus of visibility has shifted to the common individual. With the mass media, the focus of visibility is now on a few people, i.e. the elites, such as TV celebrities (Thompson, 2008, Bruno, 2013). Furthermore, one has seen the return of the visibility of common individuals, no longer of the visibility of disciplinary institutions, but in digital media environments and in other formats (Bruno, 2013). As a result, the visibility devices of contemporary media configure "... a reticular and distributed model where many watch over many or where many see and are seen in different ways" (Bruno, 2013, p. 47).

"Uni-directionality has been replaced by multi-directionality", as explained by Thompson (2020, p. 19), about how the medium changes the directionality of vision. He shows how changes in forms of interaction alter the ways in which individuals appear in front of others. "In the case of mediated online interaction, the directionality of vision is altered in other ways because many participants in the interaction may have means at their disposal to make individuals, actions and events visible to distant others" (Thompson, 2020, p. 19).

It is possible to comprehend a unique, peculiar visibility regime, which differs from previous regimes, especially in relation to interactivity. In the Panoptic model, the individual who is in the cell does not communicate with others, as described by Foucault (1975/2014, p. 194), and so "… he is the object of information, never a subject in communication". Taking that into account, it is possible to recognize a significant change in the visibility of social media, where everyone is – or can be – the subject of communication, and where everyone has the power to look at and let themselves be seen. According to Bruno (2013, p. 59), "…We have moved from the attempt to enter the media to the possibility of the individual being their own media and creating, consequently, their own audience".

"Seeing and being seen in this context is related to the idea of reputation, belonging, admiration and desire, thus giving to visibility a primarily positive, desirable connotation..." (Bruno, 2013, p. 47). This context makes surveillance acceptable or even required, because "...the same technologies that increase the possibilities of release, access and distribution of information become potential instruments of surveillance and control..." (Bruno, 2013, p. 125).

As already mentioned, visibility is related to surveillance and, according to Bruno (2013), visibility can be subjected to surveillance or act against it. An example of this are documentation techniques that use examination as a disciplinary instrument, as addressed by Foucault. The records, i.e. the documentation of ordinary individuals taken as a document for occasional use represents a form of control, a technique of power (Foucault, 1975/2014). In computer-mediated communication, the behavior of users is recorded, thus also creating a form of control given that it is possible to track their activities on the Internet. In this case, visibility makes surveillance possible. "The digital footprint of lifeworld interactions becomes a valuable commodity that is sold and used for strategic purposes, such as product marketing and political campaigning" (Hjarvard, 2019, p. 261).

This is a reality of Information Society "… which operates through technologies that communicate and control at the same time through interaction in digital networks" (Raposo, 2020, p. 79). Thus, organizations somehow also watch over the digital environment through observation and interaction with the network's users in an attempt to control and even intervene in what is said about it. For this, they also make use of "… surveillance devices, especially those that can be activated through discursive resources, to monitor what is said about them on the internet and to control the movements that Internet users carry out in their digital social network environment" (Barciehllo et al., 2017, p. 186).

It is observed, as a practice of organizations, the monitoring of their official channels (comments and direct messages) as well as the monitoring of competitors, key customers, influencers and so on.

Several social media monitoring tools are available today, including the free ones, to monitor what is said about the organization, its products or services, the use of terms (and hashtags) related to the business itself, among others.

However, the following warning should be made to communication/public relations professionals: "… the use of digital surveillance should be thoroughly considered by these professionals in order to be implemented carefully and ethically, so as not to violate the principles of privacy of individuals who use digital social networks to comment on organizations" (Barciehllo et al., 2017, p. 187).

However, visibility is also a strategy used to reduce surveillance, which is known as counter-surveillance (Bruno, 2013). It consists of an effort to build one's own representation through visibility to avoid surveillance, that is, to show oneself by selecting what is important to make visible, thus creating the sensation of being exposed and easily seen.

It can be seen, therefore, that visibility and surveillance are closely related phenomena in social media. Being visible implies undergoing a type of surveillance, but this visibility also implies the choice (or strategy) on what one wants (or does not want) to highlight/show and with what intensity.

The term "distributed surveillance" is used by Bruno (2013) to emphasize the reticular, distributed, ambiguous character of current surveillance processes. In such processes, "...the actions that constitute them are distributed among different sectors whose interests and perspectives are multiple and do not obey any unified principle" (Bruno, 2013, p. 25). This approach leads the author to reflect on distributed visibility as a term to describe visibility in the digital media, constituted from diverse flows and through actors with different interests.

This is all made possible due to convergence,

... responsible for generating our 21st century digital Panopticon, because without it the possibility of combining multiple different devices for observation, recording, memory, dissemination and exchange of data and information would not have been possible nor would the construction of operational control systems and the complex networks that exist in today's virtual world. (Vizer & Carvalho, 2013, p. 49)

Another feature to be highlighted in relation to visibility in social media is interactivity, because a mediated online interaction is dialogical in character and oriented towards a multiplicity of other recipientes (Thompson, 2020). To this end, we return to the example of newspaper reception. Owing to the press, visibility is freed from face-to-face dialogue, which is restricted to the interactions between readers who meet with each other and discuss what they have read (in cafés, clubs, etc.), even the reading of a newspaper becomes an individual act (Thompson, 2008a). In contrast, in relation to visibility created by social media, not only do users have the autonomy to express their opinion about what is visible, but the expansion of such visibility through interactions on the network depends on the users themselves. Then, it is understood that visibility in social media represents a model that considers the characteristic of visibility brought by the press, that is, of not being limited to sharing a common place and, at the same time, that approaches the pre-development visibility model of the media, which is based on the dialogic concept.

A dialogical visibility model is recognized in social media, that is, the more interaction and dialogue are promoted, the more visibility is gained. In addition, there is a receiving that is private/individual in the sense that the individuals access information from their home or from their cell phone, but that is shared at the same. That is because the actions of these individuals, while reading as well as sharing their opinions, can be recorded or retained and shared with other recipients and producers of information.

Consequently, in order to seek media visibility in the pre-internet era, the organizations had to establish relationships with the media (newspapers, TV, radio, etc.) and suggest agendas of their interest, that is, to trigger these media, provide them with information, promote strategic actions, such as press releases and press conferences. In this regime, the control of visibility relies on media outlets and/or broadcasters.

In the digital context, there is a shift in the power to make something visible, as it is known that social actors (individuals, groups, organizations) gain more autonomy, therefore, being able to create visibility spaces themselves and reach a large audience.

Of course, not everyone avails themselves of this capacity, and not everyone – or every organization – has the same power to make an image or video visible to others: like all social processes, the capacity to make visible, and the extent to which something can be made visible or kept hidden, made available or removed from view, depends on the power and resources that individuals and organizations have at their disposal. (Thompson, 2020, p.20)

However, this autonomy is also relative becouse many of these spaces – Facebook, Instagram, YouTube, etc. – belong to companies and consequently their interest is essentially guided by the logic of the market. "Today, far from being just a symbolic content, organizations are, in a broad sense, a network of relationships mediated by a digitized infrastructure, and now also organized algorithmically" (Raposo, 2020, p. 86).

Thus, it is considered that nowadays the construction of media visibility of an organization may involve different actors (the organization itself, its audiences, competitors, companies that own the means, etc.) and the interaction between all of them. However, it should be highlighted that visibility does not always have a positive effect on organizations, and may cause problems, especially if poorly managed. In times of social media, it is considered paradoxical, that is, it becomes even more complex and difficult to control visibility because its construction starts to integrate different actors with different interests. On the other hand, organizations and their interlocutors have an increasing number of means that make up the current regime of visibility, through which what becomes visible can generate interaction with the potential to strengthen their relationships.

SOLUTIONS AND RECOMMENDATIONS

Bearing in mind that visibility in the media is of great importance to communication as well as to the construction of the image and reputation of an organization, the challenges (caused by the peculiarities of the current visibility regime) and the risks involved (negative visibility, lack of control over what is visible, many actors involved in the process), it is essential that organizations adopt a strategic approach to the issue.

Based on the view of the authors aforementioned, the idea of "space of visibility" is highlighted, made possible by a multiplicity of media choices which interact with each other as components of a media ecosystem. As one can see, there are the mass or traditional media, which even nowadays are of fundamental importance to organizational communication. However, there is a growing relevance given to owned digital media, such as websites, blogs and social networks, which have been considered key elements in the construction of communication strategies in organizations.

"The sources are no longer unique and solely directed to the press. They are starting to have their own niches and subject-destinations" (Farias, 2016, p. 248). They are keeping more and more communication channels focused on their audiences, which means that: "By leaving the conventional media axis, one can find new options without completely interrupting the dialogue with the traditional media" (Farias, 2016, p. 248).

As a consequence, organizations create (or become) their own media and, thanks to the Internet, reach a wider audience. However, they should not stop using traditional means of communication, including in their digital/hybrid versions, because these means still have their relevance. After all, they represent a voice with social recognition outside the organization. Another reason why an organization should maintain its visibility in these media is based on the idea that many of the new spaces of visibility such as social networks, which can be structured by the organization, as previously mentioned, are owned by others, i.e. technology companies and, therefore, the users' autonomy is quite relative.

In addition to maintaining the visibility strategies in both traditional media and new digital spaces maintained by the organization, the author recommends thinking about the interaction between these spheres (public scenes), which are related to the construction of media visibility. That is because "[t]he dissemination of digital and interactive media, in general, does not replace the traditional media, but supplements them and interacts with them in different ways" (Hjarvard, 2013/2014, p. 103).

Therefore, one recommends a communication plan that considers the visibility of the organization in different media as well as the relationship between these media. A given situation is often seen to become an agenda of the traditional media due to its wide visibility on social media. Or, among other possibilities, an organization can use its presence on social media to expose some positions, thus responding to some of these agendas.

In addition, one also recommends to value communication based on a dialogue with the audiences in order to explore the potential to create organizational visibility in social media. Interaction is an essential element to build and expand the visibility of an organization because the more engaged the audience is by commenting and sharing, the more information that is circulating about the organization becomes visible to other media users. In other words, interaction and dialogue generate visibility in social media and vice-versa.

What is visible about an organization (data, projects, positions, etc.) also tends to guide dialogues with the audiences and, therefore, changes the attributes, such as the organizational image. The interaction between the organization and its strategic audiences in these media allows it to recognize their expectations, to monitor what they say about the organization itself and to seek harmonious communication (and a relationship) with these interlocutors as long as the organization is willing to listen to the public and, as far as possible, meet their demands.

One recognizes that, in addition to being producers and broadcasters of their own content, these users interact with the content produced by organizations in the digital space and can help disseminate it or promote new content from it. Therefore, organizational presence on social media demands an analysis in terms of strategic action since not all organizations need to build their visibility across all media, and it is part of the organizational media visibility management to recognize *when* and *how* it will be visible.

Today we live in an age of high media visibility, which means that political life now unfolds in an information environment where the capacity to reveal and conceal, to make things visible and keep other things hidden, is much more difficult to control, creating a permanently unstable arena in which leaks, revelations and disclosures are always capable of disrupting the most well-laid plans. (Thompson, 2020, p. 27)

It is also possible to see this happening in the organization's reality. Considering the political field, the author explains that the new forms of visibility create new risks as well, and that is why it is possible to try to manage the visibility of some leaders (or organizations), but it is impossible to completely control it, and this is the source of a new and distinctive kind of fragility.

Thus, in the digital context, the visibility and invisibility strategies (Silva and Baldissera, 2019), surveillance and counter-surveillance (Bruno, 2013) have become part of the communication agenda (and action) of organizations.

Organizations on social media can monitor the behavior of their audiences, the information that circulates about them on the network and the impact of their audicences' publications. However, they are subject to a type of surveillance on what they make visible, that is, other media users can follow what a given organization is doing or how it is positioning itself in the face of a wide range of issues.

As a result, organizations in general often use counter-surveillance strategies on networks (Bruno, 2013), thus creating a super exposure (of what they are interested in making visible for the purposes of image and reputation) and, somehow, distracting the audience in relation to other possible organizational matters.

Silva and Baldissera (2019) recognize invisibility, restriction and visibility targeting as "... possible organizational strategies triggered when identifying risks or the emergence of agendas (in society and/or in the media) that may go against the way organizations want to be perceived" (Silva and Baldissera, 2019, p. 18).

Based on an empirical investigation, the researchers identified a set of strategies related to the interest in not making something visible, which range from monitoring visibility to restricting it. These strategies are listed as follows: monitoring of situations, e.g. observing a crisis and its consequences; expression of an institutional position, e.g. responding to requests; shuffling facts and emphases in order to misunderstand a given situation, e.g. hiring influencers; disregard of negative associations and comments, e.g. deleting comments or posts; restriction of visibility to intended interlocutors, e.g. by selecting audience segments based on their movements and behaviors; reducing the coverage of content distributed by organizations, e.g. restricting visibility to a few channels; establishment of comfort policies, e.g. defining themes that should not be addressed by the network (Silva and Baldissera, 2019).

"It is important to highlight that the appropriation of the invisibility strategies and the reduction/targeting of the visibility can lead organizations to different levels of concealment of relevant matters to the public, which can comprehend subjects from moral issues to legal commitments." (Silva and Baldissera, 2019, p. 24). Therefore, the (in)visibility strategies demand from the organization a responsible attitude as well as an ethical and situational consideration, thus, analyzing the role that the organization plays in society, the notion of transparency and the information that is of public interest and should be made visible for everyone's good.

Due to the challenges reported here, the author finally recommends that the management of media visibility of organizations be delegated to professionals able to understand the media scenario and act in a planned way, guided by ethical principles.

FUTURE RESEARCH DIRECTIONS

Among some directions for future research, the following is suggested: The formats that promote more visibility and interaction in networks, such as images and videos; the (in)visibility strategies undertaken by organizations on each social media platform; the perception of journalists from traditional media about publications made by organizations on social media as a source for the press; the perception of users who interact with organizations on the network in order to deepen the knowledge about the potential of these interactions for the construction and consolidation of image or reputation.

CONCLUSION

Throughout this chapter, a social context of mediatization has been highlighted, in which social media have become part of the media ecosystem, so that the visibility regime presents peculiarities and is developed by means of new practices. In this scenario, the struggle for media visibility and its management are shown to be relevant to strategic organizational communication.

In particular, from social media, in which interaction and dialogue between the organization and its audiences have expanded opportunities, and organizations have greater autonomy to build or increase their visibility. Therefore, the potential of social media for the visibility and maintenance of organizational relationships is highlighted both in and out of these virtual environments.

In order to explore this possibility, organizations should value communication through dialogue with their interlocutors, i.e. media users, who are capable of acting in communication and in the construction of organizational visibility. Furthermore, they should consider their presence on social media as part of the whole process that makes up the strategy for organizational media visibility and, therefore, think about their connections with other media. Finally, it is understood that, in addition to being strategic, it is essential for organizations to act responsibly in managing their (in)visibility.

REFERENCES

Álvarez-Nobell, A.; Molleda, J. C.; Moreno, A.; Athaydes, A.; Suárez-Monsalve, A. M. y Herrera, M. (2021). *Comunicación estratégica y relaciones públicas en América Latina: crisis del COVID-19 en la gestión de comunicación, ciberseguridad, situación de las mujeres, retos éticos y nuevas competencias. Resultados de una encuesta en 20 países* [Strategic communication and public relations in Latin America: crisis of COVID-19 in communication management, cybersecurity, situation of women, ethical issues and new competences. Results of a survey in 20 countries]. Bruselas: EUPRERA.

Barichello, E. M. M. R. (2014). Midiatização e cultura nas organizações da contemporaneidade: o processo de midiatização como matriz de práticas sociais [Mediatization and culture in contemporary organizations: The mediatization process as a matrix of social practices]. In M. Marchiori (Ed.), *Contexto organizacional midiatizado* (pp. 37–45). Difusão Editora.

Barichello, E. R., Scheid, D., & Moreira, E. H. (2017). Visibilidade e vigilância nas redes sociais digitais: oportunidade e desafio para as organizações [Visibility and surveillance in digital social networks: Opportunities and challenges for organizations]. In C. M. A. Scroferneker & L. R. Amorim (Eds.), *Re) leituras contemporâneas sobre comunicação organizacional e relações públicas* (pp. 175–189). EDIPUCRS. https://editora.pucrs.br/download/livros/1224.pdf

Bruno, F. (2013). *Máquinas de ver, modos de ser: vigilância, tecnologia e subjetividade* [Seeing machines, ways of being: Surveillance, technology and subjectivity]. Sulina.

Deleuze, G. (2005). *Foucault* (C. S. Martins, Trans.). Brasiliense. (Original work published 1986)

Farias, L. A. (2016). Opinião pública, mídias e organizações [Public opinion, media and organizations]. In M. K. Kunsch (Ed.), *Comunicação organizacional estratégica: aportes conceituais e aplicados* (pp. 241–254). Summus.

Foucault, M. (2014). *Vigiar e punir: nascimento da prisão* [Discipline and Punish: The Birth of the Prison] (42nd ed., R. Ramalhete, Trans.). Vozes. (Original work published 1975)

Hepp, A. (2014). As configurações comunicativas de mundos midiatizados: Pesquisa da midiatização na era da "mediação de tudo" [The communicative figurations of mediatized worlds: Mediatization research in times of the 'mediation of everything']. *MATRIZes*, *8*(1), 45–64. doi:10.11606/issn.1982-8160.v8i1p45-64

Hjarvard, S. (2012). Midiatização: Teorizando a mídia como agente de mudança social e cultural [Mediatization: Theorizing the media as an agent of social and cultural change]. *MATRIZes*, *5*(2), 53–91. doi:10.11606/issn.1982-8160.v5i2p53-91

Hjarvard, S. (2014). *A midiatização da cultura e da sociedade* [The Mediatization of Culture and Society] (A. G. Vieira, Trans.). Ed. UNISINOS. (Original work published 2013)

Hjarvard, S. (2019). The Janus face of digital connectivity: The transformation of social dependencies. In J. Ferreira, J. L. Braga, P. G. Gomes, A. F. Neto, & A. P. Rosa (Eds.), *Between what we say and what we think: Where is mediatization?* (pp. 241–264). FACOS-UFSM. https://repositorio.ufsm.br/bitstream/handle/1/19692/betweenwhatwesayandwhatwethink.pdf

Hootsuite & We Are Social. (2021). *Digital 2021: Global Overview Report*. https://datareportal.com/reports/digital-2021-global-overview-report

Maia, R. C. M. (2003). Dos dilemas da visibilidade midiática para a deliberação política [From the dilemmas of media visibility to political deliberation]. In *Anais da XII Reunião Anual da Associação de Pós-graduação em comunicação – Compós* (v. 1, pp. 1-22). http://www.compos.org.br/data/biblioteca_937.pdf

Oliveira, I. L., & Paula, M. A. (2007). *O que é comunicação estratégica nas organizações* [What is strategic communication in organizations]. Paulus.

Raposo, J. F. (2020). Comunicação, visibilidade e organizações: reflexões e apontamentos sobre a comunicação organizacional de dados [Communication, visibility and organizations: Reflections and notes on organizational data communication]. In E. Saad (Ed.), *Caminhos da Comunicação: Tendências e Reflexões sobre o Digital* (pp. 83–96). Editora Appris.

Scheid, D., Machado, J., & Pérsigo, P. M. (Eds.). (2018). *Estrato de verbetes: dicionário de comunicação organizacional* [Strata of entries: An organizational communication dictionary]. FACOS – UFSM. https://www.ufsm.br/grupos/estrato/publicacoes

Scolari, C. A. (2013). Más allá de McLuhan: Hacia una ecología de los medios [Beyond McLuhan: Toward a Media Ecology]. In A. Rublescki & E. M. R. Barichello (Eds.), *Ecologia da Mídia* (pp. 33–39). FACOS-UFSM.

Silva, D. W., & Baldissera, R. (2019). Comunicação organizacional e as estratégias de invisibilidade e de redução/direcionamento da visibilidade nas mídias sociais [Organizational communication and the strategies for invisibility and reduction/guidance of visibility in social media]. *Organicom, 16*, 15-26. https://www.revistas.usp.br/organicom/article/view/163239

Silva, D. W., & Baldissera, R. (2020). Comunicação organizacional e estratégias de direcionamento da visibilidade nas mídias sociais [Organizational communication and visibility targeting strategies on social media]. *ECCOM*, 11(22), 187 – 199. http://unifatea.com.br/seer3/index.php/ECCOM/article/view/1123

Sodré, M. (2013). *Antropológica do espelho: uma teoria da comunicação linear e em rede* [Anthropology of the mirror: A linear network theory of communication] (8th ed.). Vozes.

Sodré, M. (2019). Between institution and organization. In J. Ferreira, J. L. Braga, P. G. Gomes, A. F. Neto, & A. P. Rosa (Eds.), *Between what we say and what we think: Where is mediatization?* (pp. 265–274). FACOS-UFSM. https://repositorio.ufsm.br/bitstream/handle/1/19692/betweenwhatwesay-andwhatwethink.pdf

Terra, C. F. (2011). *Mídias sociais...e agora?* [Social media... now what?]. Difusão Editora.

Terra, C. F. (2019). Influência digital: oportunidade para a comunicação organizacional [Digital influence: An opportunity for organizational communication]. In D. Scheid, J. Machado, & P. M. Pérsigo (Eds.), *Tendências em comunicação organizacional: Temas emergentes no contexto das organizações* (pp. 22–37). FACOS – UFSM. https://www.ufsm.br/grupos/estrato/publicacoes

Terra, C. F. (2020). Publishers de conteúdo no ambiente digital: as marcas no papel de influenciadoras digitais [Content publishers in the digital environment: Brands in the role of digital influencers]. In E. Saad (Ed.), *Caminhos da Comunicação: Tendências e Reflexões sobre o Digital* (pp. 97–112). Editora Appris.

Thompson, J. B. (2008a). *A mídia e a modernidade. Uma teoria social da mídia* [The Media and Modernity. A Social Theory of the Media] (10th ed.). Vozes.

Thompson, J. B. (2008b). A nova visibilidade [The new visibility]. *MATRIZes*, *1*(2), 15–38. doi:10.11606/issn.1982-8160.v1i2p15-38

Thompson, J. B. (2020). Mediated Interaction in the Digital Age. *Theory, Culture & Society*, *37*(1), 3–28. doi:10.1177/0263276418808592

Tironi, E., & Cavallo, A. (2006). *Comunicación Estratégica: Vivir em um mundo de señales* [Strategic Communication: Living in a world of signs]. Taurus.

Trivinho, E. R. (2011). Visibilidade mediática, melancolia do único e violência invisível na cibercultura [Media visibility, melancholy of the unique and invisible violence in cyberculture]. *MATRIZes*, *4*(2), 111–125. doi:10.11606/issn.1982-8160.v4i2p111-125

Verón, E. (1997). Esquema para el análisis de la mediatización [An approach to analysing mediatization]. *Revista Diálogos de la Comunicacion*, *48*, 9–16.

Vizer, E., & Carvalho, H. (2013). La metáfora ecológica em la era de la mediatizacion [The ecological metaphor in the era of mediatization]. In A. Rublescki & E. M. R. Barichello (Eds.), *Ecologia da Mídia* (pp. 41–58). FACOS-UFSM.

KEY TERMS AND DEFINITIONS

Media: A means of communication, a communicational environment, through which information/symbolic materials circulate that make the process of communication possible.

Media Ecosystem: The set formed by the media, which, as units of a system, affect each other.

Media Visibility: What is visible in the media about something or someone and the process that makes it possible.

Mediatization: A social stage, resulting from the emergence of the media and the expansion of its role in society, so that the logic of the media permeates other areas.

Organizational Communication: The totality of communication carried out between an organization and its audiences.

Social Media: The media made possible by the emergence of the internet, which enable the wide circulation of information by its users.

Social Networks: A type of social media organized in a network form, which allows extensive interaction between users.

Strategic Communication: An organizational communication planned in line with the organization's objectives and its management, which seeks excellence in the relationship with strategic audiences.

Section 2

Chapter 5
How Small Companies Used Shopstreaming in Their Fight for Survival in a COVID-19 Scenario:
Case Studies from Brazil and Portugal

Priscila Jaekel Krolow
https://orcid.org/0000-0001-8883-2554
Universidade Católica Portuguesa, Portugal

Patrícia Dias
Universidade Católica Portuguesa, Portugal

Sara Manuela Lopes Oliveira
Universidade Católica Portuguesa, Portugal

ABSTRACT

The digital acceleration triggered by COVID-19 was a disruptive transformation of society, which was not prepared for such quick changes in socialization, work, and consumption, among other activities. We were forced to reinvent ourselves, to pursue the continuity of our daily routines using tools already available, because there was no time to invent better ones. In this context, live performances on social media became very successful as a zero-cost (both for content producers and audiences) and highly engaging format. Brands, and particularly small companies, quickly took over this new tool, adopting a practice that had already emerged a few years ago, consisting of using live streaming as a channel for showcasing products and selling, thus being an alternative to the mandatory closure of stores. In order to better understand this emergent practice, this chapter looks into two examples: Mh2, a Brazilian fashion accessories company which used lives on Instagram to sell its products, and São Costureira, a Portuguese clothing brand which did the same using Facebook.

DOI: 10.4018/978-1-7998-9790-3.ch005

INTRODUCTION

Currently, we often speak of "going back to normal", but many argue that "normal" will not be the same anymore. Sneader and Singhal (2020) claim that we are moving on towards a "new normal" that will not resemble the pre-Covid-19 times. It is in this context that our research aims to better understand how companies reacted to the Covid-19 pandemic and quickly migrated to the digital environment, many without strategic planning or budget for this digital transformation.

When mandatory lockdowns forced stores to close, businesses, and particularly those who did not have ecommerce, struggled to find new ways to sell their products. During these periods, live transmissions on social media grew exponentially, in an attempt to provide entertainment to those confined in their homes. Brands looked at this trend as a possibility, and some came up with the new concepts of "live shopping", "live commerce" or "shopstreaming". In this modality, brands promote live showcasing of their products, during which consumers can interact, ask questions, see the products from different angles and understand its uses, and buy, all without leaving their homes or even taking their eyes off a screen. The whole consumer journey is made during the live broadcasting.

This chapter addresses this emergent shopstreaming practice, aiming to understand how and why many brands saw in this technological possibility a means to connect with their targets in a closer and more human way, contributing to a "participative culture" (Jenkins, 2006) of sales, through a bidirectional channel where brands and customers can interact in a similar way to what happens at a physical store.

We observed this phenomenon in two different settings: Brazil and Portugal. In each country we studied a case - Mh2 in Brazil and São Costureira in Portugal - focusing on how they performed these lives. The main difference was the use of different Social Networking Sites (SNS) (Boyd & Ellison, 2007): Instagram by Mh2 and Facebook by São Costureira. Our methodology included the non participant observation of lives during their transmission, and the content analysis of the corresponding comments feeds.

Our research is exploratory of an emergent phenomenon that occurred during a strong crisis, but not, in a post-pandemic period, it keeps being used and brings good results for the studied brands. Our research aims to discuss whether this practice is an ephemeral trend, or a new tool for communication and sales. The content analysis of consumers comments allowed us to understand how they perceived this innovation, and the analysis of sales and orders is evidence of the return afforded by this practice. Our results show that this initiative of the studied brands became a consolidated practice, well accepted by a high number of customers, and resulting in an increase in sales.

Physical, Online and Phygital

Before the Covid-19 pandemic, our society was already becoming phygital, that is, it was not only physical nor online, but an intermediate space built upon the alternation, overlapping or intersection of both. We are spending more and more time in this phygital space, and the barriers between these two dimensions are blurring, as Figure 1 represents. "Digital technologies are the distinctive feature of contemporary society" (Dias, 2008, p. 27), as they are ubiquitous and everpresent, even in the simplest acts of our daily lives, they are facilitators or enhancers. This new way of living has been described as phygital, "defined as the connection between two worlds - the physical and the digital" (Moravcikova & Kilestikova, 2017, p. 150).

However, the Covid-19 pandemic has blurred even more the line between physical and digital, as we began going to work, hanging out with friends, attending events, shopping, all this without leaving our

Figure 1. Cross connection of the virtual and real world (Moravcikova & Kliestikova, 2017, p. 150)

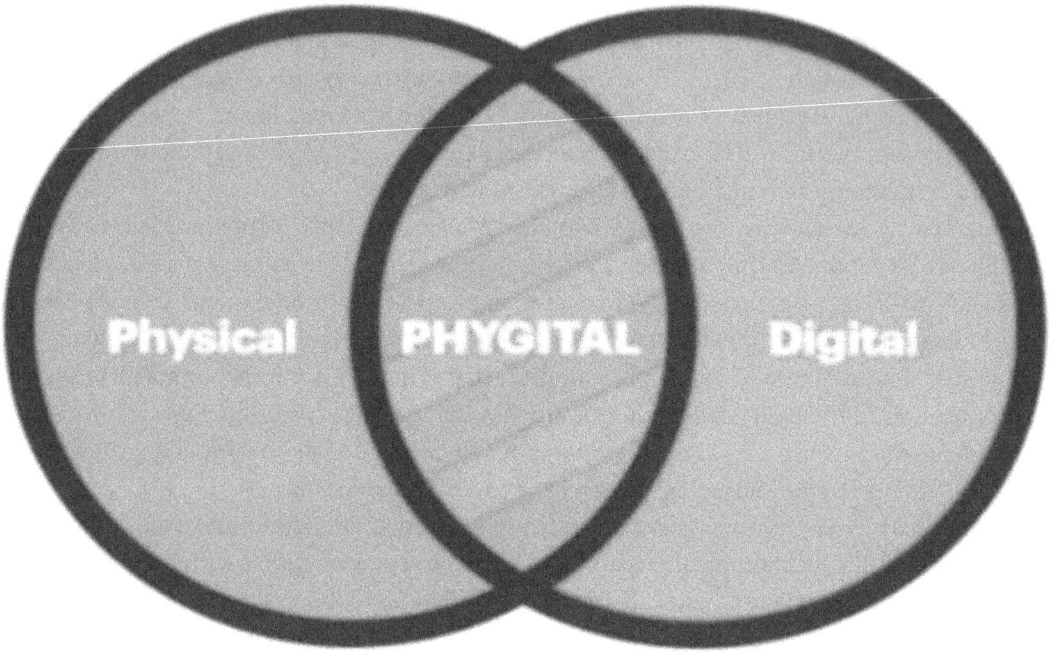

homes. We turned to digital media to satisfy our emerging needs, to social networking sites (SNS) (Boyd & Ellison, 2007), to video platforms such as Zoom, Skype and Google Meet, to Instant Messaging (IM) platforms such as WhatsApp, this was the way that people found to connect with others, making use of our networked society (Castells, 2016).

When Li (2019) describes this process as a disruption, she mentions that our safe and known world was turned upside down and the disruptive transformation is very hard because it challenges the status quo. This description certainly applies to the pandemic period, when we were forced to review several concepts, to reinvent the way we relate with each other, the way we work, and even our relationship with ourselves, and we were led to rethink about the type of content and products we consume, and the way we do so. As none of this was planned, society turned to existing tools to cope with emerging problems, such as social isolation.

According to Almeida, Santos and Monteiro (2020), digitization is helping companies worldwide to adapt and overcome the Covid-19-resultant economic crisis. The increase of the daily use of digital media is evidence of this digital acceleration. Rafiqi (2021) highlights the reinvention of shopping due to social distancing, which drove change to online platforms, leading to a significant increase of ecommerce sales and returns. Phygital environment is now intrinsic to our daily routine.

This digital acceleration process was abrupt and disruptive, and for companies which didn't have an ecommerce platform set up, SNS and video platforms became the most cost-benefit effective solution, as they are free of charge, do not require programming or other specific skills, are easy to use, and were already a big part of the lives of a great majority of consumers. Many organizations, as said by Almeida Santos e Monteiro (2020), have been forced to adopt new internal working practices and felt a strong pressure to offer products through digital channels.

As Bahl (2021) stresses, among the existing SNS, Instagram and Facebook stand out when it comes to selling and buying products, as they afford an intuitive interface, they are free of charge, and they afford sales and multi-format communication tools and options (such as stories, feed, live streaming, private messaging), both rolled out live selling support in May 2020. Live streaming took a leading role during lockdown periods, as many artists performed concerts and performances, speakers organized lectures and debates, all trying to help others cope better with this unprecedented situation. Pursuant to Dengkai, Tingxiu and Raju (2021), the "live streaming" model has become the future development direction, especially in e-commerce.

Realizing the success of this format, companies, particularly smaller ones, saw in it a solution for showcasing their products to their clients, while their stores were closed, thus inventing shopstreaming (shop + streaming). According to Sneader and Singhal (2021), which set up a research task force especially dedicated to the impact of Covid-19 on the economy reaching out to 13 countries, at least 2 out of 3 consumers tried new ways of shopping during lockdown periods. And 65% of the consumers intend to keep these practices in a post-pandemic scenario.

SHOPSTREAMING: A PANDEMIC SOLUTION FOR A POST-PANDEMIC PHYGITAL FUTURE

At a time when consumers were obliged to shop differently from the most usual ways, sales SNS lives emerged as a solution for this need. According to Gomes and Lourenço (2014), live streaming is the live broadcasting of media through the internet. This format became more relevant right at the beginning of the Covid-19 pandemic and is currently being used as a marketing and sales tool, both by companies and consumers.

Drawing on Media Studies theories and concepts, shopstreaming can be regarded as a remediation - "the logic according to which new media reform the traditional ways of previous media" (Bolter & Grusin, 2000, p. 273). For example, it is a remediation of the live broadcasting format, the live transmissions of radio or TV. More specifically, it is a remediation of the previous TV sales channels, in which products were sold live. It can also be viewed as an appropriation (Boyd & Ellison, 2007), both from companies and consumers, of the live streaming format of platforms such as Instagram, Facebook, YouTube and TikTok, for a specific and unintended purpose. This phenomenon can also be addressed as part of Jenkins (2006) social media "participatory culture".

It is a format that helps consumers advance in the different steps of their consumer journeys, recreating the sensation of being inside a physical store, able to check products from different angles and to interact closely with salespeople. According to more recent models of the consumer journey in the digital age (e.g. Edelman & Singer, 2015; Kotler, Kartajaya & Setiawan, 2017), such as the one displayed on Figure 2 (Scott et al., 2015), there are numerous possibilities for prospective customers to lose their interest and reconsider the purchase. In the face of these difficulties, shopstreaming can be a good tool for keeping prospective customers engaged throughout the journey, as many of its steps can be integrated into the same medium and moment.

As daily activities are resumed at a time when the Covid-19 pandemic seems controlled and vaccination has advanced in many countries, doubt remains about whether this trend was merely a temporary solution, or if it will continue to be integrated in business models and in sales strategies. According to Bahl (2021), live streaming commerce is still at its infancy in Europe and North America, but is cur-

Figure 2. Customer journey model for the digital age (Scott et al., 2015, p.4)

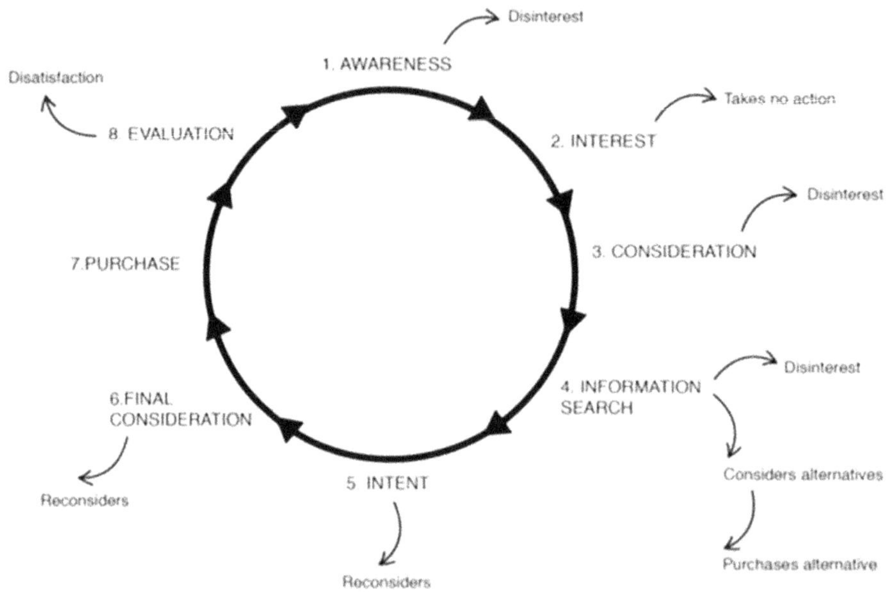

rently gaining momentum worldwide. The live streaming model can be considered a new format for ecommerce, as "Shopstreaming is not a passing fad. It will fundamentally change the way brands both sell products and connect with customers. By fusing ecommerce with live streaming, brands will have the ability to win future customers and write the next chapter of business growth" (p. n/a). In addition, the consultancy firm Hootsuite, in its 2021 report about the digital world, highlights shopstreaming as one of the most relevant ecommerce trends of the year (Hootsuite, 2021).

Even with physical stores resuming their activity, in the aftermath of lockdown periods due to Covid-19, many companies kept performing those live sales sessions, integrating them into an hybrid model that conjugates presential and digital activities. According to a report by the World Economic Forum (2020) and another by McKinsey (Lund et al., 2020), over 80% of companies accelerated their digital transformation because of the Covid-19 pandemic, and this resulted in positive outcomes, so much so that these companies are rethinking what "resuming their normal activity" actually means or could mean.

Navarini and Pereira (2021) state that "many organizations, from different sectors and of different sizes, who - verifying that their collaborators are happy with this model - are admitting to adopt a hybrid model in the next few years" (p. 30). The authors are referring to the model adopted for work, but we argue that the same applies to the way companies conduct their business, combining the physical store and online environments. As brands adapted and learnt to better use online tools for sales and for nurturing relationships with their customers, these practices tend to be kept, even with stores reopening.

Ecommerce seemed the most natural alternative for shopping while physical stores were closed, however, according to Stockdale and Standing (2004), it can be intimidating for companies, particularly for the smaller ones, as managing information systems, electronic markets and delivery logistics is still overwhelming for many SMEs (Small and Medium Enterprises). Many of these companies struggled to implement ecommerce before the pandemic, whether for lack of knowledge or resources. Creating an online store didn't seem a viable option to cope with Covid-19 lockdowns, as other problems and difficulties became a priority at this time.

Thus, these companies turned to a solution that was simpler: using the digital channels that they already had for selling online. In this sense, Almeida, Santos and Monteiro (2020) state that "simplification is a key path to a better customer experience and integration is equally crucial, both to simplify the relationship with the customer and to use data intelligently" (p. 99). And this is why shopstreaming became popular during the pandemic, it proved to be an effective way to deepen the ties between brands and consumers.

Even before the pandemic, shopstreaming was already used in China since 2016, bringing good outcomes for the companies who adhered to this practice. The biggest case of success comes precisely from China, from Li Jiaqi or Austin Li, known as "Lipstick King". This seller performed 389 live streaming sales sessions in 2019, lasting between 5 to 6 hours each, trying on lipsticks on himself. His sales record during one of these sessions is 15 000 lipsticks in 5 minutes.

This example, and others, reveal that consumers aim beyond the mere purchasing of goods, they are also seeking to satisfy other needs, such as belonging to a community and having fun. Furthermore, social capital - "the goodwill (trust and reciprocity) that is engendered by the fabric of social relations and that can be mobilized to facilitate action" (Adler & Kwon, 2002, p. 17)- is built during these transmissions. Thus, fostering emotions emerging from shared values strengthen the relationship between consumers and brands, taking it beyond the purchasing act. According to Antoniadis and Charmantz (2016), "an essential part of successful social media marketing and the development of networks and relationships with customers is the understanding of the structures of social network structures and the ways social capital is created within them" (p. 356).

In a traditional sales touchpoint (the store), according to Blessa (2015), it is possible to create an atmosphere using design, visual communication, colors, music and aromas that aim to stimulate senses and emotions. The final goal of stimulating these experiences is influencing the purchasing behavior. On the internet, namely on ecommerce. Shopstreaming is a different way of promoting purchases, when compared to other more static touchpoints, such as websites and social media posts, affording an experience that is closer to the in-store shopping experience. Shopstreaming aims to "overcome the challenge of adapting sensory experiences to virtual environments, as we, humans, are multisensorial beings: the touch, the flavour and the smell are important for us" (p. 35). This was particularly true during the Covid-19 mandatory lockdowns, a time when presencial contact and experiences were strongly restricted.

D'Andrea and Guissoni (2014) refer to recent neuromarketing research which show that images of human faces trigger stronger emotional reactions than images without people or words, and thus have a stronger effect on buyers. During shopstreaming lives, the sales process is humanized through the hosts, who provide stronger stimuli than words, images or videos. The human presence highlights the emotional appeal. Furthermore, when hosts themselves wear or try the products that they are showcasing, they appeal to the sense of touch, and make viewers feel as if they were wearing or trying the products. Lives can, therefore, engage consumers in a more immersive sensorial experience, by appealing to touch, hearing, and sight.

Shopstreaming is worth researching as a business model that will be part of the future, and which can provide huge profit. It might not be adequate for all companies, and the importance of skilled salespeople who are comfortable with this format seems crucial for its success, as, besides knowing how to showcase products, it is also important to be skilled with the video format. So far, previous research states that lives are well accepted by audiences. Research by iResearch Consulting Group (2018) shows that live ecommerce is increasingly becoming a new trend, finding that 97,2% of users revealed a positive attitude towards live marketing when watching live broadcasts. As with any other communication, marketing and sales tool, there are advantages and disadvantages which need to be considered and discussed for this practice to be improved, and this is the main goal of our exploratory study.

METHODOLOGY

Research Questions

Our study is exploratory, and it aims to explore in more depth the shopstreaming practice, mapping how it was used by companies during the mandatory lockdown periods resulting from the Covid-19 pandemic for showcasing and selling products, as well as at a post-pandemic time. Our research is guided by the following research questions:

RQ1: What are the main features of the shopstreaming practice?
RQ2: Which benefits does it afford to companies and consumers, during lockdown periods and posteriorly?
RQ3: Which risks does it entail for companies and consumers, during lockdown periods and posteriorly?
RQ4: What is the role of shopstreaming in a post-pandemic setting?

Method and Research Design

In our study, we chose the comparative case study as a method because, according to Yin (2015), it is adequate for studying in depth recent emerging phenomena. In addition, it aims to better understand complex social phenomena. It is a comparative instead of multiple case study because we are studying two units of analysis, each from a different context, aiming to compare them.

Our data collection technique is content analysis of shopstreaming emissions. Krippendorff (2013) defines content analysis as a research technique for making replicable and valid inferences from texts (or other meaningful matter) to the contexts of their use. We observed the emissions as they were broadcasted live. According to Yin (2015), live observation of studied events is an important technique for characterizing case studies. However, in the case of Mh2, the researcher had the opportunity to be present in the brand's studio during the broadcasting, and also observe what was happening "backstage". In the case of São Costureira, we were only able to follow the broadcasting as viewers. The platforms used by each brand also imposed differences in the data collection, as Facebook stores the comments made during live transmissions as if they were comments to posts, and Instagram doesn't, so we collected them using print screens of the live broadcasting.

Concerning data analysis, we used a multimodal analysis (Jewitt, 2009) grid to collect and structure our data. This grid also included inputs concerning the live comments from consumers and followers and effective live sales. Our multimodal analysis grid included the following categories: shopstreaming (actions regarding the commercial transaction of sale/purchase); entertainment (actions regarding having fun and "filling dead times"); and community (actions regarding being a part of a community, sharing the same space and time, communicating, looking for company). These categories emerged from a preliminary analysis of the data, combined with previous findings described in the literature review. Later on, for each category, excerpts of the video and the corresponding comments were isolated as units of analysis, and coded according to different subcategories which considered their duration, the content provided by the brand/host, and the interaction with the viewers.

Sampling and Sample

Our sample is purposive (Ray, 2012), as we selected cases that succeeded using shopstreaming, in order to better understand and critically reflect upon this emergent practice. We decided to study one case from Portugal and another from Brazil because these two countries share the same language, and therefore it is common that content producers from one of these countries have audiences from the other one. Also, we found it interesting that in Brazil this practice emerged more on Instagram, and in Portugal on Facebook. The selected cases were companies that were very active in shopstreaming during the mandatory lockdown periods in each country, had many followers in their lives, reached a high number of sales during each performance, and kept on with this practice even after the lifting of the Convid-19-related restrictions. The selected cases are Mh2 (@Mh2), a fashion accessories brand from Brazil, and São Costureira (@SãoCostureira), a clothes brand from Portugal.

As this is an exploratory case study, and these live broadcastings tend to be quite long, we randomly selected one emission from each of the cases studied as units of analysis. Concerning Mh2, we analyzed the live streaming emission of August 24th 2021, from its Instagram profile @mh2_bijuterias. Concerning São Costureira, we analyzed the live streaming emission of June 20th 2021, from its Facebook profile @SaoCostureira. We expect to pilot-test our methodology with this initial research focusing only on two units of analysis in order to improve it and expand it, in a subsequent stage of this research project, to more live streaming emissions and also to more companies which adopted shopstreaming. The deeper exploration of the cases will also include in-depth interviews to the leaders of companies, and also surveys to consumers and/or audiences of shopstreaming.

FINDINGS

Mh2: An experience on Instagram from Brazil

Mh2 is a fashion accessories store located in Pelotas, in southern Brazil. It is a small family company, created in 2002 by the couple Valéria Medeiros and Márcio Holz Hammes, who are the managers of the brand ever since. The brand debuted in the digital environment in 2012, creating a Facebook profile, which currently gathers 10.686 followers. In September 2020, the brand also created an Instagram profile, currently with 8.756 followers. The main target of this brand are teenagers, and this has led the managers to bet on a fun tone to their content, creating videos aimed at the Instagram Reels format, curating colourful feeds on both social media platforms, and partnering up with Brazilian digital influencers to showcase their products. Although present on social media, the brand does not have a website. Instead, the owners decided to create a digital catalogue stored on Google Drive, and they share the links on Instagram using linktr.ee. Facing the pandemic with limited digital resources and skills, this was the fastest and simplest solution that the owners found to start selling online, without having to develop an ecommerce infrastructure that was integrated with the sales in the physical store. Managing the high flux of products in stock and sold is a very intense task, as they are relatively cheap accessories, but in great variety, and sales are high. However, this solution found by the owners is working well, although they intend to invest in a more sophisticated ecommerce system in the future. As Stockdale and Standing (2004) claimed, these small company owners find the digital environment, and ecommerce in particular, intimidating, and thus are resorting to solutions that seem easier to cope with. And in the case of Mh2, these solutions included shopstreaming.

The shopstreaming live we analyzed occurred on August 24th 2021, and lasted for 2h55. It was hosted by the company owner, and counted with the participation of the collaborators who are usually the salespeople at the physical store. The way they interact with the audience online reveals that they are used to interacting with customers in the physical store. Products were showcased during the live, featuring a discount code that viewers could use by making a print screen or using the code supplied during the live, only in the following 24 hours.

Products were showcased being worn by the live hostesses, thus affording the audience an experience that is close to trying out the products at the physical store. The products were worn and then shown in different angles. Additionally, the live hostesses gave tips about how to wear them and combine them, thus starting conversations with viewers, also similar to what they would do with customers at the physical store.

In the case of this live, it was possible to follow it as it was being broadcasted from the company's setting, thus having access to its "backstage". It was notorious that the main strategy was reproducing online the experience of shopping at the store in the closest way possible.

Viewers participated actively in the live streaming, making it a true co-creation (Kotler, Kartajaya & Setiawan, 2017), as the performance adapted to the interaction with viewers. There was a script that featured the number of products to showcase, and an order to do so, but others were added impromptu, as viewers asked, or as an answer to questions, or as complements to other products. The analyzed live was the first that the brand organized, and the hostesses were a bit uncomfortable at first, but they became much more at-ease and confident as they received positive comments from the viewers during the live. We observed that they quickly overcame the technological mastery of the camera and of Instagram IGTV, as well as issues of logistics and directing. Concerning technology, they only needed a robust internet connection and a smartphone, but good lighting and a tripod to hold the smartphone were important accessories to improve the quality of the live and afford more comfort to performers. They felt that Instagram is a user-friendly platform, as you merely have to push one button to start live streaming.

Concerning the preparation of the live streaming session, the main goal was showcasing products and selling them, recreating an experience that would be similar to shopping at the physical store. In order to do so, Mh2 selected a set of products to which they could apply a 15% off discount, and which they believed would be attractive to the audience. Besides this careful selection of the products to showcase and offer, they also selected other products to feature in giveaways during the live session. These prizes included products from other partner brands, which offered them in exchange for being featured in the shopstreaming session. Thus, these partner brands were mentioned during the live performance and also in previous and subsequent Instagram posts.

We can conclude that the most differentiating features of this shopstreaming strategy were affording entertainment, discounts, and making a good previous promotion of the live transmission on Instagram. On average, the number of followers was 100, reaching peaks of 150, mainly close to giveaways.

Orders were done using WhatsApp messages or Instagram Direct, and to cope with the high number of messages received, all the Mh2 team was committed to giving feedback and organizing shipping and deliveries. The most sold product was a satin headband to wear during sleep, a new product launched during the live, that had previously been offered to many Brazilian influencers, who had already been showcasing it in their publications.

At the end of the shopstreaming session, Mh2 owners commented that the sales were similar to a "good day" at the physical store. When this live was performed, physical stores were allowed to be open, so this represented an additional effort of three extra hours of work for the whole staff. The physical store was open during its regular schedule, and the live was broadcasted after closing hours. This way, digital activities did hot interfere with the normal flux of work, it was an additional effort that also affords additional revenues. Therefore, this brand is looking at shopstreaming beyond a solution for surviving while physical stores are closed due to the Covid-19 pandemic, but as an additional touch point that affords more sales.

São Costureira: An experience on Facebook from Portugal

Our other case study is São Costureira, also a small family business, this time in Portugal. It is a clothing store located near Braga, in the north of Portugal, that offers atypical sizes, ranging from XS to XL, and thus catering to customers in the niche market of plus-size. The brand sells not only in Portugal, but also Europe-wide. It is organized in three different stores: São Costureira ready-to-wear, São Costureira shoe store and São Costureira accessories.

The current managers of the store are the siblings Anabela Carvalho and Domingos Carvalho, who are concretizing their mother's dream, who was fondly nicknamed São (first name) Costureira (seamstress/dressmaker). Before owning the physical stores, this family sold their products in markets throughout the country. Later on, Anabela Carvalho started São Costureira ready-to-wear, with the help of her oldest son, Diogo Quintela, and a few salespeople; and Domingos Carvalho started São Costureira shoe store with his wife and two collaborators. Finally, the niece Daniela Carvalho established São Costureira accessories. The three stores are located on the same street. São Costureira ready-to-wear is the one which is more involved in shopstreaming, and therefore it will be the main focus of this case.

Concerning digital presence, the brand does not have a website, and its main communication channel is its Facebook profile, with 78.368 followers. With all the stores closed due to the Covid-19 pandemic, Diogo Quintela was the first to suggest performing live streaming sessions on Facebook, which started in April 2020. For this study, we analyzed the live performed on September 8th 2021, which lasted 4 hour and 37minutes. As happens with Mh2, the products are ordered by private message, using Facebook Messenger or WhatApps, and the hosts confirm the orders live. The average audience was 280 people, reaching peaks of 300 viewers.

It is worth highlighting a differentiating feature of São Costureira's lives: its main hostess, Cátia Monteiro, a cousin of the family. Cátia suffers from a degenerative disease named Leber's congenital amaurosis, which made her go blind at the age of 13. In spite of being unable to see colour, Cátia is able to distinguish each of the brand's products by texture and details, and this captivated the audience. Cátia conveyed a message of hope and resilience, which at a troubled time such as the Covid-19 lockdown, warmed the hearts of viewers. She became a very strong ambassador for this brand.

During the live streaming sessions, Cátia was often asked about her condition, to which she answered genuinely, telling her story and generating empathy. This led to an invitation to be a guest at a TV open-channel show, in which she participated with her cousin Diogo Quintela. They both told how their goal was to honour the memory of their grandmother São with their work, and Cátia was described as "an emerging internet star during the pandemic". She was also interviewed by a local newspaper, which featured her experience of being an blind model for a clothing brand.

Also due to this media coverage, São Costureira's shopstreaming lives gained national repercussion, and their audience increased. The brand continued to perform these lives after the reopening of the stores, and they are currently hosted by Diogo Quintela and two of the store's salespeople. His mother, Anabela Carvalho, also participates sometimes. They start with music, making time for viewers to login, and Diogo welcomes every viewer. Then, the salespeople act as models, and showcase the products in an alternate way: when the first comes in and presents her look, the second changes, and vice-versa. They wear the products, showcasing them from different angles, mention the different sizes, and highlight the features of each piece that might be more flattering or better choices for certain body types. They also mention different colours available if that is the case. Every piece of clothing is presented with a code, so that viewers can order them easily. After over an year of live streaming emissions, the setting remains the same: they transformed one part of their São Costureira ready-to-wear store into a studio, and there is also a space which is now dedicated to storage for online orders. During the lives, Diogo always stimulates viewers to share the link of the live and to invite others, thus significantly increasing the audience.

The need to revinted sales channels during the Covid-19 pandemic, as Rafiqi (2021) sates, made the brand São Costureira to strengthen itself in the online environment through shopstreaming, leading to a high engagement with the audience, to an excellent acceptance of this new touch point, ant to a success in sales. This is all observable on the comments during the Facebook lives. The analyzed live had 1,1 thousand comments and was shared 753 times, and many of such comments were requests and orders.

DISCUSSION

After looking into how shopstreaming is being practiced in two different realities, Brazil and Portugal, this section recovers our research questions and discusses our findings.

About RQ1 - What are the main features of the shopstreaming practice?, we stress that the fact that supporting technology such as Facebook and Instagram, and videos, is intuitive, user-friendly and familiar to those undertaking this new strategy, is a strong motivation, as the perceived complexity of ecommerce structures is a barrier in adopting such a solution. In only a few steps, live streaming has started, and products are being sold. However, content producers feel anxious about the fact that emissions are live, a practice that they believed to be exclusive for journalists and TV and radio hosts and entertainers, but which today can be performed by any user of a social media platform.

In both lives analyzed, the hosts Valéria (Mh2) and Diogo (São Costureira) shared with their audience that they were nervous, and the audience tried to help by commenting about their good performance, and made them become more confident - thus co-constructing the shopstreaming live (Kotler, Kartajaya & Setiawan, 2017). In fact, they admitted that for showcasing products live it takes more than in-depth knowledge about the products, it also requires charisma, humour, ideas for content, and an ability to engage viewers. Both were complemented by viewers:

"Beautiful ♥ wonderful accessories 😍" (tekamunhos, Mh2 shopstreaming live viewer)

"Mh2 rocking with their accessories, customer care, and now with the live😍😍😍 👏👏👏👏👏👏 great tips" (fazzinhadapsico21, Mh2 shopstreaming live viewer)

"Everything perfect" (laureane_bbastos, Mh2 shopstreaming live viewer)

"All the best for Mh2 😍😍" (maria_ribeiro.lopes, Mh2 shopstreaming live viewer)

"I missed seeing you and listening to you, Diogo " (Cátia Silva, São Costureira live viewer)

"You're beautiful DIOGO" (Ohana Petry Torres, São Costureira live viewer)

"We missed Diogo to show us beautiful clothes and to make us laugh " (Lucília Antunes, São Costureira live viewer)

Thus, we can conclude that having hosts with charisma and resourcefulness is crucial for successful transmissions. This charisma holds viewers online, not only for making purchases, but also because of other two benefits that strongly emerged in our multimodal content analysis grid: entertainment and sense of belonging to a community. In the comments above, when viewers mention that they missed the host, as there had been some time since the last live, they reveal that they feel close to the host, and also part of a community. In addition, the reference to the host "making us laugh" stresses the importance of having fun for the viewers.

But the main goal of the brands is selling, and for that purpose it is also very important to make a careful and diversified selection of products, and showcasing them in models wearing them, as this is exactly what customers are looking for in shopstreaming. Unable to go to physical stores and try on the products, they search for being able to see the products from different angles, and not just in static photographs on websites, for example. Hosts and hostesses from both brands wear the accessories and/or clothes and show them in a detailed way, also interacting with the viewers, talking about important details, options of different colours, how to combine them in looks, and answering questions and requests.

Another observation is the similarity in format, in spite of the lives being conducted on different social media platforms, in different countries, by different brands. Accessories and clothes are picked out and prepared before the emission, they are worn during the live streaming, and hosts answer comments and interact with viewers, clarifying all doubts about the products. Thus, the viewers actively participate in the emission. Both use codes associated with each product to facilitate the orders, which are done using Instant Messaging platforms such as WhatsApp, Instagram Direct and Facebook Messenger. One significant difference is that on Facebook it is possible for viewers to share a link to the live, and this is not possible on Instagram, which might partly explain the bigger audience of São Costureira. However, the hostess Cátia Monteiro was very important to create awareness for this brand and to expand its audience.

Concerning RQ2 - Which benefits does it afford to companies and consumers, during lockdown periods and posteriorly?, findings are diverse. In Pelotas, Brazil, lockdown periods were frequent but very short, not exceeding two weeks, so the physical store closed and opened, and lives happened both at times when the store was closed and open. Lives made sense even with stores open because many people were afraid of going out to shop. Thus, since the first emission, shopstreaming lives were a success and reinforced the connection between the brand and its customers, mainly those who didn't visit the store for a long time. For the owners, the strategy was creating an additional sales channel, so lives were performed randomly, when sales were low and needed a boost, or when there was a new opportunity, such as the launch of new products or promotions, for example. On the contrary, São Costureira performed their lives with a fixed periodicity.

In Portugal, there were two long lockdown periods, one between March and May 2020, and another between January and April 2021. These strongly affected businesses, as only those which were considered "basic need" physical infrastructures, such as food and health, were allowed to be opened. For São Costureira, the shopstreaming lives were of extreme importance during these lockdown periods, as they were the only source of income for the brand. Currently, with the store open, they are still an important source of revenue, as they became a part of the customers routines. Below we present comments stating that they missed the live streaming sessions during the vacation in August 2021, which were categorized as "community" in our multimodal content analysis grid, as they reveal that viewers have formed a community that is important for them.

"Good evening, São Costureira team. I missed you a lot. Kisses (Maria dos Anjos Silva, São Costureira live viewer)

"Good evening my darlings! I missed you so much is everything ok with you all Kisses" (Elisabete Coelho, São Costureira live viewer)

"Welcome back. I hope you had a great vacation in your long absence. Kisses" (Aida Beirão, São Costureira live viewer)

In the case of Mh2 the frequency of lives is much lower than in São Costureira, but within the category "community" we perceive comments even of gratitude

We believe that shopstreaming is a beneficial option, whether as a complementary sales channel as is the case of Mh2, whether as a new business model, as is the case of São Costureira. It is a marketing tool that affords benefits for both brands. The fact that São Costureira even transformed a space of the physical store into a studio and storage for shopstreaming proofs the high numbers of online sales.

From the point of view of consumers, their comments reveal that they enjoy these shopstreaming lives as a way of observing products in more detail, when compared to photos posted on social media, or even to the website. They also enjoy the possibility of interacting directly with hostesses whenever they like a product, asking to view it from another angle or asking about more details.

"What is the price of code 29" (Patrícia Gomes, São Costureira live viewer)

"Diogo, please confirm if I got code 14, size M, in blue" (Soraia Matos, São Costureira live viewer)

"Size M is equivalent to a 38 in pants code 3?" (Maria José Pinto Ferreira, São Costureira live viewer)

"How much is this silver chain necklace?" (Jessica Fredes, Mh2 viewer)

The comments above fit into the "shopstreaming" category, as the main goal of these interactions is clarifying doubts about the products or the purchasing process, that will lead the customer into buying (or not). This interaction happens beyond the public comments, as they can choose from different ways of interacting, according to what is more comfortable for each person - beyond the text comments during the live, can also use Instagram Direct or WhatsApp. One downside is the extra step required to make the purchase, which was sending a message with the order by WhatsApp or Instagram Direct, but most viewers "walked" through this consumer journey and were not discouraged by this extra step. This is confirmed by the high number of request and order confirmations that Valéria (Mh2) and Diogo (São Costureira) make during their lives, to which customers also answer with their agreement.

Furthemore, in comparison to the physical store, it would have been impossible to welcome that many people there at the same time. It is difficult to compare the physical and the online environment, but this experience shows that finding a "middle ground" and providing a "phygital" experience (Moravcikova & Kilestikova, 2017) through shopstreaming can increase sales and also awareness about the brand. This can be reinforced by other tools and features offered by social media platforms that can be incorporated in marketing strategies (Tuten & Solomon, 2012; Kotler, Katajaya & Setiawan, 2017).

Another advantage mentioned by consumers in the comments was the lack of time that they have for shopping during their workday, so performing the shopstreaming lives at the end of the day was a viable option for them to shop. Also, they highlighted the convenience of shopping from their homes, in their own free time.

Concerning RQ3 - Which risks does it entail for companies and consumers, during lockdown periods and posteriorly?, the financial investment in shopstreaming is practically nothing, a smartphone and a good internet connection are enough. In the case of São Costureira, they invested in creating a studio, but only after testing with a few lives and being sure of the return. In the case of Mh2, as lives occured after the opening hours of the store, it was necessary to pay extra time to the salespeople who participated.

As lives last for a long time, it is difficult to have a detailed script, so it is crucial to choose hosts who are able to represent the brand well, who know a lot of details about the products and who understand the customers.

For the viewers, it is also easy and intuitive to participate in live transmissions, and it is also only required a smartphone and internet connection. Viewers can enter and leave at any time, and watch the transmissions from any place. However, they should be careful and make sure that lives are being broadcasted by credible brands, not to engage in unsafe money exchanges.

Comparing the Brazilian and the Portuguese settings, the different restrictions implemented to cope with the Covid-19 pandemic highly impacted how lives were used by both brands, and their outcomes. São Costureira bet on regular emissions because the store was closed for a long period, and this favoured them in building a wider audience and creating a routine that became a habit, essential in the relationship between customers and this brand, even when these restrictions were lifted. Mh2 transmissions were less frequent, only sporadic. This does not mean that one solution is better than the other, they are examples of different strategies that were successful in diverse conditions.

Finally, concerning RQ4 - What is the role of shopstreaming in a post-pandemic setting?, shopstreaming remains a practice for both of the brands, whether as an additional touch point (Mh2), or as a new sales channel (São Costureira). Shopstresming became a marketing and sales tool that worked really well for the studied companies, and it would be interesting to further study if the same happened to other companies. It would also be interesting to explore the role of this new routine in the lives of customers and in their consumer journey, as shopstreaming is fully integrated in the habits of São Costureira's loyal customers, for example.

CONCLUSION

From the companies' point of view, whether as an additional touch point as is the case for Mh2, or as a new sales channel as is the case of São Costureira, shopstreaming brought them benefits in sales and in improving their relationship with customers. It is a very low cost tool that can be added to the communication mix of a brand, and which is able to generate benefits not only during specific conditions as was the case of the Covid-19 pandemic, but also on the long run, as part of the "phygital" environment, being and additional layer to physical spaces (Moravcikova & Kilestikova, 2017).

From the customers' point of view, this new practice goes beyond a new way of purchasing or consuming, it also affords them entertainment and community. It created a strong bond between the hosts and the viewers, and they co-construct the live performance (Kotler, Katajaya & Setiawan, 2017). Customers use their leisure time at home to connect with a brand community through shopstreaming (Tuten & Solomon, 2012). In these lives, they find the convenience of shopping from home, without having to go to a physical store, but still having an experience which is richer to trying on the products, very different from looking at static catalogue photos on websites. In addition, these live emissions are interactive and they are able to participate, asking all their questions about the products. One very striking feature of shopstreaming is being a co-constructed (Kotler, Katajaya & Setiawan, 2017) experience between sellers and buyers, affording benefits to both.

Some issues stood out as important topics for future research. One is the group belonging feeling between the viewers of the shopstreaming live, as they reveal enjoying the presence of each other during the broadcasting session, and at times they also interact with each other in comments. Another topic is the intertwining of consumption with entertainment, as these lives are long, and we observed that, even after making purchases, many clients remained following the live streaming session, so we believe that it is also affording them other gratifications such as entertainment and sense of belonging to a community.

REFERENCES

Adler, P. S., & Kwon, S-W. (2002). *Social Capital: Prospects for a New Concept*. Retrieved from: https://bit.ly/32iacOi

Almeida, F., Santos, J., & Monteiro. (2020). *The Challenges and Opportunities in the Digitalization of Companies in a Post-COVID-19 World*. Retrieved from https://bit.ly/3AqBcqa

Antoniadis, I., & Charmantzi, A. (2016). *Social network analysis and social capital in marketing: Theory and practical implementation*. Retrieved from: https://bit.ly/3nt0vVi

Bahl, M. (2021). *Shopstreaming: The Future of Shopping*. Cognizant. Retrieved from https://cogniz.at/3oKF4jy

Blessa, R. (2015). Merchandising no Ponto-de-Venda [Merchandising at Stores] (4th ed.). São Paulo: Atlas.

Boyd, D.M. & Ellison, N. (2007). Social Network Sites: Definition, History, and Scholarship. *Journal of Computer Mediated Communication*, *13*(1), 210-230. doi:10.1111/j.1083-6101.2007.00393.x

Castells, M. (2016). *A Sociedade em Rede. A Era da Informação: Economia, Sociedade e Cultura* [The Network Society - The Information Age: Economy, Society and Culture] (5th ed., Vol. 1). Fundação Calouste Gulbenkian.

Dengkai, Tingxiu, & Raju. (2021). *Exploring the Factors that Influence Consumers Purchase Intentions in the Context of Live Streaming Commerce.* Retrieved from https://bit.ly/3oxFsSn

Dias, P. (2014). *Viver na Sociedade Digital. Tecnologias digitais, Novas Práticas e Mudanças Sociais* [Living in the Digital Society: Digital technologies, new practices and social change]. Princípia Editora.

Duarte, J., & Barros, A. (Eds.). (2005). *Métodos e técnicas de pesquisa em comunicação* [Research Methods and Techniques in Communication]. Atlas.

Edelman, D., & Singer, M. (2015). *The New Consumer Decision Journey.* McKinsey & Company. Retrieved from https://cutt.ly/EuGNIZP

Fonseca, J. J. S. (2002). *Metodologia da pesquisa científica* [Scientific Research Methodology]. UEC Apostila.

Grusin, R., & Bolter, D. J. (2000). *Remediation: Understanding new media.* The MIT Press.

Hootsuite. (2021). *Digital 2021: Global overview report.* Retrieved from https://bit.ly/3auhdwh

iResearch Consulting Group. (2018). *China Live Webcast Marketing Market Research Report 2018.* Retrieved from https://bit.ly/3anpeD5

Jenkins, H. (2006). *Cultura da Convergência* [Convergence Culture] (2nd ed.). *Aleph.*

Jewitt, C. (2009). *The Routledge Book of Multimodal Analysis.* Routledge.

Kotler, P., Kartajaya, H., & Setiawan, I. (2016). *Marketing 3.0: Do produto e do consumidor até ao espírito humano* [Marketing 3.0: From product and consumer to the human spirit]. Actual.

Kotler, P., Kartajaya, H., & Setiawan, I. (2017). *Marketing 4.0: Do tradicional ao Digital* [Marketing 4.0: From traditional to digital]. Sextante Editora.

Krippendorff, K. (2013). *Content Analysis. An Introduction to its Methodology.* Sage.

Li, C. (2019). *The Disruption Mindset: Why Some Organizations Transform While Others Fail Hardcover.* Ideapress Publishing.

Moravcikova, D., & Kliestikova, J. (2017). *Brand Building with Using Phygital Marketing Communication.* Retrieved from https://bit.ly/2pcQgJ3

Rafiqi, H. (2021). *Recreating Marketing Strategies Post Covid-19: The Marketing Word of "New Normal".* Retrieved from https://bit.ly/3BttdtT <https://bit.ly/3BttdtT>

Ray, A. (2012). *The Methodology of Sampling and Purposive Sampling.* Grin Verlag.

Rodrigues, W. (2021). *A importância do E-Commerce e das Plataformas Digitais para as PMEs: Uma reflexão à luz do contexto do COVID-19* [The importance of e-commerce and digital platforms for SMEs: A reflection on the light of Covid-19]. Retrieved from https://bit.ly/3lpSX4L <https://bit.ly/3lpSX4L>

Rosa, K. C. (2020). As experiências sensoriais dos shoppers nas compras virtuais: um estudo sobre o shopstreaming da Dengo Chocolates durante a pandemia de coronavírus [The sensorial experiences of shoppers in virtual shopping: A study about shopstreaming focusing Dengo Chocolats during de Coronavirus pandemic]. Retrieved from: https://bit.ly/3kWdo8F

Scott, T., Scott, P., Stokes, P., Moore, N., Smith, S. M., & Ward, T. (2015). *Reconceptualising the Consumer Journey in the Digital Age – An Exploratory Study of the United Kingdom Retail Sector.* Retrieved from: https://bit.ly/3HzxQ95

Sneader, K., & Singhal, S. (2020). *Além do coronavírus: o caminho para o próximo normal* [Beyond coronavirus: The path to the new normal]. Retrieved from https://mck.co/3cz9fUi

Sneader, K., & Singhal, S. (2021). *O novo normal chegou: tendências que definirão 2021 - e o futuro* [The new normal is here: trends that will define 2021 - and the future]. Retrieved from https://mck.co/3mGVoiM

Socialbakers. (2020). *State of Social Media Report: The Impact of COVID-19.* Retrieved from https://bit.ly/3qQhQHV

Stockdale, R., & Standing, C. (2004, August). Benefits and barriers of electronic marketplace participation: An SME perspective. *Journal of Enterprise Information Management, 17*(4), 301–311. Advance online publication. doi:10.1108/17410390410548715

Tuten, T. L., & Solomon, M. (2012). *Social Media Marketing*. Sage.

Yin, R. (2001). *Estudo de caso: planejamento e métodos* [Case Studies: Planning and methods]. 2nd ed.). Bookman.

KEY TERMS AND DEFINITIONS

COVID-19: Coronavirus disease (COVID-19) is an infectious disease caused by the SARS-CoV-2 virus.

Facebook: Is an American online social media and social networking service owned by Meta Platforms. Users can post text, photos and multimedia which are shared with any other users who have agreed to be their "friend" or, with different privacy settings, publicly.

Instagram: Is an American photo and video sharing social networking service. Users can like photos and follow other users to add their content to a personal feed.

Live Shopping: Have the same meaning that Shopstreaming, but in other words.

Live Streaming: Is the live broadcasting of media through the internet.

Phygital: Defined as the connection between two worlds – the physical and the digital.

Shopstreaming: In this modality, brands promote live showcasing of their products, during which consumers can interact, ask questions, see the products from different angles and understand its uses, and buy, all without leaving their homes or even taking their eyes off a screen. The whole consumer journey is made during the live broadcasting.

Chapter 6
COVID-19 Vaccination Campaign:
The Uruguayan Case – Contributions of Digital Communication

Patricia Schroeder
https://orcid.org/0000-0002-8911-7699
Universidad de Montevideo, Uruguay

ABSTRACT

Uruguay is the second country in the world with the third dose of immunization. It was notable for the population's response, which allowed for the rapid achievement of herd immunity. As vaccination progressed, there was a rapid decline in the number of severe cases and deaths. In this administration, communication has played a key role in the health strategy and now in the vaccination strategy. The credibility of the government made it possible to move forward without hard questioning. Throughout the entire process, digital communication allowed for two-way communication channels, speed, and reach in messages. In this chapter, the authors offer a theoretical framework for understanding the communication strategy, a brief account of the social climate prior to the pandemic, and finally, the main aspects of the digital communication implemented.

INTRODUCTION

In a global context of high demand for vaccines against covid-19 and a scenario of uncertainty, Uruguay has managed to position itself in the first places in the world in the advancement of vaccination. By the beginning of November 2021, 77.98% of the population had already received a dose and 73.99% had the complete vaccination schedule (Ministerio de Salud Pública – Uruguay 2021e).

In this campaign for the mitigation of the pandemic[1], government communication and the intervention of other actors in society have played a fundamental role. From the government communication, a transmedia strategy was promoted, combining all communication platforms and an intensive use of

DOI: 10.4018/978-1-7998-9790-3.ch006

social media. These aspects were central for all areas of government and especially for the Ministry of Public Health in the implementation of a health strategy. (Schroeder & Amadeo, 2021).

This chapter will present the communication strategy of the covid-19 vaccination campaign developed in Uruguay until October, 2021. Although at the time of writing the campaign has not been completed, it is possible to analyze it's design and implementation. The theoritical frame that supports the strategy will be explained, combining concepts of strategic communication with others of government communication, health communication, and risk communication.

Government communication is held with digital communication supports, offline media, and communication of authorities in territory. Digital communication channels and new technologies have played a fundamental role due to the need to carry out an unprecedented campaign in terms of the logistics required and the target audience to be reached. Digital communication allowed, among other aspects, to keep the public opinion informed in real-time about available agenda (day and time of vaccination according to their group), vaccination progress (vaccine monitor), vaccines available in the country, reports on safety and efficacy of vaccines, among other relevant aspects.

To explain the communication strategy of covid-19 vaccination, it is useful to make a brief reference to the theoretical framework, secondly explain the uncertainty framework that was at the starting point, and finally a description of the distinctive aspects of the digital communication of the covid-19 vaccination campaign in Uruguay.

RESEARCH METHODOLOGY

The purpose of this paper is to describe the Uruguayan government's communication strategy for the covid-19 vaccination plan.

A qualitative study was conducted in the period February-October 2021. First, the initial context of uncertainty is described, followed by a brief mention of the epidemiological situation, a list of the main communication challenges, and then an analysis of the development of the message in digital formats.

As already mentioned, digital communication had a preponderant place because it allowed reaching a large audience. It also enabled the segmentation of messages and contents according to specific audiences.

The pieces analyzed are those available to public opinion in the official networks of the Ministry of Public Health. Likewise, the reports of the work meetings of the communication team that participated in the communication strategy of the Ministry of Public Health were studied.

A quantitive study of the followers in the social networks of the Ministry of Public Health and their evolution was carried out. Additionally, a survey of official content published on social networks and website news was also included.

Concerning the analysis of the media, the information was monitored in the morning and evening central news programs on Channel 4, Channel 12, Channel 10 and, Channel 5; as well as the following in written press: the newspapers El País, El Observador and La República, plus the weekly newspapers Search and Brecha.

Finally, the content of the ministry's social networks and also the Twitter and Instagram of both, Minister Salinas and Undersecretary Satdjian, were also included in this analysis.

THEORETICAL FRAMEWORK

Before proceeding with the description of the vaccination communication strategy, it is pertinent to briefly develop the theoretical framework that supports it.

Different theories have been applied in health communication campaigns. Among the most frequent are, on the one hand, social science theories that explain what drives people's behavior and how these can be modified; and on the other hand, Communication theories in which what stands out is that the source, the channel, the receiver, and the message are essential components. In these two groups of theories it is stressed that information does not fall into a social vacuum but is received through processes of exposure and selective perception, prior knowledge, and macro-social levels. (Tench & Bridge 2021).

Authors Tench and Bridge highlight three theories or models: the Theory of Planned Behaviour, the Likelihood Model and the Extended Parallel Process Model.

The theory of Planned Behaviour (Ajzen, 1985) proposes that voluntary action is a function of the individual's intention to perform a behavior and perceived control. Therefore, for a successful health communication campaign, the message must consider the target audience's attitudes about the behavior, their subjective norms, and levels of perceived behavioral control.

The Elaboration Probability Model (Petty & Cacioppo, 1986) has been applied to improve health outcomes for several health problems, including smoking, nutrition, and reduction of risk behaviours concerning to acquired immunodeficiency syndrome. It focuses on asking how people will react to the messages to which they will be exposed.

The Extended Parallel Process Model, based on the health belief model (Rosentock et al., 1992), analyzes the role of emotions in behavior change. Studies on the topic show that while fear is a factor that positively influences a behavior change, it can become detrimental if people become paralyzed. (Chen et al., 2019; Witte, 1994 in Tench R. & Bridge. G., 2021) The authors conclude that fear should be used with caution in health campaigns, the sensitivity of the target audience and their ability to make changes should be taken into account.

Authors Tench and Bridge (2021) conclude that all three models emphasize that for health communication campaigns to be successful, the communication strategy must consider the target audience, their subjective norms and perceptions of health behaviour. Also, messages should be clear and understandable to the target audience. It is necessary to evaluate whether the audience is engaged in the message or it is needed to find a way to capture their attention. And, in the case of using fear to change behavior, the relationship between fear and motivation to change should be measured because fear can lead to paralysis.

Finally, it is worth to mention Schiavo's contributions. (Schiavo, R. pp. 32-46) explains the different theoretical approaches that influence the development of public health campaigns. Families of social and behavioral science theories, mass communication and social marketing theories, and other models that include medical, sociological, and anthropological models are highlighted.

The following theories and models were selected because they are usefull to understand the vaccination communication strategy.

The Innovation Theory (Rogers, 1995), addresses how new ideas, concepts, or practices can be spread within a community and defines five subgroups: innovators, early adopters, early majority, late majority, laggards. The fundamental premise is that change occurs over time and depends on the following stages: awareness, knowledge and interest, decision, testing and implementation, confirmation, and rejection.

The Health Belief Model (Becker, Haefner, & Maiman, 1977; Janz & Becker, 1984; Strecher & Rosenstock, 1997) explains that to adopt healthy patterns, individuals must be aware of the risks of serious or life-threatening illnesses. They must also perceive the benefits of behaviour change. The fundamental premise of this theory is that knowledge will bring about behaviour change.

The Social Congnivite Theory (Bandura, 1997), explains behavior as a result of three reciprocal factors: behavior, personal factors, and external events. One of the fundamental premises is its emphasis on the external factors and its major contribution to health communications is to understand the mechanisms and factors that can influence retention, reproduction, and motivation on behavior.

The Convergence Theory (Kincaid, 1979; Rogers & Kincaid, 1981; Figueroa, Kincadi, Rani & Lewis, 2002), is based on the perspective that an individual's perceptions and behavior are influenced by the perceptions and behaviors of members of the same group, such as professional associations, coworkers, family members, and people in one's social media.

Finally, the Communication for Persuasion Theory developed by social psychologist William McGuire, focuses on how people process information. According to this model, in the process of persuasive communication there are twelve steps. For a person to change their behaviour they must: be exposed to the message, pay attention, find it interesting or personally relevant, understand it, find out how this new behaviour can fit into their life, accept the proposed change, remember and validate the message, be able to think about the message in relevant situations, make decisions based on the information, behave according to that decision, receive positive reinforcement for that behavior and integrate the new behaviour into their life. (Moya, 2000).

To these conceptual frameworks of health communication models developed for risk communication and evidence-based communication must be added (Tormo, M. J., Banegas, J. R. 2001; Nespereira, J. 2014; Schwarzinger, M., & Luchini, S. 2021). It is also supported by the government communication implemented to date in the context of covid-19 (Schroeder & Amadeo, 2021).

Risk communication frames should help to avoid contradictions in order to reinforce credibility of government communication (González-Melado, F. J., & Di Pietro, M. L. 2020; Rzymski, P., Borkowski, L., Drąg, M., Flisiak, R., Jemielity, J., Krajewski, J., Mastalerz-Migas, A., et al. 2021).

Risk communication also requires permanent monitoring of the epidemiological situation in order to know the evolution of the pandemic and the reactions of the population. Specifically, in the Uruguayan case, the beginning of vaccination coincided with an increment in the number of cases. This factor required, on the one hand, reinforcing the concept that vaccines are effective in minimizing the pandemic, which would bring about a decrease in contagion and consequently a decrease in the number of deaths. On the other hand, the increment in cases elevates the perception of risk and was a factor that most likely contributed favorably to accelerating vaccination.

From the perspective of risk communication, the following issues collaborate in a successful communication (Moreno & Peres, 2020):

- The source responsible for the transmission of information must have credibility
- Honesty. What is not known must be clearly reported and clarified.
- Meaningful actions that help to understand the message.
- Participation of experts regarding medical issues and in risk communication
- Consistency in messages.

THE SOCIAL CLIMATE BEFORE THE ARRIVAL OF THE VACCINE

Uncertainty as a Starting Point

The communication of all aspects related to covid-19 has uncertainty as a common denominator. As never before, scientific knowledge has been within the reach of governments and public opinion. However, political decisions to confront a pandemic of these dimensions must be executed quickly, and the production of scientific knowledge has its deadlines, not always according to political times.

Uncertainty is compounded by Infodemic that brings with it excessive amount of information and misinformation also (Schroeder & Amadeo, 2021). In a vaccination campaign, trust in vaccines as the main measure to mitigate harm is essential. Just as communication plays a fundamental role in getting people to adopt personal protection measures (physical distance, use of masks, and hand washing, in addition to social behaviors that lead to not crowding), in this phase of the pandemic 70% of the population must agree to be vaccinated. (According to scientific recommendations, this is the percentage of vaccination necessary to reduce infections, hospitalizations, and deaths).

These aspects illustrate the double role of communication: to achieve very high levels of trust in governmental decisions and to achieve a general behavior that accompanies this vaccination process.

Epidemiological Situation Before Vaccination

Uruguay went through the first eight months of the pandemic without suffering the globally known as the first or second wave. The behavior of the virus during the first nine months was by outbreaks (Figure 1) and with almost complete social mobility. The most affected sectors of the economy were tourism and those related to festivals and parties. There was an almost total closure of borders and suspension of social activities involving more than 100 people. The rest of the economic, social, educational and sporting activities were maintained with adjustments according to the health situation.

However, in November 2020 there was an increase in cases and deaths that worsened with the presence of the P1 variant from March to June 2021. (Figure 1).

This increment in cases was the reason for more pressure from the opposition political force and also greater anxiety among the population for the arrival of the vaccine (Miranda criticized the government's slowness and said that urgent action is needed. The president of the Frente Amplio also said that the party had numerous links to accelerate the arrival of the vaccine if necessary, 2021; Vacunas: el FA suma presión al gobierno con nuevas críticas por falta de transparencia, 2021). The pressure continued for several months, even after vaccination began on 27 February 2021 due to a sustained increase in cases and deaths.

In this climate of political and social tension, the authorities of the Ministry of Public Health were summoned to give explanations about the process of study and purchase of covid-19 vaccines. On January 5, a delegation from the Ministry of Public Health and the Secretary of the Presidency attended the Senate Chamber's Health Commission (Ministerio de Salud Pública – Uruguay, 2021g).

At this Comission the Ministry of Public Health delegation explained the purchasing process managed through Covax Fund and also through bilateral negotiations. Likewise, available information was shared about the safety and efficacy of the vaccines available with Phase III studies. And the recommendations of the National Vaccine Advisory Commission and ad hoc group.

Figure 1. Number of active COVID-19 confirmed cases per day
From "Informe Epidemiológico," by Ministerio de Salud Pública Uruguay, 2021e, p. 8.

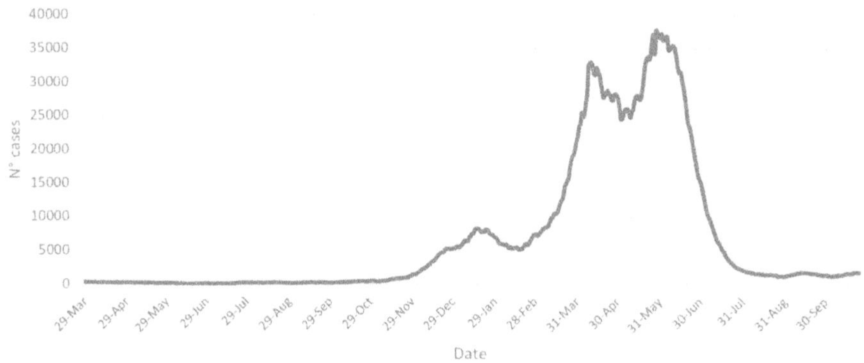

Finally, on 23 January 2021, the President Lacalle Pou announced the arrival of the first vaccines. The message was received with great acceptance and relieved partially the pressure of public opinion. The government's decision was the first major purchase of vaccines from two platforms from the laboratories Sinovac and Pfizer Biontech. (Uruguay Presidencia, 2021). With this first purchase, 70% of the target population could be vaccinated (at that date the population over 18 years of age was considered, estimated at 2:836,000 people). Later, that number was expanded with the approval of vaccination for children under 18 years old.

It is worth to mention that this purchase was made in a complex and uncertain international context, where there was a high global demand for vaccines and also the national climate of tension previous referred. There was uncertainty as to whether the vaccines would arrive on time (first and second doses in a precise period), whether logistics could be organized according to the combination of two different platforms, whether there would be a response from the population, whether there would be sufficient human resources (hiring a significant number of vaccinators), logistical requirements related to the cold chain, safety, and efficacy of vaccination.

Thus, in January 2020, a team led by the Ministry of Public Health (Minister Daniel Salinas and Vice Minister José Luis Satdjian) was consolidated to manage a complex process that includes the acquisition of vaccines, reception, distribution and vaccination in the territory (Figure 2).

It is pertinent to highlight the complexity of articulating team work to develop a task of this magnitude in a very demanding timeframe. To this end, a vaccination plan was designed that began to be implemented on March 1 (Ministerio de Salud Púbilca - Uruguay, 2021b), preceded by the vaccination of vaccinators on February 27 of the same year.

The first communication challenge was to establish permanent communication channels among all those involved to develop a seamless communication with the public opinion without contradictions.

Vaccines from Sinovac laboratory arrived first and vaccination of the prioritized groups was immediately available (Ministerio de Salud Pública - Uruguay, 2021h). Then the Pfizer vaccines arrived and all the successive arrivals were according to what was established. The vaccination plan was implemented in stages and the main events are summarized in Figure 3.

Figure 2. Integration of the team, functional areas involved in the vaccination plan

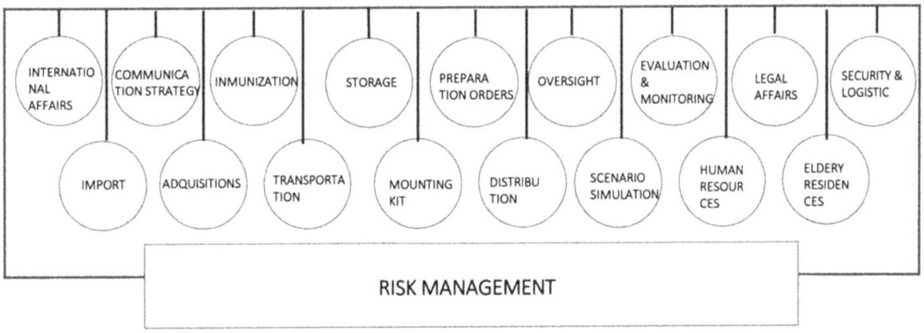

Figure 3. Main events of the vaccination plan

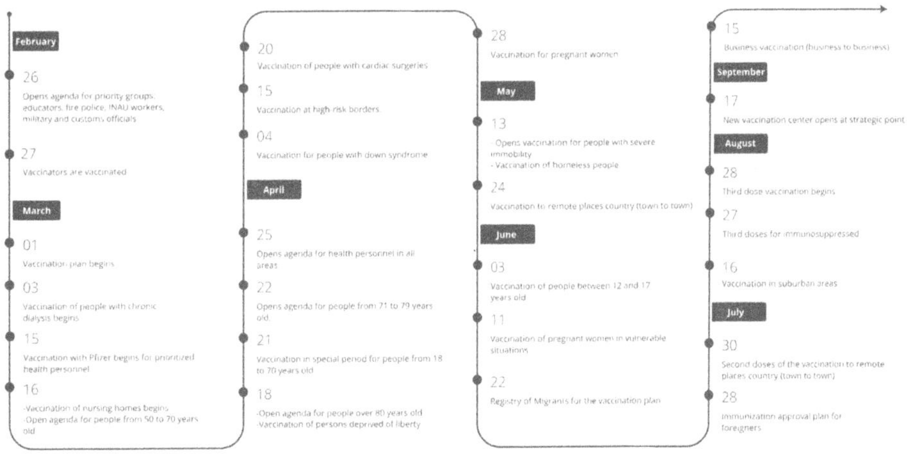

MAIN CHALLENGES IN DESIGNING COVID-19'S COMMUNICATION STRATEGY

The communication of all vaccination campaigns is challenging as it must accurately reach the previously defined target population. This is how every year since the emergence of H1N1 flu Uruguay faces the challenge of vaccinating vulnerable groups: pregnant women, children, and people over 60 years old. In 2020, in the context of the pandemic, a staggered vaccination was carried out between May and July and the objective of vaccinating these groups was achieved. More than 950,000 doses were administered, which significantly reduced the number of respiratory infections that are typical of winter time. This experience of staggering vaccination by groups, and with a previous schedule, served as experience to implement covid-19 vaccination on a larger scale.

The challenges of covid-19 vaccination are included in the recommendations of the Pan American Health Organization (Pan American Health Organization, 2021). In the uruguayan case, they are specified in the following specific challenges:

1. Vaccinate 70% of the population. This is an unprecedented number, it means administering two doses of the vaccines available in the country.
2. Vaccination in stages. The doses would be administered to the groups defined in advance and the challenge of transmitting to the population the certainty that the plan would be executed according to the initial forecast. Vaccination began in prioritized groups and the recommendations of the World Health Organization were used to define them.
3. Vaccines developed in record time. The vaccine against covid-19 are vaccines developed in a very short period, it is necessary to transmit certainty regarding the safety and efficacy of the vaccines. In all cases, the vaccines were approved with sufficient levels of efficacy (Phase III), but in all cases - and at the time of starting vaccination in Uruguay - Phase IV studies were lacking.
4. Need for adherence in the first weeks of vaccination. For the vaccination plan to be successful, the first prioritized groups must show adherence of around 70%. A positive first response is essential.
5. Infodemic. It is necessary to know how much the overabundance of information and false news about the safety and efficacy of the vaccine affects the rate of vaccination.
6. Anti-vaccine groups. It is necessary to be aware of their existence and their impact on public opinion.
7. Existence of adverse effects and how much this information may impact the vaccination campaign.
8. Maintain public confidence throughout the vaccination process, knowing in advance that there is a good chance that the plan will need to be adjusted as the epidemiological situation changes or new scientific evidence emerges.
9. Speed of vaccination. For vaccination to mitigate the pandemic, it must be carried out in an accelerated manner. This implies logistics and a territorial reach of great magnitude.

Communication Strategy

As mentioned above, the vaccination strategy has a solid base in the government's communication strategy that has sought to build trust based on the value of transparency.

There is another aspect, which perhaps goes unnoticed by the public, and that is that the Ministry of Public Health has intensively developed its own social media channels. Thus, it has deepened the work on existing networks such as Facebook, Twitter, and Youtube, and developed Instagram, and recently it is working on Tik Tok and Linkedin.

With a strategy that involves developing appropriate content for each social media, the website of the Ministry of Public Health is the government website with the most visits and its social media channels have grown exponentially in the past 18 months.

The previous work that allowed the development of the digital communication channels of the Ministry of Public Health was undoubtedly an important point of support for the communication strategy of covid-19.

Table 1 shows the exponential growth of followers in the ministry's social media, which demostrates an increase in the scope of communication. At the same time, it shows the response of public opinion to the content that is published. It also means also that official sources have proved to be reliable for different audiences.

Communication in social media is combined with public communication of authorities, news in the print media, official releases, advertisements, among others. Following the definition provided by Coffman (2002, p.2)

Table 1. Number of followers in social media of the Ministry of Public Health from February 2020 to October 2022.

	YouTube		Facebook		Instagram		Twitter		Total
February	1.797		40.410				22.313		64.520
March	2.125	25%	56.640	29%			61.313	74%	120.079
April	8.002	377%	138.000	244%	25.094		73.813	20%	244.915
May	8.425	5%	146.641	6%	33.407	25%	78.787	6%	267.260
June	8.497	1%	148.669	1%	40.930	23%	80.200	2%	278.296
July	8.535	0,5%	152.501	4%	42.150	3%	83.300	4%	286.486
August	8.665	1,5%	154.869	6%	51.679	23%	85.300	2%	300.513
September	8.728	1,0%	156.287	1%	55.557	10%	86.752	1%	307.324
October	9.063	3%	158.489	1%	60.088	11%	88.436	1%	316.076
November	9.240	2%	164.211	4%	64.242	7%	91.043	3%	328.736
December	9.540	3%	171.610	4%	74.351	14%	95.524	5%	351.025
January	9.612	1%	176.831	3%	80.333	7%	98.300	3%	365.076
February	9.737	1%	181.363	3%	84.878	5%	100.775	3%	376.753
March	10.300	6%	197.470	9%	95.799	13%	113.583	13%	417.152
April	10.800	5%	211.731	7%	101.379	5%	122.695	7%	446.605
May	11.200	4%	217.415	3%	105.813	4%	128.325	4%	462.753
June	12.000	1%	222.739	2%	109.238	3%	132.234	3%	476.211
July	12.500	4%	225.588	1%	111.298	2%	135.325	2%	484.711
August	12.900	3%	228.090	1%	112.633	1%	138.483	2%	492.106
September	13.200	2%	229.365	1%	113.143	1%	140.383	2%	496.091
October	13.400		229.803		114.573		143.277		501.053
Accumulated growth(2020-21)		746%		569%		457%		642%	

Public communication campaigns use the media, messaging, and an organized set of communication activities to generate specific outcomes in a large number of individuals and in a specified period of time. They are an attempt to shape behavior toward desirable social outcomes. To maximize their chances of success, campaigns usually coordinate media efforts with a mix of other interpersonal and community-based communication channels.

The author highlights two types of campaigns that seek individual behavioural change or promote behaviours that lead to improved individual or social wellbeing; and public will campaigns that try to mobilize society to bring about policy change.

The covid-19 campaign had a double component. On the one hand, the campaign was a call to action and, on the other hand, it sought to impose the concept of vaccination as an act of solidarity.

Undoubtedly, in this sense, the covid-19 vaccination campaign strongly marked the uruguayan society. The country proved to be an example of rapid vaccination and also showed results of vaccination

Figure 4. Number of cases per day in Intensive Care Unite and Moderate Care Unit
From "Informe Epidemiológico," by Ministerio de Salud Pública -Uruguay, 2021e, p.7.

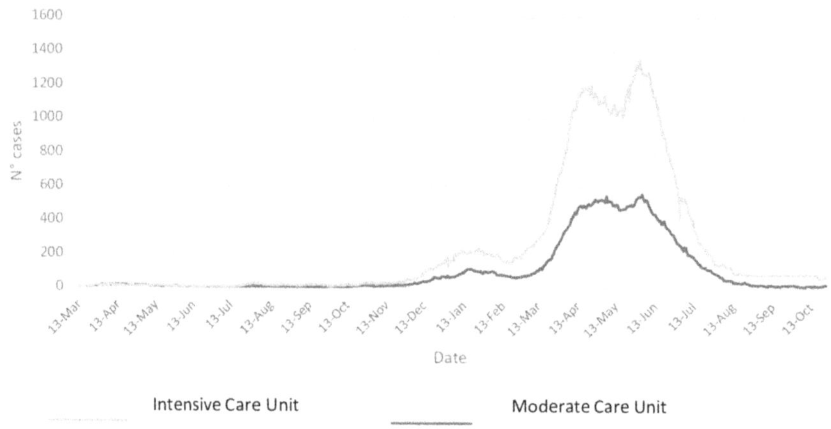

effectiveness. A negative epidemiological situation was reversed (Figure 4) and the economic activity shows a clear improvement.

To be effective, health communication campaigns must take into account the conceptual frameworks mentioned above. The following aspects stand out from the aforementioned theories:

- Information should be clear, understandable and impactful.
- Communication must be timely and promptly.
- The audience's perception of risk and its context (in this case the evolution of the pandemic) must be taken into account.
- Knowledge is a relevant factor in health decision-making.
- The influence of close groups is also relevant in health decision-making.

Concerning the covid-19 vaccination strategy in Uruguay, communication had a central place and throughout the process we sought to maintain the trust of the population. The central value is transparency, as it has been throughout the covid-19 communication. (Schroeder & Amadeo, 2021).

A 360° government communication was developed where all communication formats were taken into account to make as much information available to the population as possible.

The following issues are the main aspects of the communication strategy and its implementation on digital platforms.

Information Accessible to Public Opinion

As mentioned above, the vaccination had to be carried out in a staggered manner and for this purpose, a scheduling system was established and operated through the Ministry's website.

A landing page was developed with the main contents about the vaccination system (Figure 5):

- Schedule (day and time to receive first and second dose of vaccine).

- Frequently asked questions and answers.
- Reporting of suspicious adverse effects.
- Vaccination certificate.
- Means to make an appointment (website, coronavirus app and toll free line).
- Information for medical personnel.

Evidence-based Communication

Throughout the vaccination process, scientific information was made available to the population in an accessible way in relation to the different vaccine platforms, expected adverse effects of vaccines, questions and answers about vaccines, safety and efficacy of vaccines, effectiveness studies could be carried out, availability of vaccines, and a vaccine monitor that allowed everyone to see the progress of vaccination and its impact on pandemic mitigation.

The communication effort was focused on finding messages in accessible language and the search of interlocutors valued by society. An example of this was the campaign developed with football players where they explained with football metaphors the data on the effectiveness of vaccines.

Development of Audiovisual Contents

Audiovisual contents played an important role in the strategy. For instance, short videos were developed throughout the process to explain synthetically some relevant aspects of vaccination.

Experts, doctors, nurses were sought to develop the vaccination program message clearly. The principal concepts developed in the vaccination campaign were: Uruguay has always had high vaccination rates; vaccines are safe; they are the main tool to get out of this long process that affected all of us; they were developed in record time under exceptional circumstances and with a collaborative process of government and science and, self-care must be maintained for the vaccines to be effective.

Infographics Developments

Infographics were developed to explain in a simple way very complex concepts such as those related to the effectiveness of vaccination. These materials were disseminated in social media channels of the Ministry of Public Health and had a high impact on the public opinion. This information was also taken by local news and the main press, it was widely disseminated. Simplifying a complex message allows it to have a greater reach.

#UruguaySeVacuna

The hashtag of the campaign was #UruguaySeVacuna and had great repercussions. A global phenomenon to which Uruguay was no stranger, was the photo of the moment of vaccination, with the vaccinators, at the vaccinator's office and with messages expressing solidarity: "I am getting vaccinated for me, for my family, for my loved ones".

People from the world of art and sports, journalists, religious leaders, politicians, and others showed their support for the vaccination campaign. Social media allowed to show the images of hundreds of social referents and this not only favored the amplification of the message but also collaborated in the contagion effect.

Figure 5. Image of the landing page Vaccination Plan COVID-19
From Ministerio de Salud Pública – Uruguay, 2021a.

Figure 6. Example of a vaccine effectiveness campaign explained with football metaphors (Luis Suárez).
In this example, the text means: "Scoring goals in the National Team gives me confidence to improve myself in each game. Vaccines also give us confidence because of their effectiveness." From Noticias "Ciencia en Clave de fútbol" by Ministerio de Salud Pública – Uruguay, 2021d.

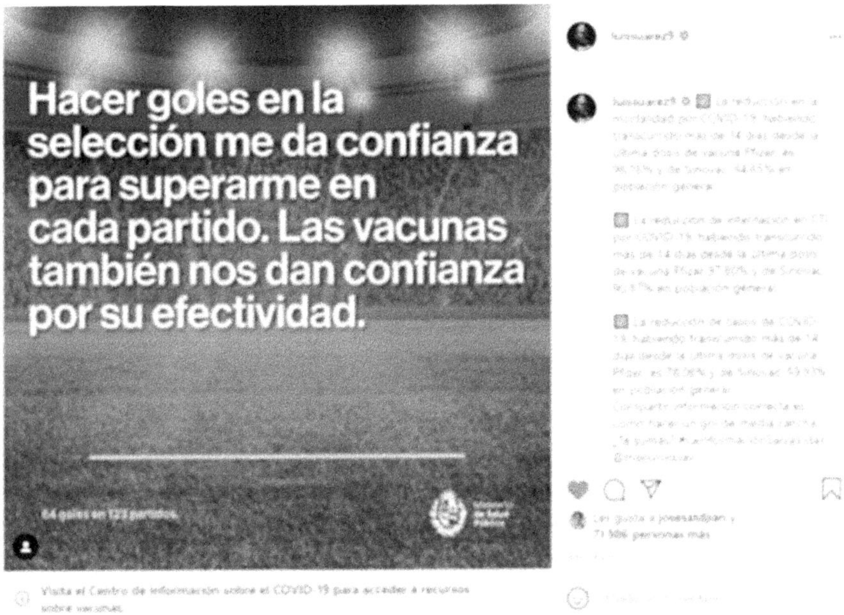

Figure 7. Infographic on the effectiveness of COVID-19 vaccines.
From "Estudio sobre efectividad vacunal" by Dirección del Departamento de Vigilancia en Salud del Ministerio de Salud Pública - Uruguay, 2021c).

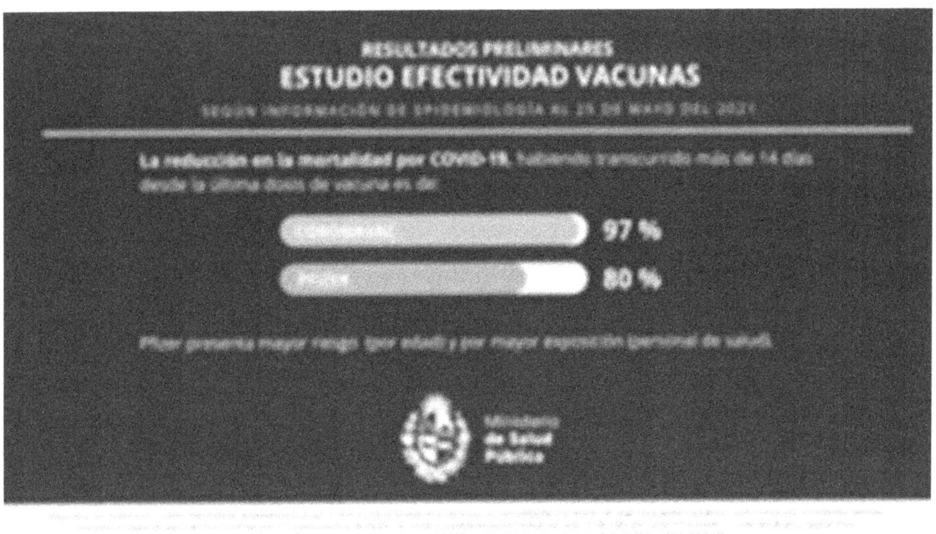

COMBATING MISINFORMATION

As already stated, the pandemic brought misinformation as a collateral effect. Globally, the most common false claims are that the vaccine modifies the human genome or implants tracking chips, induces damage to health or, contains human immunodeficiency virus particles. These false statements are also related to messages regarding the denial of the pandemic and that it is not necessary to use protective measures such as the use of masks. (Rzymski, P., Borkowski, L., Drąg, M., Flisiak, R., Jemielity, J., Krajewski, J., Mastalerz-Migas, A., et al. 2021).

Among the deniers, there is a subgroup of anti-vaccers that also have a global presence and Uruguay was not alien to this phenomenon. These anti-vaccers groups promote messages mainly on the social network Facebook, Twitter and Telegram. However, the local media did not give them relevant coverage and the social demonstrations were of little impact.

Because it is a global phenomenon and it can potentially negatively impact, it had to be monitored by the communication team of the Ministry of Public Health. This is the first misinformation phenomenon that the country has experienced on a large scale. Likewise, Uruguay is characterized by having reliable and impartial information media. Consecuently, it coins freedom of press and is one of the main strengths of the democratic system.

It is noteworthy that the media throughout the pandemic cited as their main sources of information the content provided by the Ministry of Public Health and the Presidency of the Republic. This fact shows that trust in official sources has been maintained from the beginning of the pandemic to date. This is a positive consequence of the communication policy based on transparency promoted by President Lacalle Pou.

To have a better understanding of the subject, thc Ministry of Public Health commissioned the consulting firm Civirt to conduct an analysis of misinformation on social media. The study consisted of fan analysis on Twitter indentifying the nodes of disinformation and their followers during febreruary 10 to march 10, 2021. Fifteen were detected and within this group four with greater activity. Moreover, the Facebook page that is cited by these users as a source of content was algo analyzed.

The study concludes which are the most repeated lies on social media are five:

1. There is an epidemic of false positives, tests performed with the PCR diagnostic technique are not reliable.
2. Vaccines are not safe.
3. Deaths from Covid-19 are fewer than reported.
4. Mouthpieces are not necessary, they are harmful.
5. Vaccines are not effective.

Based on this analysis, the communication strategy focused on reinforcing the information about the questioned aspects. The Ministry did not seek a form of confrontation or debate with the anti-vaccine movements but rather reinforced the information in relation to the safety, efficacy and effectiveness of the vaccine.

Mainly, it was sought to disseminate effectiveness studies that were developed very early by the Ministry of Public Health. These studies were shown through videos and infographics with the purpose of having the widest possible reach. In this regard, the amplification by the authorities (Minister and Undersecretary) were highly positive. Fundamentally, the Twitter account of Minister Salinas has a relevant scope. Salinas has the particularity of interacting personally with users and this led to building trust with the public opinion and journalists. In addition, vaccine efectivess studies were widely disseminated by referents of the scientific community, doctors and scientists who have a high reputation in Uruguay. This last aspect also contributed to reinforce trust.

The Strategy Focused on the Development of Rational Messaging

The campaign had a strong emphasis on rational messages and communication based on scientific evidence. This format was prioritized in order to provide as much information as possible about the vaccination process, vaccines, the functioning of the schedule, among others (Ministerio de Salud Pública - Uruguay, 2021i).

The content of the messages is summarized in the following concepts:

- Vaccination will be free and not mandatory.
- Vaccine doses are sufficient to achieve herd immunity.
- Vaccination is an act of solidarity, it is necessary to be vaccinated to stop the pandemic.
- It will be carried out in a staggered manner, according to prioritized groups.
- The dates when people will receive the vaccine are reported.
- The website, Coronavirus app, and call center are promoted as the main means of communication.
- It is necessary to maintain personal care while progressing with the vaccination plan.
- The different groups that should be scheduled to receive the vaccine are announced in stages.

CONCLUSION

Uruguay achieved a high vaccination rate and the expected health objectives were achieved: fewer infections, fewer seriously hospitalized patients and, consequently, fewer deaths. (Figures 1 and 4).

Both the President of the Republic and the Minister of Public Health have a high rate of approval regarding the management of the pandemic (El 84% de la población aprueba la gestión de la pandemia realizada por Lacalle, según Factum, 2021). The Minister of Public Health is the minister with the highest popular approval. (Cifra, 2021).

These data reveals the high level of confidence acquired in the past 18 months of government management. In this critical phase of the pandemic, public opinion verified that the established objectives were met, an orderly vaccination was developed and all the people who wanted to be vaccinated were able to do so. The data also showed that the vaccines are safe and effective. In general, communication was an essential issue of a very good government management, particularly digital communication was necessary to achieve an effective campaign.

Confidence in the government resulted in an excellent response from the population and other social actors such as opinion leaders, leaders from the scientific world, businessmen, among others.

Digital communication played a fundamental role in a transmedia and 360° communication strategy, it allowed having a national reach and response capacity to the concerns of the population. In this sense, it is noteworthy that digital channels allow constant monitoring of public opinion, listening to complaints and responding.

A future analysis is pending to understand the reasons that led people to get vaccinated: was it for fear of the advance of the pandemic? Was it to recover their previous social life? Was it a contagion effect? Answering these questions will be useful to face future vaccination campaigns.

REFERENCES

Ajzen, I. (1985). From Intentions to Actions: a Theory of Planned Behavior. In Action control (pp. 11-39). Springer Berlin Heidelberg. doi:10.1007/978-3-642-69746-3_2

Bandura, A. (1997). Self-efficacy: The Exercise of Control. *The Freeman.*

Becker, M. H., Haefner, D. P., & Maiman, L. A. (1977). The health belief model in the prediction of dietary compliance: A field experiment. *Journal of Health and Social Behavior, 18*(4), 348–366. doi:10.2307/2955344 PMID:617639

Cacioppo, J., & Petty, R. (1984). The Elaboration Likelihood Model of Persuasion. In T. C. Kinnear (Ed.), *NA - Advances in Consumer Research* (Vol. 11, pp. 673–675). Association for Consumer Research. https://www.acrwebsite.org/volumes/6329/volumes/v11/NA%20-%2011

Chou, W. Y. S., & Budenz, A. (2020). Considering emotion in COVID-19 vaccine communication: Addressing vaccine hesitancy and fostering vaccine confidence. *Health Communication, 35*(14), 1718–1722. doi:10.1080/10410236.2020.1838096 PMID:33124475

Cifra. (2021). *Evaluación de la Gestión de Ministros* [Evaluation of Ministers' Management]. https://www.cifra.com.uy/index.php/2021/08/10/evaluacion-de-la-gestion-de-ministros-3/

Coffman, J. (2002). *Public communication campaign evaluation: an environmental scan of challenges, criticisms, practice, and opportunities.* Communications Consortium Media Center. https://www.dors.it/documentazione/testo/200905/Public%20Communication%20Campaign%20Evaluation.pdf

El 84% de la población aprueba la gestión de la pandemia realizada por Lacalle, según Factum [84% of the Population Approves Lacalle's Handling of the Pandemic, According to Factum]. (2021, October 13). *El Observador.* https://www.elobservador.com.uy/nota/el-84-de-la-poblacion-aprueba-la-gestion-de-la-pandemia-realizada-por-lacalle-segun-factum-2021101322377

Figueroa, M. E., Kincaid, D. L., Rani, M., & Lewis, G. (2002). *Communication for social change: an integrated model for measuring the process and its outcomes.* Rockefeller Foundation and Johns Hopkins University Center for Communication Programs.

Giménez, M. P. (2017). *Aplicación de la Teoría de la Conducta Planificada en la Seguridad Vial: velocidad, alcohol y drogas* [Application of the Theory of Planned Behavior in Road Security: Speed, Alcohol and Drugs] (Doctoral dissertation). Universidad Católica San Antonio de Murcia. RIUCAM. http://hdl.handle.net/10952/2678

González-Melado, F. J., & Di Pietro, M. L. (2020). La vacuna frente al Covid-19 y la confianza institucional [The Vaccine Against Covid-19 and Institutional Trust]. *Enfermedades Infecciosas y Microbiologia Clinica.* Advance online publication. doi:10.1016/j.eimc.2020.08.001 PMID:33069493

Janz, N. K., & Becker, M. H. (1984). The Health Belief Model: A decade later. *Health Education Quarterly, 11*(1), 1–47. doi:10.1177/109019818401100101 PMID:6392204

Kincaid, D. L. (1979). *The convergence Model of Communication*. EastWest Communication Institute.

Lazarus, J. V., Ratzan, S. C., Palayew, A., Gostin, L. O., Larson, H. J., Rabin, K., & El-Mohandes, A. (2021). A global survey of potential acceptance of a COVID-19 vaccine. *Nature Medicine, 27*(2), 225–228. doi:10.103841591-020-1124-9 PMID:33082575

Ministerio de Salud Pública - Uruguay. (2021a). *Plan de Vacunación Covid-19* [Covid-19 Vaccination Plan]. https://www.gub.uy/uruguaysevacuna

Ministerio de Salud Pública - Uruguay. (2021b, March 1). *Plan de vacunación contra COVID-19: Responsabilidad cívica y solidaria* [Vaccination Plan Against Covid-19: Civil Responsibility and Solidarity]. https://www.gub.uy/ministerio-salud-publica/comunicacion/noticias/plan-vacunacion-contra-covid-19-responsabilidad-civica-solidaria

Ministerio de Salud Pública - Uruguay. (2021c, May 27). *Estudio sobre efectividad vacunal* [Study of Vaccine Effectiveness]. https://www.gub.uy/ministerio-salud-publica/comunicacion/noticias/estan-disponibles-datos-preliminares-del-estudio-efectividad-vacunal

Ministerio de Salud Pública - Uruguay. (2021d, July 12). *Ciencia en clave de fútbol* [Science in football key]. https://www.gub.uy/ministerio-salud-publica/comunicacion/noticias/campana-efectividad-vacunal-ciencia-clave-futbol

Ministerio de Salud Pública - Uruguay. (2021e, October 25). *Informe epidemiológico COVID-19 Actualización al 25 de octubre de 2021* [COVID-19 Epidemiological Report Update as of October 25, 2021]. https://www.gub.uy/ministerio-salud-publica/comunicacion/noticias/informe-epidemiologico-covid-19-actualizado-18-enero-2021

Ministerio de Salud Pública - Uruguay. (2021f, November 1). *Monitor de datos de vacunación Covid-19* [Covid-19 Vaccination Data Monitor]. https://monitor.uruguaysevacuna.gub.uy/

Ministerio de Salud Pública – Uruguay [@MSPURUGUAY]. (2021g, January 5). *En comparencia ante la Comisión de Salud Pública del @SenadoUy, el ministro @DrDanielSalinas explicó el trabajo realizado desde marzo hasta la fecha* [In appearance before the Public Health Commission of the @SenadoUy, the Minister @DrDanielSalinas explained the work carried out from March to date] [Image attached] [Tweet]. Twitter. https://twitter.com/MSPUruguay/status/1346539663104888833

Ministerio de Salud Pública - Uruguay. (2021i, February 26). *Campaña de vacunación COVID-19* [Covid-19 Vaccination Campaign] #UruguaySeVacuna. [Videos]. YouTube. https://www.youtube.com/playlist?list=PL4O9exeLSKwyeofFVi_3x3Vqcl1gZ-6Qa

Ministerio de Salud Pública - Uruguay [@MSPURUGUAY]. (2021h, February 25). *A las 23:07 hs arribaron las primeras dosis de vacunas del Laboratorio Sinovac. Funcionarios del MSP y del Laboratorio Calmette...* [At 11:07 p.m. the first doses of vaccines arrived from the Sinovac Laboratory. Officials of the MSP and the Calmette Laboratory...] [Image attached] [Tweet]. Twitter. https://twitter.com/MSPUruguay/status/1365132134697082880

Miranda criticó la lentitud del gobierno y dijo que es necesario tomar medidas urgentes. El presidente del Frente Amplio dijo además que el partido tiene numerosos vínculos para acelerar la llegada de la vacuna si es necesario [Miranda criticized the government's slowness and said urgent action is needed. The president of the Frente Amplio also said that the party has numerous links to accelerate the arrival of the vaccine if necessary]. (2021, December 14). *El País.* https://www.elpais.com.uy/informacion/politica/miranda-critico-lentitud-gobierno-dijo-necesario-tomar-medidas-urgentes.html

Montagni, I., Ouazzani-Touhami, K., Mebarki, A., Texier, N., Schück, S., & Tzourio, C. (2021). Acceptance of a Covid-19 vaccine is associated with ability to detect fake news and health literacy. Journal of Public Health. *Journal of Public Health, 43*(4), 695–702. Advance online publication. doi:10.1093/pubmed/fdab028 PMID:33693905

Moreno, A. R., & Peres, F. (2020). Comunicación de riesgos ante el Coronavirus [Communication risks in the face of the Coronavirus]. *Boletín sobre COVID-19, 1*(4), 7-9.

Moya, M. (2000). Persuasión y cambio de actitudes [Persuasion and change of attitudes]. *Psicologia e Sociedade*, 153–170.

Nespereira, J. (2014). *Estrategias discursivas en la comunicación de crisis sanitarias (retórica y teoría de la argumentación): el caso de la gripe A en 2009* [Discursive strategies in the communication of health crises (rhetoric and theory of argumentation): the case of influenza A in 2009]. (Doctoral dissertation, Universidad de Valladolid). Teseo. https://www.educacion.gob.es/teseo/mostrarSeleccion.do

Pan American Health Organization. (2021). *Guía para elaborar una estrategia de comunicación de riesgos sobre las vacunas contra la COVID-19* [Guide to developing a risk communication strategy on COVID-19 vaccines]. https://iris.paho.org/handle/10665.2/53259

Petty, R. E., & Cacioppo, J. T. (1986). The Elaboration Likelihood Model of Persuasion. In *Communication and persuasión: central and peripheral routes to attitude change* (pp. 1–24). Springer.

Rogers, E. M. (1995). *Diffusion of Innovations* (4th ed.). Free Press.

Rogers, E. M., & Kincaid, D. L. (1981). *Communication Networks: Towards a New Paradigm for Research.* Free Press.

Roozenbeek, J., Schneider, C. R., Dryhurst, S., Kerr, J., Freeman, A. L., Recchia, G., van der Bles, A. M., & van der Linden, S. (2020). Susceptibility to misinformation about COVID-19 around the world. *Royal Society Open Science, 7*(10), 201199. doi:10.1098/rsos.201199 PMID:33204475

Rosenstock, I. M., Strecher, V. J., & Becker, M. H. (1988). Social Learning Theory and the Health Belief Model. *Health Education Quarterly, 15*(2), 175–183. doi:10.1177/109019818801500203 PMID:3378902

Rzymski, P., Borkowski, L., Drąg, M., Flisiak, R., Jemielity, J., Krajewski, J., Mastalerz-Migas, A., Mastalerz-Migas, A., Matyja, A., Pyrc, K., Simon, K., Sutkowski, M., Wysocki, J., Zajkowska, J., & Fal, A. (2021). The strategies to support the COVID-19 vaccination with evidence-based communication and tackling misinformation. *Vaccines, 9*(2), 109. doi:10.3390/vaccines9020109 PMID:33535716

Schiavo, R. (2013). Health Communication. *Theory into Practice, 217.*

Schroeder, P., & Amadeo, B. (2021). Communication Strategy for COVID-19 in Uruguay. In Strategic Communication in Context: Theoretical Debates and Applied Research (pp. 295-322). UMinho Editora. doi:10.21814/uminho.ed.46.13

Schultz, É., & Ward, J. K. (2021). Public Perceptions of Scientific Advice: Towards a Science Savy Public Culture? *Public Health*, *194*, 86–88. doi:10.1016/j.puhe.2021.02.007 PMID:33866149

Schwarzinger, M., & Luchini, S. (2021). Addressing COVID-19 vaccine hesitancy: Is official communication the key? *The Lancet. Public Health*, *6*(6), e353–e354. doi:10.1016/S2468-2667(21)00108-0 PMID:33991483

Storlie, C. B., Pollock, B. D., Rojas, R. L., Demuth, G. O., Johnson, P. W., Wilson, P. M., Heinzen, E. P., Liu, H., Carter, R. E., Habermann, E. B., Kor, D. J., Neville, M. R., Limper, A. H., Noe, K. H., Bydon, M., Franco, P. M., Sampathkumar, P., Shah, N. D., Dunlay, S. M., & Dowdy, S. C. (2021). Quantifying the Importance of COVID-19 Vaccination to Our Future Outlook. *Mayo Clinic Proceedings*, *96*(7), 1890–1895. doi:10.1016/j.mayocp.2021.04.012 PMID:34218862

Strecher, V. J., McEvoy DeVellis, B., Becker, M. H., & Rosenstock, I. M. (1986). The role of self-efficacy in achieving health behavior change. *Health Education Quarterly*, *13*(1), 73–92. doi:10.1177/109019818601300108 PMID:3957687

Strecher, V. J., & Rosenstock, I. M. (1997). *The Health Belief Model*. Jossey-Bass.

Tench, R., & Bridge, G. (2021). Developing effective Health Communication Campaigns. In Strategic Communication in Context: Theoretical Debates and Applied Research (pp. 69-86). UMinho Editora. doi:10.21814/uminho.ed.46.4

Tormo, M. J., & Banegas, J. R. (2001). Mejorar la comunicación de riesgos en Salud Pública: sin tiempo para demoras [Improve risk communication in Public Health: no time for delays]. *Revista Española de Salud Pública, 75*(1). http://scielo.isciii.es/scielo.php?script=sci_arttext&pid=S1135-57272001000100001&lng=es&tlng=es

Túñez-López, M., Costa-Sánchez, C., & Valdiviezo, C. (Eds.). (2018). *Comunicación Organizacional en entornos online: gestión, actores y recursos* [Organizational Communication in Online Enviroments: Management, Actors and Resources]. Sociedad Latina de Comunicación Social. http://www.cuadernosartesanos.org/2018/cac149.pdf

Uruguay Presidencia. (2021, January 23). *Gobierno adquirió 3,75 millones de vacunas contra la COVID-19 y aspira a inocular a 2,8 millones de personas* [The Goverment acquired 3.75 millon vaccines against Covid-19 and aims to inoculate 2.8 milion people]. https://www.gub.uy/presidencia/comunicacion/noticias/gobierno-adquirio-375-millones-vacunas-contra-covid-19-aspira-inocular-28

Vacunas: el FA suma presión al gobierno con nuevas críticas por falta de transparencia [Vaccines: the FA adds pressure to the government with new criticism for lack of transparency]. (2021, February 19). *El Observador*. https://www.elobservador.com.uy/nota/frente-amplio-vuelve-a-la-carga-por-las-vacunas-y-reclama-por-su-llegada-202121817480

ENDNOTE

1 Pandemic mitigation, in terms of health strategy, involves reduction of infections, severe cases and mortality.

Chapter 7
Health Communication on Social Media:
Perceptions and Influences

Paulo Ribeiro Cardoso
Fernando Pessoa University, Porto, Portugal & Lusíada University, Porto, Portugal

Manuel José Fonseca
https://orcid.org/0000-0002-3290-8449
Polytechnic Institute of Viana do Castelo, Portugal & UNIAG, Portugal

ABSTRACT

This study aimed to analyze how social media users perceived the health-related content disseminated in this channel. Specifically, it was intended to verify how the dimensions "entertainment," "interaction," "trendiness," and "customization" impacted the "word-of-mouth" that the user could make to other users regarding health-related content. The methodological approach involved a questionnaire survey that integrated a set of statements, adapted from Kim and Ko's study. Data were collected through an online survey using a convenience sample composed of individuals from the northern region of Portugal. As result, the authors found that the dimensions "entertainment," "interaction," and "trendiness" had positive values. "Trendiness" stood out as the dimension with the greatest impact on "word-of-mouth." The dimensions "entertainment" and "customization" also showed to have an impact on "word-of-mouth" but in a more moderate way.

INTRODUCTION

Health content communication is a multidisciplinary area of influence where different theoretical approaches converge, including theories from behavioral and social sciences, mass communication, marketing, and social marketing, among others. When carried out in a rigorous and planned way, health communication can improve the way societies deal with uncertainty and fear, enlightening citizens and promoting the

DOI: 10.4018/978-1-7998-9790-3.ch007

adoption of behavioral changes. Health communication professionals have a responsibility to contribute to the dissemination of concise and valid information in different contexts (Finset et al., 2020).

Currently, research on health communication is usually structured in an applied way. That is, it is based on concrete problems of analysis of issues related to health care and issues related to its promotion and communication. This strand of communication is based on the need to reduce or even eliminate errors that endanger the quality of healthcare, to provide useful information for informed decision-making on health matters and to effectively impact the identified target segments. As health communication is an area of knowledge under construction and relatively recent, one of the main shortcomings in terms of empirical and critical reflection lies in the need to identify the main communication factors that influence critical health issues widely known and disseminated in the media (Kreps, 2012a). According to the author, there is scientific evidence that issues such as lack of consumer adherence to treatment recommendations and low levels of consumer participation in health care decision-making are directly related to the effectiveness of health communication. Thus, studies in the field of health communication should focus on the analysis of communication aimed at health care and health promotion, while also considering the influences of social communication, institutional communication, and the cultural aspects of the different target audiences.

At the same time, the use of social media has been increasing in the last decade, with about 53,6% (4.20 billion) of the world population using these platforms (Hootsuite, 2021). Individuals use social media as a source of information, as a mode of entertainment, or to communicate with other users. Social media has thus become a key channel for non-digital media, businesses, brands, and non-profit organizations.

Regarding their ability to influence, social media have played an important role in promoting a sustainable lifestyle and behavior (Strähle and Gräff, 2017) and in promoting healthy behaviors, contributing to improve the level of health literacy of the population. According to Ratzan and Parker (2006, p. 713), the concept of health literacy means "The degree to which individuals have the capacity to obtain, process, and understand basic health information and services needed to make appropriate health decisions". This means, in the authors' view, that health communication professionals must keep in mind the need to adapt information, messages and recommendations to the specificities of their target audiences, while at the same time a careful choice of appropriate media must be made to improve the quality of decision-making. Health literacy occurs when the skills and capabilities of individuals who require health information and services are aligned with the demand and complexity of information and services (Parker and Rayzan, 2010). Health literacy refers to the ability of those in the health system to accurately interpret and use relevant health information and resources to achieve their health goals (Kreps, 2017). From the author's perspective there is scientific evidence that many consumers have limited levels of health literacy to adequately understand health information considering that health literacy is both an individual characteristic (limited education, language facility, and more) and a one-time condition (based on how current physical and mental states influence abilities to communicate effectively).

In this context, social media pages oriented towards health communication and managed by non-profit organizations stand out (Kite et al., 2018). With such a high penetration rate, social media provide numerous opportunities in health communication, such as dissemination of health information, pandemic and disease monitoring, health promotion, recruitment of clinical trial participants, among others (Huo et al., 2019)

In this context, this study aims to analyze how social network users perceive the health-related contents disseminated in this channel. Specifically, we intend to verify how the dimensions of "Entertainment",

"Interaction", " Trendiness" and " Customization" have an impact on the " Word-of-mouth" that the user may make to other users regarding the contents he/she consumes.

The present research used a quantitative approach with the use of a questionnaire survey. The instrument involved a set of items adapted from previous studies on users' perceptions of social media content (Kim and Ko, 2012). Specifically, subjects were asked to express their opinion about the content published by public organizations, non-governmental organizations or other non-profit entities related to health. The aim was to find out their perception of awareness campaigns on health care, disease prevention and dissemination of useful information for the preservation of health status published by those organizations.

This study focused on young adults (18-35 years) and data were collected from a non-probability convenience sample. The inclusion of digital tools in the field of youth-oriented health communication poses a series of challenges, but also opens a potential field of work that may allow for an effective approach to this population group (Carceller-Maicas, 2016). Young people are active users of social media but poorly engaged with health-related issues and seldom users of health services (Wong et al., 2014). In this sense, and despite the research previously developed in this field, several authors warn about the need for further research on this topic (Guse et al., 2012; Goodyear et al., 2018; Plaisime et al., 2020).

Data analysis sought to analyze the dimensions that describe respondents' perceptions of health-related content on social media. Correlational analyses of the dimensions were also carried out, looking at the consequences of these perceptions on the behaviors assumed by the respondents.

The results obtained in this research may provide useful information to non-profit institutions in the management of social network pages oriented to health communication. They may also be important inputs for the creation of content related to information actions and prevention campaigns among the population, particularly in raising awareness of health care, disease prevention, and health promotion.

HEALTH COMMUNICATION AND SOCIAL MEDIA

Health communication is an evolving and increasingly relevant concept both in the public health sector and in the non-profit and commercial field. Due to the multidisciplinary nature of health communication, many of the definitions seem different from one another, but in fact virtually all point to the role that communication can play in influencing and supporting individuals, communities, health professionals, or policy makers to adopt behavioral practices, or a social or political change, aimed at improving health outcomes (Schiavo, 2013). According to the author, one of the main goals of health communication is to influence individuals and communities. This is extremely beneficial, as it is ultimately intended to optimize outcomes through the organized sharing of health-related information.

Thus, health communication is a broad and rapidly growing area of research that identifies communication as an opportunity to improve health literacy, focused on changing behaviors or perceptions. The concept has been influenced by fields such as health education, medicine, psychology, marketing, and social sciences, emphasizing dimensions such as information exchange, knowledge improvement, behavior change, well-being, and empowerment (Piculell et al, 2021). Health communication can be characterized as the set of interpersonal or mass communication activities focused on improving the health of individuals and populations (Ishikawa & Kiuchi, 2010). Concrete examples in the field of national public health were the crisis management actions, as in the situation of the Pandemic Influenza A in 2009, or Ebola in 2014/2015, or the case of the Legionella outbreak in 2014.

The broad field of health communication encompasses several interrelated areas, including the relationship between communication and care provision, health promotion, the development and use of information technology (e-health), the dissemination of information on health risks, and the functioning of health care systems (Kreps, 2012b). Thus, research in health communication may also contribute to understand the importance of the use of information technologies in an effective communication strategy capable of responding to the information needs of current consumers.

Technological developments, as a driving dimension of health communication, are creating different ways and possibilities to reach specific target groups and audiences. The development of the internet and the rapid growth of social media has allowed the emergence of different communication platforms. Today, organizations regularly communicate with their audiences using the internet through one-to-one (email), one-to-many (website), and many-to-many (social media) communication (Avidar, 2017). Thus, health communication is no longer limited to pedagogical dynamics in medical settings or media messages aimed at passive audiences. With the rapid evolution of the internet and social media, today's health communication involves dynamic information exchanges on a global scale.

According to data from Marktest (2019) social media have had a rapid growth in Portugal, from 17.1% of users in 2008 to 63.6% in 2019, and access is now quite frequent and made through cell phone. Among Portuguese users, Facebook still dominates, but loses influence, with Instagram positioning itself as a network on the rise and very relevant especially among younger people. It can also be stated that there are no differences between the two genders in the profile of Portuguese social media users. 66% of users are under 45 years old, 53% belong to the higher social classes and 36% live in the metropolitan area of Lisbon and metropolitan area of Porto. Access to social media is mainly done via cell phone, between 8 pm and midnight, with a daily average of 93 minutes dedicated to them. Saturdays and Sundays are the days on which more time is spent on social media. Among the activities performed on social media, exchanging messages is the most frequent (by 78% of users), followed by reading news on information sites (67%) and commenting on publications in the network of contacts (65%).

According to Rus and Cameron (2016), social media, defined as internet-based applications that allow for the creation and exchange of user-generated content, provide means to reach a wide audience quickly and inexpensively with health information through applications such as Facebook, Instagram, Twitter, and others. In a society where individuals more often seek health information on social media than communicate with their doctors, understanding the consequences of using these digital resources is vital to understanding the evolution of healthcare.

Thus, the use of social media by non-profit institutions acting in the health context has been analyzed in several studies and adopting different focuses of analysis, such as fundraising (Lauro, et al. 2019), the credibility and usefulness of health information published on Facebook (Kim and Syn, 2016) and Tik Tok (Zhu et al, 2020), the perception and experience of users regarding social media pages oriented to health communication (Kite et al., 2018), their impact on public sector healthcare organizations (Heldman, Schindelar & Weaver, 2013), and attitude toward health communication content shared on social media over time (Huo et al., 2019). More recently, Al-Dmou et al. (2020) examined the influence of social media on preventing COVID19. Additionally, there are also studies exploring the non-positive side of social media's role in health communication, such as the dissemination of misleading information (Syed-Abdul et al., 2013; Waszak, Kasprzycka-Waszak & Kubanek, 2018) and the tendency towards self-diagnosis, creating often conflicting relationships between clinicians and patients (Baron & Berinsky, 2019).

As regards the Portuguese scenario, we highlight the study of Espanha et. al. (2013) on internet users' attitudes and behaviors. This research involved a questionnaire survey with a sample of 808 individuals and focused on the role of the internet in health communication. The authors concluded that 82.7% of respondents conducted internet research to increase general knowledge about health and 41.7% used it to share experiences about health problems.

More recent studies on the Portuguese reality have addressed the presence of health institutions in social media. For example, Brito and Garcia (2019) analyzed the presence of Public Health Units in digital channels, specifically through websites and social media, such as Facebook. They analyzed 55 Public Health Units and found that their online presence was quite low. In view of this reality, the authors considered that it was important to understand the reasons for this scarce use, advising the training of human resources and the increase of material and financial resources that would provide an adequate use of digital channels. In this context, the authors highlighted the importance of online channels for health institutions, both in disease prevention and in health promotion and protection.

In a similar line of work, the study of Garcia and Eiró-Gomes (2020) aimed to identify the Health Care Clusters that were present on Facebook and analyze their communication on this social media. The content categories detected included health promotion and disease prevention. The research showed that these institutions have a minor presence on Facebook, either by the low percentage of institutions with a page on this social media, or by the deficient production and publication of content. These results are consistent with the study of Brito and Garcia (2019), emphasizing the need for health institutions to give more attention to this communication channel.

Pinto et al. (2020) analyzed the public health organizations as producers of content on Instagram during the pandemic. Specifically, the study included, in the international context, the analysis of the profiles of the WHO, WHO Europe, the Pan American Health Organization (PAHO), and in the national context the profiles of the health authorities of Brazil and Portugal. As results, the authors found that the social media was used strategically in Instagram as a public space for information on issues related to COVID-19.

Also, in the context of the pandemic period of COVID-19, Ramos and Jerónimo (2021) conducted a study focused on the pandemic-related contents published on Facebook. Specifically, the authors analyzed the press conferences issued on the Facebook page of the *Direção Geral da Saúde* (Portuguese department of public health) and verified, through views, reactions, comments, and shares, that the citizens' interest and involvement in this topic was clearly high.

Thus, observing some of the studies carried out in Portugal, it is possible to see that research has focused more on the analysis of published content than on the perspective of social media users. In this context, the present study gains special interest by addressing the perception of communication on social media.

DIMENSIONS OF PUBLICATIONS ON SOCIAL MEDIA

Brands and organizations use social media to disseminate content through periodic publications on their corporate or institutional pages. Kim and Ko (2012) systematized the characteristics of these publications by proposing five categories: entertainment, interaction, trendiness, customization, and word-of-mouth. This model was later applied in research related to the use of social media, associating it with brands and e-commerce. Studies have focused on topics such as e-commerce (Yadav and Rahman, 2017) and sectors such as aeronautics (Seo and Park, 2018), cosmetics (Choedon and Lee, 2020) and clothing stores (Sharma et al, 2021).

Going through the meaning of each of these dimensions, “Entertainment” stands out as one of the components that characterize social media and is one of the motivations for individuals to use them (Che Nawi et al., 2021).

In this context, “Entertainment” results from the publication of interesting, impressive, and funny content and information to consumers that can engage them and build a positive image of the brand or organization (Godey et al, 2016; Ningrum and Roostika, 2021).

Thus “Entertainment” is an important component that creates, in the minds of followers, positive emotions or feelings toward the brand or organization and stimulates their engagement and response (Ningrum and Roostika, 2021). Entertainment posts and activities, such as games and quizzes, photo and video sharing, can lead consumers to enjoy their social media experiences, motivating and reinforcing their active participation (Ashley and Tuten, 2015).

“Interaction” is another distinctive dimension of social media. In fact, social media provide an effective interaction between the brand or institution and the users through a two-way communication (Tugrul, 2014). This interaction also happens among the various users of the social media (Che Nawi et al., 2021) and can take the format of engagement, where the user not only consumes the content but also creates content himself (Schivinski et al. 2016).

Social media therefore have two interrelated roles: firstly, they allow companies and organizations to communicate with their publics secondly, they can be used by those publics to communicate with each other (Cheung et al., 2019).

“Trendiness” of information is another motivation for using social media (Abbasi and Huang, 2020). These networks provide a channel for users to stay informed about various current topics. The information is, on the one hand, transmitted by the brand or institution and, on the other hand, by the contact established with the opinions and information provided by other users (Che Nawi et al., 2021).

Social media are therefore online information sources used by citizens to gain knowledge about products, brands, services, and issues relevant to their lives (Ningrum and Roostika, 2021).

But this information and these contents will have a stronger impact if there is a “customization” to the users’ profile. The personalization consists, then, in transmitting the contents in a suitable way to the followers of a social media page, assuming their style and, in this way, seeking a closer identification with them (Ningrum and Roostika, 2021).

The “customization”, or personalization, in social media can occur in different ways. In a broader sense, this adequacy can result from a construction of the publications with characteristics that can attract more or trigger a deeper identification with the audience of a certain page. The “customization” can also occur when the brand or institution responds directly to a comment issued by a user (Che Nawi et al., 2021).

The expression of opinions also characterizes social media. In the context of Marketing this personal opinion can be formulated in the concept of “Recommendation”, or “Word-of-mouth - WOM”, which involves sharing experiences with other individuals and can play an important role in decision making (Cahyo and Roostika, 2019; Delafrooz et al., 2019). Social media has come to foster this behavior by being a medium in which interaction is encouraged, giving rise to the term e-word-of-mouth - EWOM (Ningrum and Roostika, 2021).

“Word-of-mouth” has been presented as a behavior that stems from a positive attitude toward the brand or organization or the products and services it provides (Chu and Sung, 2015; Seo and Park, 2018; Delafrooz et al, 2019).

Figure 1. Dimensions of perception regarding health-related content

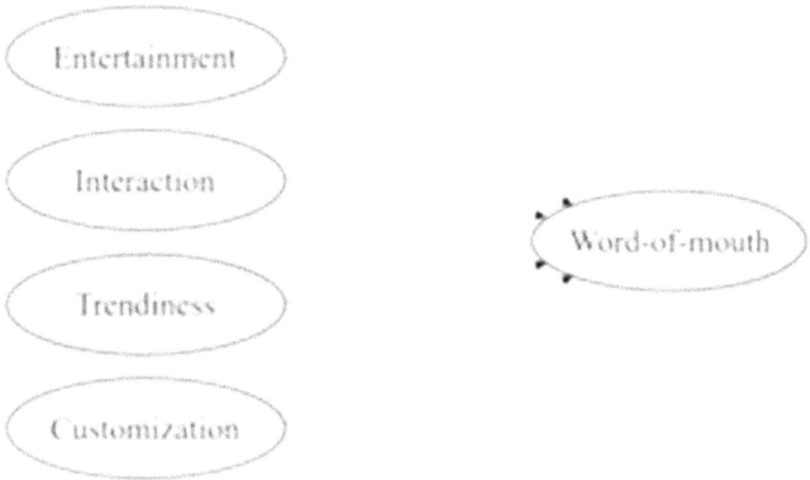

RESEARCH GOALS AND METHODOLGY

Research goals

As mentioned previously, the dimensions of social media postings proposed by Kim and Ko (2012) have been applied in research on user attitudes and behaviors, but primarily in the commercial context (Yadav and Rahman, 2017; Seo and Park, 2018; Choedon and Lee, 2020; Sharma et al, 2021). However, within the scope of the present study, no research was found that applied this model to the context of health communication.

Consequently, we propose to adapt the model to this context by analyzing how social media users perceive the health-related contents disseminated in this channel. Specifically, we intend to verify how the dimensions "Entertainment", "Interaction", "Trendiness" and "Customization" have an impact on the "Word-of-mouth" that the user may make to other users regarding the content they consume (Figure 1).

Methodology

The methodological approach involved a questionnaire survey that incorporated a set of questions about health communication on social media.

The first part of the questionnaire included questions related to the demographic profile of the respondents, such as age, gender, academic background and occupation, as well as some questions related to social media use practices.

The second part of the questionnaire used a set of statements about users' attitudes towards health-related content published on social media, adapted from the study by Kim and Ko (2012). The original study was focused on publications made by commercial brands. In the present study, as an information collection instrument, it was adapted to publications made by health-related entities. These items were measured with a 5-point Likert scale that rated each statement between "strongly disagree" (1) and "strongly agree" (5).

A sample of young adults aged between 18 and 35 years was used. Data were collected from a non-probability convenience sample residing in the Metropolitan Area of Porto of municipalities in Northern Portugal. Previous studies have addressed the issue of health communication and the use of social media focusing their analysis on young adults. For example, the study by Goodyear et al. (2018) analyzed young people's perceptions of health-related content on social media. A variety of content consumed by young people was identified as likely to be influential: content suggested by the social media itself, content created by other users, and content developed by official organizations and brands.

Plaisime et al. (2020) analyzed the potential role of social media in health promotion among young people, emphasizing that social media can be effective as a health communication channel. However, they concluded that the information should be reliable and made up of attractive messages capable of meeting the adolescents' expectations.

Barbosa, (2021) analyzed how young Z generation people perceived digital influencers as inspiring preventive behaviors towards COVID-19. The study concluded that, more important than the use of digital influencers, it is the attractiveness of the message and ease of applying the suggested behaviour that interferes with its effectiveness.

Despite the significant research already developed in this field, several authors have highlighted the need to further develop and deepen studies on this topic (Guse et al., 2012; Goodyear et al., 2018; Plaisime et al., 2020), an appeal that largely underpinned the choice of this segment.

In the operationalization stage of the research, the survey was designed in the Google Forms application and disseminated through the social networks of the researchers.

RESULTS

Respondents' Profile and Social Network Usage Habits

The sample of this study consists of 106 individuals, 60.4% female and 39.6% male. Regarding age, 55.7% were 18-25 years old and 44.3% were 26-35 years old (table 1). The sample had some diversity regarding academic background: 38.7% of the respondents had secondary school education, 34% had higher education, and 27.4% had post-graduate or master's degrees. Regarding occupation, 55.7% were students, 10.4% were self-employed, and 34% were employees. In terms of region of residence, 27.4% were from the Metropolitan Area of Porto and 72.6% were from other municipalities in the Northern region.

Concerning the time of social media use per day 33% used between 1 and 2 hours and 24.5% between 2 and 3 hours (table 2).

In terms of the preferred social network, 61.3% prefer Instagram and 15.1% prefer Facebook, with a residual preference for other social networks (table 3).

Internal Consistency and Descriptive Analysis of the Dimensions

Considering that the scale was adapted from a previous study and that the factors were kept according to the original model, the internal consistency analysis was performed (Table 4). All dimensions obtained a value equal to or higher than 0.8, which is considered adequate (Taber, 2017). After verifying that

Table 1. Sample characterization

Variables	Categories	Frequency	Percentage
Gender	Female	64	60,4%
	Male	42	39,6%
Age	18-25	59	55,7%
	26-35	47	44,3%
Academic Background	Elementary Education	41	38,7%
	Undergraduate	36	34%
	Postgraduate	29	27,4%
Occupation	Student	59	55,7%
	Self-employed	11	10,4%
	Employee	36	34%
Region	Metropolitan area of Porto	29	27,4%
	Other municipality in the North of Portugal	77	72,6%
Total		106	100%

Table 2. Time spent using social networks per day

Time spent using social networks per day	Frequency	Percentage
Less than 30 minutes	6	5,7%
Between 30 minutes and 1 hour	24	22,6%
Between 1 and 2 hours	35	33,0%
Between 2 and 3 hours	26	24,5%
More than 3 hours	15	14,2%
Total	106	100%

Table 3. Favorite social media

Favorite social media	Frequency	Percentage
Instagram	65	61,3%
Facebook	16	15,1%
Youtube	8	7,5%
WhatsApp	6	5,7%
Linkedin	4	3,8%
TikTok	3	2,8%
Twitter	2	1,9%
Other	2	1,9%
Total	106	100%

Table 4. Internal consistency and descriptive analysis of the dimension

Dimensions	Items	Mean	Standard Deviation	Cronbach's alpha
Entertainment	They are interesting. They get my attention.	3,49	0,89	0,837
Interaction	They make it possible to exchange opinions with other users. Allow you to share information with other users. They help us to express our opinion.	3,68	0,87	0,892
Trendiness	They show current information. They allow you to keep abreast of what is happening in the current health context.	3,58	0,88	0,848
Customization	They have a lot to do with me. They suit my profile.	2,80	0,93	0,941
Word-of-mouth	I recommend those advices to my family members I share those advices with others	3,00	0,99	0,833

each dimension had adequate internal consistency, a new variable was created as a result of the average between its constituent items.

To evaluate the relevance of each dimension, a descriptive analysis was performed based on the final constructs (table 4). The dimensions "Entertainment", "Interaction" and "Trendiness" present positive values, demonstrating that these dimensions are present in publications with health content. On the other hand, the dimensions "Customization" and "Word-of-mouth" present relatively neutral values.

Correlations and Multiple Linear Regression

Pearson's correlation was performed to see if dimensions were related to each other (table 5). All correlations were significant at the 0.01 level. All correlations are positive, ranging from 0.42 to 0.64.

Starting from the results obtained in Pearson's correlation, a multiple regression analysis was performed to test the relationship between the independent variables ("Entertainment", "Interaction", "Trendiness" and "Customization") and the dependent variable ("Word-of-mouth"). Table 6 shows that 3 independent variables explained the dependent variable by 38% (R2=0.387; F=17.604; p<0.001).

Table 5. Pearson's Correlation Coefficient

	1.	2.	3.	4.	5.
1. Entertainment	1				
2. Interaction	,474**	1			
3. Trendiness	,546**	,558**	1		
4. Customization	,640**	,518**	,421**	1	
5. Word-of-mouth	,546**	,419**	,538**	,540**	1

**. The correlation is significant at the 0.01 level (2-tailed).

Table 6. Multiple regression

Independent Variables	Dependent Variable		
	Word-of-mouth		
	b	t-value	p-value
1. Entertainment	0,219	2,021	0,046
2. Interaction	0,005	0,055	0,956
3. Trendiness	0,335	3,358	0,001
4. Customization	0,214	2,040	0,044
	R2=0,387; F=17,604; p<0.001		

"Trendiness" stood out as the dimension with the most impact on "Word-of-mouth" ($\beta=0.335$; $p<0.01$). The dimensions "Entertainment" ($\beta=0.219$; $p<0.05$) and "Customization" ($\beta=0.214$; $p<0.05$) were shown to have an impact on "Word-of-mouth", but more moderately. Finally, the variable "Interaction" had no influence on the dependent variable ($\beta=0.005$; $p>0.05$).

CONCLUSION

This study aimed to analyze how social media users perceive the health-related contents disseminated in this channel. Based on the model proposed by Kim and Ko (2012), we sought to verify how the dimensions "Entertainment", "Interaction", "Trendiness" and "Customization" had an impact on the "Word-of-mouth" that the user may make to other users regarding the online contents that he/she consumes.

After a literature review that addressed the concept of health communication and the use of social media to convey this type of contents, the dimensions that structure the model of Kim and Ko (2012) mentioned above were detailed and explained: "Entertainment", "Interaction", "Trendiness", "Customization" and "Word-of-mouth".

The empirical component of the study involved a questionnaire survey using a sample of young Portuguese adults living, for the most part, in municipalities in the Northern Region of Portugal and in the Metropolitan Area of Porto. The data collection instrument used intended to identify social network consumption habits and analyze the aforementioned dimensions. In this context, the scale of Kim and Ko (2012) was used, adapting it to health-related contents.

The profile of the interviewees shows individuals of both genders, aged between 18 and 35, mostly with higher education. They are frequent users of social networks, since more than 50% use them between 1 and 3 hours a day, demonstrating their ability to give their opinion about the content disseminated on these channels. Over 60% of respondents have Instagram as their preferred social media, which is compatible with their age group.

Observing the characteristics of the scale used, whose original structure was respected, it was possible to verify that the internal consistency of the 5 dimensions was adequate ($\alpha>0.8$).

As for the importance of each dimension, it was possible to verify that the dimensions "Entertainment", "Interaction" and "Trendiness" had positive values, showing that these dimensions are present in publications with health contents.

These results show that health-related content can, at the "Entertainment" level, present characteristics capable of arousing engagement and response (Ningrum and Roostika, 2021). In this sense, these contents can be interesting, impressive, and funny for consumers, engaging them and helping them to have a positive image of the organization (Godey et al, 2016; Ningrum and Roostika, 2021).

"Interaction" is a dimension that is also present in these digital contents making it possible, for companies and organizations, to communicate with their audiences and, at the same time, motivating communication between the multiple users (Cheung et al., 2019).

These contents can be perceived as informative and updated, which is one of the main characteristics and motivations for the use of social networks (Abbasi and Huang, 2020). Thus, also in the context of health, social media can be online information sources used by citizens with the purpose of obtaining knowledge about services and issues relevant to their lives (Ningrum and Roostika, 2021).

It is also important to emphasize that the "Customization" and "Word-of-mouth" dimensions present relatively neutral values.

Regarding the relationships between the dimensions, performing a Pearson correlation allowed us to verify that all correlations were positive and significant. These results led to a subsequent multiple regression analysis using, as independent variables "Entertainment", "Interaction", "Trendiness", "Customization", and as dependent variable "Word-of-mouth".

"Trendiness" stood out as the dimension with the greatest impact on "Word-of-mouth", demonstrating that above all users feel motivated to recommend information and advice that is informative and actual. This highlights a utilitarian component of this type of communication that needs to be valued: health information is important, fact-based, and properly updated.

The dimensions "Entertainment" and "Customization" were also shown to have an impact on "Word-of-mouth", but in a more moderate way. It can be seen, therefore, that users tend to recommend to their contacts contents that are interesting and that promote entertainment. Likewise, they are willing to recommend content that is somehow adapted to their profiles.

Finally, the variable "Interaction" had no influence on "Word-of-mouth" showing that the possibility to interact with other users was eventually less important with this type of content.

These results allow us to draw some practical implications, namely the importance of professionals to create digital content with features that are valued by users, seeking to publish rich and updated information.

Professionals should also make health communication contents more interesting through copywriting and visual communication, arousing users' interest and promoting, somehow, the entertainment component. Finally, the content should be appropriate to the profile of the audience to be reached, reinforcing this interaction with the dialogue that organizations can establish with their audiences through social media.

In terms of academic contribution, this study adapted a model that has been used in a business context to the area of health communication, demonstrating that some characteristics of publications on social media can be found both in the context of traditional marketing and in the context of social or non-profit marketing. Specifically, a first exploratory application of Kim and Lo's model (2012) was made to these areas in Portugal with a sample of young adults.

The study presents, however, some limitations that could be optimized in future approaches. Specifically, the age range analyzed is somewhat circumscribed, leaving out an older section of the population that may even have a greater involvement with these contents. Also, in terms of geographical coverage, the study focused on the Metropolitan Area of Porto and Northern Portugal, so that future research should open the scope of the study to a wider territory. In addition to the importance of reaching a wider geographical area, the relevance of increasing the size of the sample to increase the representativeness and impact of this study is also highlighted.

Health communication is extremely important for its informative and preventive role among the population, and social media have proven to be an essential channel for its expansion. This is a little explored area that undoubtedly deserves future studies to make these communication actions more effective among citizens.

REFERENCES

Abbasi, N., & Huang, D. (2020). Digital Media Literacy: Social Media Use for News Consumption among Teenagers in Pakistan. *Global Media Journal*, *18*, 1–7.

Al-Dmour, H., Masa'deh, R., Salman, A., Abuhashesh, M., & Al-Dmour, R. (2020). Influence of Social Media Platforms on Public Health Protection Against the COVID-19 Pandemic via the Mediating Effects of Public Health Awareness and Behavioral Changes: Integrated Model. *Journal of Medical Internet Research*, *22*(8), e19996. doi:10.2196/19996 PMID:32750004

Ashley, C., & Tuten, T. (2015). Creative strategies in social media marketing: An exploratory study of branded social content and consumer engagement. *Psychology and Marketing*, *32*(1), 15–27. doi:10.1002/mar.20761

Avidar, R. (2017). Responsiveness and interactivity: Relational maintenance strategies in an online environment. In S. C. Duhe (Ed.), New media and public relations (pp. 229-238). Peter Lang Publishing Inc.

Barbosa, C. (2021). *Understanding how Generation Z perceives social media influencers and its impact on the adoption of COVID safe behaviours* [Master Dissertation]. Universidade Católica Portuguesa. Available at: https://repositorio.ucp.pt/bitstream/10400.14/35730/1/202781453.pdf

Baron, R. J., & Adam, J. B. (2019). Mistrust in Science - A Threat to the Patient–Physician Relationship. *The New England Journal of Medicine*, *381*(2), 182–185. doi:10.1056/NEJMms1813043 PMID:31291524

Brito, D. V., & Garcia, A. (2019). Posicionamento digital das Unidades de Saúde Pública em Portugal Continental em 2019 [Digital positioning of Public Health Units in Mainland Portugal in 2019]. *Comunicação Pública*, *15*(29), 1–12.

Cahyo, P. W., & Roostika, R. (2019). Building Positive Word-of-Mouth in the Shopping Tourism. *Review of Integrative Business and Economics Research*, *8*(s4), 372–386.

Carceller-Maicas, N. (2016). Youth, health and social networks, Instagram as a research tool for health communication. *MÈTODE Science Studies Journal*, *6*, 227–233.

Cheung, M., Pires, G., & Rosenberger, P. (2019). The Influence of Perceived Social Media Marketing Elements on Consumer-Brand Engagement and Brand Knowledge. *Asia Pacific Journal of Marketing and Logistics*, *32*(3), 695–720. doi:10.1108/APJML-04-2019-0262

Choedon, T., & Lee, Y. (2020). The Effect of Social Media Marketing Activities on Purchase Intention with Brand Equity and Social Brand Engagement: Empirical Evidence from Korean Cosmetic Firms. *The Knowledge Management Society of Korea*, *21*(3), 141–160.

Chu, S., & Sung, Y. (2015). Using a consumer socialization framework to understand electronic word-ofmouth (eWOM) group membership among brand followers on Twitter. *Electronic Commerce Research and Applications, 14*(4), 251–260. doi:10.1016/j.elerap.2015.04.002

Delafrooz, N., Rahmati, Y., & Abdi, M. (2019). The influence of electronic word of mouth on Instagram users: An emphasis on consumer socialization framework. *Cogent Business & Management, 6*(1), 1–14. doi:10.1080/23311975.2019.1606973

Espanha, R., Mendes, R., & Fonseca, R. & Correia, T. (2013). O lugar e papel da internet na saúde: Contributos do caso português [The place and role of the internet in health: contributions from the Protuguese case]. *Portugal Saúde em Números, 1*, 41–49.

Finset, A., Bosworth, H., Butow, P., Gulbrandsen, P., Hulsman, R., Pieterse, A., Street, R., Tschoetschel, R., & van Weert, J. (2020). Effective health communication – a key factor in fighting the COVID-19 pandemic. *Patient Education and Counseling, 103*(5), 873–876. doi:10.1016/j.pec.2020.03.027 PMID:32336348

Garcia, A., & Eiró-Gomes, M. (2020). O papel da comunicação: a utilização das redes sociais nos cuidados de saúde primários [The role of communication: the use of social media in primary health care]. Comunicação e Sociedade, 197-217.

Godey, B., Manthiou, A., Pederzoli, D., Rokka, J., Aiello, J., Donvito, R., & Singh, R. (2016). Social media marketing efforts of luxury brands: Influence on brand equity and consumer behavior. *Journal of Business Research, 69*(12), 5833–5841. doi:10.1016/j.jbusres.2016.04.181

Goodyear, V., Armour, K., & Wood, H. (2019). Young people and their engagement with health-related social media: New perspectives. *Sport Education and Society, 24*(7), 673–688. doi:10.1080/13573322.2017.1423464 PMID:31814804

Guse, K., Levine, D., Martins, S., Lira, A., Gaardeb, J., Westmorlandc, W., & Gilliam, M. (2012). Interventions Using New Digital Media to Improve Adolescent Sexual Health: A Systematic Review. *The Journal of Adolescent Health, 51*(6), 535–543. doi:10.1016/j.jadohealth.2012.03.014 PMID:23174462

Heldman, A. B., Schindelar, J., & Weaver, J. B. III. (2013). Social media engagement and public health communication: Implications for public health organizations being truly “social”. *Public Health Reviews, 35*(1), 13. doi:10.1007/BF03391698

Hootsuite. (2021). *Digital 2021. Global Overview Report.* Available at: https://www.hootsuite.com/pt/pages/digital-trends-2021

Huo, J., Desai, R., Hong, Y., Turner, K., Mainous, A. III, & Bian, J. (2019). Use of social media in health communication: Findings from the health information national trends survey 2013, 2014, and 2017. *Cancer Control, 26*(1), 1–10. doi:10.1177/1073274819841442 PMID:30995864

Ishikawa, H., & Kiuchi, T. (2010). Health literacy and health communication. *BioPsychoSocial Medicine, 4*(1), 1–5. doi:10.1186/1751-0759-4-18 PMID:21054840

Kim, A., & Ko, E. (2012). Do social media marketing activities enhance customer equity? An empirical study of luxury fashion brand. *Journal of Business Research, 65*(10), 1480–1486. doi:10.1016/j.jbusres.2011.10.014

Kim, S., & Syn, S. (2016). Credibility and usefulness of health information on Facebook: A survey study with U.S. college students. *Information Research*, *21*(4), 1–32.

Kite, J., McGill, B., Freeman, B., Vineburg, J., Li, V., Berton, N., & Grunseit, A. (2018). User Perceptions of the Make Healthy Normal campaign Facebook Page: A Mixed Methods Study. *Social Media + Society*, *4*(July-September), 1–17. doi:10.1177/2056305118794639

Kreps, G. (2012a). Translating health communication research into practice: The importance of implementing and sustaining evidence-based health communication interventions. *Atlantic Journal of Communication*, *20*(1), 5–15. doi:10.1080/15456870.2012.637024

Kreps, G. (2012b). The maturation of health communication inquiry: Directions for future development and growth. *Journal of Health Communication*, *17*(5), 495–497. doi:10.1080/10810730.2012.685802 PMID:22571837

Kreps, G. (2017). The relevance of health literacy to mHealth. *Information Services & Use*, *37*(2), 123–130. doi:10.3233/ISU-170828 PMID:28972527

Lauro, S., Tursunbayeva, A., & Antonelli, G. (2019). How Nonprofit Organizations Use Social Media for Fundraising: A Systematic Literature Review. *International Journal of Business and Management*, *14*(7), 1–22. doi:10.5539/ijbm.v14n7p1

Marktest. (2019). *Redes sociais: números e tendências* [Social networks: numbers and trends]. Available at: https://www.marktest.com/wap/a/n/id~25a8.aspx

Nawi, N., Ghani, N., Abdullah, A., Alareeni, B., & Deraman, N., Hasan, M., & Zaato, S. (2021). Social Media Marketing to Enhance Customer Equity on Fashion Apparel Brand among University Students. *Journal of Information Technology Management*, *13*(2), 75–92.

Ningrum, K., & Roostika, R. (2021). The influence of social media marketing activities on consumer engagement and brand knowledge in the culinary business in Indonesia. *International Journal of Research in Business and Social Science*, *10*(5), 34–45. doi:10.20525/ijrbs.v10i5.1314

Nutbeam, D. (2000). Health literacy as a public health goal: A challenge for contemporary health education and communication strategies into the 21st century. *Health Promotion International*, *15*(3), 259–267. doi:10.1093/heapro/15.3.259

Parker, R., & Ratzan, S. C. (2010). Health literacy: A second decade of distinction for Americans. *Journal of Health Communication*, *15*(sup2, S2), 20–33. doi:10.1080/10810730.2010.501094 PMID:20845190

Piculell, E., Skär, L., Sanmartin, J., Anderberg, P., & Bohman, D. (2021). A concept analysis of health communication in a home environment: Perspectives of older persons and their informal caregivers. *Scandinavian Journal of Caring Sciences*, *35*(3), 1006–1024. doi:10.1111cs.12928 PMID:33145836

Pinto, P., Brasileiro, F., Antunes, M., & Almeida, A. (2020). COVID-19 no Instagram: Prácticas de comunicação estratégica das autoridades de saúde durante a Pandemia [COVID-19 on Instagram: health authorities' strategic communication practices during the Pandemic]. *Comunicação Pública*, *15*(29), 1–18. doi:10.4000/cp.11288

Plaisime, M., Robertson-James, C., Mejia, L., Núñez, A., Wolf, J., & Reels, S. (2020). Social Media and Teens: A Needs Assessment Exploring the Potential Role of Social Media in Promoting Health. *Social Media + Society*, *6*(January-March), 1–11. doi:10.1177/2056305119886025

Ramons, C., & Jerónimo, P. (2021). Conferências de Imprensa da Direção Geral de Saúde no Fcaebook: uma análise à interatividade durante a pandemia. [Directorate-General of Health Press conferences on Facebook: an analysis of interactivity during the pandemic]. In F. R. Cádima & I. Ferreira (Coords.), *Perspetivas multidisciplinares da Comunicação em context de Pandemia* (Vol. 1, pp. 126-143). Coleção ICNOVA.

Ratzan, S. C., & Parker, R. M. (2006). Health literacy—Identification and response. *Journal of Health Communication*, *11*(8), 713–715. doi:10.1080/10810730601031090 PMID:17190778

Rus, H., & Cameron, L. (2016). Health communication in social media: Message features predicting user engagement on diabetes-related Facebook pages. *Annals of Behavioral Medicine*, *50*(5), 678–689. doi:10.100712160-016-9793-9 PMID:27059761

Schiavo, R. (2013). *Health communication: From theory to practice* (Vol. 217). John Wiley & Sons.

Schivinski, B., Christodoulides, G., & Dabrowski, D. (2016). Measuring Consumers' Engagement with Brand-Related Social-Media Content - Development and Validation of a Scale That Identifies Levels of Social-Media Engagement With Brands. *Journal of Advertising Research*, *56*(1), 1–18. doi:10.2501/JAR-2016-004

Seo, E., & Park, J. (2018). A study on the effects of social media marketing activities on brand equity and customer response in the airline industry. *Journal of Air Transport Management*, *66*, 36–41. doi:10.1016/j.jairtraman.2017.09.014

Sharma, S., Singh, S., Kujur, F., & Das, G. (2021). Social Media Activities and Its Influence on Customer-Brand Relationship: An Empirical Study of Apparel Retailers' Activity in India. *Journal of Theoretical and Applied Electronic Commerce Research*, *16*(4), 602–617. doi:10.3390/jtaer16040036

Strähle, J., & Gräff, C. (2017). The Role of Social Media for a Sustainable Consumption. In Green Fashion Retail. Springer.

Syed-Abdul, S., Fernandez-Luque, L., Jian, W., Li, Y., Crain, S., Hsu, M., Wang, Y., Khandregzen, D., Chuluunbaatar, E., Nguyen, P. A., & Liou, D. M. (2013). Misleading health-related information promoted through video-based social media: Anorexia on YouTube. *Journal of Medical Internet Research*, *15*(2), 30. doi:10.2196/jmir.2237 PMID:23406655

Taber, K. (2017). The Use of Cronbach's Alpha When Developing and Reporting Research Instruments in Science Education. *Research in Science Education*, *48*(6), 1273–1296. doi:10.100711165-016-9602-2

Tugrul, T. (2014). Brand experience effects on consumer social media marketing perceptions and brand value. *Journal of Global Strategic Management*, *8*(2), 39–47.

Waszak, P., Kasprzycka-Waszak, W., & Kubanek, A. (2018). The spread of medical fake news in social media–the pilot quantitative study. *Health Policy and Technology*, *7*(2), 115–118. doi:10.1016/j.hlpt.2018.03.002

Wong, C., Merchant, R., & Moreno, M. (2014). Using social media to engage adolescents and young adults with their health. *Health Care*, *2*(4), 220–224. PMID:25984444

Yadav, M., & Rahman, Z. (2017). Measuring consumer perception of social media marketing activities in e-commerce industry: Scale development & validation. *Telematics and Informatics*, *34*(7), 1294–1307. doi:10.1016/j.tele.2017.06.001

Zhu, C., Xu, X., Zhang, W., Chen, J., & Evans, R. (2020). How health communication via Tik Tok makes a difference: A content analysis of Tik Tok accounts run by Chinese Provincial Health Committees. *International Journal of Environmental Research and Public Health*, *17*(1), 192. doi:10.3390/ijerph17010192 PMID:31892122

Section 3

Chapter 8
Beyond the Corporate Digital Newsroom 2.0

Sandra Martins Pereira
Escola Superior de Comunicação Social, Portugal

Rita Nunes Ferreira
ISCTE, Instituto Universitário de Lisboa, Portugal

ABSTRACT

The focus of this chapter is to propose a reflection on the strategic potential of corporate digital newsrooms, usually a section incorporated into corporate websites with content having in mind the journalist's interest. The central question lies in knowing whether it will be possible to identify an evolution in corporate digital newsrooms, with companies redefining their media relations strategies beyond a 2.0 model, to meet the so-called 3.0 newsrooms, typical of a cyber journalism scenario, which operates in the virtual environment. This idea was taken from an article by Neto et al. that explored newsrooms at 'O Globo' in Brazil, 'La Nación' in Costa Rica, and 'BBC' in the UK, searching for differences between newsroom models 1.0, 2.0, and 3.0. Thus, two areas in the field of communication (journalism and corporate communication) come together to assess the role that corporate digital newsrooms play in the interactions between both sides.

INTRODUCTION

It is already a widely accepted idea that we live in a very digital and dynamic world, based on network and mobile technologies, which provide us with information and knowledge 24 hours a day, 7 days a week, but also connect us to others in a way we have never experienced before. We are fascinated by interconnectivity, mobility, globalization, virtual sociability, all resulting from the unprecedented development of the World Wide Web, and powered by optical fiber, satellite communications, telecommunications and geolocation systems, which leads Wilson Dizard (2000) to say we are experiencing a third great transformation in the communicative sphere, that goes beyond the production, storage and distribution of information.

DOI: 10.4018/978-1-7998-9790-3.ch008

Technologies are so impactful in such a way that there are those who point to «the emergence of a new civility» where information and knowledge processing and storage techniques make cultural evolutions possible (Levy, 1990). Castells (1998) speaks of a rupture caused by communication and information technologies, rooted in transformation of the social forms of time and space which give rise to a new culture. Our interface with machines and technologies goes beyond a simple technical complementarity in our daily lives, being rooted in habits and routines that according to David Holmes (2005, p.2) not only help us but also imprison us, configuring a new market (technological, digital, electronic), new policies (sharing, generalized and facilitated access to all, but also control) and new behaviours (of interactivity, of integration, but also of segregation and alienation). With an interdisciplinary view that looks at contemporary communications and media through a lens that brings together sociology of communication with media studies and the perspective of cultural studies, Holmes (2005) identifies the need for a new framing to analyse the actual media architecture in a post-broadcast and interactive society, where the 'first media age' of broadcast and the 'second media age' of interactivity are no longer useful to explore the relationship between media, technology and society.

The same need to study the impact of cyberculture on the media and society is considered in the book 'Journalism, Representation and Public Sphere' by Kramp et al. (2015), that reports on how journalism is going through "tectonic shifts, turbulences and reinventions" (p. 24), in a deeply mediated world in which people have access to various forms of information without being exclusively through traditional journalistic dissemination. All this naturally changed the status of news service, the profession, the mechanisms and dynamics of research, collection and construction of news content. Adopting the concept of mediatization proposed by Friedrich Krotz (2007) and by Sonia Livingstone & Peter Lunt (2014), Kramp et al. refers to 'mediatization of everything' (2015, p. 25) as it characterizes changes in cultures and institutions in media-saturated societies, spreading across all areas of our lives. Andreas Hepp (2013) also works with this concept of media coverage to capture the interrelationship between the changes that have taken place in the media and communication ecosystem, in articulation with cultural and social transformations. "Mediatization refers to the increasing temporal, spatial and social spread of media communication. That means that over time we have become more and more used to communicating via media in various contexts. With regard to qualitative aspects, mediatization refers to the role of the specificity of certain media in the process of sociocultural change" (Hepp & Hasebrink, 2013, p.4).

It is also important, regarding this change in media roles with the loss of their power as an almost exclusive mediating force for the understanding of the different dimensions of life in society, to account for the concept of 'communicative figurations' introduced by Andreas Hepp (2013) as analytical tool to study the mediatization particularly focused on the changes that occur in the communicative constructions of the present time.

As it is not only the relationships between individuals in their daily lives or the exchange processes in cultural and social context that are affected by technological transformations (Lister et al., 2009), we also face dramatic reforms in the role of communications in the business world (Galgali, 2017) with many companies adapting values and preparing new architectures and strategic models with different priorities. The World Economic Forum in its 'Digital Culture Guidebook' (2021) shows how companies should make use of the current digital and flexible culture to achieve more sustainable action and add value to all their stakeholders through four fundamental pillars (collaboration, guidance data-driven, innovation, customer focus), proposing a review of the managers communication style.

We see Chief Executive Officers (CEOs), Chief Financial Officers (CFOs) and even Chief Information Officers (CIOs) making serious investments and relocating business resources to bet big on public relations power to navigate in this global wired world. They are aware of the gains that digital communications deliver in speed and reach for the business, while increasing the visibility among audiences in a volatile and constantly changing market (Middleberg, 2001).

But, the most impactful changes that have been verified are driven by the media, which are facing the biggest changes ever witnessed, with the blurring of borders between different media, the media/internet technological convergence (Soares, 2005) and the "almost total dissociation between 'physical place' and 'social place'" (Silveirinha, 2002, p.2). We now live in a new space, a cyberspace, which serves as a territorial basis for 'new media' or 'new information and communication technologies', where new computer-generated public and private domain relationships arise, which lead us to experience new concepts of reterritorialization, new feelings of participatory power without limits of status or social distance and new feelings of community and belonging - which necessarily lead to changes in the understanding of what the subject is, his identity and his sociability, at the limit even to visible changes in the political construction of societies and democracy (ibidem, 2002, pp. 3-4).

All these reconfigurations operated by the internet rise to a new relationship between old and new media, creating what is now called the new media ecosystem (Soares, 2005; Canavilhas, 2011; Anderson, 2013; Wlard, 2019). But what defines this ecosystem? We seek to explore these questions mainly through the view of João Canavilhas (2011). The author starts from the original concept of 'Ecology', coined in 1869 by Ernst Haeckel, which refers to the study of the relationships between different organisms in their natural environment (Odum & Barrett, 2005 in Canavilhas, 2011, p.14) and the concept of 'ecosystem', used by Arthur Tansley (1835) to explain how different elements – the abiotic component (environment) and the Biotic component (living beings) – combine and interact in a given environment (Canavilhas, 2011).

More recently Victor Wiard (2019) also speaks of two distinct terms, regarding media ecosystem, to designate journalism studies - the new ecology and the new ecosystem. The first seeks to understand the effects that technology has on social interactions and relationships and on the way in which information is consumed through the media. The new ecosystem, a more recent term, involves all actors responsible for the production and dissemination of information. The author draws two distinct perspectives on the reflection on the two terms: the first perspective of new ecology, refers to news circulation in the technological ecosystem through mediated spaces, such as social networks. The second perspective refers to the news ecosystem, with regard to the production, circulation and use of information.

Following the same reflections of other authors like Dizard, Castells, Holmes or Levy, just to name some, about the relationship between old and new media, Canavilhas (2011) speaks of 'media evolutionism' under the assumption that each media that emerges represents an improvement over the previous one by incorporating new technological applications. We thus face a media ecosystem in permanent change due to global and technological changes, with a more unstable and mobile nature, which is unbalanced and rebalanced, in constant renewal, as new resources or environments emerge, in a sort of "liquid society" - a concept recovered from Zygmunt Bauman (2000).

This new media ecosystem, with all the transformations that has taken place, leads us to stop talking about "mass media" and talk now about "masses of media", according to the vision of Rosental C. Alves, as the communication system is no longer media-centric because it has become self-centred, that is, today all individuals have gained the power to communicate, exchange information, redistribute content, mix messages, make their own videos and post them for thousands of people in an unprecedented multiplication of transmission and reception media (Elola, 2010).

Recovering João Canavilhas vision about the new media ecosystem, the intermediary factors (corresponding to the biotic factors we mentioned before in the traditional ecosystem) refer to the network society of Castells (2012) and also refer to the "symbiosis of content" promoted by the internet, which results in an overlapping or hybrid crossing of all previous media and technologies, hence its great attraction on civilization today (McLuhan, 1969 in Canavilhas, 2011, p.17). Bringing together all media, converging in a single medium – the Web – resulted from a process of media migration that blurred the distinction of boundaries between different media, with new media improving the old media and traditional media reinventing itself in a phenomenon that Bolter & Grusin (1999) called 'remediation' (Canavilhas, 2011, p.18). The second factors contextual - which come in the line of abiotics – are also related to the changes that the internet and mobile equipment have caused, namely in terms of mobility and the individualization of media consumption. The availability of these technologies contributed to a transformation in media consumption habits, which are now more individual and personalized, contributing to a new universe of reception situations, which force traditional content producers to rethink information sharing and dissemination strategies (ibidem, 2011, p.19). The new digital environment requires new answers according to the preferences of each one of us. Today we receive information when we want and where we want it. The third and last factors to consider in this new media ecosystem - the techno-environmental ones - are directly linked to the relationship between the environment and the individual, because interfaces change the relationship with the environment regardless of the content and the place where the receiver determines the information he receives. It is the instruments that take on real importance, and it is then the interfaces that change the way we interact – such as tablets, mice, e-readers, television controls or operating systems. It is the hardware and software that are assumed to promote consumer satisfaction. Basically, usability and interactivity assume their role alongside environmental elements – ways of consuming content through social networks and through friends – that also contribute to intervening in media factors (ibidem, 2011, pp.19-20).

It is also necessary to take into account that the new media ecosystem is organized in an information model that presupposes distribution of information according to algorithms. A complex scenario marked above all by mobile phone, which dictates consumption of news anytime and anywhere; by using social networks as a source and for news sharing; by streaming information facilitated by convergence between mobile phones and social networks, which contribute to information fragmentation by uninterrupted flow supported using algorithms responsible for categorizing and reclassifying information and for introducing new forms of conversation; by changes in the information distribution model, with media bringing news to readers through a multiplicity of distributors, such as Google News, Apple News, instant articles and direct-to-consumer relations; by resorting to external news delivery services where the media only function as distributors and facilitators of services and not just as content producers (Cerezo, 2017).

Today we really live in an unprecedented communication scenario under mediatized settings in which media are a constituent part of a new way of life. In an innovative vision, the anthropologist Muniz Sodré proposes the concept 'biomediatic' to characterize this effect of the media on contemporary society and culture. According to him, it is in this new 'bios' that our understanding of reality resides, going beyond language itself, technology, and even ideology. 'Biomediatic' names a new social order constituted by a real highlighted information space with new discursive formations and patterns of sociability (Sodré, 2002).

The Portuguese case has the same global reality in the appropriation logic of the online space. Soares (2005) reports that, in a space of four years (between 1999 and 2003), the Portuguese media understood the importance of adapting to new formats and forms of contact between sender and receiver. The creation of new interfaces based on technological tools allowed new forms of interaction with audiences, despite the need to study audiences to better adapt the type of platforms and content.

We then live in a media ecosystem boosted and accelerated by the advent of the internet, especially marked by the strengthening of individual's power in the dissemination of content and the proliferation of increasingly smaller, mobile and immersive media. Canavilhas (2011) even predicted that in 2020 we would reach a reality in which mobile devices would become the main device for internet access, a scenario that we ended up confirming in the highlight of the use of the smartphone as a leader in the regular use of the Internet (66%), according to data from the Marktest Group (2020). Also according to the "Portuguese Digital Life Barometer", carried out in 2021, 75% of respondents admit that they cannot do without the smartphone, a percentage that was reinforced by the global pandemic and subsequent social restrictions.

Changes are then witnessed on multiple stages, with 'audiences' becoming 'users', 'cybernauts' and 'content consumers' becoming 'content producers'. New textual experiences emerge; new ways of representing the world like immersive virtual environments or screen-based interactive multimedia; new ways of consuming media contents came to light characterised by interactivity and hypertextual formats; and a whole range of transformations occur in various already established media (Lister et al., 2009, pp.12-13).

So a distinct understanding of mass media is needed. If at some point, around the second half of the nineties, we questioned whether newspapers, television or radio could disappear with the arrival of the Internet, what is certain is that these catastrophic premonitions of the end of journalism were wrong. Today we continue to rely on written and online publications that offer a panoply of possibilities for accessing news, we have analogue and digital television in 3D, Full HD, Ultra HD and smart TV formats, radio already appears with image on social networks and diversifies into Podcasts and Web Blogs. And although citizens can compete in the production of information in parallel with the official news media, journalism knows how to reinvent itself and gain renewed impact in the news arena. The truth is that general confidence in the news increased in several countries, even during a pandemic year, and Portugal followed this trend with a 20% increase compared to 2020. It is noted that 69.3% of Portuguese believe that journalists maintain their impartiality in all situations and 41.2% believe that the State should support news brands for their financial recovery. Finland continues to be the country with the highest levels of overall confidence (65%), while the United States has the lowest levels (29%), appearing to reflect the 2020 elections that divided the country among supporters of Joe Biden and Donald Trump (Cardoso et al., 2021).

But if journalism again assumes an important role in society, it is also becoming more and more fragile, in face of a growing inequality access to news, since with the transition to digital people are exposing themselves to a greater diversity of sources that are not always credible or filtered. On the other hand, it moves towards business models that threaten the profession in the face of economic and political pressures, while the traditional role of the public agenda 'gatekeepers' also diminishes (Nielsen & Selva, 2019). In any case, today we have the best journalism ever done, considered by the Reuters Institute for the Study of Journalism.

So, it is providential to see in this scenario the relationship that organizations establish with media professionals through one of their most privileged virtual channels: the corporate website. The focus of this chapter is, therefore, a reflection on the strategic potential of digital newsrooms, usually a section or webpage incorporated in corporate websites having in mind the journalist's interest. The central question then lies in knowing whether it will be possible to identify an evolution in digital newsrooms, with companies redefining their media relations strategies beyond a 2.0 model, to meet the so called digital newsrooms 3.0, typical of a cyber journalism scenario, which operates in a virtual environment where anachronistic contents are produced in a collaborative logic? The inspiration to identify this evolution in the field of media relations in public relations came from an article entitled 'Newsroom 3.0: Managing Technological and Media Convergence in Contemporary Newsrooms', reporting on a study carried out in field trips to newsrooms of three major newspapers (*O Globo* in Rio de Janeiro - Brazil; *La Nación* in San Jose - Costa Rica; *BBC* in London - UK) (Neto et al., 2019).

This chapter intends precisely to take advantage of a time when journalism is going through the most intense transformation it has ever undergone (Cardoso, 2006; Kramp et al., 2015; Cerezo, 2016), taking in account its function and role in society. At the same time, professionals in corporate communication and public relations need to respond effectively to the new media ecosystem, adjusting their strategy and positioning regarding journalists.

Thus, two areas in the field of communication (journalism and public relations or corporate communication) come together to assess the role that digital newsrooms play in the interactions between both sides. In sum it is hoped that this chapter can contribute to broader future research and help organizations to give more strategic responses in media relations according to the digital age challenges.

DIGITAL MEDIA RELATIONS: AN ONGOING TRANSFORMATION

The advent of the internet boosted a technological leap that in the late 1980s democratized access to information and brought the convergence of media and messages, creating new efficiencies and economies of scale, both at the corporate and government levels, that radically changed notions of space and time in what became known as the Information Revolution (Middleberg, 2001). Cyberspace was born, a new space where there are no limits of borders, no time barriers and where the speed of interactions and transactions is instantaneous. Kevin Clark, Director of IBM, refers to "media collapse time, overcome distances, and extend the range of the eye, ear, and mind" despite "their fundamental role, the extensions of human perception remain unchanged" (Caywood, 1997, p. 222).

This unprecedented scenario cannot be ignored by public relations professionals, who are now faced with the need to interact, dialogue and involve multiple and new stakeholders, more informed, demanding and proactive. As the nature of work sometimes becomes confused, as the boundaries between going to work and being at home fade away, public relations professionals face a greater challenge in choosing which information best serves the purposes of organizations, such as enhancing their adaptation to the growing demands of an increasingly complex and volatile market and economy, and how to effectively deliver messages to audiences through the many media that interconnect, combining multimedia strategies, crossmedia and transmedia, as conceived by Henry Jenkins (2016) when referring to the collision of old media with new media in a convergence culture.

Thus, the full digital age of public relations is here, with some individuals, companies and agencies more committed than others. Of course, some were more perceptive in anticipating the advantages for bottom-line success, such as increased loyalty and trust of employees and other audiences, an increase in reputation and value in the market, and more sustainable economic growth (Middleberg, 2001, p.1). It is known there is still a way to go and that they are not all walking at the same speed. According to the European Communication Monitor 2021, 39.2% of PR professionals across Europe consider that there is still a "digital immaturity of communications with different stakeholders", despite large corporations are more advanced than public sector organizations and third sector institutions (Zerfass et al., 2021, p.17).

Despite everything, with the pandemic situation of Covid-19 experienced on a global scale, and the technological developments, which follow an increasingly accelerated cadence, it is possible to see among the ECM 2021 participants that 60% of corporations already use programmed digitization processes – accounting for both digitalising stakeholder communications and digital infrastructure – while a smaller percentage of only 32.3% only integrate communication routines supported by digital software and services. It seems, then, that although the level of digital maturity in Europe is not yet desirable, public relations professionals are starting to look beyond the dialogue and engagement strategies made possible by social media, websites or blogs (ibidem, 2021, p.17). The concept of CommTech is thus introduced, bringing a broader vision of what technologies can provide and enhancing the relationship with all stakeholders. Jon Iwata, executive in residence at Yale School of Management, says that today most CCOs are still at a professional stage with digital publishing, content creation and listening by using analytics. But the future of CommTech points to the pathfinder stage where communications are much more automated and sustainable to the enterprise and where PR practitioners tend to use targets to nourish and encourage stakeholders to take some kind of action (Iwata, 2021).

However, here the authors want to highlight the particular relationship with journalists, and it is interesting to note that the activity of public relations is intrinsically linked to journalism in historical terms, first with the evolution of mass media and then with the latest technological and new digital solutions. A long time has passed since Ivy Lee, considered one of the founding fathers of modern public relations, issued, on behalf of the Pennsylvania Railroad, the first recorded press release, on October 28, 1906, concerning a train accident. Since that date, what is considered the privileged tool for contacting journalists has deserved numerous praise and criticism, in addition to being commonly seen as the flag that marks the practice of public relations, limiting this function to media relations. But media relations today, particularly digital media relations, go far beyond those times.

Don Middleberg (2011) talks about five stages in the public relations development, in a way linked to the way journalists were also adjusting and embracing internet transformations. In the first stage, public relations professionals did not react actively to digital advent because they anticipated a poor adherence of journalists to electronic tools. In a second stage, as they realized the potential of the internet, fear of damaging the image of corporations became widespread with several public relations professionals having to respond to journalists about online rumours. In a third step, public relations realized that journalists and other audiences were quickly turning to online and began designing digital communication strategies and programs, opting to distribute press releases via email, creating websites and online publications to disseminate in the media lists. In a fourth stage, the internet is no longer seen as just a tool, giving rise to the foundation of a whole new dynamic of this professional activity, with both professions adjusting to new trends. The fifth phase delivered us large scale and fully networked communications, with the integration of wired and wireless functionalities, with transparency becoming mandatory and corporations having to deal with the scrutiny not only of journalists, but of an entire army of empowered citizens with an active and influential voice. Maybe the biggest revolution was the fact that it is no longer possible for corporations to rely on traditional media and on gatekeepers to decide which information gets published because of the exponential spread of information sources and the loss of control over information flows which creates a new paradigm (Cutlip & Center, 2013).

But if it is true that public relations in the interconnected and wireless world now have the power to create their own stories to target enlarged audiences that reach for those contents, this does not mean journalists and reporters are no longer important. Middleberg (2011) says that even today the 'Holy Grail' of building credibility is through a media campaign that places companies on the pages, on websites, on social media of major news media whether those are newspapers, magazines, radio stations or television channels. "Despite many challenges, professional journalism is alive if not exactly thriving" (Weiner, 2021, p. 11).

Public relations in fact embodies numerous functions, but the relationship with the media - press office - has always stood out as its main focus of activity (Cascais, 2001; Howard, 2004), especially because it points to information sharing about organizations and their projection on the media stage in search for visibility and good name. In this regard, it is up to public relations professionals to intercede for the organization in promoting its initiatives with the media, seeking to combine different interests: the organization, the media and the public (Cascais, 2001). "The central objective of public relations is to create and develop scenes (media or not), that is, places, moments, concepts, opportunities that help us transform ignorance into knowledge, apathy into interest, prejudice into acceptance, hostility in understanding" (Ries & Ries, 2008, p.9). It is therefore their responsibility to ensure a fruitful relationship with these interlocutors, by sharing information that must be factual and not manipulated, have a newsworthy character, generate interest, which requires the PR professional to distinguish newsworthy events from those that do not generate news value.

As the 'backbone' of public relations (Whatmough, 2019), the relationship with the media has always been fraught with negativity due to different needs between both professionals - on the one hand the organization interests, through PR, on the other hand, the needs of relevance, interest and topicality of the media and its audiences. The "spray and pray" approach (ibidem, 2019) reveals the need for PRs to disclose many times in quantity and not in quality, which was what affected the relationship between them and sprinkled it with some negativity.

It is accepted that not always the relationship between public relations practitioners and journalists is cordial and friendly. To succeed as the middle person who mediates both the interests and needs of their organization and those of the press is not an easy task. There is often a feeling of adversity with managers, on the one hand, launching accusations of news sensationalism, de-contextualization or poor prominence and, on the other hand, journalists countering with a lack of transparency and secrecy, difficulty in accessing more relevant sources, and flimsy contents to work with (Cutlip & Center, 2013). The truth is that journalists want relevant information that is newsworthy and easily accessible, and the role of public relations practitioners is to facilitate that information by helping them make the story. It is, therefore, about building a relationship of partnership, trust and even friendship in a win-win logic that benefits journalists in their work process and in their role of informing society and at the same time projects organizations, ideas and the subjects creating awareness and visibility.

Improved channels sophistication and the internet push, however, have brought new habits and ways of communicating for PR professionals and journalists alike. The internet has proved to be a mechanism for changing the relationship between these professionals and a great opportunity to explore new ways of contacting the public through online reputation, SEO (Search Engine Optimization), content creation and not only just through the format of personal and direct contact with the media. Today this function is not excluded, but it is complemented with new ways of communicating organizations (Lloyd & Toogoog, 2015).

In order not to be labelled as outdated and resistant to change, it became imperative that PR professionals adapt to the new formats imposed by the digital, so that organizations represented by them would benefit from this adaptation (Waters, Tindall & Morton, 2016). If in the 1990s the privileged channel was the fax, nowadays the email has become part of the routine of the relationship between PR and journalists. In addition to this channel, the website is also a means of sharing information for organizations to reach media (although apparently still less important), without forgetting other contact channels such as Social Media News Release – a more sophisticated and thought-out instrument that came to improve traditional press release (Whatmough, 2019), by incorporating photography, audio, video and text and which is sent by platforms created for promoting contact between media professionals and their information sources, but at the same time making it easier for PR professionals to reach the media. An adaptation to new forms of contact that promote more effective and fruitful relationships with the media (Waters, Tindall & Morton, 2016).

In 2009, it was said that we were facing a scenario of 'new PR' (Philips & Young, 2009, p.91) because the changes driven by the internet and social networks led to this designation. As it was already said, the internet changed the way we interact and also changed the way PR manages different channels at their disposal. It changed the management of online relationships and interactions and also provoked a new reflection on the relationship with the media, intending to make the best use for all means of communication in organizations. "Relationships with the media are not over and will not disappear, but the role changes as the vulnerability of 'command and control' models of PR activity becomes more evident" (Philips &Young, 2009, p.248).

As for the media, according to the needs of the work they perform, it also underwent an adaptation to online channels and new formats, in a time dominated by immediacy, speed, greater amount of content and by the minute-information (Philips & Young, 2009). They kept the traditional formats, but sought to adapt to digital channels, through short videos, horizontal stories, scrollytelling, structured news, liveblogs, newsletters, schedules, bots and chats, listicles and personalized content (BBC News Labs, 2017 in Whatmough, 2019).

Traditional media relations was a "push" activity to provide information for the media, in accordance with the goals and timing of the organization and to the extent of its own purposes. In other words, in traditional media relations, the objective was to make the company, the brand and the subjects of interest visible, trying to get faster results and sometimes resorting to some techniques that implied increased efforts, resources and costs. With the internet and the new digital technologies, it is now possible to have a 'pull' perspective of the relationship with journalists, ensuring they seek and remove information about the company from the website and other social media tools when they wish. Many journalists use the web as a primary tool for their research, starting by accessing the corporate website or using search engines by entering the organization's name to reach detailed information about it. Currently, as more journalists, analysts, editors and other professionals in the media field actively seek information and organizational contents, it is essential that corporate websites be prepared and optimized for main search engines, ensuring greater ease for those looking for information. By embracing a 'pull' PR media strategy, more organic and long-term projected, organizations are capable of building a digital footprint naturally over time. Most corporate websites offer today an 'about us' section but they often fail to deliver a clear and complete communication which could alienate journalists and lead them to look for other, more trustworthy and impartial sources. Kim Harrison (2020) speaks of five reasons journalists visit a corporation website: get a name, a telephone number or an email for a PR contact person; look for basic facts, numbers and stories about the organization; investigate the organization's version of issues and events; find financial information; download images to illustrate news articles.

This is why the digital newsroom should be a focal component of a public relations strategic approach in the new media ecosystem, providing relevant information, data and insights at all times not only for journalists but also to a variety of other stakeholders that work until late hours, research information during weekends, seek data during holidays and even expect an answer or enter into dialogue when the public relations team leave on health permits and are not available to provide immediate explanations.

METHODOLOGICAL OBSERVATIONS OF AN EXPLORATORY ANALYSIS

In methodological terms, the reflection presented here is based on a literature review on various concerns of modern times, which make clear the added challenges to many areas of society, especially those that are more directly linked to communication like public relations and journalism. At the same time, it delivers a systematization of the corporate digital newsroom as a media relations communication tool to which the interests of companies and journalists' converge. On one hand, through corporate digital newsrooms, corporations open another window to spread contents, inform about their mission, interests, and other issues that they want to see exposed, helping to bring together more easily information about the corporate world and the different themes launched on the agenda. On the other hand, corporate digital newsrooms provide raw material but also complete analysis and data, for journalists and other media audiences to produce and edit media contents.

As it is not common to find texts and authors who talk about the corporate digital newsroom, this chapter seeks to partially fill this gap, presenting some characteristics of this tool, which can represent a privileged channel of media relations, but go further, contributing to strengthen the cooperation and dialogue between different stakeholders in the spread of news.

The literature review is complemented with the presentation of various data collected in reports, surveys and statistical studies of reference in this subject to more easily visualize the state of the art in which the tool being analysed is found. A collection of empirical data is also carried out, in order to better support a current reflection based on the reality we face. Therefore, an analysis is performed to a set of 100 corporate websites from private companies recognized for having a responsible performance by Merco Portugal - a Corporate Reputation Business Monitor. Merco is a corporate reputation assessment tool that focuses on six main areas: economic-financial results, quality of the commercial offer, talent, ethics and corporate responsibility, international dimension of the company and innovation. The Merco methodology was created in 2000 at the Complutense University of Madrid by a team led by Professor Justo Villafañe. In a first phase, the Merco ranking was extended to several countries in Latin America due to the influence of large Spanish multinational companies that had their international presence in these countries. In a second phase, Portugal served as a Hub for the project to grow on the European continent. According to João Marques, director of Merco Portugal, the "objective of the Merco ranking in Portugal is, as in all the countries where it is present, to contribute, as an analysis and management tool, to the promotion of quality in companies, for its responsible management and improving the quality of the business fabric" (Ferreira, 2019). Choosing a sample of companies in Portugal to check whether they included a digital newsroom, and what degree of development they present on this tool, was not easy, but when Merco wanted to make the launch in Portugal coincide with the Merco Digital evaluation, it was seen as relevant to opt for a list of companies that were known to be well evaluated in terms of their digital development. In fact, Merco Digital seeks to measure and assess in the most objective way possible the corporate reputation both in the activity driven by the companies ("owned"), as in the conversation generated in the reputational dimensions ("earned"), having collected 14,711 publications and analysed 848,651 mentions to the companies present in the ranking, ensuring that the companies' score also depends on their activity, their followers, as well as the assessments carried out in digital media and on social networks by influencers and users (ibidem, 2019).

So the analysis of the corporate websites of the 100 companies in the Merco Portugal ranking serves the following purposes: (1) Assess whether companies include a corporate digital newsroom as part of their media relations strategies; (2) Check how corporate digital newsrooms are structured; (3) Compare different corporate digital newsrooms in terms of content, presentation, dynamization, topicality; (4) Register if we can currently speak of a corporate digital newsroom 3.0.

When carrying out an analysis on corporate websites, it should be taken into account that this digital tool is essential to gain competitive advantage, helping to improve the relationship with different audiences, promoting loyalty and satisfaction with the organization, while at the same time projects the organization's identity and helps to manage its reputation, with reduced costs (Ageeva et al., 2019). Therefore, when planning and creating a corporate website, companies must have a strategy to meet the expectations and needs of different stakeholders, seeking to design relevant and diversified content. "A favourable website should be more than just attractive, it should be usable, and present valuable and serviceable information" (ibidem, 2019, p.5).

But, in addition to being communication vehicles that convey the corporation identity, they also incorporate online newsrooms, an essential component to help address the challenges of the new media ecosystem. Therefore, the starting point to find out in what level of development are the corporate digital newsrooms of the 100 Portuguese companies with the highest corporate reputation index, was to search through their websites using a content analysis.

The content analysis technique is widely used in public relations studies to collect and analyse data in a structured way (Michaelson & Stacks, 2010, p.113). According to the Dictionary of Public Relations Measurement and Research, content analysis is "an informal research methodology that systematically tracks messages and translates them into quantifiable form via a systematic approach to defining message categories through specified units of analysis" (Stacks & Bowen, 2013, p.6). According to Michaelson & Stacks (2010) developing an analytic framework for the web or for applying it to social media tools does not differ much from content analysis to traditional media. Even so, any analysis carried out on digital content implies taking into account a set of precautions in the face of certain peculiarities that could endanger generalizations and representativeness of the data. For example, on the web we are faced with a different source of analysis, in which we do not control all dimensions, namely the fact that there may be content that changes, although this limitation may be overcome by rapid data collection and downloading websites. Another difficulty that can be pointed out is related to the "complexity of new features such as mixed multiple media (text, graphics, animation, video and audio etc.), interactivity, decentralized and hyperlinked structures, and its continuously evolving nature" (Kim & Kuljis, 2010, p.284).

As a way to get around some of the limitations presented, during the data recording stage a maximum limit of 5 minutes of browsing time was established for each site visited, in order to guarantee the same analysis conditions for everyone. This time limitation is particularly relevant in some of the criteria related to ease navigation and the time it takes to find information, because if journalists do not easily find relevant information they will give up this source of information and seek other alternatives, leading the company lose control of the way it tells the story and may even eventually lose the opportunity to become the target of a news story.

Once the concerns were set aside, the analysis framework was constructed based on a set of criteria adapted from "The 2013 Newsroom Report: What's The Story? - How the world's top 100 brands are using online newsrooms to tell their stories'". This report was created in 2013 by the Swedish public relations solutions company, Mynewsdesk, to discover how the world's most influential companies were setting up the digital newsroom. As the study presented in this chapter wanted to verify the state of evolution of digital newsrooms in a wide range of Portuguese companies, as mentioned above, it was considered relevant to start with a base study, as it is quite complete and was very near the intended objectives with the observation of the Portuguese reality. It should also be noticed that most companies present in the Merco Portugal ranking are large companies with global projection in terms of business, and may eventually exert some influence on the way they position their communication with the media through digital media. The study presented in this chapter occurred during the first week of October 2021.

The categories of analysis with the respective indicators are now presented - these ten categories were listed in an analysis grid where the data referring to each of the 100 websites visited were subsequently registered (see Table 1):

Category 1: Find – assess the ease with which it is possible to find the corporate newsroom, either directly by entering the corporate website or by using a search engine.

Category 2: Dimension – Number of pages and internal links within the corporate website dedicated to press information.

Category 3: Content – assess the information hosted in the pages dedicated to the press like press releases, news stories, highlights.

Category 4: Contact – register if there is a personal contact or a spokesperson with details of expertise, to elucidate if more information is needed about some issues. Verify if the corporate newsroom holds a feature allowing visitors to ask for more updates via alert applications such as the RSS feed system.

Category 5: Loading – register if the loading time functionality is synchronously, with scripts loaded sequentially, one after another, originating a more time consuming process, or it is asynchronously, allowing some scripts being loaded simultaneously thus optimizing the visitor experience accessing information.

Category 6: Navigation – rcgister if the corporate newsroom has any kind of search functionality (with a visible search box, pre-defined search categories, filters and a sort function to help manage those categories) in order to assist visitors in finding relevant information. To help visitors search information in a more targeted way, more sortable and refined the corporate newsroom should also catalogue the information hosted.

Category 7: Target – identify who is the information and resources targeting (solely journalists and other press elements or is directed to several other stakeholders?).

Category 8: Documents – register the existence of different documents and support information to better know the company like factsheets, backgrounders, Financial Reports, Press-Kits, Infographics, clipping, external studies and reports, surveys or statistics, etc.

Category 9: Multimedia – register the existence of multimedia resources like images, photos, video gallery, podcasts, animated presentations, etc.

Category 10: Social Media – register the existence of social media channels incorporated in the corporate newsroom pages.

The name given to the corporate digital newsroom by the different companies was also collected to understand the designation trend dedicated to this space for media communication on corporate websites.

Table 1. Corporate newsroom analysis grid

Category	Newsroom 1.0	Newsroom 2.0	Newsroom 3.0
1 - Find	With research / time effort and recurring to a search engine	In a few seconds after entering and searching inside the corporate website	Instantly within the corporate website
2 - Dimension	One or two pages only	More than two pages	More than five pages and both internal and external links from the corporate website
3 - Content	Press releases and a few news	Press releases, news stories	Press releases, news stories, highlights and other information/data resources
4 - Contact	No contacts	Contact telephone and email	Personal contact via telephone and email, and even access to one or more spokesperson with biographies pointing out areas of expertise
5 - Loading	Synchronous	Synchronous and Asynchronous	Asynchronous
6 – Navigation	No search functionalities	Basic search functionalities like a search box and organization plus cataloging of information	Effective navigation support with complete search functionalities and cataloging of information
7 - Target	Only journalists	Mainly journalists, reporters, editors and related other press elements	Various sorts of stakeholders interested in the company news (employees, investors, consumers, influencers, etc.)
8 - Documents	No extra documents	A few documents like factsheets, backgrounders and Financial Reports	Several documents and information like factsheets, backgrounders, Financial Reports, Press-Kits, Infographics, clipping, external studies and reports, surveys or statistics, etc.
9 - Multimedia	No multimedia resources	A Few multimedia resources like images, photos or videos	Several multimedia resources like images, photos, video gallery, podcasts, animated presentations, etc.
10 – Social Media	No links to social media channels	No links to social media channels	Links to various social media channels

COPORATE DIGITAL NEWSROOMS: A CONTEMPORARY ASSESSMENT

In general terms, corporate digital newsrooms (or digital press rooms, or website press rooms, or social media newsrooms) are a space of information that organizations make available to journalism professionals so that they can more easily find what they are looking for. Wendy Marx, president of the Marx Communications agency, defines corporate digital newsrooms as "news hubs that act as a repository of sources, information, and industry trends'' (Marx in Kowal, 2021). This tool is actually a webpage whose purpose is to present an organization's press releases and news in a single space that is more visible to journalists, influencers, potential or current customers, employees, partners, investors or other stakeholders interested in researching and obtaining systematized information about the organization and its issues. Some corporate digital newsrooms go beyond mere archives of press releases and allow access to various information materials such as fact sheets, backgrounders, photo albums, press kits, reports, studies and statistics, market and sector trends, links to more complete analysis of facts, etc..

As corporate digital newsrooms are an organization's property and responsibility, they are considered an owned media channel, which means that they are platforms that offer the organization a possibility to fully control its narrative and decide what can or cannot be made public, according to its angle. In addition to this benefit, there is the fact that 'owned media leads to earned media'. This is because, by providing journalists with online access to information about an organization, it is also easier for them to cover that information or include the organization's name in a story. And the more systematically we invest in owned media, the more confidence the organization projects as a useful and credible source of information, which can increase the likelihood of gaining earned media. In fact, one of the most important functions of the corporate digital newsroom is precisely to capture the attention of the media and facilitate its work of collecting, analysing and building news at their pace and convenience.

A report about press professionals expectations, from TekGroup (2012) - an award-winning Internet software and services company that develops solutions for the Public Relations industries – highlights that (1) 99% of journalists say it's important for a company provide access to news releases within their online newsroom; (2) it is good for journalists to have news releases organized by type of news category (93%); (3) 94% of journalists say it's important to have access to photographs – both web and print ready; (4) 90% of journalists indicate that digital product press kits would be important; (5) and 75% say video files are a relevant component of an online newsroom (The Online Newsroom Survey Report, 2012).

Depending on the features that a corporate digital newsroom integrates and how it is designed and structured, the authors consider it is possible to find three different types of working interfaces with journalists on corporate websites, ranging from digital newsroom 1.0 to digital newsroom 3.0.

The Corporate Digital Newsroom 1.0

The corporate digital newsroom 1.0 is characterized by being a simple transition from the traditional service of a press room to an online format available on a computer. It usually only contains an archive of press releases, where much of the information is made available in a disorganized way and without standardization, with the information in pdf format, without an online production of news and scripts, without a classification or thematic categorization and without search engine to facilitate interaction with the news searched. They are, therefore, somewhat static and rigid online press pages, little invested in terms of content and graphics, which frequently feature press releases with old dates and without a regular cadence. They also do not usually present links outside the page dedicated to the online room, nor do they contemplate a convergence with other applications or communication tools. The corporate digital newsroom 1.0 has synchronous loading functionality which means by default contents are loaded sequentially, one after another.

The Corporate Digital Newsroom 2.0

The corporate digital newsroom 2.0 represents an evolution compared to the first digital newsrooms, with the availability of press releases with a mixed synchronous and asynchronous loading functionality, which allows the website page to load in a search browser recognizing several elements simultaneously, improving ratios of "search visibility", and increasing search effectiveness for the user. The evolution to corporate newsroom 2.0 also already integrates categorization of stories and / or keyword tagging, but at a still undeveloped level, based only on simple keywords. These 2.0 press pages already enable greater interaction with the other features of the corporate website, which forward to the company and the brand, and are further developed by presenting scripts that share printed and online news content. They share a greater pool of information with access to corporate documents, facts and reports. They also denote more careful graphic design and identity in terms of content.

The Corporate Digital Newsroom 3.0

The corporate digital newsroom 3.0 represents a leap forward in terms of the news pages structure and conception, with more precise, rapid and complex features with a high asynchronous mode of script loading. They have many links either to other pages and tools of the corporation or to different sites and external links. They are very dynamic pages, which benefit from the evolution to the semantic web, in which "information receives a well-defined meaning, allowing computers and people to cooperate better" (Pinheiro, 2009, p.24). In this more innovative version of corporate digital newsrooms, information is presented in a more structured and organized way, making it easier for journalists to obtain information. There is also a consolidation of the social network software, creating conditions for greater interaction between the organization and journalism professionals who visit the press pages, in a logic of customization. This way it is possible to reach a better integration using meta titles and a description of the content shown in the media webpage to add a Google Analytics Tracking ID and then track the newsroom website achievements. Via customized software solutions it is also possible to combine the newsroom with different digital resources like other website pages, software, systems or platforms, according to unique needs. This most current and innovative version of the corporate digital newsrooms brings a new way of producing news and interacting with different news agents as it integrates new IoT (internet of Things) elements and tools with the ability to converge and collaborate in providing information, data and even news in a co-creation logic. It is the entry of prosumers into the news field (Neto et al., 2019). In the corporate digital newsroom 3.0 it is also possible to find an easy and direct connection to the companies' social networks, preferably with links on all news webpages, as a way to expand stories and messages. This leads to greater sharing, greater discussion and dialogue. Version 3.0 of the corporate newsrooms also includes: numerous supporting facts features such as reports, studies, surveys; a wide selection of multimedia contents that go far beyond simple photographs, with video gallery, audio records and animations; infographics to illustrate more complex information in a simplified way; email sharing buttons for sharing news via email for those who do not use social networks; social bookmarking tools, to enable, for instance, sharing and saving the news on news aggregation communities; links to other related media coverage and competitor information; contact information with clear reference to a contact person and also to a spokespeople with their biographies pointing out to different areas of expertise; email alert applications such as the RSS feed system that facilitate the subscription of visited content without the need to visit the site again; search facility to enable visitors to quickly search for information within the site; corporate calendar to reference key corporate events; background information of all sorts with access to a large variety of corporate documents and information that should be uploaded to document sharing sites like Scribd or Edocr for improving search rankings and to make easer to share those documents (Waddington, 2012).

But are corporate digital newsrooms really easy to find or use? Are they updated regularly? Do they offer a variety of materials and features in different formats (audio, video, graphic images, photos)? Are they a direct gateway for journalists to contact the organization and find a more complete response? Or, if we want to be more ambitious, the question that arises is whether corporate digital newsrooms are more than an information space and can be real dialogue rooms where communication takes place between journalists and the organization, according to a 3.0 model?

The company Mynewsdesk says the days are over when companies' press service consisted solely of sending news to a group of media publications hoping that they would publish something. Nowadays, companies are content editors and creators, developing countless communication tools to directly engage a vast realm of audiences (blogs, online communities, webpages, social media, etc.), making the way digital newsrooms are conceived change along with what is possible to make available virtually. So the Mynewsdesk report confirms that companies have essentially two goals in mind when developing their corporate digital newsrooms: (1) to become more visible in SERPs (Search engine visibility - also known as "search visibility" or "SEO visibility", meaning the share of traffic that the website receives from its organic search results), (2) build a community of devoted followers. The Report results concluded that 98% of the largest companies in the world have their own digital newsroom, with 65% of these connecting the newsrooms directly from the main corporate website, thus contributing to increase the website's traffic. With an equally relevant ratio comes the Search Visibility indicator with three quarters of the analysed newsrooms appearing on the first page of the Google search engine when searching for the terms 'company name + news'. In the analysis carried out on the 100 companies in the Merco Portugal ranking, the ratio is slightly higher than the Mynewsdesk study, with 70% of companies presenting a digital newsroom, which proves an evolution compared to 2013. Among the companies that do not have a newsroom in their corporate websites there are at least 15 multinational companies whose websites in Portuguese language are exclusively commercial and without any link to institutional information, such as, for example, Coca-Cola, Johnson & Johnson, Huawei, Toyota, La Roche Posay or Colgate-Palmolive. On the corporate website of these multinationals, there are some state-of-the-art 3.0 digital newsrooms, which were not accounted for in this study, as it was based on a ranking of companies with websites made available for Portuguese journalists.

But despite most companies delivering a positive corporate newsroom experience, there are still many areas in which they fail. For instance, in the Mynewsdesk study, 35% of corporate digital newsrooms contain out of date information, 40% failed to provide an image library, in 24% it was noticed lack of a contact phone number and 38% do not categorize, tag or optimize their news content leaving corporations missing major SEO benefits that exclusive news content can provide.

In the study carried out by us, there are also numerous flaws, especially if we want to consider the availability of 3.0 applications or functions in these corporate newsrooms. For instance, in the 'Documents' category 39% do not register any document, report or extra data for consultation and 35% do not include any 'Multimedia' resource, whether photo album, video, podcast or other tool. Only 17% of companies' present additional information and 11% show multimedia resources, adhering to the 3.0 model. Even so, these figures once again represent a significant evolution compared to the 2013 study by Mynewsdesk that reports an even higher figure of 71% of companies that do not embed multimedia within their news stories.

Three other categories that prove most companies still remain in the 1.0 corporate newsroom models, and some in the 2.0, are 'Content' (with 27% in the 1.0 model and 25% in the 2.0), 'Loading' (40% in the model 1.0 and 19% in 2.0) and 'Navigation' (30% in 1.0 and 24% in 2.0)'. Here the corporate digital newsroom 3.0 model falls far short of a prevalent presence with 18%, 11% and 16% respectively in each category. There is, therefore, still a lot of investment that can be made in categorization and filtering functions, using SEO technology, with most companies presenting synchronous or mixed search models and few companies working asynchronously, allowing some scripts being loaded simultaneously.

In the 'Contact' category, 28% of companies do not register any exclusive contact for journalists and another 28% have only a telephone and/or email contact, representing the majority of corporate newsrooms still in a 1.0 and 2.0 model, respectively. In this category, only 14% can be considered in the 3.0 model because they have direct contacts to a spokesperson or PR member, by areas of expertise, many with a photo of the people to contact.

Also in the 'Target' category we have 29% of companies only communicating to journalists (1.0), 24% who communicate to different elements of the media sector such as journalists, editors, reporters, influencers and others, and only 17% with generic content and materials relevant to various stakeholders.

There are, however, three categories that register values in agreement with the corporate digital newsroom 3.0 model: 'Find', 'Dimension' and 'Social Media'. In the first analysed category - 'Find' - it was found that only 11% of organizations with a digital newsroom 1.0 in terms of difficulty in accessing or finding it, requiring the use of the Google search engine. In terms of access, 7% of organizations still presented some difficulties in locating the corporate newsroom within the visited site, due to the lack of highly visible direct links that forced a search within the site itself, sometimes using the site map. However, most companies (52%) had a corporate digital newsroom 3.0 model, due to the ease and speed of direct access through the simple introduction of their name (which we always accompanied with 'corporate' as a second key word). Another category that shows preponderant values in the 3.0 model is 'Dimension' with 40% of the sites presenting corporate digital newsrooms with a considerable number of pages, even when the contents were just press releases or news. Finally, the category which gave the most evidence of being in a corporate digital newsroom 3.0 model was 'Social Media' with 67% companies connecting to different social networks, which is in line with the 2013 study with social media also recording a high value (55% of the companies). Note only one variation in the companies in the Merco Portugal ranking in which social media appears associated with the site where the corporate digital newsroom is hosted, but because access is made through the footer displayed on all pages of the corporate website. If we refer only to social networks directly accessible from the pages opened in the newsroom, the value drops to 22%. Interestingly, three companies did not have links to social networks.

CONCLUSION

The analysis of the corporate digital newsrooms of Merco Portugal companies allows us to observe that the 3.0 model is not yet a reality for many companies. Although it is relatively easy to find digital newsrooms integrated in corporate websites of a considerable number of companies, although they present significant pages with content available to journalists and it is still common to associate social networks with these contents, there is a whole range of more advanced functions made possible by technological developments and the logic of algorithms that escape a more effective and innovative function of digital media relations.

The biggest weaknesses found are in terms of content available, with numerous sites still offering only news of the organization (owned media) or providing press releases sometimes with old dates and without any logic of categorization or theme. Also missing documents, reports and other extra information about the organization, such as a calendar of events that only 4 organizations out of 100 analysed presented. But, above all, there is a lack of multimedia resources, which go against the needs felt by journalists themselves and listed, for example, in 'The Online Newsroom Survey Report' (2012) or evoked by Cerezo in 'The New Digital Media Ecosystem ' (2017) about audio-visuals having become one of the biggest demands for users as well as announcers. Other features attesting that most corporate digital newsrooms analysed remain in a 1.0 model are limited information loading capacities and lack of search functionalities with pre-defined search categories, filters or sort functions to help manage categories in order to assist visitors in finding relevant information.

An investment in these features would make it possible to take corporate digital newsrooms to the next level (Teter, 2021) beyond 1.0 and 2.0 models. Corporate digital newsrooms need to go beyond press releases and news produced by the organization, need to beneficiate from increased website's visibility, need a better page design that clearly highlights the newsroom and what it offers, need more applications and features that improve browsing experience and information search, putting SEO at the service of the site, and need as well a responsive news page with the possibility of gathering feedback and involvement of media professionals in the production of news and gathering of other insights. Finally they need to keep optimizing the PR content made available, as well as monitoring information access practices and visitor paths with analytics and reporting tools.

It will also be important to reach a consensus on the most suitable name to give to the space dedicated to journalists on corporate websites. From the ranking of Merco Portugal organizations, 32 different designations were found to identify the corporate newsroom, with a higher prevalence of the designation 'Media / Media Center and Press Center', followed by 'Press / Room de Press / Newsroom' or Press Office. There was also room for designations such as Actuality / News, Press releases, social communication, Media Kit, Writing, Press Club and Multimedia among others. The corporate digital newsroom should be easy to use allowing journalists and other visitors to find what they need instantly and ensuring consistency.

In short, corporate digital newsrooms aim to gain control over the facts reported by the organization, seek to achieve greater projection by targeting content for long term references, expand the business' reach quicker than other forms of media, ensure greater longevity of content and media reports because they last in the web, they are a versatile channel/tool because they serve different purposes and guarantee visibility of a great variety of themes and finally they are more cost efficient because they are free to use. For all this, we agree with Keith Childs, manager of digital and new media at Opel Europe, when he says «Newsrooms should be at the heart of the company's online presence. There's no need to have separate social media and 'traditional' newsrooms - they have or should have merged together. Companies need to think about how their news is being consumed.

REFERENCES

Ageeva, E. (2019). A Holistic Framework of Corporate Website Favourability. *Corporate Reputation Review, 25*(5). https://www.researchgate.net/publication/335312535_A_Holistic_Framework_of_Corporate_Website_Favourability

Anderson, C. (2013, May). *Media Ecosystems: Some Notes Toward a Genealogy of the Term and an Application of it to Journalism Research.* Paper prepared for the "ESF Exploratory Workshop on Mapping the digital news ecosystem: Professional journalism, new producers and active audiences in the digital public sphere." Retrieved from: https://www.cwanderson.org/wp-content/uploads/2013/04/EcosystemGenealogy.pdf

Bauman, Z. (2000). *Liquid Modernity*. Polity Press.

Broom, G., & Sha, B.-L. (2012). *Cutlip and Center's Effective Public Relations* (11th ed.). Pearson Education.

Canavilhas, J. (2011). El Nuevo Ecosistema Mediático [The New Media Ecosystem]. *Index - Comunicación, 1*, 13-24. Retrieved from: https://journals.sfu.ca/indexcomunicacion/index.php/indexcomunicacion/article/view/4

Cardoso, G. (2006). *Os Media na Sociedade em Rede* [The Media in the Network Society]. Fundação Calouste Gulbenkian.

Cardoso, G. (2021). Confiança geral nas notícias aumenta bem como importância dos meios regionais [General confidence in the news increases as well as the importance of regional media]. *EJO – European Journalism Observatory*. Retrieved from: https://pt.ejo.ch/jornalismo/confianca-geral-nas-noticias-aumenta-bem-como-importancia-dos-meio-regionais

Cascais, F. (2001). *Dicionário de Jornalismo. As palavras dos media* [Journalism Dictionary. The words of the media]. Editorial Verbo.

Castells, M. (1998). *The Rise of the Network Society*. Blackwell Publishers.

Cerezo, P. (2016). *Los Customer media - Medios líquidos para usuarios hiperconectados* [Customer media - Liquid media for hyperconnected users]. Evoca. Retrieved from: https://evocaimagen.com/dosieres/dosier-evoca-01-customer-media.pdf

Duhé, S. (2012). *New media and Public Relations* (2nd ed.). Peter Lang.

Elola, J. (2010). Entrevista: Rosental C. Alves (consultor Digital de Medios y Catedrático de Periodismo). O Futuro do Periodismo Digital - "Los medios deben aparcar su arrogancia" [Interview: Rosental C. Alves (Digital Media Consultant and Professor of Journalism). The future of Digital Journalism - "The media must park its arrogance"]. *Jornal El País*. Retrieved from: https://elpais.com/diario/2010/09/05/domingo/1283658757_850215.html

Ferreira, J. (2021). *Como está a ser o seu confinamento? 56% dos portugueses dizem que "igual" ou "mais fácil" do que primeiro* [How is your confinement going? 56% of Portuguese say "equal" or "easier" than first]. Eco. Portal Sapo. Retrieved from: https://eco.sapo.pt/2021/03/18/como-esta-a-ser-o-seu-confinamento-56-dos-portugueses-dizem-que-igual-ou-mais-facil-do-que-primeiro/

Ferreira, V. (2019). *Portugal vai ser mais um caso de sucesso do Merco. Jornal Online Vida Económica* [Portugal will be another Merco success story. Online Journal Economic Life]. Retrieved from: https://www.vidaeconomica.pt/vida-economica-1/publicacoes/edicao-num-1793-do-vida-economica-de-12072019/negocios-e-empresas/portugal-vai-ser-mais-um-caso-de-sucesso-do-merco

Fitzgerald, M., Kruschwitz, N., Bonnet, D., & Welch, M. (2014). Embracing digital technology: A new strategic imperative. *MIT Sloan Management Review*, *55*, 1–12.

Galgali, P. (2017, December). *Digital Transformation and its Impact on Organizations' Human Resource Management*. IOR and Stakeholder Management, MCM, School of Communication and Information, Rutgers University. Retrieved from: https://www.academia.edu/35595152/Digital_Transformation_and_its_Impact_on_Organizations_Human_Resource_Management

Harrison, K. (2020). *Make it easy for journalists to find information in your website*. Retrieved from: https://cuttingedgepr.com/make-easy-journalists-find-information-website/

Hepp, A., & Hasebrink, U. (2013). *The communicative figurations of mediatized worlds: Mediatization research in times of the 'mediation of everything'*. Electronic Working Paper | No. 1. University of Bremen. Retrieved from: https://www.kommunikative-figurationen.de/fileadmin/user_upload/Arbeitspapiere/CoFi_EWP_No-1_Hepp.pdf

Hepp, A., & Hasebrink, U. (2013). *Human interaction and communicative figurations. The transformation of mediatized cultures and societies.* Communicative Figurations -Working Paper No. 2. Retrieved from: https://www.semanticscholar.org/paper/Human-interaction-and-communicative-figurations-.-Hepp-Hasebrink/7c092f9dcea75b5ce6aafbf5ab264261e4156e42

Hickin, R., & Bechtel, M. (2021, April). *Technology Futures: Projecting the Possible, Navigating What's Next. Insight Report.* World Economic Forum in collaboration with Deloitte. Retrieved from: https://www3.weforum.org/docs/WEF_Technology_Futures_GTGS_2021.pdf

Holmes, D. (2005). *Communication Theory: Media, Technology, Society*. Sage Publications.

Holmes, D. (2009). New Media Theory. In Encyclopedia of Communication Theory. SAGE Publications.

Howard, C. (2004). Working With Reporters: Mastering The Fundamentals To Build Long-Term Relationships. Public Relations Quarterly, 49(1), 36-39.

Internet 2020: cresce a liderança dos smartphone [Internet 2020: Smartphone leadership grows]. Retrieved from: https://www.marktest.com/wap/a/n/id~269e.aspx

Iwata, J. (2021). *Getting Started in CommTech: From Professional to Pathfinder.* Arthur W. Page Society. Retrieved from: https://commtechguide.page.org/getting-startedincommtech-from-professional-to-pathfinder/a-new-profession-emerges/

Jenkins, H. (2016). *Convergence Culture - Where Old and New Media Collide*. University Press.

Kim, I., & Kuljis, J. (2010). Applying Content Analysis to Web based Content. *Proceedings of the ITI 2010 32nd International Conference on Information Technology Interfaces*. Retrieved from: https://www.researchgate.net/publication/220066206_Applying_Content_Analysis_to_Web-based_Content

Kowal, E. (2021). What Is an Online Newsroom & Why Do You Need One*? Prowly Magazine*. Retrieved from: https://prowly.com/magazine/need-online-newsroom/

Kramp. (2015). *Journalism, representation and the Public Sphere*. Bremen: Edition lumière.

Lévy, P. (1990). *As Tecnologias da Inteligência - O Futuro do Pensamento na Era da Informática* [Intelligence Technologies - The Future of Thinking in the Information Age]. Instituto Piaget.

Lister, M. (2009). *New Media: a critical introduction* (2nd ed.). Routledge.

Lloyd, J., & Toogood, L. (2015). *Journalism and PR. News media and public relations in the digital age. Reuters Institute for the Study of Journalism*. Oxford University.

Michaelson, D., & Stacks, D. (2010). *A Professional and Practitioner's Guide to Public Relations Research, Measurement, and Evaluation.* New York: Business Expert Press.

Middleberg, D. (2001). *Winning PR in the Wired World*. New York: McGraw-Hill.

Neri, A. (2021, June). *Digital Culture Guidebook*. World Economic Forum. Retrieved from: https://www3.weforum.org/docs/WEF_Digital_Culture_Guidebook_2021.pdf

Neto, B. (2019). Newsroom 3.0: Managing Technological and Media Convergence in Contemporary Newsrooms. *Proceedings of the 52nd Hawaii International Conference on System Sciences*. Retrieved from: https://www.researchgate.net/publication/330467967_Newsroom_30_Managing_Technological_and_Media_Convergence_in_Contemporary_Newsrooms

Newman, D. (2017, June 6). How Shifting Communication Trends Are Impacting Digital Transformation. *Forbes*. Retrieved from: https://www.forbes.com/sites/danielnewman/2017/06/06/how-shifting-communication-trends-are-impacting-digital-transformation/#12a070b3408f

Nielsen, R., & Selva, M. (2019). *More Important, But Less Robust? Five Things Everybody Needs to Know about the Future of Journalism*. Reuters Institute Report. Retrieved from: https://reutersinstitute.politics.ox.ac.uk/our-research/more-important-less-robust-five-things-everybody-needs-know-about-future-journalism

Phillips, D., & Young, P. (2009). *Online Public Relations - A Practical Guide to Developing an Online Strategy in the World of Social Media*. Kogan Page.

Pinheiro, J. (2009). Semantic Web: A Network of Concepts. *Cadernos UniFOA, 9*, 23-27. Retrieved from: https://revistas.unifoa.edu.br/index.php/cadernos/article/download/930/854

Porter, M. (2018). *The second Media Age*. John Wiley & Sons.

Ries, L., & Ries, A. (2008). *A queda da Publicidade e a ascensão das Relações-Públicas* [The Fall of Advertising and the Rise of PR] (2ª ed.). Lisboa: Notícias Editorial.

Rose, S. (2016). *12 Features of a Great Site Search Function*. SilverDisc. Retrieved from: https://www.silverdisc.co.uk/blog/2016/02/19/12-features-great-site-search-function

Schwarzmüller, T. (2018). How Does the Digital Transformation Affect Organizations? Key Themes of Change in Work Design and Leadership. *Management Revue - Socio-Economic Studies, 29*(2), 114-138.

Silveirinha, M. J. (2002). *Novos Media, Velhas Questões* [New Media, Old Issues]. BOCC - Biblioteca Online de Ciências da Comunicação. Retrieved from: http://bocc.ufp.pt/pag/silveirinha-maria-joao-novos-media-velhas-questoes.pdf

Soares, T. (2005). Os Meios de Comunicação Social na Internet: Contributos para a Análise Sociológica dos Cibermedia [The Means of Social Communication on the Internet: Contributions to the Sociological Analysis of Cybermedia]. *Livro de actas - 4º SOPCOM*, 1485-1494. Retrieved from: http://www.bocc.ubi.pt/pag/soares-tania-meios-comunicacao-social-internet.pdf

Sodré, M. (2002). *Antropológica do Espelho - Uma Teoria da Comunicação Linear e em Rede* [Mirror Anthropology - A Theory of Linear and Networked Communication]. Editora Vozes.

Stacks, D., & Bowen, S. (2013). *Dictionary of Public Relations Measurement and Research*. IPR Measurement Commission. Institute for Public Relations.

The Online Newsroom Survey Report. (2012). *TekGroup*. Retrieved from: https://www.tekgroup.com/online-newsroom/list-of-things-journalists-expect-in-online-newsroom.htm

Velasquez, A. (2018). From the mass media to social media: reflections on the new media ecology. *Revista Latina de Comunicación Social*, *73*, 583-594. Retrieved from: http://www.revistalatinacs.org/073paper/1270/29en.html

Waddington, S. (2012). *Share This - The Social Media Handbook for PR Professionals*. Wiley. doi:10.1002/9781119207856

Waters, R., Tindall, N., & Morton, T. (2010). Media Catching and the Journalist–Public Relations Practitioner Relationship: How Social Media are Changing the Practice of Media Relations. *Journal of Public Relations Research*, *22*(3), 241–264. doi:10.1080/10627261003799202

Weiner, M. (2021). *PR Technology, Data and Insights - Igniting a Positive return on Your Communications Investment*. Kogan Page.

What's The Story? (n.d.). *The 2013 Newsroom Report: how the world's top 100 brands are using online newsrooms to tell their stories*. MyNewsdesk. Retrieved from: https://pages.mynewsdesk.com/rs/mynewsdesk/images/The%202013%20Newsroom%20Report%20by%20Mynewsdesk.pdf

Whatmough, D. (2019). *Digital PR. PRCA practice guides*. Emerald Publishing Limited.

Wiard, V. (2019). *News Ecology and News Ecosystems. In Oxford Research Encyclopedia of Communication*. Oxford University Press.

Zerfass, A. (2021). *ECM - The European Communication Monitor 2021*. Retrieved from: https://www.communicationmonitor.eu/2021/05/21/ecm-european-communication-monitor-2021/

Chapter 9
Bridging Journalists and PR Practitioners in a Digital Context:
A Good Practice Case Study

Romina Surugiu
https://orcid.org/0000-0003-2731-2058
University of Bucharest, Romania

ABSTRACT

The chapter presents a project that aims at bridging journalists and public relations practitioners in Romania. In the introductory part, the author reflects on the characteristics of the PR-journalism relationship in the historical context. Then, the chapter analyzes several digital challenges that influence the contemporary communication industry. The concept of hybridity between journalism and strategic communication, and the solution of educating journalists in public relations literacy will be unpacked. The empirical research focuses on the case study (the campaign "#RespectJurnalistii" [Respect Journalists], the digital platform "2Value Reporters," and the app "2Value") that is informed by document analysis, participatory observation, and semi-structured interviews with the initiators of the project.

INTRODUCTION

The relationship between journalism and public relations has always been problematic for media practitioners. Journalists and media managers expressed motivated concerns over the public relations domain from its very beginning. While embracing the ideology of objectivity, news values, and public interest, reporters felt that public relations practitioners' efforts to protect public figures and companies' image and reputation were a menace for their professional activity.

As the American sociologist Michael Schudson explained in his book, "Discovering the News. A Social History of American Newspapers" (1978), the public relations agents were criticized – from the early 1900s – for their efforts to present as "news" a content that should have been sold to newspapers as

DOI: 10.4018/978-1-7998-9790-3.ch009

advertising (p. 136). The editors' and journalists' response to public relations was described by Schudson (1966) as "uneasy" ("a mix of distaste, disgust, rivalry, and grim affection"), and "unambiguous" (they were "inevitable enemies") (p. 137).

Referring to the situation of British press in the '60s, Jeremy Tunstall (1971) wrote that public relations' activity of arranging news "events" (quotation marks in original) co-existed with the ideology of facts' disclosure as the primary goal of journalists (p. 72). However, as Tunstall noticed, the work practices of journalists mixed the gathering of news with "'press visits', 'facility trips', or 'junkets'" (p. 72). Tunstall observed that, despite the criticism of public relations in general, journalists preferred to work with organizations that had public relations departments, and they tended to appreciate honesty and productivity from the part of PR practitioners ("by helping specialists [journalists] to cover 'all' the news, to work at speed, to meet deadlines, and to present lively material briefly, public relations has much success", Tunstall, 1971, p. 181).

However, public relations practitioners did not produce such a negative character as it was argued. On the contrary, research by Craig Aronoff in the '70s in the US underlined that public relations practitioners shared the same understanding of news values as journalists did. Yet, while public relations practitioners displayed a positive attitude toward journalists and had confidence in them as a professional guild, the journalists considered PR specialists as "low credibility sources" and had negative feelings toward them (Aronoff, 1975, pp. 54-55).

Other academic studies – covering the '80s and '90s – continued to portray the public relations – journalism relationship as "antagonist" (Ryan & Martinson, 1988) or "colonising" and "destructive" (Moloney, 2000). In a sense, the journalists' critique of public relations could be understood as legitimate, especially if it is linked with the ideal image of the journalist as a mythical defender of objectivity and truth. Nevertheless, this critique ignores the efforts made by the public relations domain to institutionalize, to professionalize, to apply ethical codes, and to respond to the needs and expectations of the public and society, not only to the ones of clients and companies. From this point of view, the work of James E. Grunig and his collaborators toward what they called "Excellence in public relations and communication management" (1992) should be taken into consideration and acknowledged.

Many contemporary voices (L'Etang, 2007, Morris & Goldsworthy, 2012, Gregory, 2015, Koch et al., 2017 *inter al.*) underline the mutually profitable and beneficial relationship between journalism and public relations and open the path to understanding its digital dimension. "Neither journalists, nor PR practitioners see their professions as antagonistic and that both groups are aware that the other side plays an important role in them doing their job", argue Koch *et al.* (2017, p. 11). However, several discourses on the intricate journalism-PR relationship coexist: discourse of denial, discourse of spin, discourse of victimhood, discourse of honest brokers and discourse of symbiosis (Macnamara, 2016).

The contemporary approach to journalism and PR relations has also to take into consideration several aspects related to the digital dimension of media communication such as: (1) the reconfiguration of audience and its digital presence (the quest for interactivity, building a social presence, considering the user's experience and participation), (2) the emerging technological capabilities (the introduction of new tools, apps, devices), (3) the ever-growing importance of social media and its diverse and innovative possibilities of communication, and (4) the new features of the communication industry (the global decline of trust in journalists and media, and the emerging strategies of content integration, embedded marketing, native advertising).

This chapter's aim is to present and critically assess: the characteristics of the PR-journalism relationship in the context of digital communication challenges, the concept of hybridity in relation to journalism and public relations, and to unpack the concept of "educating journalists in public relations literacy" (Macnamara, 2020). The chapter will then focus on presenting a good practice case study from Romania, the campaign "#RespectJurnalistii" [Respect Journalists], the digital platform "2Value Reporters" and the app "2Value". The empirical research is informed by document analysis, participatory observation, and semi-structured interviews with the initiators of the project.

PUBLIC RELATIONS, JOURNALISM, AND THE CHALLENGES OF DIGITAL COMMUNICATION

For journalism and public relations, the digital world came with the destruction of the myth about the control of the flow of information, as Grunig (2009) has argued. Communication professionals and journalists had previously shared the idea that they can exert power through messages transmitted by their organizations. "Anyone now can be a journalist, members of the public can talk freely to each other about organisations, and information is widely available to everyone with little cost and effort", explained Grunig (2009, p. 4).

Although Grunig (2009) considered that the control of messages was an illusion even before the advent of new technologies, one can observe a clear shift in digital communication, a rupture from the analogical world. This rupture has technological roots (relying on the possibilities of the new media and social media to produce, store, share, modify, etc., content) and social roots (with a focus on communities and users' experience and participation).

The web 2.0 is characterized by a "radical decentralization, radical trust, participation instead of publishing, users as contributors, rich user experience, the long tail, the web as platform, control of one's own data, remixing data, collective intelligence, attitudes, better software by more users, play, undetermined user behaviour" (Tim O'Reilly, quoted by Fuchs, 2014, p. 32). The idea of the "unlimited", "rich" participation of users to Internet and social media belongs to an ideology that should be always critically analysed (Fuchs, 2014). However, its reality cannot be ignored by communication specialists. Users and their attitudes toward products and messages are in the centre of traditional and experimental research studies that focus on media use, social interactions, users' experience (UX), the mix between production and consumption (prosumers), and also on forms of resistance and contestation.

For Grunig (2009), the new digital media (with their "dialogical, interactive, relational, and global properties") offer the possibility for PR practitioners to enter the "strategic management paradigm of public relations", i.e., to abandon the "traditional one-way, message-oriented, asymmetrical and ethnocentric paradigm of practice" and to adopt the two-way symmetrical model of communication. One condition is that PR practitioners stop using the new media "in the old way", and focus on the possibilities to broaden "the number and types of media and communication activities and fits them into a framework of research and listening", developing messages that "reflect the information needs of publics as well as the advocacy needs of organisations" (Grunig, 2009, p. 9). Moreover, PR practitioners should make use of the digital tools available at present, such as: communication programmes (from social media use to online meetings), environmental scanning (using the cyberspace to identify issues important for the public and for organizations), segmenting stakeholders and publics, anticipating and dealing with issues and crises, measuring relationships and reputation, and evaluation of communication programmes (see Grunig, 2009, pp. 13-15).

On the other hand, PR companies have to look closely to their traditional partner, media, which is confronted nowadays with a global decline of trust, which could make room for fake news or conspiracy theories. The levels of trust differ from one country or region to another, but it is clear that public support diminished in the last decades (van Dalen, 2020, p. 356). A low level of trust undermines the legitimacy of the press and the watchdog function, allows politicians and governmental institutions to make decisions without the media to hold them accountable, increases polarization and extremism in society, and encourages biased narratives (such as fake news) (van Dalen, 2020, p. 363-365). One possible ethical dilemma of the situation described above is the possibility of PR practitioners to take advantage of the "journalistic defenselessness", and of the journalists' lack of resources to organize professional agencies as "newsrooms" of corporate communication (Iturregui-Mardaras *et al.*, 2020, p. 10).

From this point of view, the hybridity between media and PR, advertising or marketing, conceived as a mixture between journalism practice and strategic communication does not encourage the audience to trust the journalists and the media institutions. Media is nowadays confronted with the emerging strategies of content integration, embedded marketing, and native advertising.

"The integration of media and advertising is not new but it is intensifying", argues Hardy (2022, p. 4), explaining that this is possible as a result not only of technological conditions (which make possible the convergence across digital platforms), but also of the pressure of brand communication (which sponsors, co-creates, and tries to exercise full control on content). Other authors (Ghorbanzadeh, 2020, Koch *et al.*, 2021) critically assess the hybridity between the journalism and communication industries, be it PR, advertising or marketing, which takes the shape of "brand journalism". The brand journalism places itself at a crossroads between journalism and strategic communication, and could encourage "role conflicts", between journalists and communication professionals (Koch *et al.*, 2021).

To sum up, there is growing evidence that the digital dimension brings disruptive transformation to the field of media and communication. It triggers changes in journalistic and PR professional practice, undermining traditional ways of action or procedures. The keywords in describing the current situation of media are "emerging", "disruptive", "challenge", "pressure", "polarization" and "extremism". It is a period characterized by uncertainty, and reconfiguration, and the prognosis is rather negative, with many reasons for a skeptical approach.

EDUCATING JOURNALISTS AND PR PRACTITIONERS

The analyse of the "problematic and paradoxical" relation between journalists and public relations practitioners, led Jim Macnamara (2020, p. 350) to four major themes of reflection for the future of both professions: (1) transparency – which has to replace negative discourses of journalists vs. PR, and the unethical persuasion actions of PR practitioners, (2) educating journalists to properly understand public relations as practice and industry, (3) educating PR practitioners in ethics and social responsibility and (4) further research on the main area of interest and concern both for journalists and PR practitioners: native advertising, content marketing, brand journalism, ethics, public interest, and, last but not least, the fake news phenomenon.

For the present chapter, it is of interest to unpack the concept of educating journalists in public relations literacy (Macnamara, 2016, Macnamara, 2020). Jim Macnamara (2020) uses the concept of "public relations literacy" via Holladay and Coombs (2013) who described it as an empowerment of the public by the use of knowledge and evaluation tools needed to identify the good and bad practices in public relations (p. 143).

Holladay and Coombs (2013) openly address the "strong persuasive aspect" of public relations, which in their opinion should be clearly recognized by the profession and by academics. "When a public relations message appears in a legacy news story, the message appears to be coming from the news media rather than the public relations source" explain Holladay and Coombs (2013, p. 133). Similar to media literacy, public relations literacy – argue Holladay and Coombs, 2013 – includes the understanding of PR messages as "constructions" (not simple reflections of reality) with a purpose. The public should be educated to look for sources of messages, and to reflect on the motivations and values behind the strategic communication: "Public relations messages are strategic; they reflect the particular values and goals of their source and are designed to influence people." (Holladay and Coombs, 2013, p. 129).

Although Holladay and Coombs (2013) aimed in their article to argue for the importance of public relations literacy for the public, the discussion is also of interest for the journalists-PR practitioner's relationship. In this sense, Macnamara (2020) considers that by educating journalists to understand the importance and also the shortcomings of the PR industry, the discourse of denial toward PR will be downplayed. By understanding how PR work, journalists will increase their capacity to identify, analyse and critically asses the messages and the actions of the communication industry. In addition, stereotypes and prejudices about public relations will be minimized.

The journalists' education in public relations literacy is not the only solution to forge a better relation between journalism and PR. At the same, the education of PR practitioners in regard to ethics and social responsibility is also needed. Macnamara (2020, p. 350) underlines the following: "concept of social responsibility should be expanded to address the increasing role of PR practitioners in the contemporary public sphere through social media and digital communication including the practices of native advertising, content marketing, and brand journalism". PR practitioners should also focus their professional development in order to develop the industry in an ethical and responsible way.

The educational role of public relations is part of the "core of advanced public relations capabilities" (Verčič *et al.*, 2001, in Ruão, Fernández-Souto, 2020, p. 9), and should be taken into consideration for "the construction of socially relevant standards and values and for the communicative education of internal publics in contemporary organizations, as citizens within our communities" (Ruão, Fernández-Souto, 2020, p. 9). By educating journalists and the general public in public relations literacy, the companies build a stronger social dimension, and better integrate in their communities.

Moreover, the focus on public relations literacy becomes even more important in the digital context of the present-day communication industry. The companies' efforts to educate the public and journalists challenges the skeptical approach related to the media and communication current state in the disruptive online climate.

METHODOLOGY

This study is based on a case study research, developed in Romania, between July and October 2021. The methodological approach was chosen based on Yin (2009) and Hartley (2004) contributions to the understanding of case studies in an organizational context.

Previous research conducted in Romania was quantitative, and substantiated their results on questionnaires applied to journalists and/or PR practitioners (Dolea, 2012, Grasu et al., 2014).

The present research chooses as its unit of analysis a public relations company (Tudor Communication) and its projects (the campaign "#RespectJurnalistii", the digital platform "2Value Reporters" and the app "2Value") used to create a mutually beneficial and positive relation between journalists, PR practitioners and small and medium-sized companies. As the research takes into consideration an organization, and its projects, the more appropriate research strategy was to build an exploratory single-case research (see Hartley, 2004).

To ensure the construct validity (Yin, 2009, p. 41), the findings are drawn from multiple sources of evidence: document analysis (the websites and Facebook page of the project: https://2value.ro/, https://2valuereporters.ro, FB 2ValueApp), participant observation of the online trainings organized by the company, and four semi-structured interviews: two with the representatives of the company (Tudor Communication), and two with trainers who facilitated training sessions for journalists. The interviews were conducted on e-mail (n=3) and by phone (n=1), and had 11 questions that referred to the ideal and present relationship between journalists and PR practitioners, the description of the project (objectives, stakeholders, beneficiaries, expected results), and the influence of the digital environment. One key informant reviewed the draft of the case study and formulated remarks.

The documents, the observation notes and the transcription of the interviews were analysed inductively in order to identify the motivations, the rationale, the practices, and the possible effects of the project.

The study explores four research questions:

1. What are the motivations for a PR company to create bridges between journalists and PR practitioners?
2. What strategies could be used by a PR company to encourage mutually beneficial collaboration between journalists and PR practitioners?
3. How does the social responsibility dimension of the company relate to the business side?
4. How is the digital dimension included in the analysed project?

The limitation of the study consists in its focus on the company and its projects, motivated by the descriptive feature of the present research. However, for a continuation of this case study, following an explanatory approach, a necessary addition would be a questionnaire applied to the journalists who took part in the trainings. Also a gender perspective related to the influence of women in PR practice would be of interest for future research.

BRIDGING JOURNALISTS AND PR PRACTITIONERS: FINDINGS AND DISCUSSIONS

The campaign #RespectJurnalistii [Respect Journalists] and the digital platform "2Value Reporters" were launched on November 2019 by a PR, communication, and branding company from Romania (Tudor Communication). Founded in 2012, Tudor Communication is a small size company, based on Romanian capital, and led by a woman with entrepreneurial skills and with experience in the fields of journalism, public relations and strategy – Mihaela Raluca Tudor (Paul, 2016).

The aim of "#RespectJurnalistii" is to build a community of Romanian journalists interested in acquiring new skills for digital communication and the practice of quality journalism (2Value Reporters, 2020).

The campaign is designed to respond to the need of Romania journalism to overcome the obstacles of media based on sensationalism, manipulation of facts and fake news. Also, the campaign takes into consideration that social media and other alternative sources aspire. and in many cases succeed, to take the place of journalism, without being able to replace the quality of journalism. The campaign's initiators observed that in Romania newsrooms have fewer and fewer full time journalists. The journalists are suffering because of important time pressures and incredible workloads, and this situation prevents them from doing fieldwork, face-to-face interviews and quality reporting (M. R. Tudor, interview (by e-mail), October 12, 2021; D. Palade Teodorescu, interview (by e-mail), October 11, 2021.

Also, another trend observed by the campaign's organizers is that print media is in decline, and many outlets closed down in the last ten years. Many journalists had to find another work place in the field, and for this they needed new skills – digital skills. Moreover, journalists from all types of media suffer from the lack of professional recognition and wanted to be part of a respected trade.

"The newsrooms have fewer and fewer journalists, which are overwhelmed by a multitude of tasks. Time and workload have become a very important challenge. Online events have solved the problem of in situ participation, but journalists remain extremely selective with the events they participate in, which leads to a decrease in their visibility. Hence a decrease in their recognition on the market, later translated into stagnation or declining revenues and increasing frustrations.

The excessive marketization of information and the avalanche of fake news increase the distrust on both sides of the barricade: journalists and companies. The fragmentation of communication media and the explosion of social networks have changed mass communication" (D. Palade Teodorescu, interview (by e-mail), October 11, 2021).

As a matter of fact, recent research projects carried out in Romania identified the diminishing credibility of journalists, the media agenda influenced by political or economic interests, the (self) censorship of journalists, the lack of media ethics, the de-professionalization of the field, as the main characteristics of national and local media systems (CJI, 2015, Avadani, 2017, Lupu, 2021). Precariousness, poor working conditions, and economic vulnerability affect both journalists and media institutions (Apostol, 2018, Popescu *et al.*, 2021)

Moreover, journalists in Romania are skeptical of the possibility of joining trade unions which they do not consider to be powerful institutions that could offer protection to media professionals (Ghinea & Mungiu-Pippidi, 2010, 326, Surugiu, 2016). Local media is captured by political forces that put pressure on journalists and media outlets (FreeEx, 2014).

From the technological point of view, media is caught in the middle of a disruptive process of digitalization and the use of artificial intelligence, so journalists need access to information and skills to anchor themselves in the midst of these disruptive changes. "Both sides [journalists and PR practitioners] face a common threat and challenge – Data & Digital – to which they must adapt quickly. In the VUCAD context (volatility, uncertainty, complexity, ambiguity, diversity, disruption), technology rewrites the way in which communication takes place in journalism and, also, in public relations." (D. Palade Teodorescu, interview (by e-mail), October 11, 2021).

The campaign's idea was to build a community of journalists relevant to their field of activity, who communicate their activity honestly and transparently. This community of journalists should be linked by networking to the business environment, in direct contact with company representatives. The motivation of the community of journalists is to encourage good practices in journalism, that is a journalism without fake news, dubious sources, unverified or truncated information, or sensationalism (2Value Reporters, 2020).

The platform "2Value Reporters" was launched through an awareness-raising campaign which consisted of public events, press releases, interviews given by the representatives of Tudor Communication, a webpage, https://2valuereporters.ro, and an active social media presence, Linkedin, Facebook, Youtube.

The awareness-raising campaign underlined two key messages: the support and training for quality journalism, and the previous experience as journalists of the representatives of Tudor Communication. One example is the video interview with the manager and CEO of Tudor Communication, Mihaela Raluca Tudor, broadcasted by paginademedia.ro, a well-known Romanian website and platform specialized in media and communication industry. The video is accompanied by a headline and a lead paragraph which present the project as follows:

"#RespectJurnalistii. A campaign for journalists, started by a former journalist (…), now a PR practitioner. What does it aim for? (…) 'To sound the alarm on the problems faced by media because of time constraints, lack of funds for newsrooms, because of managerial abuses, the declining confidence of society in journalists, political pressures and the fragile trade union solidarity, and, also, because of the inefficiency of associations representing the rights of professional [journalists].'" (Bambu, 2019)

In January 2020, the project founded the Academy of Journalists that organized - on a regular basis and with no participation fee - professional and personal development trainings supported by top trainers in the communication industry or business, and also by experienced journalists. The trainings were mainly organized online (on the Zoom platform), as the campaign was launched near the outbreak of the COVID-19 pandemic, and were also offered during the state of emergency (which lasted in Romania between March and May, 2020).

Between January 2020 and September 2021, 22 training sessions for journalists were organized; one was face-to-face and 21 were online. The topics covered four major areas of interest for journalists: (1) media (and social media) developments (video and mobile journalism, SEO); (2) professional practice (interviewing techniques, investigative journalism, fake news exposure, public speaking techniques), (3) entrepreneurial skills (sales, leadership, networking) and (4) personal development (resilience, adaptation, decision-making techniques, lifelong learning). (https://2valuereporters.ro/calendar-traininguri-gratuite/)

More than 200 professional journalists and students in media and communication attended the training sessions. The journalists belonged to the Romanian national and local media and work for a variety of media institutions: news agencies, newspapers, online publications, glossy magazines, television stations, radio stations, based in the capital city, Bucharest and in other important cities and towns such as: Iaşi, Constanţa, Cluj, Timişoara, Braşov, Baia Mare, and Reşiţa. (D. Palade Teodorescu, interview by e-mail, October 12, 2021).

According to an internal analysis made by the company, the average participant to the trainings is 35 years old, with at least 10 years' experience as a journalist. Two thirds of the participants are from the capital city Bucharest and one third from other cities of Romania. The journalists belong to public radio (approx. 30 percent), and online media (approx. 30 percent). The least represented media outlets are print media, television and alternative media. Also, specialist journalists are rarely present, the majority of the participants belonging to national mainstream media (D. Palade Teodorescu, personal communication, December 28, 2021).

One important advantage of the online trainings was the possibility to join journalists from national and local media in professional debates over the situation of Romanian media. Moreover, they gave the local media representatives from distant locations (400-500 km from Bucharest) the possibility to meet top trainers from the capital city.

All trainers offered their services *pro bono*. One of the trainers, a former journalist who specialized in human resources development and business consultancy, pointed out that *pro bono* involvement represents a constant presence in her professional activity and that it is of great importance for the society to have strong professional communities.

"I think it is important to recognize that each of us, regardless of profession, must develop continuously and to do our best by constantly networking with people from our own profession, but also from other professions. In what regards this project, it is important for journalists and PR practitioners to discover common points of interest and to analyse together different aspects of society, both at the grassroots and in organizations. The role of the media has always been complex one - finding out the truth, signalling problematic aspects, but also providing positive examples, giving a voice to the public (...), watchdog. At the same time, society can have a real dialogue with the business people that we all want to be more and more involved in communities. What I want to say is that I see the role of the PR professional not only as a person responsible for the image of a company - as it is perceived by people and media –, but also as a useful interface that permanently translates the pulse of society (...) for the represented organizations. The PR professionals, like the journalists, should promote values inside and outside the organizations they represent." (D. Voicu, interview (by e-mail), October 8, 2021).

Another trainer, a journalist specialized in investigation, explained his willingness to offer a *pro bono* session by underlining the necessity for journalists to learn or update the "tools of the trade" from other professionals in a relaxed and friendly environment ("with calm and patience"). (A. Nedea, interview by phone, October 6, 2021)

From the perspective of trainers, the participants to the trainings – journalists and students in Media and Communication - have also the opportunity to network with fellow colleagues and to reconsider their opinion on PR.

The participants enjoyed the partnership and support, and they were happy to discuss, to work and to network with colleagues and, perhaps, they also understood that PR is not only concerned with embellishing with golden embroidery the company's image (...) - but it does produce added value responsibly, both for the journalists and for the public. (D. Voicu, interview (by e-mail), October 8, 2021).

In addition to the trainings, the project organized the "Media Responsibility Month" (May 2020), that consisted of online talk shows and interviews with renowned journalists on the state of media during pandemic. In May 2021, the journalists were offered the possibility to join workshops led by international coaches during the International Coaching Week "Defying Challenging Times." All the events and trainings were organized with zero budget, with the sustained effort of the Tudor Communication team and its partners. The impact of the campaign exceeded the expectations of the organizers: more than 200 journalists as active participants in the trainings and 100,000 viewers of the recordings of the training sessions on different social media platforms. In two years, the project managed to form a community of active journalists, who may pass on to their colleagues from the newsrooms the skills and information acquired during the training sessions. The aim of the project for the future is also to facilitate the organization of an international association dedicated to quality journalism (D. Palade Teodorescu, interview by e-mail, October 11, 2021).

As a recognition for the quality of the campaign "#RespectJurnalistii", Tudor Communication was awarded the prize "Best Communication in the Public Sector" by "Romanian PR award 2020".

In addition to the campaign, Tudor Communication also developed in 2019 an innovative digital app "2Value", which gives companies with no public relations department the possibility to produce PR tools (such as press releases). 2Value is described by the company as being "an app that creates synergy between companies and journalists, automatically offering them the first virtualized space for standardized communication, with information value. 2Value thus gives power to SMEs … and offer the journalists valuable information about the business world" (M. R. Tudor, interview by e-mail, October 12, 2021).

The app offers small and medium-sized companies relevant and highly accessible media content, written by journalists, as well as access to relevant communities and multiple tools to write their own press releases, interviews or events. For these services, the companies have to pay a monthly fee. By using the app, the companies have the possibility of sending quality content directly to journalists. On their turn, journalists have free unlimited access to the content generated by the app. Basically, access to the platform is possible by creating an account that is free for journalists. They have filters at their disposal to help them quickly find news in their areas of interest (M. R. Tudor, interview by e-mail, October 12, 2021).

The app could be considered the business side of the project, that focuses on the SMEs in an effort to convince them of the necessity of developing professional public relations campaigns.

"The 2Value platform valorises the SMEs, this engine of the economy which, unfortunately, is not stimulated to reach its greatest potential. 2Value concretely helps entrepreneurs to promote themselves in a context in which SMEs are often ignored by the press, but still need promotion. Many entrepreneurs have moved their business online - in part or in full. 2Value thus becomes a bridge that reinvents the way journalists and entrepreneurs communicate". (M. R. Tudor, interview (by e-mail), October 12, 2021).

The SMEs' representatives were also offered the possibility to take part in a training session specially organized for entrepreneurs. The impact of the training sessions for entrepreneurs was also important: tens of participants in physical presence trainings and more than 25,000 views on live transmissions on 2Value and TUDOR Communication Facebook pages. The online talk shows (the 2ValueTALKS debates and Brands that Value interviews) mediatized the voice of business professionals who talked about the importance of values in business. "We are practically a new form of media, with clear values in everything we do, and oriented towards education" argued the initiator of the project, M. R. Tudor (interview (by e-mail), October 12, 2021).

In 2021, the app continued to be developed and improved by the help of the InnovX-BCR bootcamp (aimed at innovative startups) and by the partnership with Women in Tech. "2value" app was also nominated for the Webstock Awards 2021 competition, Best Applications section. The next step in developing the application is the internationalization of the platform. (M. R. Tudor, interview (by e-mail), October 12, 2021).

The case study identified that the need to have reliable communication partners in the media companies was the motivation for the PR company to create bridges between journalists and PR practitioners. A strong journalistic community would ensure not only quality journalism for the public, but also a stronger and healthier business environment, one that communicates efficiently with media and the consumers.

The analysed company chose to involve itself in building a community of journalists by organizing free trainings and other related events that encouraged journalists to develop professionally, but also to understand better the work of PR companies. The novelty and the social relevance of the "#RespectJurnalistii" / "2ValueReporters" project were publicly acknowledged by the PR community in Romania (see *supra* the information of the prize offered by the "Romanian PR award 2020").

In this respect, it is important to underline that the social responsibility dimension of the company is accompanied by a business side, that focused on the development of an application to be used by SMEs companies. The digital dimension of the project is clearer in the application that uses the digital resources in an innovative way, and that allows the development of an international business. Nevertheless, the training activities for journalists also make use of the digital infrastructure. The pandemic context accelerated the acceptance of online meetings and also revealed the new possibilities brought by new technologies. The recordings of all the online meetings are available on YouTube, and can be accessed by journalists and students in Media and Communication as learning tools.

CONCLUSION

The campaign "#RespectJurnalistii" and the digital platform "2Value Reporters" are examples of good practice in bridging journalists and PR practitioners in the digital world. The project's initiators are former journalists who – according to their statements – "converted" themselves into public relations practitioners. In developing the PR business, they closely analysed the situation of media in the national and digital context, and identified structural problems (such as underfinancing of media or the economic and political pressures over journalists) that affect the socio-professional status of journalists and influence their receptivity to cover events and get involved in business coverage.

At the same time, the project's initiators observed that small and medium size companies need support in organizing the communication campaigns and have to professionalize in developing messages for media (e.g. press releases). Also, as it was underlined by one of the trainers from the program, the whole society would benefit if strong professional organizations existed in media and in business.

The campaign "#RespectJurnalistii" was involved in creating and mobilizing a community of journalists. The main activities were to organize professional debates and regular training sessions. The PR company that organized everything *pro bono* acted as facilitator and moderator of the meetings. From this point of view, it can be characterized as a Social Responsibility Campaign aimed at supporting quality journalism, professional journalists, and the development of a democratic society. The PR company argues that this initiative is unique at the national level, and from a certain point of view this information is accurate (no other company organized for journalists so many events, on a regular basis). Nevertheless, other companies from Romania support the media by offering prizes and trainings for professional journalists.

The second project, "2Value" app, was meant to encourage SMEs to develop professional PR campaigns and to allocate funds in their budget for communication and marketing. The representatives of the companies are offered the possibility to opt for different types of subscriptions for the app that automatically generate PR content, while journalists get the information (under the form of press releases) for free.

The campaign "#RespectJurnalistii", the platform "2ValueReporters" and the project "2Value" make use of the advantages of digital communication (platforms for sharing content, digital communication programs, scanning the environment at accessible costs). They can be seen as part of the effort to educate journalists, and also business managers in "public relations literacy" (Holladay, and Coombs, 2013, Macnamara 2020). From this point of view, the campaign and the project could also be considered as activities that belong to "advanced public relations" (Ruão, Fernández-Souto, 2020), which require a combination of the use of new technologies with understanding the power of education for enhancing the social role of public relations in the 21 century.

ACKNOWLEDGMENT

The author would like to express her gratitude to Elizabeth DuVerlie who proofread this text.

REFERENCES

Apostol, N. (2018). *Dimensiune de gen si munca in journalism* [Gender and work dimension of journalism]. Editura Universitatii din Bucuresti.

Aronoff, C. (1975). Credibility of public relations for journalists. *Public Relations Review*, *1*(2), 45–56.

Avadani, I. (2017). Of Journalists and Money: The Employment of Journalists in Romania and its Influence on Media Freedom and Quality. *International Journal of Communication*, *11*, 1975–1997.

Bambu, R. (2019, November 15). *Interviu Video. Campanie #Respectjurnaliştii. Cine a lansat-o şi ce-şi propune?* [Video Interview. #Respectjurnaliştii Campaign. Who launched it and what's the aim?]. https://www.paginademedia.ro/2019/11/interviu-video-campanie-respect-jurnalistii-cine-a-lansat-o-si-ce-si-propune/

CJI (Centrul pentru Jurnalism Independent). (2015). *Starea sectorului mass-media din România în 2014 - Vulnerabilități și posibile soluții* [The status of the mass media sector in Romania in 2014 – Vulnerabilities and possible solutions]. CJI&Centras.

Dolea, A. (2012). Institutionalizing government public relations in Romania after 1989. *Public Relations Review*, *38*(2), 354–366.

Evans, T. (2010). We are all in PR now. *British Journalism Review*, *21*(2), 31–36. doi:10.1177/0956474810374531

FreeEx. (2014). *Harta politică a televiziunilor locale* [The Political Mapping of the Local TV stations]. FreeEx, Active Watch, Agenția de Monitorizare a Presei.

Fuchs, C. (2014). Social Media: A critical introduction. *Sage (Atlanta, Ga.)*.

Ghinea, C., & Avadani, I. (2011, December). *Does media policy promote media freedom and independence? The case of Romania*. Hertie School of Governance (HERTIE).

Ghorbanzadeh, K. (2020). L'agence de communication, une rédaction comme une autre ? Interroger la frontière entre information et communication au prisme des routines de travail [The communication agency, a newsroom like any other? Questioning the boundary between information and communication through the lens of work routines]. *Questions de Communication*, *38*, 351-370.

Grasu, N., Tasențe, T., & Sandu, M. (2014). Perception of Journalists on the Role of Public Relations. *Acta Universitatis Danubius*, *8*(2), 54–68.

Gregory, A. (2015). *Planning and managing public relations campaigns a strategic approach* (4th ed.). Kogan Page.

Grunig, J. E. (Ed.). (1992). *Excellence in public relations and communication management*. Lawrence Erlbaum Associates.

Grunig, J. E. (2009). Paradigms of global public relations in an age of digitalisation. *Prism*, *6*(2). http://praxis.massey.ac.nz/prism_on-line_journ.html

Hardy, J. (2022). *Branded content. The fateful merging of media and marketing*. Routledge.

Hartley, J. (2004). Case study research. In C. Cassell & G. Symon (Eds.), *Essential Guide to Qualitative Methods in Organizational Research* (pp. 323–333). Sage.

Holladay, S. J., & Coombs, W. T. (2013). Public relations literacy: Developing critical consumers of public relations. *Public Relations Inquiry*, *2*(2), 125–146.

Iturregui-Mardaras, L., Gutiérrez-Cuesta, J.-J., & Cantalapiedra-González, M.-J. (2020). Journalists and Public Relations professionals: From influence and dependence to journalistic disintermediation. *El Profesional de la Información*, *29*(3). https://doi.org/10.3145/epi.2020.may.20

Koch, T., Obermaier, M., & Riesmeyer, C. (2017). Powered by public relations? Mutual perceptions of PR practitioners' bases of power over journalism. *Journalism*, 1–17. doi:10.1177/1464884917726421

Koch, T., Viererbl, B., & Schulz-Knappe, C. (2021). How much journalism is in brand journalism? How brand journalists perceive their roles and blur the boundaries between journalism and strategic communication. *Journalism*. Advance online publication. doi:10.1177/14648849211029802

L'Etang, J. (2008). Public Relations – Concepts, Practice and Critique. *Sage (Atlanta, Ga.)*.

Lupu, C. (2021). *Journalism: An obstacle race, with fewer and fewer winners*. Center for Independent Journalism.

Macnamara, J. (2016). The Continuing Convergence of Journalism and PR: New Insights for Ethical Practice from a Three-Country Study of Senior Practitioners. *Journalism & Mass Communication Quarterly*, *93*(1), 118–141.

Macnamara, J. (2020). Journalism, Public Relations and Spin. In K. Wahl-Jorgensen & T. Hanitzsch (Eds.), *The Handbook of Journalism Studies* (2nd ed., pp. 341–355). Routledge.

Moloney, K. (2000). *Rethinking Public Relations: The Spin and the Substance*. Routledge.

Morris, T., & Goldsworthy, S. (2012). *PR Today – the authoritative guide to public relations*. Palgrave Macmillan.

Paul, A. (2016). *Forța economică a femeilor* [The economic force of women]. Polirom.

Popescu, M., Bodea, R., & Toma, R. (2021). Monitoring Media Pluralism in the Digital Era. Application of the Media Pluralism Monitor in the European Union, Albania, Montenegro, The Republic of North Macedonia, Serbia & Turkey in the year 2020. Country report: Romania. Center for Independent Journalism.

reporters. (2020). *Cine suntem* [Who are we?]. https://2valuereporters.ro/cine-suntem/

Ruão, T., Fernández-Souto, A. B., (2020). Advanced public relations: enhancing a reflexive and educational approach. *Comunicação e Sociedade*, 9-15.

Ryan, M., & Martinson, D. L. (1988). Journalists and Public Relations Practitioners: Why the Antagonism? *The Journalism Quarterly*, *65*(1), 131–140.

Schudson, M. (1978). *Discovering the News: a social history of American newspapers*. Basic Books.

Surugiu, R. (2016). The Fragile Professional Identities of Digital Journalists in Romania. In J. Webster & K. Randle (Eds.), *Virtual Workers and the Global Labour Market* (pp. 179–198). Palgrave Macmillan.

Tunstall, J. (1971). *Journalists at Work: specialist correspondents: their news organizations, news sources, and competitor-colleagues*. Constable London.

Van Dalen, A. (2020). Journalism, Trust, and Credibility. In K. Wahl-Jorgensen & T. Hanitzsch (Eds.), *The Handbook of Journalism Studies* (2nd ed., pp. 356–371). Routledge.

Yin, R. K. (2009). *Case Study Research. Design and Methods* (4th ed.). Sage.

Section 4

Chapter 10
Empathic Brands:
Proposing a Model for Its Measure and Evaluation

Alexandre Duarte
https://orcid.org/0000-0002-2665-864X
CECS, Universidade do Minho, Portugal

Mafalda Sotto Mayor Gregório
Universidade Católica Portuguesa, Portugal

ABSTRACT

In a world where brands are becoming ever more ubiquitous, competition is increasing, and consumers are, every day, more demanding, creating and maintaining powerful, emotional, and reciprocal relationships between brands and their stakeholders is no longer just an ambition, but an imperative call. This can potentially be accomplished by focusing on a brand purpose that consumers identify with and can be stimulated through the creation of unique and distinct experiences and by the development of interpersonal feelings, such as empathy. This chapter proposes a new model for measuring and evaluating brand empathy. For this study, the automotive sector was chosen to test the proposed model. Through a quantitative study, divided into two periods, the awareness of the automotive brands was evaluated, after which the proposed model was applied. This investigation concluded that the majority of automotive industry are characterized by consumers as not very empathetic, as well as the advertising campaigns created by these brands.

INTRODUCTION

With the increasing number of brands, it has become fundamental that each one finds its own space, in order to stand out from their competitors, develop a reciprocal identification with its stakeholders and built strong and long-lasting relationships. In the pursuit of this goal, many brands attempted to humanize not only themselves, but also the products they produce through communication (Golossenko, Pillai & Aroean, 2020). This phenomenon is commonly called "anthropomorphism". The way brand anthropo-

DOI: 10.4018/978-1-7998-9790-3.ch010

morphism changes consumers judgements and behaviors has been subject of extensive research in the consumer behavior field (Kim & McGill, 2011).

In its identity construction, beyond the physical and visual aspects, brands need to be recognized as a set of ideas, values, feelings and personality, among others (Chandler & Owen, 2002; Lindon, Lendrevie, Lévy, Dionísio, & Rodrigues, 2004). This is where empathy fits in. Hoffman (2008, p. 440) defined empathy as "an emotional state triggered by another's emotional state or situation, in which one feels what the other feels or would normally be expected to feel in the same situation."

The perception of brands as "humans" has increased considerably recently, with several authors labelling it "brand anthropomorphism" and other scholars demonstrating that is possible to understand the existing and growing relationship between brands humanization and the empathy generated by them for consumers (Chen, 2017).

Through humanization and personalization of the brand, consumers proceed understanding them as their partners, originating a closer, deeper, lasting, empathic, social, emotional and loving relationship (Fournier, 1998; Puzakova, Kwak & Rocereto, 2009; Rauschnabel & Ahuvia, 2014; Yang et al., 2019). This means that brands that behave as humans will have a bigger chance to be successful, since "brands create value for organizations" and "one way to enhancing that value is through brand anthropomorphism" (Portal, Abratt & Bendixen, 2018, p. 367).

Despite this growing perception, this theme has not been studied further within the Marketing and Advertising field.

This study tries to deepen the knowledge one consumer's relationship with brands, in a way that brands are positioned not only as service providers or carriers of the symbolism of products, but rather as entities within which consumers feel some kind of concern and interpersonal relationship.

This way, the authors propose the creation of an instrument for measurement and evaluation of empathy in brands, applied to the automotive industry in Portugal.

Starting from the research question: "*In what way automotive brands can be considered empathic for consumers?*" a positioning model was developed to rank the automotive brands, so that one can perceive the level of empathy they generate on their consumers.

ANTHROPOMORPHISM

The greek words "anthropos" and "morphe" (respectively "human" and "form") created the word "anthropomorphism", which is the representation of mental and physical characteristics, intensions and objectives, motivations, desires, feelings and human emotions in non-human objects, whether real or imaginary (Delgado-Ballester, Palazón & Pelaez-Muñoz, 2017; Yang, Aggarwal & McGill, 2019; Waytz, Cacioppo & Epley, 2010). But one should not confuse this concept with animism. Although commonly used as synonyms, animism is the simple attribution of life to a non-living entity (Epley, Waytz & Cacioppo, 2007). Meaning, attributing human characteristics to a non-human object (animism) is different than seeing these objects as complete human beings (anthropomorphism) (Puzakova et al., 2009).

Brands Anthropomorphism

It's increasingly frequent that brands are no longer seen as a set of meanings and are now observed as living entities (Kniazeva & Belk, 2010), with who consumers can interact, communicate or even connect to build long-term relationships (Kaufmann, Filho, Silva & Monteiro, 2019). Among researchers and marketing professionals, there is the belief that brands can be understood as humans (Guido & Peluso, 2015) and research has shown that by associating human characteristics to brands and/or to their products, they become active players in the consumer experience, standing out significantly from those who are observed only as objects (Yang et al., 2019). This way, brand anthropomorphism becomes an increasingly valued perception amongst marketing professionals and organizations (Aggarwal & McGill, 2007).

MacInnis & Folkes (2017) explain the "humanized brands" as adopting three main domains:

1. A human perspective on brands, imbuing them with human qualities (being the detainer of human characteristics or products physiognomy; a human mind; and a human personality);
2. A more focused consumer perspective, analyzing the way that it specifically identifies with "I" (that is, the connection between brand and consumer and not exactly how the brand behaves as a person);
3. A focused perspective on the relationship between brand and consume (understanding how this relationship seems like an interpersonal behavior).

Anthropomorphism incorporates distinct combinations of human characteristics and qualities, such as: the ability to communicate, imagination and sensory interaction. These are transmitted by communication strategies to enrich further brand-consumer interactions, achieving paramount competitive advantage (Golossenko et al., 2020).

Furthermore, anthropomorphized brands are understood by consumers as having a mind, soul and various emotional states and conscious behaviors; acting as important agents in the creation of social ties (Puzakova et al., 2009). Some characteristics, such as empathy, are developed through anthropomorphism, making them act as powerful active agents of social and human connection for consumers (Epley et al., 2007; Yang et al., 2019).

Although being positively related concepts, there is a distinction between anthropomorphism and brand personality. The first one is related to brands and/or their product's perception as real human beings, by consumers (Guido & Peluso, 2015); the latter, personality, concerns the consumers' metaphorical perception about the brand images (Caprara, Barbaranelli & Guido, 2001) and the human characteristics associated with it (Aaker, 1997). Thus, brand personality represents only a portion of the various components of brand anthropomorphism (Puzakova et al., 2009).

Anthropomorphism Scales

Although there have been several anthropomorphism measuring scales over time (e.g. Waytz, Cacioppo & Epley, 2010; Guido & Peluso, 2015) more recently these have been developed in brands, from which we highlight the Brand Anthropomorphism Scale (BASC) (Golossenko et al., 2020) and the Brand Anthropomorphism Questionnaire (Huang, Zhou, Ye & Guo, 2020).

Golossenko et al. (2020), after reviewing several previously constructed scales, developed the Brand Anthropomorphism Scale (BASC), which is a scale used as a diagnostic tool to perceive the level of humanization that brands have and in what degree of anthropomorphism they are. This scale evaluates a set of twelve items, divided into four main dimensions: Appearance, which refers to the understanding of external characteristics identical to human ones; Moral Virtue, where the measuring of a brand as a moral entity is made; Conscious Emotionality, which measures the perception of a brand's ability to experience cognitive and complex emotions such as shame and guilt; and Cognitive Experience, that is, the understanding of a brand's ability to develop cognitive tasks such as thinking or reasoning (Golossenko et al., 2020).

The Brand Anthropomorphism Questionnaire was developed recently by Huang et al. (2020) whit the purpose to develop a scale through the attribution of a human consciousness to brands by consumers. Thus, the goal was to measure two dimensions: Thinking (where the brand is seen as an agent possessing autonomy, aware of its own goals and intentions and able to have cognitive thoughts) and Feeling (which involves the ability of a brand to have feelings and emotions and to be able to provoke emotions as well). This scale consists of a set of fourteen items, divided into two sub-scales (Think and Feel), answered on a Likert 7-Point scale based on the statement: "Please rate the extent to which you think Brand X (specific brand name) can performance the following actions" (Huang et al., 2020, p. 6).

EMPATHY

"Empathy in the broadest sense refers to the reactions of one individual to the observed experiences of another." (Davis, 1983, p. 113)

Emergence and Definition of Empathy

Although there is not an exact notion of either the emergence or the very definition of empathy, it is thought that this term may have arisen from the German word *Einfühlung*. According to Aring (1958) *Einfühlung* means the act of someone projecting themselves into someone else's body or environment, that's "feeling into" someone and their feelings towards something, being able to feel the same in things contemplated or in the observation of people.

For Vischer (1873, cited by Ganczarek, Hünefeldt, & Belardinelli, 2018), the term represents a certain "imaginary body perspective" in which the objective is predisposed to understand what it would be if someone lived in another person's body or environment, understanding in this way what the other person's sensation would be. Some authors (e.g. Ganczarek et al., 2018) argue that this concept was developed between the end of the 19th century and the beginning of the 20th century, by Robert Vischer (1873), others (e.g. Riess, 2017) claim it was developed by Theodore Lipps (1903, 1906) and there still those who claim (e.g. Mercer & Reynolds, 2002) that it was Titchener (1909) who developed it, by joining the Greek words "*em*" and "*pathos*", which means "to feel in".

The present-day definition of "empathy" was given by Rogers (1951, p. 129, cited by Carré, D'Ambrosio, Bensalah, Stefaniak, & Besche-Richard, 2013, p. 680) who defined it as "the concept of 'as if'", that is, through empathy is possible to understand the visions and feelings of others, that includes the ability to feel similar emotions and to understand the causes of those same emotions. This definition, given by Rogers, highlights the main characteristic of empathy - a process of identification, where a differentiation between "me" and the "others" is based.

One can affirm that empathy is a capacity that allows individuals to understand and predict the entire social world (Baron-Cohen, 2002) thus creating compassion-driven behaviors (Riess, 2017). Beyond understanding, it also involves the attribution of certain mental states to someone else, that is, a cognitive consciousness, experiencing what the other feels, thinks or perceives. In this way, a concern is developed towards what others feel, which in turn leads to an indirect affective response to another

(Hoffman, 2000; Riess, 2017). Following this idea, Baron-Cohen (2002), defines "empathizing" as the desire to recognize someone's emotions and thoughts, and respond to them through an appropriate emotion. Generally, individuals tend to have a higher level of empathy when they act or look like each other (Riess, 2017), yet empathy between distinct groups is also possible (Reeder, Temple, Petheram, Marks, & Stephens, 2016).

Empathy vs. Sympathy

The concepts "empathy" and "sympathy" are constantly used as synonyms, but they should not be confused (Bove, 2019), since they are two distinct psychological procedures. Although both have as "object" someone's emotions, "they should not be called by the same word" (Wispé, 1986, p. 314), yet opinions are divided in this distinction. There are authors who claim that these concepts are distinct (Aring, 1958; Carré et al., 2013; Hojat et al., 2001; Mercer & Reynolds, 2002; Stepien & Baernstein, 2006), although the latter claim that there are authors who consider sympathy to be the same as the emotional component of empathy, such as Baron-Cohen & Wheelwright (2004). Jolliffe & Farrington (2006) support the same idea adding that sympathy can be associated with cognitive empathy, since it is a cognitive processing, where it is expected an understanding of someone else's emotions and a "perspective taking" (Eisenberg, Eggum & Giunta, 2010). Other authors, such as Batchelder, Brosnan, & Ashwin, (2017) argue that sympathy derives from empathy, as both involve a kind of affective response by someone else's emotions. Aring (1958), Bove (2019) and Stepien & Baernstein (2006) distinguish the two concepts, describing sympathy as the act of experiencing someone's emotions or having the ability to share that person's feelings, feeling "pity" for the subject. Sympathy translates into a way of relating, where the sympathizer is "moved" by another person and where the objective is that person's well-being (Wispé, 1986). Empathy is about understanding the other person. We can characterize it as the same act or capacity to share feelings, without "joining" that person, having the consciousness of a separation between the person who observes and the one who is observed (Aring, 1958; Hojat et al., 2001), that is, in this way there is only the possibility to imagine or examine these same emotions (Bove, 2019; Stepien & Baernstein, 2006). Unlike sympathy, empathy is referred when one substitute herself for others, trying to understand the other person without judging them (Wispé, 1986), or, as Aring (1958, p. 449) states the "appreciation of another's feelings and problems is quite different from joining in them".

Advantages of Empathy for Organizations

Moreover, as seen before, anthropomorphized brands are an increasingly common trend (Kniazeva & Belk, 2010). Since being empathic is an inherent characteristic of tracing a personality (Lee, 2016) and associate it to a way of knowing or understanding another person (Duan & Hill, 1996), it becomes evident the possibility of empathy between consumers and the brands.

Through the organization of different services and products, a company is capable to develop and market various experiences (Kotler & Keller, 2012). These experiences are developed through the interaction between the consumers and the company, or a product, provoking a certain reaction, whether emotional, rational, sensory, physical, or even spiritual (Lywood, Stone, & Ekinci, 2009). Due to its great competitive advantage, it is becoming more common and necessary to create value through experiences for their consumers, potentially raising awareness within consumer insight managers. To achieve it, brands should understand how their clients think and feel, not only about the previous expectations, but also on the post-experience evaluations (Berry, Carbone, & Haeckel, 2002).

Considering that empathy is a fundamental issue in customer experience (Lywood et al., 2009) and an essential element in building relationships and human interactions in the social world (Batchelder et al., 2017), it is important to ensure its presence in all brand interactions with stakeholders, as well as to ensure that it receives as much attention as any other technological advance (Bove, 2019). Empathy should be considered one of the criteria when building a quality service of an organization and its products (Parasuraman & Grewal, 2000). When there is a capacity to understand and create relationships with the feelings, thoughts or experiences of other people, there is a greater probability of forgiving mistakes (Wieseke, Geigenmüller, & Kraus, 2012).

When a consumer feels empathy for a certain brand, their perceptions about service quality improve, and if there are some problems in that service, there is a greater facility for forgiveness, thus ensuring a certain protection as to the brand's reputation (Bove, 2019). In other words, the social bond between the client and the organization is enhanced by empathy. Marketing professionals should, therefore, venture on the use of empathy to improve relationships with consumers and their brands (Hassan, Belanche, & Casaló, 2019) since once the emotional connection between companies and consumers is assured, it is much more difficult to overcome or be broken by competitors (Berry, Carbone & Haeckel, 2002; Lee, 2016). As Godin (2019, p. 17) states, "Effective marketing is now based on empathy and service, instead of selfish mass strategies".

Evaluating Empathy

As Neumann, Chan, Boyle, Wang, & Westbury (2015, p. 257) wrote:

The measurement of empathy presents a serious challenge for researchers in disciplines ranging from social psychology, individual differences, and clinical psychology. Part of this challenge stems from the lack of a clear, universal definition for empathy.

In fact, empathic responses can be measured in many different of ways, not only because of the various ways in which the term "empathy" can be defined (Duan & Hill, 1996) but also because the measurement differs widely between studies (Gerdes, Segal & Lietz, 2010).

Almost of the existing measurement scales has its origin in Rogers' work, which focused on patient therapy in the 1950's and, as such, were developed to evaluate in a medical environment (Mercer & Reynolds, 2002). Nevertheless, more and more measures have been developed to evaluate empathy in general population (Fields et al., 2011) such as self-report measures, behavioral observation measures, measures of neuroscientific approaches and physiological measures (Neumann et al., 2015).

Measuring Scales

One of the most used techniques in the evaluation of empathic responses is the self-report (Zhou, Valiente & Eisenberg, 2003), which are measures where respondents make their own evaluation (Duan & Hill, 1996). There have been several self-reporting measures developed over the years, however not all of them address the same components. While some only address the emotional component of empathy (e.g. Mehrabian & Epstein, 1972), and others address purely the cognitive component (e.g. Hogan, 1969), there are some that address both components (e.g. Davis, 1980; Jolliffe & Farrington, 2006).

Behavioral observation measures are based on reports of verbal and non-verbal behavior of the observed person (Gerdes et al., 2010) and include evaluations of the performance of those observed in tests and their experimental stimuli. An example of a behavioral observation measure is the Kids' Empathic Development Scale (Reid et al., 2013).

The measures in neuroscience are constructed by techniques capable of measuring empathy by the production of neuroimaging in the magnetic field (Morin, 2011) where it is possible to observe the intern structure of the body and the central nervous system (Neumann et al., 2015). Some examples are the Magnetic Resonance Imaging (MRI) and the Functional Magnetic Resonance Imaging (fMRI).

Finally, there are also physiological measures, which use methods such as Heart Rate and Skin Conductance (Zhou et al., 2003) during observation of the respondent. These measurements are more difficult to deceive, since they are physical reactions of the organism, most of the times, consciously uncontrollable.

METHODOLOGY

This study used quantitative research instruments, more specifically questionnaire surveys, since this is a type of research capable of reaching a larger number of respondents (Apuke, 2017; Slade-Brooking, 2016), divided in two periods: a top-of-mind questionnaire and a new model of empathy measuring scale.

Questionnaire 1 (Top-of-Mind Automotive Brands)

Participants

In this sample, 155 participants responded to the first questionnaire, of which five were eliminated since they were considered inconclusive.

Of the 150 respondents considered valid, 63% were female, 37% male, and the sample belonged mostly (53%) to the age group of 18 and 30 years.

Instruments and Development

In the first questionnaire it was requested, to a random sample, to indicate the first five car brands respondents remembered. The objective was to understand which are the top-of-mind brands in this sector, thus assessing the five with greater awareness to be used as an example for the second questionnaire.

Questionnaire 2 (New Model of Empathy Measure)

Participants

This questionnaire was distributed online, similarly, to a random sample from where 162 answers were collected, of which ten were eliminated since these participants were considered invalid for the study, mainly because they did not answer values within the scales or because they did not complete the questionnaires until the end.

Of the 152 respondents, 57% were female, 43% were male, and of the 152, 53% were between 18 and 30 years old.

Instruments and Development

After identifying the five most familiar car brands, the second questionnaire was distributed where the new empathy scale model was placed, along with an anthropomorphism scale. This scale was chosen because it is used as a diagnostic tool for the perception of the level of humanization that brands have. Through it, it is possible to understand how these levels of anthropomorphism influence the performance of the brand, its value, loyalty to it and its positioning.

It is a scale that addresses several dimensions of anthropomorphism, not just focusing on the cognitive part.

The use of a second scale served for an in-depth detailed data analysis and to understand how the empathy of brands was related in some way with the humanization that consumers observed in them.

Have analyzed all the scale measures, it was concluded that the indicated scales to be used in this proposed model would be the Interpersonal Reactivity Index (IRI) by Davis (1980) and the Brand Anthropomorphism Scale (BASC) by Golossenko et al. (2020).

The main scale of this new model - Interpersonal Reactivity Index (Davis,1980) – is divided into four sub-scales (Fantasy, Perspective-taking, Empathic Concern and Personal Distress). For an easier and more coherent adaption of this scale to the theme in question, it was decided to modify the items of the Fantasy sub-scale in order to understand how the respondents felt in relation not to the brand itself, but to the advertising pieces they conveyed.

The model is composed by five main questions: the first is from the Anthropomorphism Scale, with twelve items; and the remaining four questions represented the Empathy Scale, where the first, second and third question contained six items each and the fourth only four.

In this questionnaire, respondents were asked to rate each question on a Likert type scale. In the first question, each respondent would have to answer each item on a 7-point scale, where 1= Strongly Disagree and 7= Strongly Agree. In the remaining questions on a 5-point scale, from 0 to 4, where 0= Doesn't Describe Me Very Well and 4= Describes Me Very Well.

Thus, the total scores on the Anthropomorphism Scale could be between 12 (minimum) and 84 (maximum) and on the empathy scale between 0 (minimum) and 88 (maximum).

RESULTS AND DISCUSSION

Questionnaire 1

To the question "Which five first brands do you remember when talking about the automotive industry?" each respondent were asked to give five distinct answers. The five most present brands in the mind of the respondents were Mercedes-Benz (112 answers), BMW (109 answers), Audi (60 answers), Renault (58 answers) and Peugeot (55 answers).

Questionnaire 2 (New Model of Empathy Measure)

Besides the main question of this study – to understand if brands in the automotive industry are (or not) considered empathic for consumers – other analysis were conducted such as: understand the differences between under-18's and the other age groups in both scales; Understand the difference between genders, in relation to the empathy scale; Analyze the differences between the empathy scale and the anthropomorphism scale on the five brands and understand if the most empathic brands are also the most human for consumers; And finally, since betting on advertising that has the ability to impact their consumers by generating empathic responses from them is important for companies, as the creation of empathic responses is precisely what advertisers are looking for so that more involvement can be developed, deep and attractive (Mooradian, Matzler & Szykman, 2008), it was also decided, in this study, to try to understand whether the advertising of each brand is able or not, and to what extent, to generate empathy in consumers.

The analysis of the data obtained was conveyed in two main ways:

1. Initially, the sum of scores of the questions concerning the anthropomorphism scale and the empathy scale, for each brand, were calculated per respondent, thus obtaining new variables relating to these sums: a) Sum of the scores obtained on the anthropomorphism scale, for each brand; b) Sum of the scores of empathy scale, for each brand.
2. Then, a sum of the five scores of each brand was made, through the total scores previously obtained. The objective of this sum was to make, on a later stage, an average of these final scores (of the five brands), obtaining a single empathic and anthropomorphic score, in each respondent. The purpose was to understand the total average score of each respondent, in each scale.
3. In addition to these, sums of scores obtained on each of the sub-scales of the empathy scale (of the five brands) were also taken following the same norms as previously explained, using them later, in the same way as average, for each respondent.

Empathy and Anthropomorphism in people <18

To be able to make a comparative observation between the current and future consumers of this sector, the average total scores for each group in both scales were analyzed, as well as the brand considered more empathic by each group.

People under 18 obtained a total average of empathic scores higher than any other age group, as well as on the anthropomorphism scale.

As such, in view of all other age groups, it is possible to conclude that those who are considered as "future buyers" have a greater empathic relationship with the automotive industry and are able to understand brand more as "Human" than current consumers.

Gender Empathy and Anthropomorphism

The differences between genders regarding the empathic level are noticed in several studies (Baron-Cohen, 2002; Baron-Cohen & Wheelwright 2004; Davis, 1980; Hogan, 1969; Hojat et al., 2002), therefore it's aimed to understand if the present study corroborated or not these previous results.

Looking to the data, it was possible to confirm that the female gender, on average, obtained higher scores than the male gender in all brands.

After analyzing the empathic scores of each brand, an average of the sum of the five individual scores (within the five brands) was made, to understand the differences, in general, between genders. Throughout this analysis, it was concluded that the female gender had an average of total empathy scores higher than the male gender.

This way, it is possible to confirm that, despite being a sector traditionally more connoted with male gender, the obtained results are in line with those already existing (e.g. Baron-Cohen & Wheelwright, 2004; Hogan, 1969; Reniers, Corcoran, Drake, Shryane & Völlm, 2011), in which it is stated that the female gender obtains higher empathic scores than the male gender.

Empathy and Anthropomorphism of the Five Brands

For a perception of the proximity between the two variables (empathy and humanization of the brands) the total scores of each brand in both scales were studied.

According to the results, Mercedes-Benz is the brand characterized as the most human of the five brands, followed by BMW. The same brands also obtained the highest average scores on the empathy scale. Although very close, BMW achieved a higher average than Mercedes-Benz in the anthropomorphism scale. In contrast, Renault was the brand with the lowest average scores on both empathy and anthropomorphism scale, with values very close to those obtained by Audi. Peugeot does not stand out in any of the scales obtaining, on average, intermediate values compared to the other brands.

Thus, it is concluded that the brands that obtained the highest average scores in both scales were Mercedes-Benz and BMW, so it can be assumed that the two variables (empathy and anthropomorphism) are related in some way.

Empathy in general in the Automotive Industry Brands

Considering that the brands used in this study were chosen based on awareness, the authors reinforce that these brands are used merely as examples for this study. Nevertheless, it is possible to conclude that, in general, the brands in the automotive industry analyzed in this study are not characterized as highly empathic, since the obtained values on the empathy scale, on average, are relatively low, as in the maximum total scores possible to achieve (88 points), none of which exceeds the average value of 44 points.

Based on the values obtained, it is possible to affirm that, represented by these five brands, the automotive industry has not yet been able to develop products and services with the necessary empathy so that consumers feel connected and related with it in some way.

Advertising effectiveness

The sub-scale Fantasy, belonging to IRI (Davis, 1980) was the most modified in this study, in order to adjust the adaptation of the empathic scale to brands, as previously mentioned. Thus, this sub-scale serves to understand how consumers perceive the empathy generated by advertising campaigns of the represented brands.

Respondents evaluate, on average, BMW as the brand with the most empathetic advertising campaigns, followed by Audi. The remaining brands presented smaller values, although not far from the previous one. In general, the brands obtained intermediate values, taking into account the total possible scores to obtain on this scale (24 total points).

The authors can conclude, from the obtained results that the advertising made by these brands is not empathic enough for the respondents.

Empathy in Individuals Under 18 Years Old

The Internet is nowadays used daily for the most diverse purposes, and the panoply of information increases exponentially every day. This gigantic network of information and communications is used mainly by teenagers, who are the biggest users of it (Saboor, Jan, Raheem & Rizwan, 2011). Moreover, this is an age group characterized as a strong influence in the decision-making processes of purchasing in a family context, and since they are the consumers of the future, it is relevant to understand the differences between these and other age groups. After analyzing the collected data it is possible to conclude that it is this segment who feels both a greater empathy for these brands, as well as a superior capacity to observe and understand them as human, thus becoming a new and relevant data for the market. This way, it can potentially be a market opportunity, within which brands can aim to connect in a deeper way to these consumers and, therefore, to their families, friends, and acquaintances.

Gender empathy

Despite the fact that women obtain higher empathic scores than men, the conclusions of this study corroborate these previous investigations (e.g. Baron-Cohen, 2002; Davis, 1980; Hojat et al., 2002). Although the automotive industry has traditionally been associated with greater interest from male rather than female elements, it is important to note that women influence almost 85% of new car sales and are willing to pay more for a vehicle than men (Lezotte, 2014), so this conclusion is also relevant.

Empathic advertising

Create advertising campaigns that impacts the consumers by generating empathic responses is also something important for companies, because advertising has the ability to generate cognitive, affective and behavioral responses in their receptors, and the creation of empathic responses could be one option for advertisers in order to develop a deeper and more attractive involvement with their consumers (Mooradian, Matzler & Szykman, 2008).

CONCLUSION

Developing a good and solid relationship between a brand and their consumers is essential to any brand to distinguish itself from their competitors, generating new and unique experiences (Loureiro & Lopes, 2012) but also feelings like empathy.

This research aimed to design a new evaluation model that would allow brands to understand how their consumers felt (or not) empathy towards them as well as their advertising campaigns.

The authors chose the automotive industry because it is a sector focused on creating experiences with the consumer, which allow the existence of a differentiation between the various brands (Konrad,

2019). Also, automobiles are more than a simple product, representing a symbol of social ascension, power and social status (Júnior, Lima & Freire, 2016) and therefore the feelings associated with cars are sometimes greater or stronger in relation to other products, as the identity they have is transmitted to the people who use it (Lindon et al., 2004). On the other hand, the automotive sector is still widely used for studies related to anthropomorphization, especially regarding the physical appearance of the products they develop (Aggarwal & Mcgill, 2007; Guido & Peluso, 2014; Windhager et al., 2008).

This study concluded that automotive brands' approach is characterized as low empathic, as well as their advertising campaigns. Although the small sample and the fact that one cannot assume these five brands as representative of the whole automotive industry (even these were the ones chosen by its awareness), the results allow us to conclude that the top-of-mind brands were those that obtained the highest average empathic scores (Mercedes-Benz and BMW), even if the advertising made by automotive brands in general doesn't reach higher levels of empathy with consumers. This study also allowed us to conclude that people under 18 years old are the ones that shows greater empathy for brands in the automotive industry. In line with the literature, we also corroborate the fact that women have higher empathy scores than men.

From a practical and managerial point of view, the instrument proposed here allows brands a new way of measuring the empathy that consumers feel about them and their communication actions. As seen above, empathy is an extremely relevant factor in the relationship between the brands and the consumers - everyday more demanding, so the use of this model in this or any other sectors of activity can prove to be an asset for countless organizations that, with this valuable information, will be able to define and implement strategies to maintain or improve the engagement with their diverse audiences and thus stand out in this ultra-competitive market in which we live.

Q1 – Age:

7) 7)<18
8) 8)18>30
9) 9)31>50
10) 10)>50

Q2 – Rate on a scale of 0 to 4, where 0= Does Not Describe Me Very Well and 4= Describes Me Very Well

Q3 – Rate on a scale of 0 to 4, where 0= Does Not Describe Me Very Well and 4= Describes Me Very Well

Q4 – Rate on a scale of 0 to 4, where 0= Does Not Describe Me Very Well and 4= Describes Me Very Well

Q5 – Rate on a scale of 0 to 4, where 0= Does Not Describe Me Very Well and 4= Describes Me Very Well

Q6 – Gender:

- Feminine
- Male

Q7 – Level of education (highest level of complete education):

- Basic Education
- High School

Table 1.

	0	1	2	3	4
When I'm reading an interesting advertising piece, of this brand, I imagine how I would feel if the events of this piece were happening to me.					
I really get involved with the feelings of the characters of an advertisement of this brand.					
I'm usually objective when I watch an ad or any other type of advertising piece, and I don't often get completely caught up in them. (-)					
After seeing an ad of this brand, I feel as if I was one of its characters.					
Becoming extremely involved in a good advertisement or advertising piece of this brand is somewhat rare for me. (-)					
When I watch a good ad of this brand, I can very easily put myself in the place of a leading character.					

Table 2.

	0	1	2	3	4
Before criticizing this brand, I try to imagine how I would feel if I were in its place.					
If I'm sure I'm right about something, I don't waste much time listening to this brand's arguments. (-)					
I sometimes try to understand this brand better by imagining how things look from its perspective.					
When this brand is exposed to a certain issue, I believe that there are two sides to it, and try to look at them both.					
I sometimes find it difficult to see thing from this brand's point of view. (-)					
When I'm "upset" with this brand, for some reason, I usually try to "put myself in its shoes" for a while.					

Table 3.

	0	1	2	3	4
When I see this brand being taken advantage of, I feel, in some way, protective towards it.					
When I see this brand being treated unfairly, I don't feel very much pity for it. (-)					
I would describe myself as a "soft heart" person in relation to this brand.					
Sometimes I don't feel very sorry for this brand when it's having problems.					
The misfortunes of this brand do not usually disturb me a great deal. (-)					
I'm often touched by thing that I see happening to this brand.					

Table 4.

	0	1	2	3	4
When I see that this brand badly needs help, in an emergency, I got devastated.					
I sometimes feel helpless when I'm in the middle of a very emotional situation of this brand.					
Being in a tense emotional situation of this brands, scares me.					
When I see this brand being hearted, I have the tendency to remain calm. (-)					

- Degree
- Professional Course
- Pos-Graduation
- Master's Degree
- PhD

REFERENCES

Aggarwal, P., & McGill, A. L. (2007). Is That Car Smiling at Me? Schema Congruity as a Basis for Evaluating Anthropomorphized Products. *The Journal of Consumer Research*, *34*(4), 1–12. doi:10.1086/518544

Apuke, O. D. (2017). Quantitative Research Methods: A Synopsis Approach. *Arabian Journal of Business and Management Review*, *10*(6), 40–47.

Aring, C. D. (1958). Sympathy and Empathy. *Journal of the American Medical Association*, *167*(4), 448–452. doi:10.1001/jama.1958.02990210034008 PMID:13538722

Baron-Cohen, S. (2002). The extreme male brain theory of autism. *Trends in Cognitive Sciences*, *6*(6), 248–254. doi:10.1016/S1364-6613(02)01904-6 PMID:12039606

Baron-Cohen, S., & Wheelwright, S. (2004). The Empathy Quotient: An Investigation of Adults with Asperger Syndrome or High Functioning Autism, and Normal Sex Differences. *Journal of Autism and Developmental Disorders*, *34*(2), 163–175. doi:10.1023/B:JADD.0000022607.19833.00 PMID:15162935

Batchelder, L., Brosnan, M., & Ashwin, C. (2017). The Development and Validation of the Empathy Components Questionnaire (ECQ). *PLoS One*, *12*(1), 1–34. doi:10.1371/journal.pone.0169185 PMID:28076406

Berry, L. L., Carbone, L. P., & Haeckel, S. H. (2002). Managing the Total Customer Experience. *Sloan Management Review*, *43*(3), 1–6.

Bove, L. L. (2019). Empathy for service: Benefits, unintended consequences, and future research agenda. *Journal of Services Marketing*, *33*(1), 31–43. doi:10.1108/JSM-10-2018-0289

Caprara, G. V., Barbaranelli, C., & Guido, G. (2001). Brand personality: How to make the metaphor fit? *Journal of Economic Psychology*, *22*(3), 377–395. doi:10.1016/S0167-4870(01)00039-3

Carré, A., D'Ambrosio, F., Bensalah, L., Stefaniak, N., & Besche-Richard, C. (2013). The Basic Empathy Scale in Adults (BES-A): Factor Structure of a Revised Form. *Psychological Assessment*, *25*(3), 679–691. doi:10.1037/a0032297 PMID:23815121

Chandler, J., & Owen, M. (2002). *Developing Brands with Qualitative Market Research*. SAGE Publications. doi:10.4135/9781849208840

Chen, K.-J. (2017). Humanizing Brands: An Examination of the Psychological Process of Anthropomorphism and its Effects on Consumer Responses. *Journal of Marketing Management*, *5*(2), 75–87.

Davis, M. H. (1980). A Multidimensional Approach to Individual Differences in Empathy. *Journal of Personality and Social Psychology*, 1–19.

Davis, M. H. (1983). Measuring Individual Differences in Empathy: Evidence for a Multidimensional Approach. *Journal of Personality and Social Psychology*, *44*(1), 113–126. doi:10.1037/0022-3514.44.1.113

Delgado-Ballester, E., Palazón, M., & Pelaez-Muñoz, J. (2017). This anthropomorphised brand is so loveable: The role of self-brand integration. *Spanish Journal of Marketing - ESIC, 21*, 89-101.

Duan, C., & Hill, C. E. (1996). The Current State of Empathy Research. *Journal of Counseling Psychology*, *43*(3), 261–274. doi:10.1037/0022-0167.43.3.261

Eisenberg, N., Eggum, N. D., & Giunta, L. D. (2010). Empathy-Related Responding: Associations with Prosocial Behavior, Aggression, and Intergroup Relations. *Social Issues and Policy Review*, *4*(1), 143–180. doi:10.1111/j.1751-2409.2010.01020.x PMID:21221410

Epley, N., Waytz, A., & Cacioppo, J. T. (2007). On Seeing Human: A Three-Factor Theory of Anthropomorphism. *Psychological Review*, *114*(4), 864–886. doi:10.1037/0033-295X.114.4.864 PMID:17907867

Fields, S. K., Mahan, P., Tillman, P., Harris, J., Kaye, M., & Hojat, M. (2011). Measuring empathy in healthcare profession students using the Jefferson Scale of Physician Empathy: Health provider – student version. *Journal of Interprofessional Care*, *25*(4), 287–293. doi:10.3109/13561820.2011.566648 PMID:21554061

Fournier, S. (1998). Consumers and Their Brands: Developing Relationship Theory in Consumer Research. *The Journal of Consumer Research*, *24*(4), 343–373. doi:10.1086/209515

Ganczarek, J., Hünefeldt, T., & Belardinelli, M. O. (2018). From "Einfühlung" to empathy: Exploring the relationship between aesthetic and interpersonal experience. *Cognitive Processing*, *19*(2), 141–145. doi:10.100710339-018-0861-x PMID:29766344

Gerdes, K. E., Segal, E. A., & Lietz, C. A. (2010). Conceptualizing and Measuring Empathy. *British Journal of Social Work*, *40*(7), 2326–2343. doi:10.1093/bjsw/bcq048

Godin, S. (2019). *Isto é Marketing* [This is Marketing]. Ideias de Ler.

Golossenko, A., Pillai, K. G., & Aroean, L. (2020). Seeing brands as humans: Development and validation of a brand anthropomorphism scale. *International Journal of Research in Marketing*, *37*(4), 1–19. doi:10.1016/j.ijresmar.2020.02.007

Guido, G., & Peluso, A. M. (2015). Brand anthropomorphism: Conceptualization, measurement, and impact on brand personality and loyalty. *Journal of Brand Management*, *22*(1), 1–19. doi:10.1057/bm.2014.40

Hassan, M., Belanche, D., & Casaló, L. V. (2019). *The Relevance of Empathy on Facebook Brand Communities*. Academic Press.

Hoffman, M. L. (2000). Empathy, Its Arousal, and Prosocial Functioning. In Empathy and Moral Development: Implications for Caring and Justice (pp. 29-62). Cambridge University Press.

Hoffman, M. L. (2008). Empathy and Prosocial Behavior. In Handbook of Emotions (3rd ed., pp. 440-455). New York: The Guilford Press.

Hogan, R. (1969). Development of an Empathy Scale. *Journal of Consulting and Clinical Psychology*, *33*(3), 307–316. doi:10.1037/h0027580 PMID:4389335

Hojat, M., Gonnella, J. S., Nasca, T. J., Mangione, S., Vergare, M., & Magee, M. (2002). Physician Empathy: Definition, Components, Measurement, and Relationship to Gender and Specialty. *The American Journal of Psychiatry*, *159*(9), 1563–1569. doi:10.1176/appi.ajp.159.9.1563 PMID:12202278

Hojat, M., Mangione, S., Kane, G. C., & Gonnella, J. S. (2005). Relationships between scores of the Jefferson Scale of Physician Empathy. *Medical Teacher*, *27*(7), 625–628. doi:10.1080/01421590500069744 PMID:16332555

Hojat, M., Mangione, S., Nasca, T. S., Cohen, M. J., Gonnella, J. S., Erdmann, J. B., & Veloskyi, J. (2001). The Jefferson Scale of Pshysician Empathy: Development and Preliminary Psychometric Data. *Educational and Psychological Measurement*, *61*(2), 349–365. doi:10.1177/00131640121971158

Huang, R., Zhou, X., Ye, W., & Guo, S. (2020). Think versus feel: Two dimensions of brand anthropomorphism. *Journal of Product and Brand Management*, *29*(7), 1–15. doi:10.1108/JPBM-11-2018-2125

Jolliffe, D., & Farrington, D. P. (2006). Development and validation of the Basic Empathy Scale. *Journal of Adolescence*, *29*(4), 589–611. doi:10.1016/j.adolescence.2005.08.010 PMID:16198409

Kaufmann, H. R., Filho, C. G., Silva, C. R., & Monteiro, P. R. (2019). Consumer-brand relationship development in the automotive market: An integrative model. *International Journal of Automotive Technology and Management*, *19*(3/4), 321–340. doi:10.1504/IJATM.2019.10022009

Kim, S., & Mcgill, A. L. (2011). Gaming with Mr. Slot or Gaming the Slot Machine? Power, Anthropomorphism, and Risk Perception. *The Journal of Consumer Research*, *38*(1), 1–15. doi:10.1086/658148

Kniazeva, M., & Belk, R. W. (2010). If This Brand Were a Person, or Anthropomorphism of Brands Through Packaging Stories. *Journal of the Academy of Marketing Science*, *20*(3), 231–238.

Kotler, P., & Keller, K. L. (2012). *Administração de Marketing* (14th ed.). Pearson Education.

Lee, E.-J. (2016). Empathy can increase customer equity related to pro-social brands. *Journal of Business Research*, *69*(9), 3748–3754. doi:10.1016/j.jbusres.2015.05.018

Lezotte, C. (2014). Automotive knowledge, auto activism, and women's online car advice. *Feminist Media Studies*, 691–706.

Lindon, D., Lendrevie, J., Lévy, J., Dionísio, P., & Rodrigues, J. V. (2004). *Mercator XXI: Teoria e Prática do Marketing* (10th ed.). Dom Quixote.

Loureiro, S. M., & Lopes, R. (2012). Brand Credibility And Self-Brand Connection As Drivers To Cool Brands. *Global Marketing Conference*, (pp. 1551-1569). Academic Press.

Lywood, J., Stone, M., & Ekinci, Y. (2009). Customer experience and profitability: An application of the empathy rating index (ERIC) in UK call centres. *Database Marketing & Customer Strategy Management*, *16*(3), 207–214. doi:10.1057/dbm.2009.24

MacInnis, D. J., & Folkes, V. S. (2017). Humanizing brands: When brands seem to be like me, part of me, and in a relationship with me. *Journal of Consumer Psychology*, *27*(3), 355–374. doi:10.1016/j.jcps.2016.12.003

Mehrabian, A., & Epstein, N. (1972). A measure of emotional empathy. *Journal of Personality*, *40*(4), 525–543. doi:10.1111/j.1467-6494.1972.tb00078.x PMID:4642390

Mercer, S. W., & Reynolds, W. J. (2002). Empathy and quality of care. *The British Journal of General Practice*, *52*, S9–S12. PMID:12389763

Mooradian, T. A., Matzler, K., & Szykman, L. (2008). Empathetic responses to advertising: Testing a network of antecedents and consequences. *Marketing Letters*, *19*(2), 79–92. doi:10.100711002-008-9032-7

Morin, C. (2011). Neuromarketing: The New Science of Consumer Behavior. *Society*, *48*(2), 131–135. doi:10.100712115-010-9408-1

Neumann, D. L., Chan, R. C., Boyle, G. J., Wang, Y., & Westbury, H. R. (2015). Measures of Empathy: Self-Report, Behavioral, and Neuroscientific Approaches. In Measures of Personality and Social Psychological Constructs (pp. 257-289). Academic Press.

Parasuraman, A., & Grewal, D. (2000). The Impact of Technology on the Quality-Value-Loyalty Chain: A Research Agenda. *Journal of the Academy of Marketing Science*, *28*(1), 168–174. doi:10.1177/0092070300281015

Portal, S., Abratt, R., & Bendixen, M. (2018). Building a human brand: Brand anthropomorphism unravelled. *Business Horizons*, *61*(3), 367–374. doi:10.1016/j.bushor.2018.01.003

Puzakova, M., Kwak, H., & Rocereto, J. (2009). Pushing the Envelope of Brand and Personality: Antecedents and Moderators of Anthropomorphized Brands. *Advances in Consumer Research. Association for Consumer Research (U. S.)*, *36*, 413–420.

Rauschnabel, P. A., & Ahuvia, A. C. (2014). You're so lovable: Anthropomorphism and Brand Love. *Journal of Brand Management*, *21*(5), 372–395. doi:10.1057/bm.2014.14

Reeder, L., Temple, E., Petheram, L., Marks, K., & Stephens, L. (2016). *Empathy Conversations-Testing their effectiveness as a policy-making instrument: A Pilot Study*. Academic Press.

Reid, C., Davis, H., Horlin, C., Anderson, M., Baughman, N., & Campbell, C. (2013). The Kids' Empathic Development Scale (KEDS): A multi-dimensional measure of empathy in primary school-aged children. *British Journal of Developmental Psychology*, *31*(2), 231–256. doi:10.1111/bjdp.12002 PMID:23659893

Reniers, R. L., Corcoran, R., Drake, R., Shryane, N. M., & Völlm, B. (2011). The QCAE: A Questionnaire of Cognitive and Affective Empathy. *Journal of Personality Assessment*, *93*(1), 84–95. doi:10.1080/00223891.2010.528484 PMID:21184334

Riess, H. (2017). The Science of Empathy. *Journal of Patient Experience*, *4*(2), 74–77. doi:10.1177/2374373517699267 PMID:28725865

Saboor, F., Jan, M. A., Raheem, T., & Rizwan, M. (2011). Impact of Teenagers on Family Purchase Decisions: Considering the role of Internet. *Journal of Business and Management*, •••, 101–105.

Schleyer, T. K., & Forrest, J. L. (2000). Methods for the Design and Administration of Web- based Surveys. *Journal of the American Medical Informatics Association: JAMIA*, *7*(4), 416–425. doi:10.1136/jamia.2000.0070416 PMID:10887169

Slade-Brooking, C. (2016). *Creating a Brand Identity- A Guide for Designers*. Laurence King Publishing Ltd.

Stepien, K. A., & Baernstein, A. (2006). Education for Empathy: A Review. *Journal of General Internal Medicine*, *21*(5), 524–530. doi:10.1111/j.1525-1497.2006.00443.x PMID:16704404

Waytz, A., Cacioppo, J., & Epley, N. (2010). Who Sees Human? The Stability and Importance of Individual Differences in Anthropomorphism. *Perspectives on Psychological Science*, *5*(3), 219–232. doi:10.1177/1745691610369336 PMID:24839457

Wieseke, J., Geigenmüller, A., & Kraus, F. (2012). On the role of empathy in customer-employee interactions. *Journal of Service Research*, *15*(3), 316–331. doi:10.1177/1094670512439743

Wispé, L. (1986). The distinction between sympathy and empathy: To call forth a concept, a word is needed. *Journal of Personality and Social Psychology*, *50*(2), 314–321. doi:10.1037/0022-3514.50.2.314

Yang, L. W., Aggarwal, P., & McGill, A. L. (2019). The 3 C's of anthropomorphism: Connection, comprehension, and competition. *Counselling Psychology Review*, *3*(1), 3–19.

Zhou, Q., Valiente, C., & Eisenberg, N. (2003). Empathy and Its Measurement. In S. J. Lopez & C. R. Snyder (Eds.), *Positive psychological assessment: A handbook of models and measures* (pp. 269–284). American Psychological Association. doi:10.1037/10612-017

Chapter 11
Place Branding, Digital Communication, and Citizenship

Adriano de Oliveira Sampaio
Federal University of Bahia, Brazil

José Gabriel Andrade
Minho University, Portugal

ABSTRACT

Since the 1990s, studies have been developed with the aim of understanding citizen participation in e-government, e-citizenship experiences, etc. Motivated by this context of reflexivity, governments began to be questioned about their management, to account for public debates and implement public policies through digital communication. Also strongly, and in this same time frame, city governments start to invest in self-promotion strategies in these territories in order to attract tourists in place branding strategies. Faced with this phenomenon, this chapter intends to reflect on the existing tensions between digital communication strategies focus on citizens and tourists in Brazil. It intends to identify the approximations and distances in the strategic communication developed by some Brazilian city governments, in one side, to animates citizen's public opinion in order to constructs public policies and, in the other hand, to position the cities as attractive tourist destinations for visitors.

INTRODUCTION

The Latin American researcher Nestor Garcia Canlicini (1998) develops two key notions to understand the interdependence of globalization with space and time.

"The most radical searches for what it means to be entering and leaving modernity are those that acknowledge the tensions between deterritorialization and reterritorialization. By this I refer to two processes: the loss of the "natural" relationship of culture with geographic and social territories and,

DOI: 10.4018/978-1-7998-9790-3.ch011

at the same time, certain relative, partial territorial relocations of old and new symbolic productions" (Canclini, 1998, p. 37).

At the same time, as the barriers between time and space are softened, the production of knowledge becomes even more specialized and makes expert systems emerge (Giddens, 1991). Advances from a technological point of view are linked to communication and the social and our relationship with space and time is increasingly relativized. This entire paradigm shift led to the appearance of "non-places": "(...) by "non-place" we designate two complementary but distinct realities: spaces constituted in relation to certain purposes (transport, transit, commerce, leisure) and the relationship that individuals maintain with these spaces (...) (Augé, 2012, p.87) These spaces are also: "(...), those we borrow when we drive on the highway, shop at the supermarket or we wait at an airport for the next flight (...)" (Augé, 2012, p.88).

We are increasingly tied to shared spaces that are similar across the globe. Airport lounges, subways, elevators, movie theaters, shopping malls, among many other spaces, are not endowed with local particularities and could be anywhere in the world. The Vinci Airport Network, for example, helps to spread these non-places. This organization operates more than 36 airports worldwide, including: 13 in France, 10 in Portugal, three in Cambodia, two in Japan, six in the Dominican Republic, one in Chile and Brazil. The consumption of goods and services, in turn, and because they are increasingly similar, make us part of the same group of consumers, like fast food companies. To some extent, these marks and not places (Augé, 2012) help to make common symbolic productions that could, on the contrary, stimulate symbolic exchanges between identity/alterity (Hall, 2006) in these territories.

These dynamics described so far are likely to be observed in "late modernity". For Anthony Giddens (1991) and Stuart Hall (2006), it is characterized in some axes of discussion that can be related to issues of cultural identities. Among them, we highlight: a) the accentuation in the reflexivity of individuals added to the processes of deterritorialization and disembedding that configure the discussions about cultural identities because, "(...) it removes social activity from localized contexts, reorganizing social relations through large time-spatial distances" (Giddens, 1991, p.58); b) the presence of online media and social networks, and in particular advertising, as a form of interaction and circulation of cultural products; c) the discussions and the clash between the global and the local that mark cultural identities in late modernity; and finally, d) a new interest in the 'local', since among the globalization strategies is the creation of market 'niches', in the relationship between the regional and the global, providing and demanding the negotiation of identities.

In Brazil, the geographer Milton Santos (2003) presented a good part of these criticisms pointed out so far, but related to peripheral countries. Santos (2003) proposes another Globalization to territories in which it is necessary to revisit local dynamics in order to better relate to these global issues. Even with all the advances in communication technologies, this did not reduce social problems and the world continues to be unequal.

Like the maritime globalization of the 15th century, Santos (2003) calls our attention to the fact that the current globalization model continues to reinforce unequal logics of access and appropriation of technologies that have been used by large nations and companies as ways of appropriating the symbolic and of the material of territories and people with a view to developing complex processes of commodification of things to be offered to people under the logic of consumption. It is no coincidence that Firat and Venkatesh (1993) claim that marketing becomes the main form of understanding reality in the 21st century. What are the impacts of this issue on the relationship of societies with public communication and territories?

PLACE, TOURISM AND CITIZENSHIP BRAND

In Invisible Cities Italo Calvino (1990) presents the stories told by the Venetian traveler Marco Polo (1254-1324) about the cities conquered by Emperor Kublai Khan, whom he served for many years. Marco Polo's narratives replace the eyes, more than that, they become the production of meaning for a ruler who is unaware of his surroundings and the very territory he inhabits. This novel describes an experience that we know is also part of our days, but today, Marco Polo's eyes are replaced by Communication Strategies and Marketing.

In the contemporary world, more precisely, from the end of the 1970s onwards, a communication campaign in the United States offers visibility at a global level to a phenomenon that starts to influence the management of cities, states and countries around the world: (I Love NYC, I love New York). With this slogan, the city of New York built a vast campaign of place brand and managed to offer visibility to this destination, by articulating three other domains which are: communication, culture and tourism. By place brand we mean:

"The communication and marketing efforts developed by the territories (cities, states, countries) in a brand positioning that seeks the development of visibility strategies for the tourist market, in addition to the positioning of products and services by countries in international markets" (Kotler, 2006).

But it was only after the 1990s that the local brand developed more strongly around the world, and motivated by the emerging processes of globalization. Milton Santos (2009, p.55) argues that: "In a globalized world, regions and cities are called to compete, and given the current rules of production and current consumption imperatives, competitiveness also becomes a rule of coexistence between people".

In the 1990s, governments (municipals, states and nations) began to understand Tourism as an important industry and source of income for these territories. In 1990, the world collected 268.9 billion dollars from tourism and in Brazil, U$ 1,492.3 which represented 0.55% of the share of this world market that year (Rabahy, 2006).

This new context, linked to the need for social distinction (Bourdieu, 1999), makes tourism become an attractive industry for governments. With this, public administrations begin to explore the dimension of strategic communication applied to the place brand, which we understand as the efforts made by public managers on territories, from the 1970s onwards, as presented by Michalis Kavaratzis (2004).

"The context in which marketing became accessible to city administrators was provided by the rise of the so-called "Entrepreneurial City" and the marketing of places has been one of the defining characteristics of the business modes of urban governance that have been prominent since the 1970s" (Kavaratzis, 2004, p.59)

According to data from the World Travel & Tourism Council – WTTC, which is the world tourism and travel council in Portugal, whose economic recovery is attributed to tourism, Travel & Tourism represented 16.5% of the total economy. The sector's GDP grew by 4.2%, outpacing the economy's global GDP growth almost three times in 2019. This continued growth in the Travel & Tourism sector accompanied the government's success in implementing an ambitious tourism strategy, which resulted in strong growth of visitors from non-traditional markets such as USA, Canada, China and Brazil. (WTTC, June 2020).

In the same year in Brazil, according to data from the same source, in 2019, it occupied 12th place in a world ranking of tourism share in Gross Domestic Product - GDP. The country has established itself as the largest travel and tourism economy in Latin America, growing 3% in 2019, this percentage surpassed the general economy of the country, which grew, in the same year, only 1.2%. This growth was driven by spending by Brazilians on travel in the country, which accounted for (94%) of total investment in tourism. International tourism represented only 6% of revenues in the country. This curve was general in several countries, but Brazil is the country with the greatest dependence on domestic tourism (WTTC, 2020).

Due to the serious health, social and political crisis that resulted in more than 600,000 deaths, the country is heavily exposed to economic recession. Even so, and so far, in 2021, according to a report by the Brazilian Association of Tourism Operators - (Braztoa, 2021), the Northeast region was responsible for 70% of tourism revenues in Brazil, with the cities of Maceió, Natal and Salvador the main tourist destinations in the country. In relation to the Human Development Index - HDI (Atlas, 2021), the states where these capitals are located are among the worst in the country, namely: Alagoas 26th, Rio Grande do Norte 16th; Bahia 22nd, respectively. Here, the contradiction between the choices made by public administrations in favor of the construction of tourist destinations in opposition to public policies aimed at the citizen is presented. This contradiction is the discussion of the political plan of this research. We understand as citizenship: "(...) a law of society that, without distinction, affects everyone and invests each with the strength to see respected against force, in any circumstance". (Santos, 2014, p.19)

We know that public management builds its territory brand positioning and how this is implied in a communication logic that also interferes in the territory, which is a type of public communication, political communication (Duarte, 2012; Gomes, 2016). Two models of public communication interfered in a very marked way in the country, the American model and the European model. The first is marked by the capitalist bloc and by the establishment of the perspective of consumption, mainly during the beginning of the Cold War. The second model, on the other hand, is based on a relationship between communication, the social (the citizen) and the territory and is related, in Brazil, to the period of political opening in 1985 with the social movement, named by, Diretas Já, when social movements developed in the country an important process of rebuilding democracy, after the dictatorial regime (Peruzzo, 2012).

The Brazilian Constitution is considered a Citizen Constitution as it is the 10th in the world in Constitution of Rights, there are a total of 79 of them, according to CPP (Comparative Constitutions Project) (Schreiber, 2020). This magna letter also enhances the action of the councils in the most different areas, such as health (SUS system), culture, education, communication, tourism, among others. In addition to a commitment to massive and predatory tourism, we established a dialogue, in this research, with a sustainable concept linked to Public Communication (CP).

"(...), tourism development, from the perspective qualified as "sustainable", requires a joint effort, involving academia, public management, the social movement, and the private sector, so that tourism can be reinterpreted as a contemporary phenomenon, according to a new paradigm, guided by the incorporation of ethical principles and values (...)" (Irving, 2019, p.23)

In Brazil, many cities, especially in the Northeast, have invested in strategic communication in the recent years. The definition of Strategic Communication, for Margarida Kunsch (2018, p.20):

"(...) strategic communication applied in different social segments, both within public institutions and organizations of organized civil society, as well as in private organizations, depending on the training and vision of the actors involved, may adopt more conservative or more interactive forms."

In order to attract new visitors, we saw that the communication guidelines of the cities that are part of the research corpora manage to earn about 70% of resources in Tourism (Braztoa, 2021), however public policies aimed at the citizen are not well implemented in the country. This could be verified by the HDI of the states of the Northeastern cities as we presented, above, which are the worst in the country. That said, we start from the hypothesis that the choice of managements for strategic communication that promotes commodity cities (Harvey, 1989) are not equated in relation to communication efforts and discursive practices with those aimed at public communication. The concept of Public Communication that we use in this research is related to:

"(...) acting in Public Communication (CP) requires: a) commitment to privilege the public interest over individual or corporate interests; b) centralize the process on the citizen; c) treat communication as a broader process than information; d) adaptation of the instruments to the needs, possibilities and interests of the public; e) assume the complexity of communication, treating it as a whole" (Duarte, 2012b, p.59)

The current context in which we live due to the serious health/political crisis and the ineffectiveness of inclusive public policies in our country have caused changes in our daily lives. The relationship with brands, businesses and public management of territories has also changed drastically. Certainly, we will not leave the same after this global crisis that has been more devastating in Brazil. What to think about our relationship with tourism and citizenship, after the pandemic and its future consequences? How is it possible to develop participatory models of public communication with a view to citizen participation in more inclusive communication practices?

A PROPOSAL TO OBSERVE THE RELATIONSHIP BETWEEN PLACE BRANDING AND CITIZENSHIP IN BRAZILIAN CITIES.

In recent studies carried out on the place brand and public communication in Brazil (Freitas; Porto, 2014; Porto; Santos, 2015; 2016; Moreira; 2020; Melo, Gotardo; Freitas 2019) we have observed that the construction of a positioning of the places brands and also of the public communication guidelines for the citizen are pointed out by the researchers as being unilateral in their majority. Generally, communication models come from governments through specialists in strategic communication and related areas, such as: communication and marketing advisors, public relations, advertising, etc. towards society and to the market". This type of perspective brings as obstacles the absence of public discussion and the risk of anchoring these representations in stereotypes and/or social stigmas (Goffman, 1988).

Different from these types of approach, we propose in this research a comparative investigation in two moments, the first being qualitative and the second quantitative. In the first of them, under the aegis of the qualitative approach, we seek to discursively analyze these universes of meaning around the manifestations of the brands places (Semprini, 2006) of the cities to be observed with a view to promoting these cities for tourism in: a) brand campaigns place aimed at tourists and; then, when these same discursive enunciators, the governments, develop: b) public communication campaigns aimed at the citizen. Therefore, we propose to analyze the plans, campaigns and pieces of communication that according to Semprini (2006; 2005, 2000; 1996) can be understood as the "manifestations of the brand project" in these cities.

In a second moment, inspired by the quantitative approach, we intend to analyze this same issue in a comparative way: a) public communication and b) strategic communication for tourism, mark place, having as methodological support the documental analysis (Moreira, 2009). For this purpose, the corpora of this phase of the research will be official documents and data, namely: communication and tourism plans, the amount of resources allocated by the departments of communication, culture and tourism in: a) public communication campaigns for confrontation of the pandemic aimed at the citizen and b) in the strategic communication campaigns of self-promotion of these cities. This proposal is anchored in the classic analytical proposal of discourse analysis studies (Verón, 2013; Foucault, 2012; 2004; Fairclough, 2001; Maingueneua, 2001) which suggests the relationship between textual and contextual analysis that was recently re-signified by Fairclough (2001) in: textual, discursive and social practices. In summary, this proposal is structured in:

1. **Discourse analysis** (discursive positioning) of the "possible world" (Verón, 2012; Semprini, 2006;2005,1992; Floch, 1990; 1985; 1995; Jost, 1997; 1997; Sampaio, 2012) of: a) communication public in the cities to be observed and b) tourist communication campaigns, mark the place of these Brazilian cities.
2. **Documentary** (Moreira, 2009) and contextual (Fairclough, 2001) analysis of data and official documents: namely communication and tourism plans the amount of resources, among other material and symbolic resources, destined by the communication and tourism secretariats in: a) public communication campaigns aimed at citizens and b) self-promotion campaigns in these cities, to promote their local brand.

This convergence of theoretical-methodological fields, presented in this research project, highlights the interdisciplinary characteristics of the communicational field, as highlighted by Maria Immacolata Vassallo de Lopes (2004)

"What is noticed is a movement of convergence of specialized knowledge about communication, understood more as an intersection movement that is not, under any circumstances, an amalgamation or synthesis of knowledge. It is, rather, a product of the relations between the object of study, the specificity of the analytical contributions and the particularity of the historical evolution between them." (Lopes, 2004)

ANALYTICAL GRID, DISCURSIVE POSITIONING AND BRAND ANALYSIS PLACE ITS MANIFESTATIONS (PLANS, CAMPAIGNS AND COMMUNICATION PIECES)

We have seen previously that the concept of "place brand" is related to the construction of universes of meaning through discursive positioning (Vitorio; Andrade, 2021; Semprini, 2006;2005,1992; Floch, 1990; 1985; 1995; Jost, 1997 Ferreria; 1997; Sampaio, 2012) tourist destinations, through their self-promotion and public communication campaigns.

By discursive positioning we understand as being the domain of studies on discourse analysis (VERÓN, 2012) that seeks to account for the strategies and discursive structures of meaning production of brands in general, as well as their products. Therefore, we must comparatively analyze the brand identity projects (Semprini,2006;2005;2000;1996) of northeastern cities that, for the purposes of these strategic communication efforts aimed at attracting tourists, behave as competitors and in the same scenario of symbolic dispute. In this field, we find the theoretical proposals of Jean Marie-Floch (1995;1990;1985;) and Andrea Semprini (2006;2005;2000;1996;1992).

In studies on discourse and brand analysis, such as Andrea Semprini (2006;2005;2000;1996;1992) and Jean-Marie Floch (1995, 1990, 1985) "(…) there are three properties that since the moment the public recognizes them in a brand, they seek adhesion, the same, with great strength and with greater ease; it is about credibility, legitimacy and seduction (our translation)" (Semprini, 1992, p.70).

For the author, these three concepts guide the brand identity of several products, such as cosmetic products and brands known around the world. This is because these characteristics are also present in the discourse towards strategic communication (Kunsch, 2018). Each brand through these guidelines seeks to build, discursively, a universe of meaning - that is, a possible world (Semprini, 2006, Floch 1995) - harmonic through its self-promotion strategies.

The possible world proposed in your brand project must be coherent so that the public can find the same indemnity brands as the campaigns, for example, in each placement. The loyalty of the audience ends up being built through the expectations launched around the place brand and also in the creation of a discursive unit, translated into a positioning (Semprini, 2006;2005,1992; Floch, 1990; 1985; 1995; Jost, 1997 Ferreria; 1997; Sampaio, 2012).

That said, the elements that constitute this context can relate both to the spaces in which these brand manifestations are circulated – online social networks, billboards, television commercials, in weekly magazine ads, etc. – as well as the "ways of saying" (Benveniste, 1989) which constitute the type of strategic marketing communication discourse (Kunsch, 2008) whose ultimate purpose is to explore seduction and persuasion.

As Aristotle (2011) suggests, both seduction and persuasion are present in Rhetorical Art and are developed, in particular, from three horizons of expectations: Ethos, the construction of the enunciative subject, Pathos, a seduction strategy that takes place through of affects and Logos, the argumentative basis of the statement.

This triad, therefore, is based on the rhetoric that, according to Paul Ricouer (2007), is the oldest discipline on the study of language. Aristotle defines it as: "(...) the art of human discourse, more human" (Aristóteles apud. Ricouer, 2007, p.106). A first criterion of rhetorical art is knowing that: 1. it is audience-oriented, 2. it is argument-oriented, and 3. it aims at persuasion.

The rhetorical approach is also present in any form of speech, or enunciation if we want to use a term closer to discourse analysis, and is also governed by three perspectives: 1. a way of managing faces (Ethos), 2. a treatment given in function of a practical end (Logos) and 3. a correlative treatment of affections (Pathos).

We thus observe that Semprini's (1992) proposal for analysis - anchored in the observation of the discursive construction of credibility, legitimacy and seduction - is inspired by Aristotelian Rhetoric, more specifically, by the three types of arguments or proofs intended to produce persuasion, which are: Ethos, Logos and Pathos. These three instances are also developed by discourse analysis, through the production of perlocutory effects: Please, Inform/Convince and Commove (Charaudeau, Maingueneau, 2004).

It is noteworthy that these three types of effects production have as their main objective the persuasion through the discursive construction of evidence within the discourse. We take as a working hypothesis that it is from these three variables that the possible world of the brands in reference is developed and through it seeks to retain the public (be it the tourist or the citizen) through the construction of a discursive subject that pleases the modalities from Ethos, informs and convinces thanks to Logos and moves through Pathos.

It is through this process of symbolic construction (Semprini, 1996) that the possible world is created and its audiences can be associated, from an identification process, through discursive strategies elaborated by contemporary brands.

We intend, therefore, with this proposal to establish a critical analysis of this symbolic construction strategy, verifying how it collaborates or breaks with constructions that reproduce social stigmas (Goffman, 1988) about the cities analyzed, as well as evaluating its relevance in relation to the context cultural in which they are inserted.

For the development of the discursive analysis of the campaigns, we will take as a proposal the "project/manifestation model" developed by Andrea Semprini (1996; 1992). In it, campaigns are analyzed through three milestones, namely: textual (analysis of strategic communication pieces of campaigns), discursive (positioning), values (social and discursive practices).

In summary, this analysis grid is based on the analysis of the textual, possible and "real" worlds. Anchored in this premise, each brand builds a possible world in each brand manifestation, but based on a specific way of dealing with its audience. The first one comes from the construction of a particular mode of enunciation (Ethos) in relation to its audience, which can also be understood as the search to make people please through the discursive construction of credibility.

In a second moment, there is a particular form of construction of his point of view that can be observed from the discursive construction strategies of legitimation (persuasion) explored from the level of the utterance (Logos).

Finally, discursive positioning is also developed from a specific way of building an affectionate relationship with your audience, through seduction (Pathos). The disaggregation of these three facets of discursive positioning is merely didactic, since both complement and are interdependent.

We have seen that the operations of constructing the meaning effect of enunciators towards co-enunciators aim to legitimize the possible world constructed, discursively, by the first. In short, the real world, the possible world and the textual world are involved in a process of social semiosis (Verón, 2012).

In discourse analysis, the textual world must be observed from a dialogical relationship (Bakhtin, 2002). The enunciator, who speaks through his speech, foresees a co-enunciator. As Benveniste (1989) teaches us: "As a form of discourse, the enunciation places two equally necessary 'figures', one the origin, the other the end of the enunciation. It is the structure of the dialogue". (Benveniste, 1989, p. 87). We assume as a presupposition that every enunciation aims to unite the listener and the speaker (enunciator/co-enunciator) through some bond of feeling (Benveniste, 1989).

Some authors, like Maingueneau (2001), use the term guarantor to show this relationship of co-responsibility between the one who speaks and the one who is questioned by the discourse. Place brands, when they propose their possible world, through strategic communication campaigns, seek to build a relationship of trust in relation to their audience, be it tourists or citizens, through the production of the meaning of an Ethos, a particular way of organizing his speech (Logos) and through his persuasion and seduction strategies (Pathos). Because of these discursive strategies, the enunciator is also involved in the discourse by suggesting a promise (Jost, 1997) to his co-enunciator. The enunciator, when he promises, is also involved in the co-enunciator's discourse through the debt of keeping what was promised.

Once involved in the possible world suggested by the brand, the public must be convinced of the belief (Querré, 2005) that this system represents the interpretive schemes that surround them.

CONCLUSION

Nowadays, strategic communication has given new meaning to the relationship between people and territories and how this has influenced the applicability of the notion of brand in different types of businesses, products, services and even in the management of territories (Freitas; Porto, 2014; Porto; Santos, 2015; 2016; Moreira; 2020; Melo, Gotardo; Freitas 2019). In the field of political communication, during the first decade of this millennium, the world witnessed the strength of these technological devices that were used by the political field. The presidential elections of Barack Obama, Donald Trump and, in Brazil, Jair Messias Bolsonaro are a symptom of these changes in the scope of strategic communication.

Despite this exacerbated exposure mediated by online social networks, there is also space to encourage participation in public forums and debates through communication technologies. Since the 1990s, studies have been developed in another direction and seek to understand citizen participation in experiences of e-government, e-citizenship, etc. (Gomes, 2016). Motivated by this context of reflexivity, governments began to be questioned about their management and the population began to use information and communication technologies to account for public debates.

Here it is worth noting that the meanings of Public Communication (PC) are different all over the world. As Brandão (2012, p.1) reminds us: "(...) In many countries, the understanding of PC is clearly identified with organizational communication, that is, the area that deals with analyzing communication within organizations and between it and its audiences, seeking strategies and solutions. As previously mentioned, the concept of public communication that we take as a parameter in this study is ascendant and bilateral and its efforts aim at the realization of public participation, proposed by Duarte (2012), and anchored in the Federal Constitution of 1989 in its model of democracy participatory, with the institutionalization of communication, culture and tourism councils, for example.

Following this perspective, in 1989, Porto Alegre developed a benchmark governance model that was recognized by the UN as one of the 40 best urban public management practices in the world (OP, 2020). In it, the government worked together with the local population to discuss participatory budgeting.

What institutionally allows the development of these forms of management is the Federal Constitution itself, whose federative model offers autonomy to the states of the country and, at the same time, encourages the construction of municipal and state plans based on specific councils and legislation, as is the case. The case of the organic laws of culture and the constitution of funds, in Brazil, and other forms of promotion for the development of public policies. Such experience was used, for example, in the administration of Gil and Juca (2003-2011) in front of the then Ministry of Culture through the Culture Conferences (Rubim, Barbalho; Calabre, 2015).

In this model, there is the CPF (Council, Plan and Fund). In it, in a collegiate manner, citizens can constitute their representatives from organized civil society, build together with the state the plan of the sector involved (culture, tourism, communication, etc.) and propose allocation of resources within the development funds for each one of those segments. These models of participation of third sector organizations (Peruzzo, 2012) can also be intensified using communication and new information technologies.

These e-governance designs also make people follow their leaders' profiles and pages on Facebook, Twitter, Instagram, etc. The use of comments, likes, memes, emojis, etc. have had numerous impacts on the reputation of these leaders, as well as their governments. At the same time, it encourages them to have the provision of services from professionals from the most diverse areas of Communication, from journalists, public relations and advertisers. This high reflexivity (Giddens, 1993) has caused great impasses and new challenges to management.

There are many types of interventions in the territory that can come from this practice of new information technologies linked to territories. Gomes (2016) presents us with some of them in a survey he conducted on this field of studies.

"(...) the concentration on public services had to give way to other agendas, such as citizen consultation (e-petitions, e-consultations); cooperation with citizens to develop projects, initiatives and policies (crowdsorcing) [sic]; the use of embedded and integrated technological solutions in urban planning to improve the lives of people living in cities (smart cities); the involvement of citizens in the planning and preparation of public budgets (digital OPP); the offer of public, raw or filtered data (open data) for citizens, social organizations and private corporations to produce data-driven technological solutions. As can be seen from the set of themes, in mid-2010 the interfaces between digital government and digital democracy have a number of applications that go far beyond what the traditional pair "electronic governance"-"online public services" would allow us to imagine . And it is also very clear that there is a huge confluence, which is likely to grow even more in the future, between digital government and digital democracy." (Gomes, 2016, p.64-65)

Despite advances in the use of new technologies in urban areas (IBGE, 2020), a look at the interior of Brazilian states and following data from this same source, only 41% (less than half) of the entire rural population of the country is connected to the internet. Meanwhile, in urban centers, telephone and high-speed internet operators are still not able to deliver the signal to all Brazilians, especially in locations that are not part of the public policy view of the administrations, such as in the case of favelas.

On the other hand, some cities that have the highest figures in the world in their economy, have already managed to advance in the use of information technologies to build smart cities. In them, the communication between people and things and vice versa, as well as between things-things and people-people (Lemos, 2013) cause symbolic exchange processes and participation in cities to be mediated using these technologies. In Brazil, some cities have developed local integration strategies based on the use of mobile applications and some other tools that enable this type of practice, as in Curitiba and Salvador.

Some successful examples of public policies already developed in the country, using PC as an instrument of participation, were developed in a collegiate manner, such as Health and Culture and municipal management linked to the participatory budget (OP, 2020). These experiences date back to moments before the pandemic, more precisely between the years 2003 to 2016. Our working hypothesis suggests that if the administrations manage to establish this look towards the citizen, more inclusive communication models may emerge for the territories in favor of citizenship.

We start from the working hypothesis that when the citizen can take a leading role in the referrals of management plans, councils and funds for the design of public policies in the territory they inhabit, Public Communication (CP) in the territories can be carried out. In a context of reflexivity (Giddens, 1991) it is essential that the dimension of the CP, mainly by Public Relations, be implemented and that transparency and mutual understanding between the publics are obtained (Kunsch, 2003;2008). This will be the great differential of the management of territories in the future, especially for public administrations, with regard to public communication policies.

REFERENCES

Aristóteles. (2003). Retórica das paixões [Rhetoric of Passions]. São Paulo: Martins Fontes.

Atlas Brasil, I. D. H. M. (2021). *Atlas Brasil* [Atlas Brazil]. http://www.atlasbrasil.org.br/ranking

Augé, M. (2012). Não lugares [No places]. In Introdução a uma antropologia da supermodernidade. São Paulo: Papirus.

Bakhtin, Ml. (2002). Marxismo e Filosofia da Linguagem [Marxism and Philosophy of Language] (10th ed.). São Paulo: Hucitec.

Benveniste, É. (1989). *Problemas de linguística geral II* [Problems of general linguistics II]. Pontes.

Bourdieu, P. (1999). O Poder Simbólico [Symbolic Power] (2nd ed.). Rio de Janeiro: Bertrand Brasil.

Brandão, E. (2012). Conceito de Comunicação Pública [Concept of Public Communication]. In *Comunicação Pública. Estado, mercado, sociedade e interesse público*. Atlas.

Braztoa, Associação Brasileira das Operadoras de Turismo. (2021). *Anuário* [Yearbook]. https://drive.google.com/file/d/15dqqAnlX1kROS3QVFG-BZxhAIBBa8qwW/view

Calvino, Í. (1990). *As Cidades Invisíveis* [The Invisible Cities] (D. Mainardi, Trans.). Companhia das Letras.

Canclini, N. (1998). *Culturas híbridas* [Hybrid crops]. EDUSP.

Canclini, N. (2010). *Consumidores e cidadãos: conflitos multiculturais da globalização* [Consumers and citizens: multicultural conflicts of globalisation]. Ed. UFRJ.

Charaudeau, P., & Maingueneau, D. (2004). *Dicionário de análise do discurso* [Dictionary of discourse analysis]. Contexto.

Dinnie, K. (2008). *Nation Branding: concepts, issues, practices*. Elsevier.

Duarte, J. (2012) Instrumentos de comunicação pública [Public communication tools]. In Comunicação Pública. Estado, mercado, sociedade e interesse público. São Paulo: Atlas.

Duarte, J., & Barros, A. (Orgs.). (2009). Métodos e técnicas de pesquisa em comunicação [Research methods and techniques in communication]. São Paulo: Atlas.

EMBRATUR. (2020). *Plano Aquarela 2020: marketing turístico internacional do Brasil* [Aquarela 2020 Plan: international tourism marketing of Brazil]. Disponível em: http://www.embratur.gov.br/lai_embratur_secom/export/sites/lai/galerias/download/Plano_Aquarela_2020.pdf

Fairclough, N. (2001). *Discurso e mudança social* [Discourse and social change]. Editora Universidade de Brasília.

Ferreira,G. (1997). *O posicionamento discursivo de "A Gazeta" e "A Tribuna" (Vitoria-ES / Brasil): uma explicação para entender a evolução de suas tiragens* [The discursive positioning of "A Gazeta" and "A Tribuna" (Vitoria-ES / Brazil): an explanation to understand the evolution of their circulation]. Academic Press.

Ferreira, G., Sampaio, A., & Fausto Neto, A. (2012). *Mídia, discurso e sentido* [Media, discourse and meaning]. Edufba.

Firat, A., & Venkatesh, A. (1993). *Postmodernity.* The age of marketing. *International Journal of Research in Marketing, 10*(3), 227–249. doi:10.1016/0167-8116(93)90009-N

Floch, J. (1985). Le changement de formule d'un quotidien approche d'une double exigence: la modernité du discours et la fidélité du lectorat [The change of formula of a daily newspaper approaches a double requirement: the modernity of the discourse and the loyalty of the readership]. In Les Medias - Expériences recherches actuelles applications. Paris: IREP.

Floch, J. (1990). Sémiotique, marketing et communication [Semiotics, marketing and communication]. Paris: Presses Universitaires de France.

Floch, J. (1995). *Identités visuelles* [Visual identities]. Presses Universitaires de France.

Foucault, M. (1985). *As palavras e as coisas. Uma arqueologia das ciências humanas* [Words and things. An archaeology of the human sciences.]. Martins Fontes.

Foucault, M. (2004). *A ordem do discurso* [The order of the discourse]. Loyola.

Foucault, M. (2012). *Arqueologia do Saber* [Archaeology of Knowledge]. Forense Universitária.

Freitas, R., & Porto, A. (2014). Nas ondas do Copacabana Palace: sobre a importância do Hotel na Constituição da Marca Rio [On the waves of Copacabana Palace: on the importance of the Hotel in the making of the Rio brand]. In *Congresso Brasileiro Científico de Comunicação Organizacional e de Relações Públicas*. Abrapcorp. Disponível: https://portal.abrapcorp.org.br/anais/

Furtado, C. (1974). *O mito do desenvolvimento econômico* [The myth of economic development]. Paz e Terra.

Giddens, A. (1991). *As consequências da modernidade* [The consequences of modernity]. Editora Unesp.

Giddens, A. (1993). *A transformação da intimidade. Sexualidade, Amor e Erotismo nas Sociedades Modernas* [The Transformation of Intimacy. Sexuality, Love and Eroticism in Modern Societies]. Unesp.

Gnoth, J. (2002). Leveraging export brands through a tourism destination brand. *Brand Management, 9*(4-5), 262-280.

Goffman, E. (1988). Estigma. Notas sobre a manipulação da identidade deteriorada [Stigma. Notes on the manipulation of deteriorated identity] (4th ed.). São Paulo: LTC.

Gomes, W. (2016). 20 anos de política, Estado e democracia digitais: uma "cartografia" do campo [20 years of digital politics, state and democracy: a "cartography" of the field]. In Democracia digital, comunicação política e redes. Teoria e prática. Rio de Janeiro: Folio Digital: Letra e Imagem.

Goodman, N. (1978). *Ways of Worldmaking*. Hackett Publishing Company.

Greimas, A. (1976). *Semântica Estrutural* [Structural Semantics]. Cultrix.

Hall, S. (2006). *A identidade cultural na pós-modernidade* [Cultural identity in post-modernity]. DP&A.

Harvey, D. (1989). From Managerialism to Entrepreneurialism. The Transformation in Urban Governance in Late Capitalism. *Geografiska Annaler. Series B, Human Geography, 71*(1), 3–17.

IBGE. (2021). *O IBGE apoiando o combate à Covid*-19 [IBGE supporting the fight against Covid-19]. Disponível em: https://covid19.ibge.gov.br/pnad-covid/trabalho.php

IBGE. (2021). *População estimada* [Estimated population]. https://www.ibge.gov.br/pt/inicio.html

Irving, M. (2019). Para sustentabilizar o turismo na contemporaneidade. Ética e políticas públicas globais [To sustain tourism in contemporary times. Ethics and global public policies]. In Turismo: Ressignificando sustentabilidade. Rio de Janeiro: Folio Digital: Letra e Imagem.

Jost, F. (1997). La promesse des genres [The promise of genres]. Réseaux, 81.

Kavaratzis, M. (2004). *From city marketing to city branding: Towards a theoretical framework for developing city brands. In Place Branding* (Vol. 1). Henry Stewart Publications.

Keller, K., & Machado, M. (2006). *Gestão estratégica de marcas* [Strategic brand management]. Person Prentice Hall.

Kotler, P., & Keller, K. (2006). Marketing de lugares [Seat Marketing]. In Como conquistar crescimento de longo prazo na América Latina e no Caribe. São Paulo: Prentice Hall.

Kunsch, M. (2018). A comunicação estratégica nas organizações contemporâneas [Strategic communication in contemporary organisations]. Media & Jornalismo, 33, 13-24. doi:10.14195/2183-5462_33_1

Kunsch, M., & Krohling, M. (Org.). (2009). Comunicação organizacional [Organisational communication] (vol. 2). São Paulo: Editora Saraiva.

Lemos, A. (2013). *A comunicação das coisas. Teoria ator-rede e cibercultura* [The communication of things. Actor-network theory and cyberculture]. Annablume.

Lopes, M. (2004). *As fronteiras entre as ciências sociais vistas da comunicação. Uma aproximação aos estudos sociais das ciências* [The boundaries between the social sciences as seen from communication. An approach to social science studies]. http://www.compos.org.br/e-compos

Maingueneau, D. (2001). *Análise de textos de comunicação* [Analysis of communication texts.]. Cortez.

Melo, F., Gotardo, A., & Freitas, R. (2019). A (re)construção da Marca Rio e seus discursos: medo, comunicação e megaeventos [The (re)construction of the Rio Brand and its discourses: fear, communication and mega events]. In *Congresso Brasileiro Científico de Comunicação Organizacional e de Relações Públicas*. Abrapcorp. Disponível: https://portal.abrapcorp.org.br/anais-abrapcorp/2019/

Moreira, A. (2020). Rio Media Center: comunicação e produção de sentidos sobre a Cidade Olímpica [Rio Media Center: communication and production of meaning about the Olympic City]. In *Congresso Brasileiro Científico de Comunicação Organizacional e de Relações Públicas*. Abrapcorp. Disponível: http://portal.abrapcorp2.org.br/anais-abrapcorp/2020/gts.php/

Moreira, S. (2009). Análise documental como método e como técnica [Documentary analysis as method and as technique]. In *Métodos e técnicas de pesquisa em comunicação*. Atlas.

Novelli, A. (2006). O papel institucional da Comunicação Pública para o sucesso da governança [The institutional role of Public Communication for successful governance]. *Organicom*, 4.

Péninou, G. (1976). *Semiótica de la publicidade* [Semiotics of advertising]. Editorial Gustavo Gili.

Peruzzo, C. (2012). Comunicação e terceiro setor [Communication and the third sector]. IN Comunicação Pública. Estado, mercado, sociedade e interesse público. São Paulo: Atlas.

PIAUÍ. (2021). https://www.pi.gov.br/noticias/wellington-dias-firma-parceria-com-a-franca-em-evento-de-turismo-sustentavel-pos-covid-19/

Porto, A., & Santos, M. (2015). Rio 450 anos: a celebração como estratégia da campanha comemorativa em homenagem à Cidade Maravilhosa [Rio 450 years: the celebration as strategy of the commemorative campaign in honor of the Marvelous City]. In *Congresso Brasileiro Científico de Comunicação Organizacional e de Relações Públicas*. Abrapcorp. Disponível: https://ebooks.pucrs.br/Ebooks/Pdf/978-85-397-0751-5.pdf

Quéré, L. (2005). "Dispositifs de confiance" dans l'espace public [Confidence-building devices in the public space]. Reseaux, 132.

Rabahy, W. (2006). Aspectos do turismo mundial, situação e perspectivas desta atividade no Brasil [Aspects of world tourism, situation and perspectives of this activity in Brazil]. *Observatório de Inovação do turismo – Revista Acadêmica, 1*(1).

Ricouer, P. (1994). Tempo e Narrativa [Time and Narrative]. Campinas: Papirus.

Ricouer, P. (2007). Les références du langage [The language references]. Seuil.

Rubim, A., Barbalho, A., & Calabre, L. (Org.). (2015). Políticas culturais no governo Dilma [Cultural policies in Dilma's government]. Salvador: Edufba.

Sampaio, A. (2012). A marca em produtos midiáticos: o estudo do posicionamento discursivo aplicado ao telejornalismo [The brand in media products: the study of discursive positioning applied to telejournalism]. In *Mídia, discurso e sentido* (pp. 217–236). Edufba.

Sampaio, A. (2020). Comunicação social em territórios [Social communication in territories]. Salvador: UFBA, Escola de Administração; Superintendência de Educação a Distância.

Sampaio, A., & Caliman, L. (2015). Brasil, "o mundo se encontra aqui": manifestações discursivas da marca país rumo à copa de 2014 [Brazil, "the world meets here": discursive manifestations of the country brand towards the 2014 World Cup]. In *Temas Contemporâneos*. Edufba.

Sampaio, A., & Oliveira, J. (2020). Posicionamento da marca Barcelona. Uma disputa de sentidos entre as nacionalidades espanhola e catalã [Positioning the Barcelona brand. A dispute of senses between the Spanish and Catalan nationalities]. *Organicom*, *17*(32), 2020.

Sanches, R., & Sekles, F. (2008). From country-of-origin and national identity to nation branding - Country Case Insight – Brazil. In *Nation Branding: concepts, issues, practices* (pp. 131–160). Elsevier.

Santos, M. (2003). Por uma outra globalização. Do pensamento único à consciência universal [For another globalisation. From the single thought to universal consciousness]. *Record*.

Santos, M. (2009). *Metrópole corporativa fragmentada: o caso de São Paulo* [Fragmented corporate metropolis: the case of São Paulo]. Edusp.

Santos, M. (2014). *O espaço do cidadão* [The citizen's space]. Edusp.

Schreiber, M. (2020). *30 anos da Constituição: a Carta Magna brasileira é generosa demais?* [30 years of the Constitution: is the Brazilian Magna Carta too generous?]. https://www.bbc.com/portuguese/brasil-45754119

Semprini, A. (1992). El marketing de la marca [The marketing of a brand]. In Una aproximación semiótica. Barcelona: Paidós.

Semprini, A. (1996). Analyser la communication [Analysing communication]. In Comment analyser les images, les médias, la publicité. Paris: L'Harmattan.

Semprini, A. (2000). *CNN et la mondialisation de l'imaginaire* [CNN and the globalisation of the imagination]. CNRS.

Semprini, A. (2005). La marque [The mark]. In Une puissance fragile. Paris: Vuibert.

Semprini, A. (2006). A marca pós-moderna. Poder e fragilidade da marca na sociedade contemporânea [The postmodern brand. Power and fragility of the brand in contemporary society]. São Paulo: Estação das Letras.

Verón, E. (1983). *Il est là, je le vois, il me parle. Communications* [He is there, I see him, he speaks to me. Communications]. Academic Press.

Verón, E. (1985). *L'analyse du "contrat de lecture": une nouvele methode pour les etudes de positionnement des supports presse* [The "reading contract" analysis: a new method for media positioning studies]. IREP.

Verón, E. (2013). La semiosis social, 2. Ideas, momentos, interpretantes [Social Semiosis, 2. Ideas, Moments, Interpreters]. Buenos Aires: Paidós Planeta.

WTTC. (2021). *Economic impact reports*. Disponível em: https://wttc.org/Research/Economic-Impact

Section 5

Chapter 12
Internet Marketing:
Factor of Improving SME Business in Serbia

Ivana Domazet
https://orcid.org/0000-0002-3493-4616
Institute of Economic Sciences, Belgrade, Serbia

Marija Lazarević-Moravčević
Institute of Economic Sciences, Belgrade, Serbia

ABSTRACT

This chapter aims to analyze the presence of modern technology solutions in the marketing communication of small and medium enterprises (SMEs) in Serbia. The chapter points out the role of information and communication technology in business improvement and identifies certain issues faced by the SME sector in Serbia, which, among other things, hinder the implementation of modern communication forms. The chapter examines the representation of modern approaches in the marketing communication of SMEs in Serbia and in the form of proposals offers certain solutions for their more effective and efficient implementation. The findings presented in this chapter can contribute to improved SME marketing communication practices and accelerate the transformation of their business from a physical to an online environment.

INTRODUCTION

With the affirmation of marketing orientation as a business concept, market communication is gaining more and more importance for creating business success and competitive advantage. Through market communication, marketing-oriented organizations establish long-term and quality relationships with key stakeholders and strive to create a positive image in the public, and for this purpose use a large number of communication tools and instruments. In fact, when it comes to marketing communication, one cannot avoid the fact that it is an extremely dynamic instrument of the marketing mix, which is constantly changing and improving under the influence of numerous technological and market conditions (Lazarević-Moravčević, Domazet, Lazić, 2021).

DOI: 10.4018/978-1-7998-9790-3.ch012

One of the key factors that lead to drastic changes in the field of communications is the development of modern information technology, i.e. the emergence of interactive media, especially the Internet. Thanks to the Internet, communication becomes dynamic, interactive, targeted, and the effects are measurable. Increasingly intensive reliance on the Internet as a channel of communication has resulted in the emergence and development of a new form of marketing - Internet marketing. Internet marketing is a basic part of digital marketing that has seen impressive growth and development in recent years.

By moving to online business, modern companies are trying to adapt to new changes, which are reflected in the behavior and habits of consumers, and which are significantly intensified by the emergence of the covid-19 pandemic. The increasing use of the Internet as a communication channel by companies is certainly encouraged by the constant growth in the number of Internet users. According to estimates by Datareportal (2021), about 59.5% of the world's population uses the Internet. Additionally, such a situation required companies to find new ways to establish and maintain relationships with stakeholders, which meant accepting the Internet as the dominant channel of communication.

The pandemic that the world faced gave digitalization a completely new dimension and meaning. In the period of isolation, digital media become an integral part of every individual's life. There is a significant increase in the number of Internet and social network users, as well as digital customers. Mobile devices have taken on the role of the most important channel for internet access. These, as well as many other changes in consumer behavior have necessitated the abandonment of traditional forms of communication and the application of various tools and instruments of Internet marketing. In the period of isolation, digital, i.e. online communication is becoming the only possible form of communication between companies and consumers.

The Covid-19 pandemic has induced significant challenges to almost all of the aspects of business activities. In order to overcome the negative effects of the ongoing health crisis, the business sector has turned to digital technologies and application of advanced ICT solutions due to their potential to significantly improve competitiveness and business processes (Domazet et al., 2018). Along with the increased usage of digital technologies in everyday lives, the world population spend most of their time being connected. During a pandemic, digital marketing plays a vital role among different types of customers, regardless of their gender, age, income, qualifications (Kumari, 2021). According to official data (Statista, 2021), as of January 2021 the total number of active internet users on the global level accounts for 4.66 billion with 4.2 billion in social media alone. It is estimated that approximately every second person in the overall global population uses at least one social network. Also, due to the accelerated digitalization, there has been an expansion of e-commerce and a soar in content created for digital channels since social distancing measures have shifted all focus of communication and money transactions to the digital environment.

The pandemic also significantly affected digitalization in Serbia, because it accelerated the process of transformation from traditional to digital business. During the state of emergency, companies were forced to adapt to new circumstances, especially to the trends identified in consumer habits, which relate to the time, type and manner of consumption of certain media.

In this chapter, the authors analyze the representation of the Internet, i.e., online marketing tools in the marketing communication of SMEs in Serbia. The question is to what extent this form of communication is accepted by SMEs, as well as whether the basic conditions for the transformation of business from traditional to online forms are met in these companies. The authors of the paper are of the opinion that the size of a company significantly determines the process of digitalization. While on the one hand there are factors that stimulate this process and make it simpler compared to large systems, on the other hand there are also factors that limit and slow down the digitization process. In fact, the author's position is that small organizations, as extremely flexible systems, can fully or partially switch to online business, i.e., their marketing communication strategy can be based on various internet marketing tools, assuming that two key barriers are removed - lack of financial and human resources.

The desk-research method was applied in the paper, where the sources of secondary data were primarily papers and publications from scientific journals and other professional literature in the field of marketing, as well as official data and reports of relevant institutions.

LITERATURE REVIEW

Modern society is inextricably linked to technology. Technology and modern technological solutions are the result of society and social transformations. Technology is evolving in society and integrates more than ever into the daily life of the individual. According to Castells (2005) society shapes technology in accordance with the needs, values and interests of people who use technology. Moreover, information and communication technologies are particularly sensitive to the effects of social uses on the technology itself. Actually, information and communication technologies (ICT) are not some spontaneous and unprovoked inventions. They are the product of numerous social factors, but they are also the initiator of numerous changes in society.

New technologies are emerging in society, and determine all its subsystems: economy, culture and politics. They help develop a number of sectors in the economy, such as retail (e-commerce), transportation (automated vehicles), education (massive open online courses), health (electronic record and personalized medicine), as well as social interactions (social networks). On the other hand "many of the same technologies that drive the digital economy are also disrupting key industries and upsetting major incumbents (Kotler, 2006). Modern technologies are used to lead revolutions, but also as a means of creating new values and norms, creating new cultures and manipulation.

Due to technological changes, the business environment has also changed significantly. Thanks to the appearance of virtual companies and stores on the Internet, as well as virtual advertising space, a new online market has been created. It is a market that has no borders (Živadinović and Želić, 2014). The changes have also affected the field of marketing, and especially the marketing communication. New technological solutions have led to the emergence of new, but also the improvement of existing approaches in communication between companies and stakeholders.

In modern business conditions, the Internet plays a significant role in marketing communication. As an interactive and multimedia medium, the Internet enables dynamic and two-way communication. Clay Shirky in his work The Political Power of Social Media points out that "as the communication landscape becomes more complex, dense and participatory, the networked population is gaining greater access to information, more opportunities to engage in public speech, and an enhanced ability to undertake collective action (Shirky, 2011). Communication that takes place via the Internet has both the characteristics of interpersonal and mass communication (Ognjanov, 2013). According to Gurau (2008) what makes the Internet specific compared to any other communication channel is interactivity, transparency and the ability to store information. According to Pierre Levy (2019) with the internet we reach a a new point, a new threshold in the history of collective intelligence. We now have the media "with the almost complete disappearance of the constraints of a physical space, and the memory is accessible from any point on earth, a full kind of ubiquitous memory. Also, everybody has the ability, at least theoretically, to add something to the common memory (Lévy, 2019)."

Thanks to the Internet, communication has become targeted, efficient, and the effects are measurable (Lazarević-Moravčević, Domazet, Lazić, 2021). It is necessary to point out the fact that communication via the Internet takes place in real time, has a higher level of flexibility and coverage, and allows a far greater range compared to traditional forms of communication. (Domazet, 2018). In the process of communication, the position of the consumer changes significantly. Internet user, i.e. the consumer takes a proactive and extremely active role in the communication process. Actually, modern information technologies are introducing numerous changes. One of the key is the constant movement of market power from creators and advertisers to customers (Rani, 2019). The view of the authors Peterson, Balasubramanian & Bronnenberg (1997) is that the Internet provides numerous opportunities, not only as a communication channel, but also as a means of transaction and distribution channel. The use of the Internet reduces transaction costs, makes products / services available to consumers, sales are tailored to individual requirements and becomes flexible. The use of the Internet as a distribution channel not only reduces costs, but also ensures the immediate delivery of products / services.

Chaffey, Ellis-Chadwick, Mayer and Johnston (2009) in their work *Internet Marketing: Strategy, Implementation and Practice*, as the basic forms of internet marketing state the following: Search Engine Optimization (SEO), Search Engine Marketing (SEM), Social Media Marketing (SMM), Email Marketing, and Affiliate Marketing. These online marketing techniques are tools for guiding Internet users to websites where it is possible to perform further activities - buying or ordering products. (Schwarzl & Grabowska, 2015). It is necessary to point out the fact that internet marketing is a part of digital marketing. Compared to digital marketing that uses various offline tools - advertising on any electronic medium, internet marketing relies solely on internet advertising (Amirova, 2019). Actually, digital marketing as a broader phenomenon compared to online marketing represents the promotion of a company through different types of digital media (Diyana, 2018). Chaffey (2009) also points to the fact that successful internet marketing requires the integration of these techniques with traditional media such as TV, print, direct mail. In fact, in the professional literature, there is an opinion that each new technology has certain advantages over the previous ones, but it also lacks some characteristics that the previous one possessed (Fletcher, 2003). Stanković, Ćurčić, & Dragićević (2010) believe that these techniques are not equally important for all companies and their choice is conditioned by marketing strategy, company activity, product life cycle, brand recognition, Internet development. Chaffey (2009) also points to the fact that successful internet marketing requires the integration of these techniques with traditional media such as TV, print, direct mail. In fact, in the professional literature, there is an opinion that each new technology has certain advantages over the previous ones, but it also lacks some characteristics that the previous one possessed (Fletcher, 2003). Stanković, Ćurčić, & Dragićević (2010) believe that these techniques are not equally important for all companies and their choice is conditioned by marketing strategy, company activity, product life cycle, brand recognition, Internet development. Kotler (2016) concludes that despite the growing dominance of online communication, they will not completely replace offline business. Coulter believes that "they need a coexist to deliver the best customer experience."

The modern marketing literature is dominated by the standpoint that the Internet, compared to traditional marketing, offers numerous advantages. The key advantage is two-way and interactive communication. Based on the established dialogue, it is possible to identify the needs and habits of consumers more easily, solve the identified issues, and adequately promote products / services. (Domazet, Neogradi, 2019). Two-way communication enables efficient implementation of the promotional campaign, as well as obtaining accurate information on the effects achieved (Chaffey & Chadwick, 2016), which creates the possibility for further improvements in parts of the campaign that do not provide satisfactory results (Lazarević-Moravčević, Domazet, Lazić, 2021). One of the main advantages of using digital technology is greater interaction with customers and the growth of the ability to meet personal expectations, which in the coming period may play a key role in creating a sustainable competitive advantage (Vidas-Bubanja, Madžar, 2019). As an advantage of this type of marketing, it is necessary to point out the fact that it usually does not require large investments. Bala & Verma (2020) point out that online communication brings lower costs compared to conventional and expensive advertising methods, such as print media, radio, television and magazines. Also, the authors state that the amount of the budget intended for Internet marketing primarily depends on the choice of elements that will make up the marketing strategy, i.e., on whether the strategy is based more on inbound (input) or outbound (output) techniques.

According to research by Opren and Vinerean (2015), the application of digital inbound marketing strategies is the most efficient way to reach consumers with less investment. In fact, the goal of inbound marketing is to attract customers based on high-quality content (Dakouan, Benabdelouahed & Anabir, 2019), i.e. to guide interested customers to specific websites. Unlike outbound techniques, that aim to find customers, inbound marketing focuses on methods that affect the visibility of the company and its activities, as well as on creating quality relationships with potential customers. The most used inbound marketing techniques are content marketing, blogs, search engine optimization (SEO), social networks, etc. Due to the numerous benefits offered by the application of these techniques, and especially social networks, their use has grown in recent years.

Social media marketing is the latest trend that has evolved in recent years and has begun to dominate online communication. The use of social media has changed customer behavior and consequently the way companies operate (Akay and Badlo, 2021). Many authors in the field of marketing are increasingly emphasizing the importance of social networks as channels of communication. According to Kapoor (2018) social media have become part of marketing tactics and are significantly integrated into marketing strategies.Social media allows companies to connect with their customers, improve awareness of their brands, influence consumer attitudes, receive feedback, help improve current products and services and sales increase (Algharabet, 2018). Marketing on social networks is used for commercial purposes, ie attracting customers to the site, creating demand, increasing sales. It is also used for branding purposes - increasing brand awareness, audience loyalty, working with reputation.

Baird and Parasnis (2011) point out the fact that it is advisable for companies to be present on the networks, given that they represent a gathering place for many people. In addition, it is necessary to consider the fact that the number of users of social networks is constantly increasing and it is estimated that 56.8% of the world's population is currently active on social networks. The fact that in 2021, compared to the previous year, the number of active users of social networks at the global level increased by 13.2%, indicates the role they play as a channel of communication during the pandemic crisis. (Datareportal, 2021). Krstić and Đurđević (2017) point out the great marketing potentials of Facebook and note that this social network must not be neglected in creating the marketing strategy of any organization. As the most popular network, Facebook currently records close to 2.8 billion active users monthly (Dataportal, 2021). Domazet et al. (2019) point to the growing popularity and role of Instagram, pointing to its potential in the advertising segment. The authors point out that activity on Instagram provides a broad marketing presence thanks to the capability that content can be shared on other networks as well. Despite the numerous opportunities that these social networks provide, according to Gardašević et al. (2018) for successful communication through social networks, it is necessary to understand the ways in which they function, as well as the motives for its use by its users, i.e., consumers. It is necessary to point out the fact that the use of social networks carries certain risks due to the disclosure of personal data, which most users are not even aware of or consider themselves a low-risk target (Tow, 2010).

The reasons for using social networks and internet marketing as communication channels are numerous. According to the Eurostat (2020) survey, companies in the EU use social networks mainly to build their image and promote their products. In addition to the above, there are other reasons such as: getting opinions or customer reviews, answering questions, hiring, involving customers in product development, etc. In addition, digital communication as the basis of internet marketing is simpler than traditional because it simplifies buying and selling processes. The Internet is available to both: to consumers for their research, and to sellers for their campaigns - 24 hours 7 days a week.

In addition, internet marketing precisely targets the target audience according to location, gender, age, interest. This is the purpose of site and social media analytics, which directs digital marketing campaigns. Also in a digital marketing campaign, you have complete control over the content of you post, when you will post it and what the dynamics of the posts will be. You can correct the strategy at any time, and the speed of reaction during the campaigns you conduct is immense and incomparable with any other type of promotion or marketing. In addition, during and after the campaign, you receive feedback from the target segment in the form of their reaction to your activities, and you can measure the achieved result immediately (Domazet, 2018).

Finally, digital marketing allows you to build and maintain quality relationships with your customers. Marketing tools such as posts, auto responders, blogs, social media posts... have proven their power in magnetizing new customers. Using these and many other tools, you can easily find, and interest customers and build long-term relationships with them. (Vukmirović, Domazet, Kostić-Stanković).

In the current business conditions, the transition from traditional to modern communication approaches is important for every company, regardless of its size or activity (Lazarević-Moravčević, Lazić, Kaličanin, 2019). Respecting the characteristics of smaller companies, primarily their flexibility, it is considered that the transformation of business from physical to online environment should not be a problem for these organizations and would certainly bring numerous benefits (Vidas-Bubanja, 2021). By applying modern and interactive media such as the Internet, small businesses have numerous opportunities to promote, offer and sell their products / services (Lazarević-Moravčević, Lazić, Kaličanin, 2019). On the other hand, SMEs that do not invest constantly in innovation have a higher risk of marginalization of products and services by technologically superior competitors (Bogavac – Cvetković, Pavlović, Cvetković, 2015).

In his work Guerrilla Marketing, Levinson (2009) highlights the fact that the relationship between small businesses and the environment is established based on fast, dynamic and unconventional methods of communication. Moreover, these new methods of communication imply the application of modern technology and enable high business results to be achieved with minimal investment (Levinson, 2009).

Despite the numerous benefits offered by modern information technology, certain research has shown that SMEs lag behind large systems with the application of modern technological solutions, i.e., that "SMEs in Serbia lag behind in taking over advanced digital solutions (European Commission, 2021)". The non-acceptance of modern technological solutions is the result of the influence of numerous factors. Phyllis, Johansson, & Wagner (2003) believe that SME owners are not sufficiently aware of all the possibilities of applying modern technologies and are less willing to support changes within the company to enable the implementation of ICT. In his research, Denić (2018) proves that SME managers in Serbia are not sufficiently familiar with all the advantages offered by internet marketing. In the professional literature, there is also the opinion that the lack of resources (financial and human) may be one of the key issues that hinders the transformation of SMEs from traditional to online business (Vidas-Bubanja, 2021). As the main reasons for the slower introduction of ICT in the SME sector, Deakins and Freel (2012) enumerate high costs of procurement and implementation of ICT, limited Internet speed and availability, time and effort to acquire new ICT skills, real or apparent lack of needs for new technologies, aversion to innovative practices, etc.

APPLICATION OF INFORMATION AND COMMUNICATION TECHNOLOGY IN THE SME SECTOR IN SERBIA

Companies of all sizes, including small and medium-sized ones, use a variety of digital channels, such as search engines, social networks, email, webpages, as well as mobile phones to connect with existing and potential customers. These digital media open new opportunities for marketers, primarily in the field of customer targeting, how to create a message and shape the offer. Unlike them, traditional media are so present in our lives that we are simply confused when we need to define or list them, because traditional media include television, radio and print media (newspaper, magazines, leaflets, flyers, etc.)

In today's world, which is increasingly striving for digitalization and automation of business processes, it is necessary to adapt to this and other trends that prevail in the market. The technological revolution, which began with Web 2.0 to today's 5.0, has changed the way we communicate in terms of speed and interactivity of communication. Communication via digital, internet media and platforms is now very fast and feedback is expected. Companies need to adapt to this way of digital communication, and to do so efficiently, they use a simple three-phase concept that includes 1. Defining business goals, 2. Setting a campaign budget and 3. Targeting a group of consumers to dominate their marketing activities.

The trends that have led to the exponential development of digital communications include (Domazet, Neogradi, 2019; Vukmirović, Domazet, Kostić-Stanković, 2020):

- Growth of internet access via mobile phones
- Growth of advertising through mobile phone applications
- Visual content becomes more important in communication than textual content
- Increasing consumer bargaining power, through global online communities
- Cheaper internet services as well as mobile devices used for this
- Development of the "open innovation" model
- Intensification of communication between individual users (sites for software exchange, videos; group shopping sites; company evaluation, etc.)
- Development of Cloud Computing (reducing the importance of geographical location to Internet users)
- Development of analytical methods and tools for processing a huge amount of data collected in a virtual environment (Big data)
- A major challenge in addressing privacy, security and copyright issues.

The main goal of marketing has always been to connect with its target group in the right place and at the right time. Today, this means that you must look for customers and get to know their habits and problems where they mostly spend their time: on the Internet. This is where internet marketing comes into play.

Table 1. Companies with internet access and own website in Serbia (shown in %)

	2017	2018	2019	2020
Companies with internet access	99.7	99.8	99.8	100
Companies that own website	80.4	82,6	83.6	84.4

Source: Statistical Office of the Republic of Serbia (2020). Use of information and communication technologies in the Republic of Serbia, http://publikacije.stat.gov.rs/G2020/Pdf/G202016015.pdf

Today, most customers start searching for products or services online. They ask for information about a new product, service or location, they have questions, they ask for help, additional information about a certain case. They want more information about certain brands, companies, etc. The way of buying has changed drastically, so - offline, or traditional marketing based on TV, radio and outdoor advertising is not as effective as before. In contrast to traditional marketing, internet marketing is characterized by constantly evolving activities, following the habits of internet users who are very often online, via their mobile phones, tablets, laptops or desktops. Hence, we can say that the Internet is the most important factor in the development of digital marketing. It has opened new, faster, and more selective opportunities for companies to do business and communicate with clients. Most importantly, the Internet has virtually abolished the physical boundaries that exist between people who buy and sell.

Accordingly, and due to the numerous benefits that can be achieved, digital forms of communication have become a practice of many companies in Serbia. This position is also confirmed by the results of the research on the use of information and communication technologies in Serbian companies, which was conducted at the beginning of 2020 by the Statistical Office of the Republic of Serbia. The survey was conducted on a sample of 1571 companies, of which 79.3% belong to the SME category.

According to the results of the research, all companies in the sample have an internet connection. Of the total number of companies that have an Internet connection, 98.4% of companies have a broadband Internet connection. About 77% of companies use a mobile internet connection using portable devices (smartphone, laptop, tablet, etc.) At the sample level, 27% of companies sold products / services via the Internet in 2019, 20.9% of companies employ ICT professionals, and about 77% use external suppliers to perform the ICT function (Statistical Office of the Republic of Serbia, 2020).

Research by the Statistical Office of the Republic of Serbia also points to the fact that the number of companies that own websites is constantly growing. During 2020, this segment grew by 0.8% compared to 2019, or 1.8% compared to 2018. On the other hand, a relatively small number of companies have chat service and pay cloud services over internet (Statistical Office of the Republic of Serbia, 2020).

According to Thelwall (2020) there are five types of business websites: 1) Company information and contacts, 2) Company information, contacts and information about specific products and services, 3) On-line catalog with details of product groups, 4) an online catalog that allows online ordering, 5) cyber stores, which allow online payment (Thewall, 2000). The following chart shows the services that companies in Serbia provide through the website.

A website is an extremely powerful means of communication. This internet-marketing instrument is a center for collecting effects, achieved based on other online promotion techniques. In fact, websites are not just platforms for digitally presenting a company and its products but serve as a basic way of generating revenue and a basic point of contact between seller and buyer (Abdallah & Jaleel, 2015). In order to achieve optimal results, it is necessary that this communication channel is supported by other

Figure 1. Services provided by companies in Serbia through the website
Source: Statistical Office of the Republic of Serbia (2020). Use of information and communication technologies in the Republic of Serbia, http://publikacije.stat.gov.rs/G2020/Pdf/G202016015.pdf

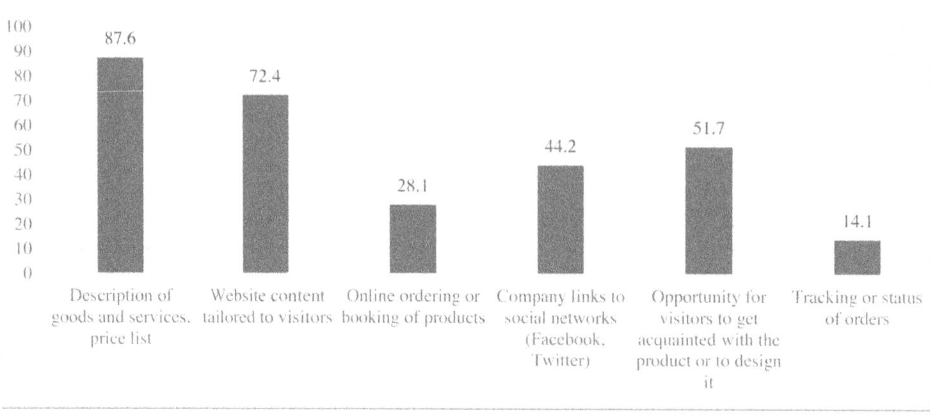

online marketing techniques, especially the active presence of companies on social networks (Lazarević-Moravčević, Domazet, Lazić, 2021).

Eurostat (2020) surveys conducted in 2019 indicate that 47% of companies in Serbia use one of the social networks as a communication channel. In this segment of communications, significant progress was made compared to 2013, when about 30% of companies were active on social networks. Comparing the result with the EU level standard, which is about 51%, we can conclude that Serbia according to this indicator does not lag behind developed economies (Eurostat, 2020).

Based on the analysis of the results of a small number of researches that dealt with the topic of the presence of ICT in SMEs in Serbia, it can be concluded that these systems, compared to large organizations, lag behind in the application of modern technological solutions. On the other hand, this is an extremely important segment of the economy. The SME sector has a dominant share in employment, GDP creation and total turnover. According to the latest data from 2018, this sector accounts for 99.9% of total active enterprises, employs 2/3 of employees and participates with 57.5% in the GVA of the non-financial sector (Ministry of Economy, 2020).

SMEs make up the dominant share of companies in the Serbian market, and this segment of the economy that went through numerous challenges over the years. Therefore, creating a business environment that would stimulate small business development is one of the main goals of economic policy makers in Serbia. The results of numerous researches and studies, which were conducted with the aim of assessing the quality of the business environment in Serbia show that despite certain positive tendencies, in the segment of macroeconomic stability, infrastructure and legal regulations, the quality of the business environment in Serbia cannot be assessed as satisfactory (Kamenković, Lazarević-Moravčević, 2019). According to the research of the World Economic Forum, certain factors that discourage business in Serbia are still present, and according to the report from 2019, one of them is the adoption of information and communication technologies (WEF, 2019).

According to the data from the report of the World Economic Forum in 2019, Serbia took the 72nd position on the ranking list, with the value of the Global Competitiveness Index of 60.9 (the maximum is 100). The report ranks 141 economies based on 103 indicators in 12 areas. Compared to previous years, progress has been made in institutions, education, business dynamics, etc. In the area of macroeconomic

Table 2. Use of social networks by companies in selected EU economies (shown in %)

	Social networks	Enterprise blog or microblogs	Multimedia content sharing websites	Use at least one tipe of social media
EU – 28	51	13	21	53
Belgium	70	16	30	71
Bulgaria	33	4	9	34
Germany	45	8	21	48
Greece	53	11	15	55
Croatia	47	7	20	52
Italy	46	7	21	47
Austria	55	10	27	60
Romania	32	4	7	33
Slovenia	49	8	23	50
United Kingdom	68	32	25	72
Bosnia and Herzegovina	48	6	13	49
Serbia	47	12	17	49

Source: Eurostat (2020) Social media - statistics on the use by enterprises, https://ec.europa.eu/eurostat/statistics-explained/index.php?title=Social_media_-_statistics_on_the_use_by_enterprises#Use_of_social_media_by_enterprises

stability, Serbia has maintained the same position as in previous years. On the other hand, an extremely negative trend was observed in the field of ICT. According to this indicator, Serbia fell by 17 positions compared to the previous year, based on the criteria - the number of mobile telephony and broadband Internet subscribers (World Economic Forum, 2019).

In addition to certain factors that come from the external environment and limit the innovative capacity of SMEs, it is necessary to point out the fact that SMEs face numerous internal constraints, such as lack of financial and human resources, outdated equipment, lack of knowledge and skills in cash flow management, lack of business planning, strategic thinking, marketing orientation, etc. (Lazarević-Moravčević, Erić, Kamenković, 2018).

The characteristics of SMEs significantly determine their relationship to marketing activities. In smaller companies in Serbia, there is no practice of forming a department in charge of marketing activities, and often not even an individual specialist in this field exists. The owner of the company has a key

Table 3. Number of enterprises and employees in the SME sector (2018-2020)

SME	**Medium enterprises**			**Small enterprises**			**Micro enterprises**		
Year	2018	2019	2020	2018	2019	2020	2018	2019	2020
Number of enterprises	1.387	1.497	1.815	10.387	11.036	11.617	93.689	93.085	92.257
Number of employees	232.991	253.876	273.115	313.435	321.391	316.247	236.575	236.639	237.035

Source: APR (2020) Annual bulletin of financial statements, https://www.apr.gov.rs/upload/Portals/0/GFI_2021/Godisnji_bilten_2020/BiltenSI2020.pdf

Table 4. Changing the rank of the pillars of competitiveness in the period 2017-2019 in Serbia

	2017	2018	2019	Change in %
Institutions	65	76	75	+1
Infrastructure	50	48	51	-3
Addoption of ICT	57	60	77	-17
Macroeconomic stability	95	64	64	=
Healthcare	67	67	76	-9
Education and skills	58	56	55	+1
Commodity market	78	66	73	-7
Labor market	54	52	54	-2
Financial system	97	79	82	-3
Market size	74	75	74	+1
Bussiness dynamics	59	59	54	+5
Ability to innovate	65	56	59	-3

Source: WEF, The Global Competitiveness Report 2019, 2018, 2017

role in planning and implementing marketing activities. Marketing agency services are rarely used, and formal market research is uncommon (Lazarević-Moravčević, Erić, Kamenković, 2018). The research conducted by the market research agency *Smart Plus Research* in cooperation with the portal *Marketing Network*, on a sample of 400 small and medium enterprises, indicates that small business owners in Serbia mostly equate marketing with advertising and sales. Advertising comes down to printing and distributing promotional material, as well as owners 'expectations that a nice word from a satisfied customer will be enough to strengthen the brand. Neither the benefits of internet marketing (Domazet, Đokić & Milovanov, 2017), nor business gatherings and advertising on social networks (Marketing mreža, 2017) are fully used. Obradović et al. (2018) in their research also points to the fact that the potentials of email marketing are not used either. According to the mentioned research, employees in SMEs in Serbia are aware of all the benefits of e-mail marketing and use this type of communication on a daily basis in order to increase sales. However, this online marketing tool is most often used for sending messages of an informative rather than a promotional nature.

The limitations faced by small organizations force these companies to find new, unconventional ways to implement marketing activities, especially in the field of communication (Lazarević-Moravčević, 2019). In fact, small business owners often do not need to rely too much on marketing theory but adapt marketing activities to the needs of the business. For them, formal research is not of great importance. They are more focused on gathering information through informal methods, especially through contact networks (Collinson and Shaw, 2001). However, the fact that despite all the benefits that internet marketing can provide to these companies, its potentials are not used enough, is worrying.

The crisis caused by the corona virus has further aggravated business conditions in Serbia. The consequences of the crisis are being felt by all organizations, regardless of their size. The largest resistance to the crisis was provided by large and medium-sized enterprises, while the micro-enterprise sector was the most affected. The sensitivity can be explained by the fact that these are companies that mainly

Figure 2. Measures taken or planned in response to the crisis
Source: USAID (2020) Annual Survey of 1.000 Serbian businesses, https://saradnja.rs/wp-content/uploads/2020/11/Anketa-1000-preduze%C4%87a-2020.pdf

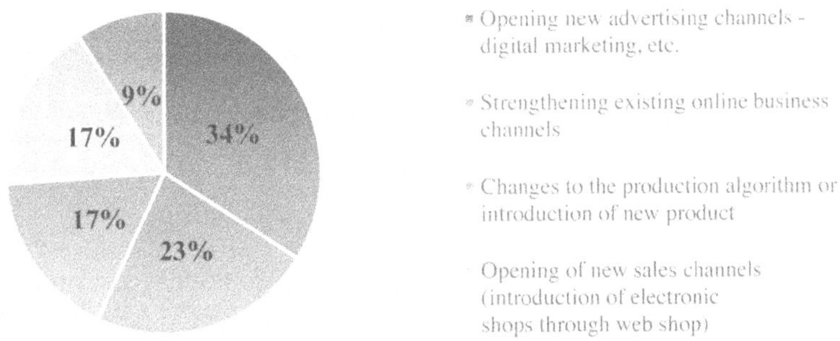

operate in the most vulnerable sectors, face a lack of financial resources and have little opportunity to diversify their operations (CEVES, 2020).

A survey conducted by USAID in cooperation with the Serbian Chamber of Commerce during 2020, indicates that optimism regarding future business, volume of activities and income, abandons businessmen in Serbia to a certain extent. As in previous years, lack of funding and inaccessibility to external sources of funding have been identified as a major problem facing the SME sector. In addition to the mentioned problem, the following issues were also identified: unfair competition, legal uncertainty due to unclear regulations and lack of transparency in the adoption of regulations, lack of qualified human resources, etc. (USAID, 2020).

On the other hand, according to the results of the USAID survey from 2020, the crisis has significantly changed the attitudes of businessmen in Serbia regarding the digitalization and acceptance of modern technological solutions in business, that is, it has accelerated the transformation process. According to the above research, every third company in the sample believes that it is possible to, partially or completely, adapt to doing business over the Internet, and certain activities are already being undertaken in this segment.

According to the results of this research, large and medium-sized companies are more willing to accept e-commerce. One-fifth of these companies are already part of the e-commerce chain. The companies most affected by the crisis, which had a significant drop in revenue, see the greatest importance in e-commerce. The absolute majority of companies in the sample (82%) rated the web shop as important or more important than the traditional business model. As for the companies who utilize a webstore, we notice a significant increase of those that offer the online payment option. In addition, it is extremely important to note that most SMEs believe that they lack additional ICT skills (USAID, 2020).

The growth in the number of companies that own websites indicates the fact that SMEs in Serbia have realized the importance of this communication channel. On the other hand, the fact that this internet-marketing tool is not used by more than 43% of micro and 24% of small businesses in the sample is also distressful.

The expansion of the digital economy has continued intensively with the outbreak of the Covid-19 pandemic, both in developed and developing economies. The pandemic conditioned the accelerated acceptance of digitalization and encouraged companies to reorient themselves towards digital business models, as well as to invest more in modern information technologies and digital skills.

Figure 3. Presence of online business in SMEs
Source: USAID (2020) Annual Survey of 1.000 Serbian businesses, https://saradnja.rs/wp-content/uploads/2020/11/Anketa-1000-preduze%C4%87a-2020..pdf

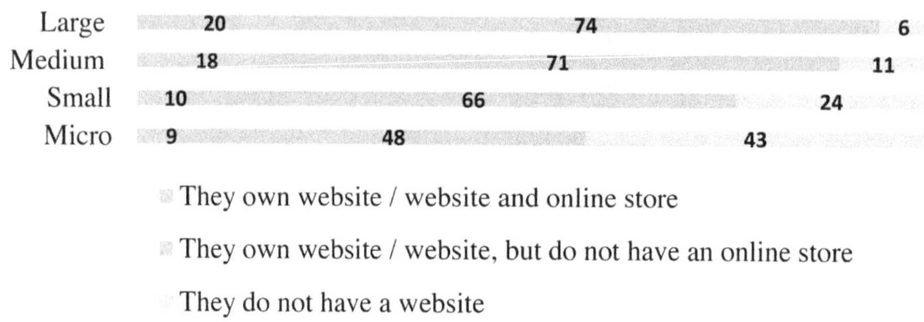

The authors of the paper believe that SMEs in Serbia must adapt to the identified trends in the coming period. In fact, the marketing communication strategy in these systems must be readjusted to the situation in which the companies operate. This situation is determined not only by internal, but also by numerous factors from the external environment (Lazarević - Moravčević, 2019). When creating a marketing communication strategy, it is necessary for SMEs to consider the changes that occur in consumer behavior, which are primarily related to the choice of information and communication channels.

During the pandemic, and especially in the period of isolation, people's behavior and lifestyle were drastically changed and attuned to the measures that were introduced with the intention of preventing the spread of the disease. New circumstances have caused changes in the habits of consumers in Serbia in terms of the manner and type of consumption of certain media. During the isolation, the growth of consumption of digital channels was identified - TV, Internet, social networks (IPSOS, 2020). Moreover, according to the latest data (January 2021), the number of Internet users in Serbia amounted to 6.89 million and compared to the previous year, an increase of 4.9% was recorded (Datareportal, 2021). According to the data of the Statistical Office of the Republic of Serbia, in 2020 81% of households in Serbia have a broadband internet connection, 78.4% of the population use the Internet, 94.1% mobile phones and 37% of Internet users use e-government services (Statistical Office of the Republic of Serbia, 2020).

During the previous year, Serbia recorded a significant increase (8.1%) in the number of active users of social networks. Despite the fact that the number of users of social networks is constantly growing, it is necessary to point out that according to this indicator, Serbia still lags behind developed countries in Europe. In Serbia, about 52.8% of the population currently actively uses social networks, which is below the current European average, which can be estimated at 60-70%.

Similar to the global level, the dominant social network in Serbia is Facebook with 3.2 million users, followed by Instagram with 2.6 million users. In recent years, other platforms have become increasingly popular - TikTok, Twitter, Snapchat and YouTube. There is also a growing trend of reviews of advertisements published by these networks (Lazarević-Moravčević, Domazet, Lazić, 2021).

A survey conducted in Serbia in 2020, on a sample of 1,000 respondents, indicates that a large number of users (42%) use social networks to search for people, companies and brands (Pioniri, 2020). According to Datareportal (2021), an average user of social networks in Serbia likes about 16 posts on Facebook

Figure 4. Number of internet users and active users of social networks in Serbia (in thousands)
Source: Based on Datareportal data, 2017,2018, 2019, 2020, 2021

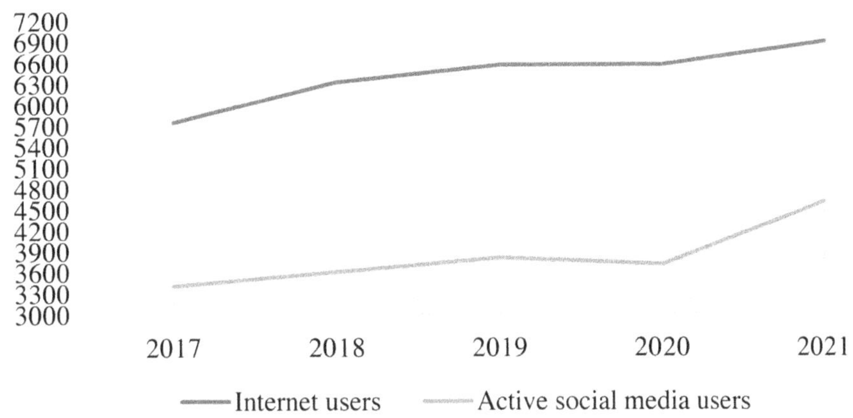

per month, creates three comments, and views about 26 ads. These data indicate that social networks have significant marketing potential, which SMEs should use more intensively in the coming period.

RECOMMENDATIONS AND FUTURE RESEARCH DIRECTIONS

The analysis conducted in this chapter showed that Internet marketing in SMEs in Serbia is in the development phase. In addition, we identified certain factors that prevent more intensive acceptance of online communication tools: lack of financial and human resources, especially skills and knowledge in digital technology and marketing, resistance of entrepreneurs to changes, aversion and fear of innovative solutions, etc.

Figure 5. Number of users of social networks in Serbia and surrounding economies (in %)
Source: Based on Datareportal data, https://datareportal.com/

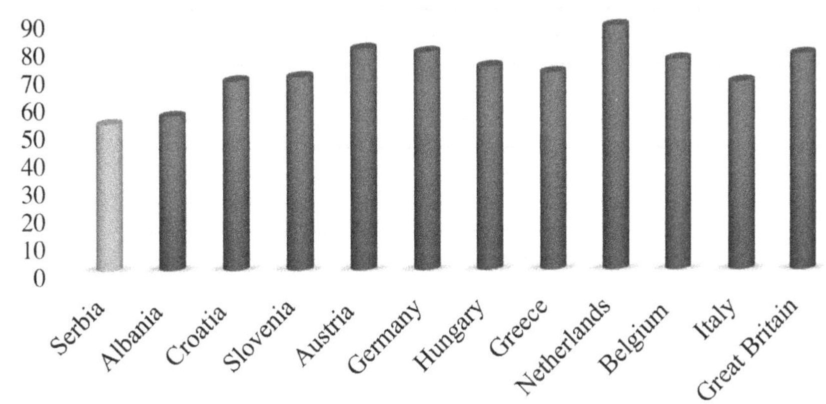

Figure 6. Ranking of social networks in Serbia according to the number of users
Source: State of social media - Serbia 2020, https://pioniri.com/sr/socialserbia2020/

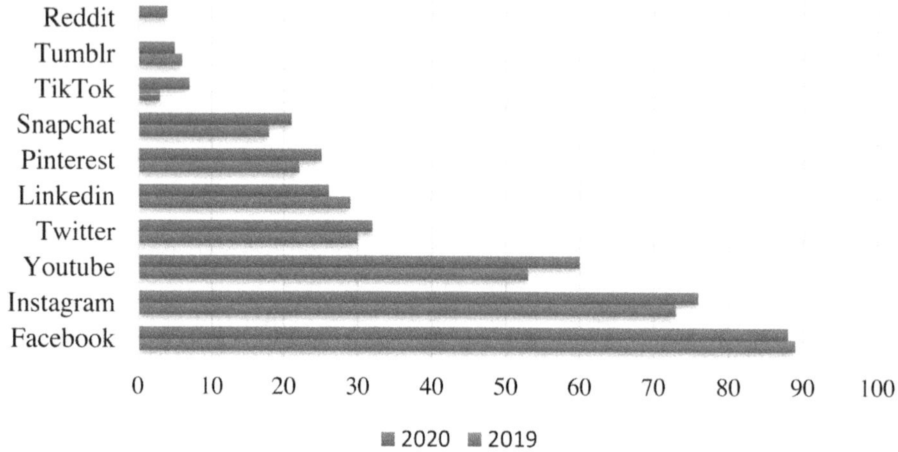

The authors of the paper believe that the challenges that limit the modernization of business in SMEs, and especially those related to human resources, can be overcome by launching various business education programs in Serbia. In that way, knowledge in the field of marketing and digital skills would be acquired and promoted. Innovative capabilities of companies can also be improved by encouraging cooperation between scientific institutions and companies, as well as through the process of incubation and cluster formation.

In addition, the authors emphasize the fact that state support in this domain would be extremely important. Recognizing the importance and role of information and communication technology in the development of the economy and society, the Government of the Republic of Serbia adopted a new Strategy for the Development of the Information Society and Information Security for the period from 2021 to 2026. The Government also defined a vision for the development of the Information Society in the Republic of Serbia. The strategy covers important areas that can contribute to the development of the information society, and which relate to: electronic communications, e-government, e-health and e-justice, ICT in education, science and culture, e-commerce, ICT business sector, information security, and other important areas.

Given that the lack of financial resources, as well as difficult access to external sources of funding, significantly reduce the potential of SMEs in the segment of innovation and implementation of ICT, the focus in the coming period should be on the introduction of new financial support mechanisms. By developing alternative and promoting non-banking sources of financing, funding would become available to SMEs.

Assuming that some of the proposed measures will be implemented, and the identified barriers to the implementation of modern ICT removed in the coming period, some future research may focus on analyzing the presence of internet business in SMEs in the post-covid-19 period. The analysis would look at the real impact of the pandemic on the adoption of modern technology solutions in the field of communication.

CONCLUSION

Small and medium enterprises have certain specifics that make them significantly different compared to large business systems. Certain characteristics put SMEs in a privileged position in relation to large organizations, while there are also specifics that act as a restriction on their growth and development (Kamenković, Lazarević-Moravčević, 2018), as well as the adoption of modern technological solutions in business. Advantages over large organizations can be found in the segment of innovation, simple organizational structure, opportunities for networking and cooperation. Smaller companies are more prone to entrepreneurial ventures and, compared to large systems, accept new technological solutions faster, especially if they do not require significant investments.

Despite the fact that the generalization in terms of determining the common characteristics of small and medium enterprises is not completely correct, we can conclude that flexibility is something that determines both categories of enterprises. Small and medium-sized enterprises, unlike large systems that are mostly preoccupied with achieving economies of scale, which negatively affects their flexibility, have the ability to adapt more easily and quickly to new circumstances and market demands. Thanks to that flexibility, the SME sector in Serbia has shown a certain level of resistance to the impact of the crisis.

Based on the research conducted in this paper, we can conclude that in Serbia, Internet entrepreneurship is in the development phase. The research confirmed that organizations that belong to the category of medium-sized companies rely more on online marketing tools in marketing communication, compared to smaller systems. The explanation can be found in the fact that these are companies that have the characteristics of both small and large organizations and based on that meet the basic requirements for the implementation of ITC, especially in the segment of financial and human resources. The problem has been identified in small, and especially in micro enterprises, where a significant percentage of enterprises do not use basic internet marketing tools.

In the coming period, it is necessary for companies to adopt the basic tools of online marketing. This especially refers to those that belong to the category of small and micro enterprises and have not yet entered the world of digital business. Primarily, it refers to the implementation of the website and interactive applications. The website is an extremely powerful means of communication, which can significantly improve the visibility of the company. Even if it is not possible to conduct an online store, one should not ignore the fact that the Internet certainly provides great opportunities in the exchange of information with potential consumers and is an adequate advertising tool.

The assumption of the authors is that in the coming period, in order to adapt the business to the new circumstances, SMEs will more intensively accept modern communication solutions. In addition, the opinion of the authors is that the state can play a key role in removing certain barriers to the acceptance and implementation of ITC. Significant use of advanced technologies will have a positive impact on the performance of the SME sector, as well as on the overall economic development.

ACKNOWLEDGMENT

This chapter is financed by the Ministry of Education, Science and Technological Development of the Republic of Serbia.

REFERENCES

Abdallah, S., & Jaleel, B. (2015). Website appeal: Development of an assessment tool and evaluation framework of e-marketing. *Journal of Theoretical and Applied Electronic Commerce Research*, *10*(3), 45–62. doi:10.4067/S0718-18762015000300005

Akay, Ü., & Badlo, Y. (2021). Digital Marketing and Social Media: A Review. *International Conference on E-Business Technologies (EBT)*. Available at: https://ebt.rs/journals/index.php/conf-proc/article/view/83

Algharabat, R., Rana, N. P., Dwivedi, Y. K., Alalwan, A. A., & Qasem, Z. (2018). The effect of telepresence, social presence and involvement on consumer brand engagement: An empirical study of non-profit organizations. *Journal of Retailing and Consumer Services*, *40*, 139–149. doi:10.1016/j.jretconser.2017.09.011

Amirova, D., & Zaporozhets, O. (2019). Social media marketing as an effective tool promotion. *The Eurasian Scientific Journal*, *11*(2), 1–8.

APR. (2020). *Annual bulletin of financial statements.* Available at: https://www.apr.gov.rs/upload/Portals/0/GFI_2021/Godisnji_bilten_2020/BiltenSI2020.pdf

Baird, H. C., & Parasnis, G. (2011). From social media to social customer relationship management. *Strategy and Leadership*, *39*(5), 30–37. doi:10.1108/10878571111161507

Bala, M., & Verma, D. (2018). A Critical Review of Digital Marketing. *International Journal of Management, IT & Engineering*, *8*(10), 321–339.

Bogavac-Cvetković, N., Pavlović, R., & Cvetković, T. (2015). Strategic Importance of Innovation in Small and Medium Enterprises in the Era of Information Technology. In *Proceedings of the 3rd International Conference New Functional Materials and High Technology* (pp. 137-144). Tivat.

Castells, M. (2005). *The Network Society From Knowledge to Policy, The Network Society: From Knowledge to Policy Manuel Castells.* Center for Transatlantic Relations.

CEVES. (2020). *Preduzeća u Srbiji i Agenda 2030* [Business in Serbia and Agenda 2030]. Available at: https://ceves.org.rs/wp-content/uploads/2021/04/Preduzeca-u-Srbiji-i-Agenda-2030-prioriteti-izazovi-i-kriza-COVID-19-1.pdf

Chaffey, D., & Chadwick, E. (2016). *Digital marketing: Strategy, implementation and practice*. Pearson.

Chaffey, D., Ellis-Chadwick, F., Mayer, R., & Johnston, K. (2009). *Internet Marketing: Strategy, Implementation and Practice.* Available at: https://books.mec.biz/tmp/books/5G7BGE3Z6KNWFOHBFCWN.pdf

Collinson, E., & Shaw, E. (2001). Entrepreneurial Marketing - a historical perspective on development and practice. *Management Decision*, *39*(4), 761–766. doi:10.1108/EUM0000000006221

Coman, C., Popica, M., & Rezeanu, C.I. (2020). The Adoption of Digital Marketing by SMEs Entrepreneurs. *International Conference on Digital Science 2018.* Available at: https://link.springer.com/chapter/10.1007/978-3-030-37737-3_37

Dakouan, C., Benabdelouahed, R., & Anabir, H. (2019). Inbound marketing vs. outbound marketing: Independent or complementary strategies. *Expert Journal of Marketing*, *1*, 1–6.

Datareportal. (2021). Available at: https://datareportal.com/reports/

Deakins, D., & Freel, M. (2012). *Entrepreneurship and Small Firms*. The McGraw Hill Higher Education.

Denić, N., Petković, D., Vujović, V., Spasić, B., & Vujućić, I. (2018). *A survey of internet marketing by small and medium-sized enterprises for placing wine on the market*. Available at: https://www.sciencedirect.com/science/article/abs/pii/S0378437118305235

Diyana, A., & Dolah, J. (2018). How Digital Marketing Affects Consumer Behavior. *Advances in Social Science, Education and Humanities Research Journal.* Available at:https://creativecommons.org/licenses/by-nc/4.0/

Domazet, I. (2018). Digital transformation of business portfolio through DCRM. In *Digital Transformation-New Challenges and Business Opportunities* (pp. 214–235). Silver and Smith Publishers.

Domazet, I., Đokić, O., & Milovanov, O. (2018). The Influence of Advertising Media on Brand Awareness. Management. *Journal of Sustainable Business and Management Solutions in Emerging Economies*, *23*(1), 13–22.

Domazet, I., Neogradi, S., & Simović, V. (2019). Značaj društvenih mreža kao digitalnih kanala komunikacije u srpskim bankama [The importance of social networks as digital communication channels in Serbian banks]. *Marketing.*, *50*(4), 289–297. doi:10.5937/markt1904289X

Domazet, I. S., & Neogradi, S. (2019). Digital Marketing and Service Industry: Digital Marketing in the Banking Industry. In *Managing Diversity, Innovation, and Infrastructure in Digital Business* (pp. 20–40). IGI Global. doi:10.4018/978-1-5225-5993-1.ch002

European Commission. (2021). 2021 *SME Country Fact Sheet*. Available at: https://ec.europa.eu/neighbourhood-enlargement/sites/default/files/serbia_-_sme_fact_sheet_2021.pdf

Eurostat. (2020). *Social media - statistics on the use by enterprises.* Available at: https://ec.europa.eu/eurostat/statistics-explained/index.php?title=Social_media_-_statistics_on_the_use_by_enterprises#Use_of_social_media_by_enterprises

Filis, I., Johansson, U., & Wagner, B. (2003). A Conceptualisation of the Opportunities and Barriers to E-business Development in the Smaller Firm. *Journal of Small Business and Enterprise Development*, *10*(3), 336–344. doi:10.1108/14626000310489808

Flečer, K. (2003). *Upravljanje marketingom i informaciona tehnologija* [Marketing management and information technology]. Clio.

Gardašević, J., Ćirić, M., & Carić, M. (2018). Razumevanje motiva koršćenja društvenih mreža u funkciji unapređenja komunikacije sa potrošačima [Understanding the motives for using social networks in the function of improving communication with consumers]. *Marketing*, *49*(4), 311–320.

Gurau, C. (2008). Integrated online marketing communication: Implementation and management. *Journal of Communication Management (London)*, *12*(2), 169–184. doi:10.1108/13632540810881974

IPSOS Srbija. (2021). *Mediji u Srbiji* [Media in Serbia]. Available at: http//www.ipsos.com/

Kamenković, S., & Lazarević-Moravčević, M. (2018). Ocena kvaliteta okruženja i njegov uticaj na poslovanje sektora MSPP u Srbiji [Assessment of the quality of the environment and its impact on the business of the SME sector in Serbia]. Institute of Economic Sciences.

Kapoor, K., Tamilmani, K., Nripendra, P., Pushp, P., Yogesh, K., & Sridha, R. (2018). *Advances in Social Media Research: Past, Present and Future*. Available at: https://link.springer.com/article/10.1007%2Fs10796-017-9810-y

Kotler, P., Hermawan, K., & Setiawan, I. (2016). *Marketing 4.0: Moving from Traditional to Digital*. Wiley.

Krstić, A., & Đurđević, B. (2017). Marketing na društvenim mrežama [Social media marketing]. *Marketing*, *48*(4), 254–260.

Kumari, K. (2021). Impact of digital marketing during pandemic period with special reference to north Chennai city. *Turkish Journal of Physiotherapy and Rehabilitation*, *32*(3), 17357-17368.

Lazarević-Moravčević, E. D., & Kamenković, S. (2018). Uticaj poslovnog okruženja na performanse sektora MSPP u Srbiji [The impact of the business environment on the performance of the SME sector in Serbia]. *Business Economics (Cleveland, Ohio)*, *12*(1), 33–53.

Lazarević-Moravčević, M. (2019). Characteristics of marketing communication strategy of a small enterprise. *Economic Analysis*, *2*, 104–112.

Lazarević-Moravčević, M., Domazet, I., & Lazić, M. (2021). Characteristics of Market Communication in Modern Business. *Proceedings of the 26th International Scientific Conference Strategic Management and Decision Support Systems in Strategic Management*, 142-149. 10.46541/978-86-7233-397-8_134

Lazarević-Moravčević, M., Lazić, M., & Kaličanin, T. (2019). Primena marketing koncepta u malim preduzećima [Application of marketing concept in small businesses]. *International Scientific Conference: Challenges of modern marketing*, 242-249.

Levinson, J. C. (2009). *Gerila Marketing – jednostavne i jeftine strategije za ostvarivanje velikog profita od vašeg malog biznisa* [Guerrilla Marketing - Simple And Cheap Strategies To Make Big Profits From Your Small Business]. IPS Media.

Lévy, P. (2019). Collective Intelligence, the Future of Internet and the IEML. *Humanist Studies & the Digital Age*, *6*(1), 6-31. Available at: http://journals.oregondigital.org/index.php/hsda/article/view/4620/4513

Marketing Mreža. (2017). Available at: https://marketingmreza.rs/svega-25-srednjih-malih-preduzeca-ima-osobu-zaduzenu-samo-za-marketing/

Ministry of Economy. (2020). *Report on small and medium enterprises and entrepreneurs*. Available at: https://privreda.gov.rs/wp-content/uploads/2021/05/Izvestaj-MSPP-2018_FIN.pdf

Obradović, M., Alčaković, S., & Pavlović, O. (2018). Effective Use of E-Mail Marketing on Example of Small and Medium-Sized Enterprises in Serbia. *Proceedings of the International Scientific Conference on Information Technology and Data Related Research – SINTEZA 2018*, 79-84. 10.15308/Sinteza-2018-79-84

Ognjanov, G. (2013). Integrisane marketinške komunikacije [Integrated marketing communications]. Faculty of Economics.

Oprena, A., & Vinerean, S. (2015). A New Development in Online Marketing: Introducing Digital Inbound Marketing. *Expert Journal of Marketing*, *3*(1), 29–34.

Peterson, R. A., Balasubramanian, S., & Bronnenberg, B. (1997). Exploring the implications of the internet for consumer marketing. *Journal of the Academy of Marketing*, *25*(4), 329–346. doi:10.1177/0092070397254005

Pioniri. (2021). *Stanje društvenih medija u Srbiji* [The state of social media in Serbia]. Available at https: //pioniri.com/sr/socialserbia2020/

Rani, S. (2019). Digital marketing and social media – a step to thrive in business, *International Journal of Management, IT & Engineering*, *9*(3), 394–415.

Republički zavod za statistiku [Republican Bureau of Statistics]. (2020). *ICT in Serbia*. Available at: https://www.stat.gov.rs/sr-latn/vesti/20200922-godisnje-istrazivanje-o-ikt/?a=27&s=0

Schwarzl, S., & Grabowska, M. (2015). Online marketing strategies: The future is here. *Journal of International Students*, *2*(2), 187–196. doi:10.14254/2071-8330.2015/8-2/16

Shirky, C. (2011). *The political power of social media: Technology, the public sphere, and political change. Foreign affairs.* Available at: http://sites.asiasociety.org/womenleaders/wp-content/uploads/2010/05/The-Political-Power-of-Social-Media-Foreign-Affairs2.pdf

Stanković, U., Ćurčić, N., & Dragićević, V. (2010). On-line promotivne tehnike kao faktor unapređenja promotivnih mogućnosti veb sajtova [Online promotional techniques as a factor in improving the promotional capabilities of websites]. *Ekonomske teme, 3,* 421-435.

Statista. (2021). *Global digital population as of January 2021*. Available at: https://www.statista.com/statistics/617136/digital-population-worldwide/

Thelwall, M. (2000). Effective Websites for Small and Medium-Sized Enterprises. *Journal of Small Business and Enterprise Development*, *7*(2), 149–159. doi:10.1108/EUM0000000006836

Tow, W., Dell, P., & Venable, J. (2010). Understanding information disclosure behavior in Australian Facebook users. *Journal of Information Technology*, *25*(2), 126–136. doi:10.1057/jit.2010.18

USAID. (2020). *Anketa "1000 preduzeća"* [Survey "1000 companies"]. Available at: https://saradnja.rs/wp-content/uploads/2020/11/Anketa-1000-preduze%C4%87a-2020.pdf

Vidas-Bubanja, M. (2021). Uticaj pandemije COVID -19 na digitalnu transformaciju privrede Srbije [The impact of the COVID-19 pandemic on the digital transformation of the Serbian economy]. *Ekonomski vidici, 1-2*, 47-62.

Vidas-Bubanja, M., & Madžar, L. (2019). Importance of Innovation and Knowledge for Economic Development of the Country and the Competitive Business of Company. *Journal of Social Sciences*, *11*(11), 157–173.

Vukmirović, V., Domazet, I., & Kostić-Stanković, M. (2020). Personalized Social Media Communication based on Millennials' Attitudes. *Conference Proceedings - International Scientific Conference Strategic Management and Decision Support Systems in Strategic Management*, 97-103. 10.46541/978-86-7233-386-2_13

World Economic Forum. (2019). *The Global Competitiveness Report 2019*. Available at:https://www.weforum.org/reports/how-to-end-a-decade-of-lost-productivity-growth

Živadinović, V., & Zelić, M. (2014). *Uticaj online-tržišta i digitalnih tehnologija na reputaciju preduzeća* [The impact of online markets and digital technologies on a company's reputation]. Infoteh-Jahorina. Available at: https://infoteh.etf.ues.rs.ba/zbornik/2014/radovi/RSS-3/RSS-3-4.pdf

KEY TERMS AND DEFINITIONS

Digital Communication: Communication that involves the use of all available communication channels, including online channels, as well as traditional if they are digital, and do not involve the use of the internet.

Digital Marketing: Is a way of advertising in which digital media are used to promote products or services on the market.

Digital Transformation: Improvement of business processes based on the application of modern technology solutions.

Inbound Marketing: Communication based on the use of certain internet marketing tools (SEO, social networks, e-mail marketing, blogs, etc.) to lead interested customers to a specific website.

Interactive Marketing Communication: Communication based on dialogue and free exchange of information through modern communication technologies and internet marketing tools.

Internet Marketing: Represents the application of the Internet, accompanying digital technologies and services to achieve marketing goals.

Outbound Marketing: Application of traditional methods of promotion (advertisements in newspapers, magazines, electronic media, banners, mass sending of e-mails, etc.) characterized by sending a message by the company regardless of whether there is interest from potential consumers.

Social Networks: Are online web services that provide users with various forms of communication and the possibility of personal presentation.

Chapter 13
The Use of CRM in Marketing and Communication Strategies in Portuguese Non-Profit Organizations

Maria Inês Magalhães Rodrigues
ISAG – European Business School, Portugal

Manuel José Serra da Fonseca
https://orcid.org/0000-0002-3290-8449
Polytechnic Institute of Viana do Castelo, Portugal

Jorge Esparteiro Garcia
https://orcid.org/0000-0001-5710-5557
Polytechnic Institute of Viana do Castelo, Portugal

ABSTRACT

The truth is that competitivity has gained a strong growth in business, and it is important that companies pay attention to the practice of their relational marketing strategies. Technology, innovation, and digital have been transforming the way society operates in the market. Organizations must look for current opportunities in order to add value of their business and negotiation process and of course in the way they act and interact with the target. This way, the current research demonstrates the importance of CRM in relational marketing practices, particularly in non-profit organizations. Regarding the methodology, a case study was developed using a qualitative methodology through semi-structured interviews in a convenience sample, with the aim of retaining the opinion fundraising and marketing responsible department between the different organizations under study. The main result of this exploratory study appears to prove the importance of using CRM for the good practice of relational marketing strategies in order to attract, retain, and build trust with their stakeholders.

DOI: 10.4018/978-1-7998-9790-3.ch013

INTRODUCTION

In a globalized market where consumers are increasingly concerned in interacting and supporting social issues, Non-Profit Organizations must also outline a set of practices and marketing strategies in order to increase their performance in the market and consequently reach the intended target audience.

The awareness actions that each organization entails and the fact that it has a non-profit character aroused an interest in understanding how marketing tools would work in an association with several specificities and inserted in a differentiated sector.

In this sense, non-profit organizations are no exception and need to incorporate in their actions and strategic planning a technological aspect that is able to meet their needs in marketing and fundraising strategies, as well as in building a good image and reputation, and transmit their social projects, ideas and values to society. Ultimately, to fulfill the goals they set themselves, ensuring a better quality of life for the community to develop positively.

The choice of this topic was aimed at understanding the Importance of CRM in Relational Marketing Strategies and Practices in Non-Profit Organizations. Since CRM implementation is quite present in commercial companies, this study aims to understand the strategy behind a sector that is different from the rest.

It is observed that managers/administrators/directors at the level of non-profit organizations still seem to have little sensitivity to the subject and to the consequent advantages in optimizing the performance of the daily functions of this type of organization.

Throughout this research, it will be important to recognize that the third sector should also take advantage of tools used in other areas of the economy, especially in the implementation of a CRM platform that will create opportunities in these organizations, whether in the practice of relational marketing strategies or in the attraction, retention and loyalty of its target - donors, partners and volunteers and, consequently, understand whether the application of a CRM software will have a differentiation in responding to the goals of organizations.

In the current context of the COVID-19 pandemic, many of these organizations, which conducted their actions mostly face-to-face, had to adapt and take advantage of technologies that allowed them to reach their segment in a non-face-to-face manner.

In this context, and in the scope of the work of this chapter, we started by analyzing empirical and research papers, thus defining the different subjects to be addressed in the literature review.

In order to fulfill the general objective of the study, five specific objectives were defined: The first consists in understanding the characteristics and identity of the non-profit organization; the second intends to understand how the entity was organized before the implementation of CRM; the third intends to understand the importance and experience of CRM in the organization, and, the fifth and last objective aims to understand the role of CRM in the adaptation of organizations to the pandemic context COVID-19.

With regard to the methodological approach that underlies this research, it should be noted that a qualitative methodological approach was used, based on exploratory interviews with leaders of the organizations.

This chapter consists of five sections, the first of which refers to the introduction and identification of the research problem containing a brief background of the theme mentioned the research objectives.

The second section is a literature review of the core concepts addressed.

The third section, called research methodology, is based on the exposition of the methodological approach, the detailed description of the general and specific objectives, and the selected collection instrument.

The fourth section analyzes the data and presents the results.

Finally, the fifth and last section presents the conclusions and general contributions of the research, as well as the recognition of its limitations and recommendations for future research.

LITERATURE REVIEW

Over the years the primordial concepts of marketing have been changing, Kotler et al. (2017) state that in the current marketing scenario we should consider individuals as human beings and not as mere consumers. In an initial phase of marketing the center was only in the management of the product and/or service, alreadý in a transitional phase and with the emergence of the internet and the explosion of information the importance has shifted to the management of the consumer. In the current technological reality, the key concept becomes centered in the mind of the human being, consisting of informed and active consumers in the digital environment who consider the values transmitted by organizations.

Marketing assumes a growing importance not only for the good adaptation to the market but also in a differentiation aspect of the companies. Information technology management emerges in order to reduce costs and add productivity for marketers (Lindon et al., 2018).

It is in this context that marketing shows all its comprehensive capacity, particularly in its aspect of optimizing the performance of non-profit organizations. Thus arises the concept of social marketing, which is often confused with other areas of knowledge such as nonprofit marketing, public sector marketing, and education. Although it uses commercial marketing techniques, contains a relational and service marketing dimension, often operates at the service of the social economy and uses commercial marketing tools to enhance its performance (e.g. CRM tools), the principles and techniques of social marketing are mostly used to promote public health, prevent accidents, protect the environment, increase community involvement and improve financial well-being (Kotler & Lee, 2015).

Social Marketing

Lindon et al. (2018) state that social problems are extremely complex and are related to various sectors on a social, educational, environmental level and therefore solutions need to be developed considering socioeconomics, historical, religious and cultural factors. By adjusting society's awareness, it is necessary to bring about changes in people's attitudes and behaviors, habits, interests, feelings and beliefs. What is important in social marketing is the ability of its agents to appeal to the social, civic, and solidarity consciousness of citizens, so social campaigns aim to educate and prevent. The specificity of social marketing occurs essentially at the level of its object (social awareness) and in the objectives it proposes (to awaken this awareness, modify attitudes, and change behaviors).

According to Kotler and Lee (2011) there are four fundamental ideals that characterize social marketing: in addition to its influence on society's behaviors it uses a planning process that applies marketing principles and techniques in view of its audience and benefits to society.

In order to minimize the difficulties in the development of behaviors to be promoted in social marketing, the authors Martins et al. (2014) state that marketing actions should be strategically developed through clear, measurable and defined long-term objectives. Damn (2010) attributes a key role to social marketing in the adoption of positive behavior and consequently reduce the negative. In addition to promoting change and redirecting an individual's preference to a particular cause, social marketing provides positive and beneficial outcomes for the individual and society as a whole. Mihăilă (2017) states that social marketing is a promising framework for planning and implementing programs related to social change, far beyond social advertising this type of marketing is fully related to social causes, corporate and community volunteering with the aim of promoting changes in society's behavior and attitude. Nancy et al., (2011) define social marketing as the process that uses commercial marketing principles and techniques with the goal of influencing behavior, all depending on the creation, communication, delivery and exchange of offers that have a positive value to society.

Social marketing involves changing behavior whether in environmental, economic, social, and political circumstances, with the major goal being in meeting society's desire and consequently improving their quality of life (Serrat, 2017). Social marketing is advantageously positioned in the fight against problems on a global, national and local level, however it is necessary to think long term and with a related development of appropriate principles and techniques (Serrat, 2017). According to Peattie and Peattie (2009) social marketing underlies accessibility, engagement costs to media interconnecting with partnerships, funding, politics and people.

Classical definitions of marketing carry associated appreciations such as satisfaction of needs and wants, demand, market, value and exchange. In social marketing these expressions are also applicable as: social demand, social needs, social exchange and social market, however these factors have different goals than traditional marketing (Souza et al., 2018). According to Meira and Santos (2012) social marketing aims to raise awareness and sensitize people about a social cause in the search for behavior change.

In the same perspective, the authors Basil et al. (2019) define social marketing as the integration of marketing concepts with other approaches in order to influence behaviors that benefit individuals and the community. The practice of social marketing is guided by ethical principles that aim at a research development, practice improvement, public overview in order to maintain an integrated and informed society in social programs that are effective, efficient, equitable and sustainable. It is essential that these professionals know their competition in order to understand behaviors and where the efforts of these actions should go.

According to Bernhardt et al. (2012) in social marketing there are several points to keep in mind beyond individual and behavioral change: 1) Harnessing the power of markets and marketing to improve well-being; 2) Maximizing well-being with access to means; 3) Developing and enhancing marketing techniques that support consumer well-being. Social marketing is a planned approach to social innovation, i.e., it is the application of marketing principles to shape markets to be more effective, efficient, sustainable, and fair in supporting well-being and social causes (Phills et al., 2008)

Lefebvre (2012) believes that the focus of social marketing is on facilitating and supporting value creation processes in which people are seen as targets in changing behaviors, thus social marketing aims to propose the possibilities of this change, for the author the importance lies in achieving a dynamic participation and learning for both society and marketers. Bach and Enas (2016) state that the core of social marketing is in the orientation to the general public in an analysis of their reasons, actions and habits in society. In this way social marketing empowers and motivates people to adopt a desired and positive behavior as part of their daily lives. Despite the significant challenges in measuring the practice of social marketing in causes the goal is in the dissemination of actions and behaviors to adopt in various social areas. Author Lefebvre (2011) identified six challenges that apply to social marketing: heritage, social networks as behavioral determinants, critical marketing, sustainability, scalability, and market approach. Social marketing must address such challenges by showing the effectiveness and efficiency of supporting each cause.

It should also be noted that there are several studies and areas that demonstrate the relevance of social marketing in Portuguese non-profit organizations. Studies can be highlighted in the areas of Tourism (Araújo &Sá, 2017), Portuguese League Against Cancer (Santos, 2018), Road Prevention (Fonseca, 2012), Breastfeeding (Martins et al., 2014), Domestic Violence (Machado, Antunes and Miranda, 2016), Public Health (Dançante, 2017), among others.

Services Marketing

Lindon et al. (2018) state that services have some particular characteristics that lead to a differentiated marketing approach the intangible nature of services does not allow it to be easily appreciated by the consumer, because they do not have a physical and material component that allows for prior observation and analysis it is necessary to use a service to understand if it is suitable to expectations. A service consumer contributes to the quality of that service, by his good or bad mood, by his level of demand, by his competence, by his experience and by the way he gets involved in the act of consuming that service. Each customer is different, so a service is less homogeneous than an industrialized product.

The service sector has had a significant growth in the world economy and for this the concepts and strategies of service marketing have had a great development to respond to the market. The evolution in the sector has drawn attention to the challenges that organizations come to face be this change at the organizational level, commercial, distribution and consumer experience in service delivery (Zeithaml et al., 2014). Gummesson et al. (2012) defined services marketing as a concept that includes the firm's performance in the value proposition, in addition to dissolving the division between goods and services. Among other concepts that have been emerging the most interesting are that of value creation and service and the integration of resources among stakeholders, giving an active role to customers. Bateson and Hoffman (2016) distinguish service marketing from product marketing mainly by the function of its intangibility. The authors believe that this new era of global services is characterized by greater customer involvement in strategic business decisions; the development of technologies that have come to enable both customers and employees to assist in service delivery; as well as employees with greater freedom to develop customized and immediate solutions.

Lovelock and Wirtz (2009), further add that a major responsibility of management is to ensure that managers and their employees do not isolate themselves between departments but work together to achieve goals. Operations is the primary function of a service company, as they are responsible for all delivery management (equipment means, facilities, systems, and even employees who have direct contact with the customer).

According to Kotler (2000) there is a set of tools that companies must follow to achieve their goals in the market: the marketing-mix that will drive managers to sell their products and innovate according to their market. Each of the marketing strategies must adopt four elements: price, product, promotion, distribution, and communication. Since the services sector presents certain characteristics in the form of performance there was the need to expand the components for a better practice of the strategies, these being: people, physical evidence, and processes. In this way, the 7 Ps represent a set of variables of decisions with the purpose of offering help to companies so that they can achieve their goals and consequently, satisfy and retain customers (Lovelock & Jochen, 2011). Thus, companies must be prepared to ensure the quality and value of the service provided in order to increase the success of the organization (Marangoni, 2015).

Throughout the 20th century, one begins to see many companies investing in initiatives to promote the quality of their services aiming to achieve differentiation and build competitive advantages. Based on instinct and intuition, managers quickly understood the importance of serving their customers with maximum efficiency, this dedication became the basis for the success of most companies in various sectors. Today, one of the strongest factors observed in service marketing is the influence of technology. The growth of the Internet has brought with it a range of new services, especially for companies focused on the online environment, where in addition to offering opportunities for new products and services, it provides the means to offer existing services in a more accessible, convenient, and productive way. The presence of technology results in an empowerment in reaching customers worldwide in every possible way by keeping in touch easily and sharing information. The globalization of technology facilitates efficiency in the service sector, and the tasks that produce and support these activities can be conducted virtually anywhere in the world (Zeithaml et al., 2014).

Following the ideas of the author mentioned above, the emergence of technologies can also hinder some processes, such as the lack of customer readiness to technology, often there are customers who have no interest in the existing technological advances having failure to adapt. As well as the return on investment in technology is often uncertain, in addition to the time that can be achieved, the management of gains in productivity and customer satisfaction is uncertain since it creates dependence on other factors.

Relational Marketing

The concept of relational marketing arises with the purpose of responding to the growing need that companies have to satisfy their customers, considering them more and more informed and demanding. Relational marketing aims to establish and maintain relationships between the brand and the consumer based on personalized, interactive, and measurable actions, creating a constant knowledge of evolution for brand building. To establish and maintain good relationships with customers it is crucial to know, be relevant, communicate, listen, reward for their loyalty, and associate them to the life of the company or brand. The strategies defined for relational marketing actions go much further than direct contact with the customer based on the knowledge of those customers' needs and service perception (Lindon et al., 2018).

Most of the marketing theories are developed through product markets, however, the analysis of industrial and services markets emerges with a new perspective: the relational marketing, with the aim of building long-lasting and stable relationships with customers. The business model becomes customer-centric, supported by technological development, information management and service (Antunes & Paulo, 2008).

Berry (1995) began by defining the concept of relational marketing as a means to attract, maintain and develop relationships with customers. The goal of relational marketing is in building profitable and beneficial relationships for both companies and consumers (Antunes & Paulo, 2008). In a further opinion, Cruz (2017), states that due to increased competition and a rapid evolution of markets, it becomes essential to add value to consumers through channels that connect with each other in order to establish business processes at the level of buying and selling, aiming for organizations to have all kinds of information from each customer to adapt new offers tailored to their needs. Thus, the major indicator of strategic positioning becomes the customer portfolio instead of market share.

Relationship marketing seeks to establish ongoing relationships with customers in order to achieve loyalty and fidelity between the company and the consumer. The benefit of these long-lasting relationships lies mainly in the fact that the company passes on a good brand image and builds customer loyalty, with the aim of these customers having no interest in competitors (Martínez et al., 2017).

Casais et al. (2019) state that relational marketing is a central aspect of business models and an incentive for innovation. Relational marketing focuses on customer loyalty, its focus is on the individual customer for which a unique value proposition is sought to be developed. One of the indicators for the performance of relational marketing is in customer retention as well as profitability (Brito & Lencastre, 2014).

In a world in constant change and evolution, both on the supply and demand side, there are several factors that increase the strategic importance of approaches directed to relational marketing: the advancement in the areas of technologies, not only in terms of communication, but also in production and logistics departments. Thus, technology came to allow means to identify and maintain this commitment with the customer (Brito, 2011).

Relationship marketing emerged as the rapid result of changing consumer needs and intense competition in the market (Agariya & Singh, 2011). New technologies have enabled a capacity of data storage and extraction in order for organizations to deal with a vast amount of customer information that would have been unthinkable before, from the marketing point of view this evolution has allowed the ability to individualize and manage the relationship with the customer (Brito, 2011).

Miquel-Romero et al. (2014) believe that relationship management between companies and partners should be viewed in the long term. As long as both parties are willing to maintain this relationship, the lower the risk of relationship dissolution, since it requires investments that are often unrecoverable (Scheer et al., 2014). According to Miquel-Romero et al. (2014) trust and commitment is a strategic goal and a source of profitability for the business in the long run.

Agariya and Singh (2011) states that the key elements for relationship management beyond trust and commitment is also in the cooperation conveyed. Palmatier et al. (2006) further adds that a good relational marketing practice makes partners more likely to share information and consequently increase security and reduce opportunism.

Social Economy

The Social Economy was defined by the Commission of the European Communities in the Communication to the Council of December 18, 1989, as follows: an enterprise belongs to the Social Economy if its productive activity is based on organizational techniques based on the principles of solidarity and participation among members, whether producers, users or consumers, and on the values of autonomy and citizenship. In general, these enterprises adopt the legal form of a cooperative, mutuality, or association (Afonso, 2018).

Ávila and Campos (2018) define the social economy as the response to social problems in which its character is quite different from private and traditional enterprises based on the logic of capital.

Third sector organizations are characterized, as those that do not have any aspect in providing goods or services, but rather a focus on human beings and their issues, their product is in changing human beings to positive activities, that is, non-profit organizations are agents of human change (Drucker, 1999). Andrade and Franco (2007) state that there are several denominations and characteristics that exist in the nonprofit sector that also impose clarity as to their definitions.

CRM (Customer Relationship Management)

Nowadays the goal of organizations is not only to satisfy customers, but equally to have chances to compete in the market to achieve their goals. Customer satisfaction is often seen as a central and determining point for customer retention, Rahimi and Kozak (2017) argue that the most important goal for an organization is to maintain the loyalty of its customer and centralize all information about the customer, in this way anticipating their organizational and marketing strategies will enable organizations to perform better in the market with the aim of meeting customer needs and exceeding their expectations.

Henrique and Miake (2017) state that the CRM process is supported by relationship orientation and customer knowledge management derived from data collection, data consolidation, data analysis, and knowledge distribution to support decision making.

CRM can be seen as the systematic and automated application of relationship marketing concepts as CRM adoption will enable an improvement in customer knowledge management from an appropriate technology infrastructure, but mainly a review of management processes at the operational and customer level (Henrique & Miake, 2017).

Parvatiyar and Sheth (2001) define CRM as a comprehensive tool and process in customer acquisition and retention. Beyond this consumer focus it encompasses areas with integration in marketing, customer service, sales and after-sales with the goal of achieving efficiency and effectiveness as two main dimensions in customer value delivery performance.

Yim et al. (2004) state that CRM originates from the combination of three fundamental aspects: customer orientation, relationship marketing and database marketing.

Regarding the use of CRM tools in optimizing communication strategies (namely in non-profit organizations) the contributions of Kristoffersen and Singh (2004), Wu and Hung (2008), Courchesne et al (2019), Wang (2019), Idzikowski (2019), among others, can also be highlighted.

METHODOLOGY

This chapter details the methodological approach used during the research carried out in the context of the importance of CRM in non-profit organizations.

In order to respond to the general objective of this research and since it is a little explored theme in Portugal it was considered relevant to know the opinions and experience in CRM strategies within non-profit organizations according to the view of their professionals, through an exploratory case study.

This chapter presents a description of the procedures carried out in the investigative path for which, in an initial phase, the bibliographical survey, previously presented, was relevant for a greater perception of the theme to be investigated. Next, we proceeded to a qualitative methodological approach based on semi-structured exploratory interviews presenting a set of dimensions in order to obtain a diversity of relevant and complete opinions.

Research Questions and Analysis Model

In order to meet the proposed objectives, an interview script was developed. Complying with the good practices of conducting an interview, the study's general objective was to analyze the opinion of the representatives of the marketing and fundraising departments of the different organizations under study, specifically:

1. Characterization of the organization
2. The organization before the CRM implementation
3. Importance and experience of CRM in the organization
4. Role of CRM in adapting the organization to the pandemic context COVID 19

In a collection of clear and concise objectives, the intention was to analyze the relationship between the different variables presented and determine the different behaviors of social economy organizations in the application of CRM.

The questionnaire merely responds to open-ended questions (discussion topics) with the aim of the interviewee expressing their ideas and opinions regarding the study. In this sense, in addition to answering data such as: name of the organization, number of employees, position held, area of operation and time in the organization.

Sample

According to Oliveira (2001) the sample is a stage of great importance in the development of research capable of determining the validity of the data obtained. For this study, the sample under analysis is a sample by convenience that comprises a professional position of marketing and/or fundraising manager, where 5 non-profit organizations in Portugal were interviewed. Convenience sampling is appropriate and often used for idea management in exploratory research where the researcher selects a sample from the most accessible population (Oliveira, 2001).

Prior to the interview process, this questionnaire was sent by email in January 2021 with the aim of contextualizing the professionals in the study and scheduling the day for the exploratory interview. Given the impossibility of a face-to-face interview due to the current context of the global pandemic, we chose to conduct the interview online via Google Meet.

The interviewees' answers were later transcribed, and the audio of the interview is available for consultation. Thus, in this research it was interviewed the people responsible for Marketing and Communication (or equivalent) of the institutions Ajuda em Ação; Cáritas Portuguesa; Associação Salvador; Nariz Vermelho, and Médicos do Mundo".

ANALYSIS AND DISCUSSION OF THE RESULTS

Dimension 1: Characterization of the Organization

Although the five organizations under study fall within the third sector the way they act and support their mission is quite diverse among them.

When and how did the organization come about? What were the main motivations that led to the creation of this organization?

Ajuda em Ação

Based in Lisbon, Ajuda em Ação is a non-profit organization that operates at an international level. Its mission is to promote the solidarity of people around the world with the aim of helping children, families and people who suffer from poverty, exclusion and inequality, but who want to develop the capacity to achieve a dignified and sustainable way of life. Its values are governed by a commitment to human rights and the dignity of people, transparency, independence, and collective effort.

We are an NGO working to combat poverty and social exclusion and this year we are celebrating our 40th anniversary, that is, our work began with this very purpose of working in cooperation and development to combat poverty and social exclusion. At this moment we work in 21 countries. We've only been in Portugal for 1 year and 3 months – Ajuda em Ação

Cáritas Portuguesa

With 65 years of history, Cáritas Portuguesa, based in Lisbon, aims to act in places of proximity, in parishes and communities, a work that is carried out in a network gives this institution the ability to be present throughout the national territory. The mission of Cáritas in Portugal passes mainly by the integral human development and the defense of the common good intervening in order to transform the society, with the support of the animation of the social pastoral, encourages the sharing of goods and the assistance in situations of calamity and emergency. Its values are based on the centrality and dignity of the person, mercy, equal opportunities, the option for the poor, the care of creation, the universal destination of the goods of the earth, solidarity and subsidiarity, cooperation and fraternal communion.

One of the great questions when creating Cáritas was to have the social part of the church, that is, the church has several pillars of ritual, of masses, the part of mythological production, and this more social aspect was entrusted to Cáritas. Meanwhile, the various diocesan Cáritas were created by each district, by each diocese, basically to respond to all the social action requests that came to the different parishes at a more local level or to the different dioceses that articulate the parishes, or even to the Portuguese Cáritas that is the coordinator – Cáritas Portuguesa

Associação Salvador

With its headquarters in Lisbon and delegation in Porto, the Associação Salvador has as its mission to promote the inclusion of people with motor disabilities in society and improve their quality of life, enhancing their talents and raising awareness of equal opportunities. Its vision is above all equality for all regardless of their differences. Its values are driven by commitment, dynamism, collaboration and excellence.

The Associação Salvador has the goal of full inclusion and integration of people with motor disabilities and reduced mobility in society in two ways, therefore empowering the talents and promoting the talents of our beneficiaries, technical skills, personal, self-esteem, confidence and independence and then also the other side which is the awareness and therefore be agents of change in this sense, we have a project dedicated only to accessibility and advocacy and enforcement requirement so that laws are met and Portugal is a more accessible and inclusive country – Associação Salvador

Nariz Vermelho

Founded in 2002 and based in Lisbon, Operação Nariz Vermelho aims to ensure a continuous intervention program within the pediatric services of Portuguese hospitals through the visit of professional clowns. These artists have specialized training in the hospital environment and work closely with health professionals, performing performances adapted to each child and each situation. In this way, its mission is to bring joy to hospitalized children, their families, and health professionals, through the art and image of the Clown Doctor.

Operação Nariz Vermelho was officially born on June 4, 2002 and started with volunteer work before its constitution by its founder Beatriz Quintela and two other colleagues doing volunteer work specifically in Estefânia hospital and it was mainly a work that was more dedicated at Christmas, volunteer work through clowns' intervention in children hospitalized in Estefânia. And then they realized that it could be a continuous work, because otherwise no one would go there. So that's when the official work was established - the mission is to bring joy to hospitalized people through the art of clown doctors. And this, currently, we are in 17 hospitals, so throughout these 18 years, we have been able to expand our space – Nariz Vermelho

Médicos do Mundo

Based in Lisbon, the association Médicos do Mundo is an international network that was born in 1980 with the purpose of establishing the fundamental right of all human beings to have access to health care, independently of their nationality, religion, ideology, race or economic possibilities. Médicos do Mundo acts in several areas, from medical and social assistance to the denouncement of social injustices before public opinion, the media and competent entities, fighting discrimination against vulnerable populations, in order to increase their quality of life and well-being.

Médicos do Mundo is the name of the organization. We belong to an international network, Doctors of the World, and we have been in Portugal since 1999, but the organization was created in 1980. We do, it's not only, but free health care and it's always going to the people and the most vulnerable – Médicos do Mundo

The Organization's Main Challenges

Since these are non-profit organizations, for most of these types of entities the main challenge lies in their sustainability throughout the year. Once the budget is defined the big challenge is in this ability to sustain the projects and causes for which they are involved. In addition, raising people's awareness to their causes ends up being a challenge to provide answers to the different areas of the organizations.

Main Intervenient in the Organization's process

Since these are non-profit organizations, their main stakeholders are the beneficiaries, donors (individuals and companies) and volunteers, the organizations believe that the support of these stakeholders is a key factor for the proper functioning of the various areas. organization's main challenges.

Dimension 2: The organization before CRM implementation

It is fundamental to understand how the non-profit organizations were working prior to the implementation of CRM and thus understand what led them to have the need for a technological tool in the development of their strategies and actions.

When did you implement a CRM system in your organization? How did this initiative arise?

After analysis of the interviews, it was noted that the need for CRM implementation arose in several ways: By the growth of non-profit organizations, by the need to simplify processes in one area with the use of CRM and by the fact that international non-profit organizations are already using and mirroring this for their delegations. Throughout the interviews it became clear that the implementation of CRM is intertwined with the area of fundraising and marketing since it is an area that requires contact management, loyalty of donors whether individuals or companies and segmented communication

Was a company contracted to provide support during the implementation process?

For the good functioning of the CRM system most of the organizations have used a consulting company to provide support, training and support in the development of the CRM applied to the social economy. With the exception of one organization that relies heavily on international support and therefore has international colleagues helping in the implementation and development of the system. However, in general we realize that there is no database manager within the organizations, it is always necessary to have someone with a role behind them, in this case a consulting firm capable of providing this CRM support.

Before using the CRM did you use any kind of system? If you did not have any kind of system in place, where did you store your volunteer/donor information?

It is underlined that all organizations, before the CRM implementation, stored their data only in Excel or else they used pro bono projects designed by Portuguese companies that made tailor made implementations for these organizations to take advantage of the technology and optimize their processes. It is considerable that the initial investment in a CRM tool leads organizations to opt for other solutions, especially pro bono, but in the medium/long term and with the continuous growth of the entities in terms of contacts and beneficiaries, they need to adapt to a tool with greater responsiveness to their tasks and from there they have moved on to other solutions, as was the case with the CRM platform Salesforce.

Before the implementation how was the cost-benefit ratio of a CRM system perceived by the organization? And currently, in an overall assessment, do you consider that the investment was profitable for the organization?

Although the non-profit organizations only use CRM for one of their intervention areas: fundraising and marketing, they feel that there is a positive cost-benefit relationship for the effectiveness and efficiency it has given to their daily work. However, it is necessary to consider the budget impossibilities of the third sector and there are some limitations, especially in the use of the remaining features that CRM allows.

Dimension 3: Importance and experience of CRM in the organization

In this dimension we will deepen the importance and experience of CRM from understanding its benefits to how it helped in the definition and development of strategies. With some practical cases in order to understand the usefulness of this tool in the social economy.

What are the benefits obtained so far with the use of CRM?

Throughout the interviews it was clear that when there is a specialized person with time to use CRM the benefits are much greater, although these organizations do not always have the financial investment to invest in human resources with CRM expertise. One of the biggest benefits of using CRM is seen in the fundraising department in terms of growth of new donors, number of donors, information management, work organization, obtaining data reports, and tailoring responses to incoming requests

What are the main limitations of the CRM solution implemented in the organization?

The main limitations of CRM are the lack of human resources with skills and expertise in the CRM area. On the other hand, they are rooted in the time that is necessary to devote to this tool in order to understand all its features and how they can be applied to the daily work of organizations, in addition to the constant updates in the digital world. From another perspective there are functionalities that require a very high investment, which is seen as an obstacle to continue the CRM development process.

What changes have been made in your role and in the organization with the use of CRM?

Throughout the study factors that influenced the CRM practice in the organizations were perceived, one of them being the fact that there is a recurrent change of people between the various non-profit organizations under study and this way, since they already used CRM in other institutions, they end up bringing this knowledge. It is clear that a large part of the hiring in recent years in the organizations was with the aim of enhancing the CRM tool with experienced people in other organizations and consequently bring results for the fundraising department.

Was there a need to adapt any process of the organization's operation when CRM was implemented? Why?

Since CRM is only used by one area of the non-profit organization (fundraising and marketing department) the adaptation of processes was mainly the transfer of the use of Excel to the CRM software as well as the use of CRM in the accounting area to issue receipts, however they state that not all staff is able to take advantage of this tool.

Have short, medium and long term goals been defined? By whom?

The goals are defined mainly in the fundraising department and consequently in the use of the database, as well as in the measurement of indicators that will mainly dictate the performance of campaigns in fundraising: from number of donations, donors and loyalty rates.

Has the CRM implementation improved the definition of strategies in the marketing/communication and fundraising department? How has it?

One of the advantages of using CRM is the fact that it has interconnection with other digital tools, in this case social networks and e-mail marketing, which will help in the implementation of both communication and marketing campaigns as well as fundraising.

It is mainly to make a segmented communication that these tools help in defining their strategies, in addition to prior consultation that fundraisers do in CRM to have a better perception in defining the next strategies and therefore achieve greater success in its implementation

The implementation of a CRM system requires relationship management. Which relationships do you consider to be the most important for your organization (beneficiaries, volunteers, donors, etc.)?

Generally speaking, donors, volunteers and beneficiaries are the main profiles of these non-profit organizations allowing to create relationships according to the type of intervention they have to perform.

How are the databases made? And how are the assumptions of the GDPR (General Data Protection Regulation) taken care of?

As soon as the data protection system was implemented, the organizations started to comply with the requirements, mostly by filling out the consent in their online forms, or even when the information is provided by letter, email or telephone. They also have the system in place to remove the person from their database if they express that intention.

When you have doubts regarding the use of CRM, how do you clarify them? Who do you ask for support?

As we can analyze throughout the study the consulting partner for these organizations has a fundamental role of support, and any doubt about the use of CRM is referred to the partner in question. In addition, one of the advantages of the Salesforce CRM platform is access to learning modules with some explanations about the various areas of CRM implementation which can boost these organizations to take greater advantage of the tool.

Have there been any difficulties in human resources adapting? To what extent are employees prepared to make the best use of CRM?

It is important to understand that for those who already use this tool or had initial training the way to use it is very practical and accessible, but on the other hand passing this information to other employees of the organization can be a challenge. The CRM practice in institutions requires time and learning and it is clear from the interviews that employees often leave aside that training and learning, mostly because there are priority tasks in which it is not possible to stop to learn more about the tool.

What are the main features that you value in a CRM system?

Despite the limitations that exist in the third sector, the CRM system is seen by the majority as something fundamental in their daily work. In addition to enjoying a centralized database with all the information accessible to all employees, it allows them to export a set of reports on key indicators of their department that they can easily present to management, which will later help in decision making, in addition to saving hours in manual work and allow automation of processes.

What do you think needs to be improved in the organization's CRM?

It is important to understand that the use of CRM in non-profit organizations is quite different from the business sector, not only by the capacity of financial resources as the processes of the various areas. Most nonprofit organizations in Portugal only use CRM to automate and optimize the fundraising department and even within this department there are still processes that are not fully linked to CRM. Some organizations still want to improve the use of CRM in a single department and slowly and with the help of globalization move the processes to other relevant areas within the organization.

Dimension 4: Role of CRM in the organization's adaptation to the pandemic context COVID 19

Non-profit organizations mostly work with a physical presence in the territory. With the current pandemic situation COVID-19, we wanted to understand how these organizations adapted and what were the benefits of having a CRM platform that helped them to mark their presence also in a digital and technological environment.

Due to the current pandemic situation in Portugal have they needed to adapt to a more digital world? What kind of changes occurred in the organization?

Despite the setback that the year 2020 had for non-profit organizations, they were able to adapt easily in most areas of intervention. Since they already had some practice in online campaigns, they began to use this medium in its entirety. Throughout the interviews, some examples of adaptations were mentioned that contributed to the continuity of support to their causes.

Do you believe that the future of the organization will continue to be digital?

Since it is important for non-profit organizations to be on the ground and participate face-to-face, they believe that there will be a balance between digital and face-to-face depending on the actions they take.

How have employees reacted to this change?

The adaptation to digital has occurred worldwide, so in one way or other employees have automatically had to mark their presence in digital. Despite some initial difficulties, they believe that in general the entry into the digital world was an inevitability that had been talked about for some time within the organizations but that had not really happened yet.

What impact has the organization had in joining a more technological and digital world?

The organizations impact to a more digital world has occurred both on a personal and organizational level. On a personal level it has led employees to take trainings in the area of digital to enjoy technology as much as possible in the organization. On the other hand, at the organizational level, it brought a cost reduction and the fact that the whole country could be present in the various activities that were going to be carried out online, which otherwise would not be possible.

How has your CRM system allowed you to respond to this context?

It is observed that CRM allowed easily to respond to the pandemic context in the organizations, namely by using their databases to implement campaigns, carry out segmented communication, extract reports to make important decisions linking online forms with CRM for online campaigns

Based on your experience, what changes would you suggest in adapting a CRM system to the context of COVID-19?

The context of COVID-19 opened up new opportunities for non-profit organizations to modernize and see pre-pandemic campaigns continue to be successful and hence adaptations had to be made during the year.

DISCUSSION OF THE RESULTS

After analyzing these interviews, it was possible to understand the perspective of the third sector in the use of technological tools and digital tools. The adaptation of these organizations in joining a digital world has several challenges, from available financial resources to human resources with knowledge and skills in the use of technological tools. However, it is notable that due to the growth of donors and beneficiaries, these entities seek tools that are able to have a greater perception of stakeholders, and, to this end, the use of CRM can meet the current needs.

During the research it became clear that CRM has a fundamental role in relational marketing strategies, especially in the fundraising department. The practice of segmented communication will mirror the quality of their fundraising actions, which consequently leads to an increase in donations and a good level of commitment and loyalty from their donors.

The centralization of information has enabled not only the successful implementation of a CRM, but also the strategies of non-profit organizations, placing the donor as the center for any decision making in their campaigns. Having a broad knowledge of their target audience makes it easier to raise awareness of their causes and to create medium- and long-term loyalty commitments.

Although these institutions still don't use CRM as much as they would like, not only in the department where they work, but also in the others, they make a significant effort to gradually move to optimized and automated processes, in order to improve their daily work and expand their time, especially in the management and implementation of their campaigns. In the course of this research, it was identified that many of the organizations have recently started with someone specialized in the CRM practice. Depending on the characteristics of these institutions, in terms of resources, it is believed to be a long and time-consuming process to allocate CRM to all areas, as well as to allow all features to be active in order to take full advantage of the tool. The third sector needs to see people involved in their cause and for this it is essential that they use tools that can dictate their actions, that help and support them to have a personalized message for their target audience.

LIMITATIONS AND FUTURE RESEARCH DIRECTIONS

With this research we believe to have deepened knowledge related to third sector entities and, thus, to understand the importance of CRM in the application of relational marketing practices and strategies.

A limitation of this research is the lack of updated and recent bibliography on CRM applied to non-profit organizations. It is believed that social marketing in general is still little explored in terms of deeper strategies in the development of its actions. Another limitation was the fact that the interviews were conducted online: it is believed that with a face-to-face interview one would have a greater perception and more openness of the relationship between the moderator and the interviewee. But the current pandemic context in which we find ourselves (COVID 19), dictated it.

For future studies it is recommended to expand the research to non-profit organizations of international level, since Portugal is still at an early stage in the importance it gives to CRM within the third sector.

It is also recommended and with the aim of enriching the study, the application of methodological approaches of a quantitative nature in order to understand the majority view of the beneficiaries and donors of these organizations in the application of CRM and the impact that these actions have in the way of reaching their stakeholders.

CONCLUSION

The main objective of this research work presented in this chapter was to understand the relationship between non-profit organizations and CRM and how this interferes in the definition of marketing strategies, relational marketing and communication.

The first step was to review the literature in order to deepen the knowledge of marketing, relational marketing, social marketing and CRM concepts. Then the exploratory study was based on a methodological approach of qualitative nature, based on the realization of semi-structured interviews to five non-profit organizations in Portugal - Caritas Portuguesa, Associação Salvador, Nariz Vermelho, Médicos do Mundo, Ajuda em Ação.

The current context of the COVID-19 pandemic and the consequent use of CRM tools has shown non-profit organizations much of what this transformation to digital should have already been. Adaptation and presence in digital were fundamental to continue with ongoing actions and consequently respond to society's aid. Therefore, it is believed that there should be a balance in the strategies of these entities, in which they will somehow remain digital since they can reach any place in the country, but due to the characteristics of these organizations the presence on the ground will continue to be fundamental so as not to create new isolations and emergency needs.

It is fundamental that non-profit organizations think about the promotion of an adequate training of practices and tools that enhance the value of these entities. The promotion, dissemination and recognition of non-profit organizations by society may have a positive impact, especially in the area of fund raising. that allow entities to reach a certain level of sustainability. It is therefore important that, in addition to continuing their support in society, they can take advantage of technological solutions capable of improving their results, obtain efficient and effective processes, and, even more importantly, know how to measure their social impact throughout the year. It is believed, therefore, that the areas of marketing and communication are those that most need investment and development by organizations in terms of technology, so that, consequently, they can take advantage of automatisms that will improve their day-to-day service delivery.

REFERENCES

Afonso, O. (2018). *Economia Social: conceito e características* [Social Economy: concept and characteristics]. Dinheiro Vivo.

Agariya, K., & Singh, D. (2011). What Really Defines Relationship Marketing? A Review of Definitions and General and Sector-Specific Defining Constructs. *Journal of Relationship Marketing*, *10*(4), 203–237. doi:10.1080/15332667.2011.624905

Andrade, M., & Franco, R. (2007). *Economia do conhecimento e organizações sem fins lucrativos Sociedade Portuguesa de Inovação* [Knowledge economy and non-profit organizations Portuguese Innovation Society]. Princípia Editora.

Antunes. J., & Paulo, R. (2008). O marketing relacional como novo paradigma [Relationship marketing as a new paradigm]. *Revista Portuguesa e Brasileira de Gestão*, 36-46.

Araújo, C., & Sá, E. S. (2017). A importância do marketing social no turismo: Revisão da literatura [The importance of social marketing in tourism: a literature review]. *Revista Turismo & Desenvolvimento*, *1*(27/28), 713–731.

Ávila, R. C., & Campos, J. L. M. (2018). The social economy facing emerging economic concepts: Social innovation, social responsibility, collaborative economy, social enterprises, and solidary economy. *C.I.R.I.E.C. España*, *93*(93), 5–50.

Bach, C., & Enas, A. (2016). View of The Impact of Social Marketing on Public Behavior. *Journal of Engineering Research and Science*, *1*(5), 17–22.

Basil, D. Z., Diaz-Meneses, G., & Basil, M. D. (2019). Social Marketing in Action. Springer. doi:10.1007/978-3-030-13020-6

Bateson, J., & Hoffman, D. (2016). *Princípios de Marketing de Serviços* [Services Marketing Principles]. Cengage Learning.

Bernhardt, J. M., Mays, D., & Hall, A. K. (2012). Critical social marketing: Investigating alcohol marketing in the developing world. *Journal of Social Marketing*, *2*(2), 94–102.

Berry, L. L. (1995). Relationship Marketing of Services-Growing Interest, Emerging Perspectives. *Journal of the Academy of Marketing Science*, *23*(4), 236–245. doi:10.1177/009207039502300402

Brito, C. (2011). Relationship marketing: Old wine in a new bottle? *Journal Innovative Marketing*, *7*(1).

Brito, C., & Lencastre, P. (2014). *Novos Horizontes do Marketing* [New Horizons of Marketing]. Córdova: D. Quixote.

Caeiro, J. M. C. (2008). Economia social: Conceitos, fundamentos e tipologia [Social economy: concepts, foundations and typology]. *Revista Katálysis, 11*(1), 61–72. doi:10.1590/S1414-49802008000100006

Casais, B., Fernandes, J., & Sarmento, M. (2019). Tourism innovation through relationship marketing and value co-creation: A study on peer-to-peer online platforms for sharing accommodation. *Journal of Hospitality and Tourism Management, 42*(42), 51–57.

Courchesne, A., Ravanas, P., & Pulido, C. (2019). Using Technology to Optimize Customer Relationship Management: The Case of Cirque du Soleil. *International Journal of Arts Management, 21*(2).

Cruz, I. (2017). Aplicación de la mercadotecnia relacional en una empresa de venta de café de Baja California [Application of relationship marketing in a coffee company in Baja California]. *Journal Región y Sociedad, 30*(71), 3–20.

Dançante, D. S. D. S. G. C. (2017). *O marketing social aplicado à saúde pública: as duas campanhas de sensibilização em Portugal* [Social marketing applied to public health: the two awareness campaigns in Portugal] (Master's thesis). Universidade de Évora, Portugal.

Fonseca, M. J. (2012). *As campanhas de comunicação de marketing no âmbito da prevenção rodoviária portuguesa: um contributo para a análise da sua eficácia* [Portuguese road safety marketing communication campaigns: a contribution to the analysis of their effectiveness] (Doctoral dissertation). Universidade Fernando Pessoa, Porto, Portugal.

Gummesson, E., Mele, C., Polese, F., Gummesson, E., & Grönroos, C. (2012). The emergence of the new service marketing: Nordic School perspectives. *Journal of Service Management, 23*(4), 479–497. doi:10.1108/09564231211260387

Henrique, A., & Miake, S. (2017). *Gestão do Conhecimento do Cliente (GCC): Proposta e Avaliação de um Modelo em um Grande Grupo Privado de Ensino Superior Brasileiro* [Customer Knowledge Management: Proposal and Evaluation of a Model in a Large Brazilian Private Higher Education Group]. Universidade Tecnológica Federal do Paraná.

Idzikowski, A., Kuryło, P., Cyganiuk, J., & Ryczko, M. (2019). Customer Relationship Management (CRM)-philosophy and its significance for the enterprise. *System Safety: Human-Technical Facility-Environment, 1*(1).

Kotler, P. (2000). *Marketing Management, Millenium Edition*. Pearson Custom Publishing.

Kotler, P., Kartajaya, H., & Setiawan, I. (2017). *Marketing 4.0: Mudança do Tradicional para o Digital* [Marketing 4.0: Moving from Traditional to Digital]. Conjuntura Actual Editora.

Kotler, P., & Lee, N. R. (2011). *Social Marketing: Changing Behaviors for Good*. SAGE Publications.

Kotler, P., & Lee, N. R. (2015). *Social Marketing: Changing Behaviors for Good* (5th ed.). SAGE Publications.

Kristoffersen, L., & Singh, S. (2004). Successful application of a customer relationship management program in a nonprofit organization. *Journal of Marketing Theory and Practice*, *12*(2), 28–42. doi:10.1080/10696679.2004.11658517

Lefebvre, C. (2011). An integrative model for social marketing. *Journal of Social Marketing*, *1*(1), 54–72. doi:10.1108/20426761111104437

Lefebvre, C. (2012). Transformative social marketing: Co-creating the social marketing discipline and brand. *Journal of Social Marketing*, *2*(2), 118–129. doi:10.1108/20426761211243955

Lindon, D., Lendrevie, J., Lévy, J., Dionísio, P., & Rodrigues, V. (2018). *Teoria e Prática do Marketing*. Lisboa: D. Quixote.

Lovelock, C., & Jochen, W. (2011). *Understanding Digital Marketing*. Kogan Page Limited.

Lovelock, C., & Wirtz, J. (2009). *Service Marketing: people, technology, and strategy*. Pearson.

Machado, A. T., Antunes, A. C., & Miranda, S. (2016). *Marketing social através de campanhas de comunicação: o caso da Associação Portuguesa de Apoio à Vítima (APAV)* [Social marketing through communication campaigns: the case of the Portuguese Association for Victim Support]. Revista Portuguesa de Marketing.

Marangoni, S. M. (2015). *Marketing de Serviços* [Services Marketing]. Estácio.

Martínez, A. M., Monserrat, J. M., & Campillo, A. C. (2017). El paradigma relacional en las estrategias de las organizaciones de marketing de destinos: Interactividad y función social en las webs turísticas oficiales. *Revista Latina de Comunicación Social*, *4*(72), 374–396.

Martins, O., Dourado, M., Paço, A., Mainardes, E. W., & Rodrigues, R. G. (2014). O marketing social e a promoção de mudanças estruturais no aleitamento materno [Social marketing and the promotion of structural changes in breastfeeding]. *Revista de Administração de Empresas*, *54*(4), 370–380. doi:10.1590/S0034-759020140403

Meira, P., & Santos, C. (2012). Programas de marketing social: Proposição e exame de uma estrutura conceitual de avaliação de resultados [Social marketing programmes: proposing and examining a conceptual framework for outcome evaluation]. *Revista de Administração Pública*, *46*(2), 493–522. doi:10.1590/S0034-76122012000200008

Mihăilă, V. (2017). The changing nature of innovation-based social marketing programs: The case of health promotion programs. *Manager Journal*, *25*(1), 176–184.

Miquel-Romero, M. J., Caplliure-Giner, E. M., & Adame-Sánchez, C. (2014). Relationship marketing management: Its importance in private label extension. *Journal of Business Research*, *67*(5), 667–672. doi:10.1016/j.jbusres.2013.11.025

Nancy, R., Michael, L., & William, S. (2011). *A Declaration of Social Marketing*. Sage Publications.

Oliveira, T. M. V. (2001). Amostragem não Probabilística: Adequação de Situações para uso e Limitações de amostras por Conveniência, Julgamento e Quotas [Non-Probability Sampling: Suitability of Contexts for Use and Limitations of Convenience, Judgmental and Quota Sampling]. *Administração Online*, *2*(3), 1–7.

Palmatier, R. W., Dant, R. P., Grewal, D., & Evans, K. R. (2006). Factors influencing the effectiveness of relationship marketing: A meta-analysis. *Journal of Marketing*, *70*(4), 136–153. doi:10.1509/jmkg.70.4.136

Parvatiyar, A., & Sheth, J. (2001). Customer relationship management: Emerging practice, process, and discipline. *Journal of Economic and Social Research*, *3*(2), 1–34.

Peattie, K., & Peattie, S. (2009). Social marketing: A pathway to consumption reduction. *Journal of Business Research*, *62*(2), 260–268. doi:10.1016/j.jbusres.2008.01.033

Phills, J., Deiglmeier, K., & Miller, D. (2008). Rediscovering Social Innovation. *Stanford Social Innovation Review*, *6*(4), 36–42.

Rahimi, R., & Kozak, M. (2017). Impact of Customer Relationship Management on Customer Satisfaction: The Case of a Budget Hotel Chain. *Journal of Travel & Tourism Marketing*, *34*(1), 40–51. doi:10.1080/10548408.2015.1130108

Santos, F. de A. O. G. dos. (2018). A *comunicação estratégica em organizações sem fins lucrativos: A Liga Portuguesa Contra o Cancro como estudo de caso* [Strategic communication in non-profit organizations: The Portuguese League Against Cancer as a case study] (Master's thesis). Universidade Nova, Lisboa, Portugal.

Scheer, L. K., Miao, C. F., & Palmatier, R. W. (2014). Dependence and interdependence in marketing relationships: Meta analytic insights. *Journal of the Academy of Marketing Science*, *43*(6), 694–712. doi:10.100711747-014-0418-1

Serrat, O. (2017). The Future of Social Marketing. Springer. doi:10.1007/978-981-10-0983-9_17

Souza, S., Pitombo, T., Zaccaria, R., & Monteiro, T. (2018). Social Responsibility and Social Marketing at Monsanto. *Responsabilidade Social e Marketing Social na Monsanto.*, *8*(2), 6–20.

Wang, C. S., Lin, S. L., Chou, T. H., & Li, B. Y. (2019). An integrated data analytics process to optimize data governance of non-profit organization. *Computers in Human Behavior*, *101*, 495–505. doi:10.1016/j.chb.2018.10.015

Wu, S. I., & Hung, J. M. (2008). A performance evaluation model of CRM on non-profit organizations. *Total Quality Management*, *19*(4), 321–342. doi:10.1080/14783360701591978

Yim, F. H. K., Anderson, R. E., & Swaminathan, S. (2004). Customer relationship management: Its dimensions and effect on customer outcomes. *Journal of Personal Selling & Sales Management*, *24*(4), 263–278.

Zeithaml, A., Dwayne, G., & Bitner, M. (2014). *Os Fundamentos do Marketing de Serviços* [The Fundamentals of Services Marketing]. McGraw-Hill.

ADDITIONAL READING

Dewnarain, S., Ramkissoon, H., & Mavondo, F. (2019). Social customer relationship management: An integrated conceptual framework. *Journal of Hospitality Marketing & Management*, *28*(2), 172–188. doi:10.1080/19368623.2018.1516588

Galan-Ladero, M. M. (Ed.). (2021). *Cause-Related Marketing: Case Studies From a Global Perspective*. Springer Nature. doi:10.1007/978-3-030-65455-9

Liston-Heyes, C., & Liu, G. (2013). A study of non-profit organisations in cause-related marketing: Stakeholder concerns and safeguarding strategies. *European Journal of Marketing*, *47*(11/12), 1954–1974. doi:10.1108/EJM-03-2012-0142

Nair, S. R. (2020). Cause-Related Marketing and Consumer Buying Behavior: Opportunities and Challenges. *Emotional, Sensory, and Social Dimensions of Consumer Buying Behavior*, 324-348.

Rathi, D., & Given, L. M. (2017). Non-profit organizations' use of tools and technologies for knowledge management: A comparative study. *Journal of Knowledge Management*, *21*(4), 718–740. doi:10.1108/JKM-06-2016-0229

Rosnerova, Z., & Hraskova, D. (2021). The Application and Importance of Marketing and its Tools in the Conditions of Non-profit Organizations on a Global Scale. In *SHS Web of Conferences* (Vol. 92). EDP Sciences. 10.1051hsconf/20219202055

Chapter 14
Social Media Reputation, Corporate Reputation:
Social Media Risks on Corporate Reputation and Precautions

Kevser Zeynep Meral
https://orcid.org/0000-0002-2514-8744
İstanbul Bahçeşehir University, Turkey

ABSTRACT

Corporates create and protect their corporate reputation and identities through social media. At the same time, they use internal (like meeting with zoom) and external communication methods via social media along with marketing through social media. However, they face the risk of destroying their corporate reputation via social media. Social media and social media platforms such as Facebook, Instagram, Twitter, etc. have become essential communication tools with the customers and affect corporates' reputation as well. This study aims to explain the role and risks of social media on the corporate reputations via literature review. Results show that institutions need to know how to use social media tools very well in order to create and protect their reputation. Corporates need managers and social media specialists who know how to use social media and how to avoid the potential risks of social media.

INTRODUCTION

Communication with social media platforms (Facebook, Instagram, twitter, etc.) has changed and continues to transform the way of life not only of individuals but also of all institutions and even the world. Mutual interaction, content sharing and social media accounts in social media are no longer belonging to individuals or institutions but have turned into a common space. Social media, with the help of information technologies, has changed the fundamentals of communication, consuming and creating methods in the world. It transforms not only individuals, but also institutions with its internal and external use. Social media creates new opportunities for all functions of the business, from marketing, finance, op-

DOI: 10.4018/978-1-7998-9790-3.ch014

erations and human resources management, while at the same time causing challenges. Once seen as a communication tool for young people, social networking sites have now become the main communication tools for all age groups. For example, in the United States, social media usage rates among adults by age group as of February 2019; It is 90 percent in the age group 18-29, 82 percent in the 30-49 age group, 69 percent in the 50-64 age group, and 40 percent above 65+ (Statista.com, 2020). The aim of this study is to investigate the effects of social media and social media on corporate reputation through the literature review method. In addition to the importance of the social media on corporate reputation also aim to define what can be done by communication / social media experts in institutions on use of social media and to present importance of social media for managers. At the same time to enable corporates to prevent possible application errors in social media platforms, which have become a common area for their customers with examples from real life based on experiences, focusing on commercial communication and interaction with customers through corporate social media platforms. Social media and social media aspects will be given in the first part, followed with corporate reputation and lastly corporate reputation risks and precautions will be given.

SOCIAL MEDIA

Social media enables online interaction via platforms where contents are created by users on real time among participants (Dwivedi, Kapoor and Chen, 2015). The real time created contents are very important for organizations as results of Cone Communications about consumers show that four out of five consumers stated that they changed their purchasing decision when they saw negative news about a product on the internet, and 89% of consumers stated that they found internet sources reliable to get information about products. On the other hand, 59% of consumers stated that they prefer to read online product reviews because they can be reached very easily from their mobile phones. When all these data are evaluated, it is seen that the reputation of institutions in the online world has a great impact on consumers (Cone Communications, 2011). As an important factor which affects consumers decisions, along with organizations, scholars are focusing on social media relationships via social media as well. According to Harrigan et.al (2020) major brands all over the world are active in social media. Some of the leader brands followers numbers are:

- GoPro (@gopro) with 18.6 million Instagram, 10.9 million Facebook, and 2.1 million Twitter followers.
- Nike with 184 million Instagram, 36.4 million Facebook, and 8.8 million Twitter followers.
- Spotify with 7,3 million Instagram followers,
- Starbucks with 17.8 million Instagram, 35 million Facebook, 10.9 million Twitter followers.
- National Geographic with 195 million Instagram, 49.2 million Facebook, 26.6 million Twitter followers

Although number of followers is one of the important measures for success, another measure is the engagement rate, of which a post receives actions for examples sharing, comments and likes which is related with the organizations followers in social media (Hootsuite, 2020).

All these actions (like, share, comment) actually are customer's voluntary contribution to the organization's marketing, in other words like a reflection of customer's engagement to the organization beyond financial patronage (Harmeling, Moffett, Arnold, & Carlson, 2017). Nike's engagement rate sits around 0.67 per cent, while Adidas' is around 0.20 per cent (Rival IQ, 2020). Nike has more number of followers, compared to Adidas (Adidas.com) with 26 million followers in Instagram, where Nike has 184 million followers as of 08.December.2021.

Social media is used especially in human resources by organizations as well, according to Statista (Statista.com, 2021), large-sized companies use approximately three social media applications and eighty percent of medium sized companies used LinkedIn for job applications. Social media along with organizational effect at the same enables companies to find out their customers' ideas and at the same time increase publicity of the companies and organizational satisfaction (Reitz, 2012).

Becker ve Lee (Becker and Lee, 2019), study about 198 organizations findings show that

1. Large firms have more social media accounts than smaller firms,
2. Large firms respond more frequently and quickly to their use of social media than smaller firms,
3. Firm size structure for online reputation management is less related to response styles in social media. According to research data, most organizations lack a strategic framework in the use and monitoring of social media communication for reputation management.

CORPORATE REPUTATION

Corporate reputation is a tangible asset and relationship between emotions, experiences and attitudes affect reputation. Reputation is also affected from value of corporation. Emotion is a reflection of feelings and expressed as a reaction, based on Scherer's (2005) work, Ramos et al. (2020) argued that an attitude can be defined as a set of beliefs or predispositions towards specific people or objects which are associated with an intention and behaviour (Ajzen and Fishbein, 2005) and (Ponzi et al., 2011). Wepener and Boshoff (2015) and Fombrun et al. (2000) defined "emotional appeal," as customer's feelings of empathy, trust, pride, and admiration to company.

Scholars have focused on most important aspect of corporate reputation, stakeholders or consumers, some scholars investigated 'consumer experience' (Lemon and Verhoef, 2016).

Scholars have investigated main variables of their customers' experiences with their customers via customer evaluations (Casado and Pelaez, 2014). Consumer experience via expressed in digital environment where they can communicate and engage interactively, helps organizations to maximise performance (Ferreira and Zambaldi, 2019).

Online reputation management does not delete negative information in internet, tries to reduce the negative impacts and is a tool to combat against negative online reputation. Online reputation management is based on following the key words in search engines and replying the contents correctly (Mikulaskova et al. 2016).

Sometimes a crisis can occur outside of social media, and social media can be used to alleviate this crisis. According to the research conducted by PWC in 2013, 57% of companies see social media as the main source of crisis solutions (Stránská ve Stříteský, 2015).

According to Sofranec (Sofranec, 2016), Online Reputation Management rules are:

1. Monitoring what customers are talking about on online platforms: Signing up to online platforms and monitoring what is being said about the company, to ensure that the organization is informed

about all the comments about the brand by using the Google Alert feature for social platforms without membership.

2. Understanding the cause of negative comments: Before a negative comment can be answered, it is essential to understand what the cause of the problem is; it is important to talk to the employees and check the service; Then the appropriate response to the situation should be given.
3. Giving appropriate answers: If the customer is right, organization must definitely apologize; indicate that the situation will be corrected. If there is a misunderstanding, it should be shared how the situation is perceived in terms of the business, by expressing regret.
4. Setting the business's response tone: The business's responses are a reflection of the company's values and professional experience. Slang words should be avoided, the answer tone should be moderate. The response should emphasize the firm's strengths.
5. Obtaining support from offline tools when necessary: If the customer's complaint is not resolved; organization must contact him by e-mail or phone. It is important to ask the client directly how to fix the situation in private.

Corporate Reputation and Corporate Image

Corporate reputation has been defined by researchers (Fombrun, Ponzi, and Newburry, 2015).

Corporate reputation and corporate image terms are usually used interchangeably (Chun, 2005). Some researchers argued that corporate reputation is a dimension of corporate image (Yadav, Dokania, and Pathak, 2016) or opposite (Cian and Cervai, 2014), (Loureiro and Gonzalez, 2008). Corporate reputation is usually confused with corporate image (Fillis, 2003). Relationship between corporate reputation and projected corporate image is a dynamic bilateral relationship (Gotsi and Wilson, 2001).

Corporate image is designed by company (Villena-Manzanares and Souto-Perez, 2016) to create a public emotional feeling towards company (Barich and Kotler, 1991). Walker (2010) defines corporate image as desired image for which an organization would like public to think about them.

Gardberg (2017) has suggested that there is a relationship between corporate reputation and corporate image. Image and reputation relationship in Lai's (2019) research about hotel industry has found that hotel image is an antecedent of hotel reputation and that to increase loyalty hotel management must establish customer loyalty. Some researchers have found that corporate image affects perceived value and satisfaction and loyalty in hotel and tourism sector (Ryu, Han, and Kim, 2008).

Corporate Reputation and Corporate Identity

Wei, (2002) suggests that corporate reputation is confused with corporate identity. Corporate reputation relationship with corporate identity aspects has been investigated by (Harris and De Chernatony, 2001), (Urde and Greyser, 2016). In Devereux et al., (2017) study on impact of social media use on corporate identity, it is suggested that organizations can improve and define how they can focus on commercial communication through corporate social network platforms. With help of information technologies, social media, which carries risks of creating and protecting corporate identity and reputation, but also losing reputation, also contains risks as well as finding new opportunities, jobs and customers.

Corporate Reputation and Trust

Reputation and trust are also confused with each other because they are both subjective and social (Marwick, 2013), reputation is an economic source as a metric, however trust is a public good, gives feeling of trustworthiness (Gandini, 2016).

Huang and DiStaso (2020), in their experimental research about timing and message affects organization perception and intentions in social media, found that response one day after in Facebook has initiated more trust to hospital than response posted one week later and emotional approach also initiated more trust, and more intention to 'like' post.

United Airlines and Trust Case

As in United Airlines incident, in April 2017, three security guards dragged a random passenger in aisle of United Airlines plane, forced out of plane, however two passenger with their mobiles, filmed event, and shared it via YouTube. videos were instantly shared from social media platforms like Twitter and Facebook. Immediately following films shared in social media, many passengers who flew before with United Airlines, share it in all social media platforms, with angry comments, adding their experiences with United Airline's poor service, with mocking United Airlines slogans, sarcastically like "If we cannot beat our competitors, we beat our customers" (Moneycnn.com, 2017). Finally, major news media like Guardian, CNN, New York Times also published event, increasing access, as a result, United Airlines 800 million dollars market value in one day and forced to implement expensive policies to prevent more loss of reputation and a drop in ticket sales (Lazo, 2017). United Airlines example shows social media's with help of new information and communication technologies (Kaplan and Haenlein, 2010) – how social media users can be connected over Internet and share their experiences, ideas and opinions in a publicly accessible way - of quality, competence or characteristics of organizations. It shows how it is produced, propagated, and modified in open access. Also, as in this example, social media enables users with public access to reach large audiences connected via online social networks by assigning roles and bypassing barriers of traditional news media (Castells, 2011). After crises scholars researched crise, Cheng and Shen (2020) and found that from customers' trust was affected by company's negative ethical judgements and were negatively affected in terms of trust.

Corporate Reputation and Corporate Communication

Corporate reputation relationship with corporate communication also searched in literature (Balmer and Greyser, 2006), Wickert and Cornelissen, 2017).

Social media reputation is created through "reputation resources", such as enabling managers to find content through social media tools and search engines, according to research results on impact of reputation through corporate communication (Van Riel and Fombrun, 2007), (Grützmacher, 2011).

Organizations need to manage their social reputation as well as they manage their other assets (Edmunds, Turner, 2005). Studies on reputation, which consist of abstract judgments, and their results are still at an estimate level (Budd, 1994). Reputation is sum of images and consists of corporate performance, corporate behavior and corporate communication (Doorley and Garcia, 2007).

Corporate reputation definition is based on process of interpretation and processing of clues of factors such as analytical, evaluative and judgment (Bitektine, 2011) about quality or reliability of institution

(Highhouse, Brooks, and Gregarus, 2009). Organizations spread some of these clues when they strategically reflect their positive image through corporate communication or symbolic actions (Petkova, Rindova, and Gupta, 2013). It is produced by other actors, such as news media (Deephouse, 2000).

Combined with diminishing impact of institutions on knowledge production and dissemination, which are no longer decentralized in a number of origins where organisations are partially dependent for their income and access to information, this diversity increases difference to formal corporate communication (MacKay and Munro, 2012) and to evaluations exposed to news media reports (Etter and Vestergaard, 2015).

Corporate Reputation and Corporate Performance

Walsh and Beatty (2007) focused on a reliable and financially strong company, and service and product quality. Walker (2010) on profitability and product and service quality, wherelse Fombrun et al. (2000) on financial performance and quality of service and product and Wepener and Boshoff (2015) only on service points.

Corporate Reputation and Employees/ Employers

Lee and Kim (2020) found that organization-employee relationship effects on employees' negative communication intentions are affected by their social media motives. Schaarschmidt and Walsh (2018) tested a model where employees' being aware that they can affect online reputation of company.

Top managements's reputation like CEO is found to influence organizations reputation in general (Conte, 2018). However employees' acting opposite may create negative actions and harm reputation of corporate.

New York Daily News Newspaper Case

When New York Daily News newspaper laid off half of its social media employees in 2018, one of social media team that left wanted revenge by posting strange GIFs on newspaper's Twitter account. Due to this incident that may lead to a social media crisis, institutions need to ensure their publishing authority and control on social media (Slate.com, 2018).

Corporate Reputation and Social Responsibility

In their study about about corporate social responsibility, Grover, Kar and Ilavarasan, (2019) state that corporate social responsibility impact corporate reputation and searched how corporate social responsibility messages on social media affected corporate reputation and found that social influencer CEOs posted 5,97 times more corporate social responsibility messages on twitter compared to Fortune CEOs.

Campa and Zijlmans (2019) have investigated whether corporate social responsibility activities covered corporate support for arts, and found that they have been rewarded for art support and that social reports are best communication channel to communicate about corporates support for art.

BP-Oil Company Case

In terms of environmental responsibility corporates must be very careful as in BP-Oil Company, following oil spill (Bloomberg, 2020), for example, social media, yellow-green sun stained with black-oil with retouched versions of oil company BP logo, dying seabirds, etc. scandal produced a Google search for "BP logo", these cramped images as a constant condemnation of insincerity and irresponsibility (Logomyway, 2020).

However corporates must be careful about using this as a communication strategy because as in Onur Air case in Turkey, it might create a social media crisis.

Onur Air

In Turkey as well due to media literacy, such cases are seen (Untila Kaplan, 2019) in social media as well. When fundraising campaign was launched following Van earthquake, in Turkey, airline company, Onur Air also caused an extraordinary reaction by announcing that it would participate in aid campaign and declared 50 kurus for each new follower. For this reason, social media experts should carefully make every post carefully (Mikail and Yurtseven, 2014).

Corporate Reputation and Mergers and Acquisitions

Ethical behaviour is not only important in hotel sector, researchs show that ethical behaviour increases company's moral capital (Zhang, Wiersema, 2009), (Connelly, Certo, Ireland and Reutzel, 2011), ethics is considered as a valuable source of reputation (Portes and Sensenbrenner, 1993) and in mergers as well (Lin and Wei, 2006).

Especially in international Mergers and Acquisitions, ethical behaviour is more important as it is related with company's reputation, as international mergers and acquisitions are more complex and with higher asymmetric information (Martynova and Renneboog, 2008), (Rani, Yadav and Jain, 2014), with more risks (Erel, Liao and Weisbach, 2012).

Maung, Wilson and Yu (2020), in their research claim that in international merger and acquisitions, target company, is usually have lower acquisition premiums especially when negative behaviour is reported in media.

In banking sector, Ramos and Casado-Molina (2020), in their study have found that in banking sector, ethics experience has most affecting factor on intangible asset in terms of online corporate reputation management.

Social Media and Cultural Differences

Tansey and O'Riordan (1999) argued that socially constructed realities may differ from culture to culture as in Starbuck case.

Starbuck Case

Wang and Laufer (2020) have investigated in their research difference between Eastern and Western countries, in case of China and found out that due to cultural differences, there are different crisis management strategies in China.

Hence in Osakwe et al (2020) study on bank reputation in Africa, they have found that customer care and service offering affect bank's reputation positively and positive bank reputation is important in customer's loyalty and trust. Furthermore, there are differences among countries, and that management must take into consideration institutional differences in internationalization and reputational strategies.

Corporate Reputation and Humor

Kentucky Fried Chicken (KFC) Crisis

Internet memes that break traditional forms (mem: a video or phrase spread over Internet, often with humorous and creative modification, an internet sharing format that combines images with short words and interprets everyday situations) (Guadagno et al., 2013) flexible multimodal text, images, by trying audio and video combinations (Jenkins, 2006), it is seen as a tool to develop creative side of users (Papacharissi, 2012), and it is observed that original, creative content internet memes content is encouraged due to higher likelihood and higher transmission of it on social media (Jenkins, Ford and Green, 2013).

Social media users can use sarcasm and humor for popularity (Zappavigna, 2012). In fact creative use of humor has been shown to trigger emotional responses that encourage individuals to search, discuss, and share information that motivate individuals to share this content online (Nelson-Field, Riebe, and Newstead, 2013) and encouraged its spread to social networks (Dobele et al., 2007). Humorous words in social media change format to culture jamming, which occurs like in using corporate materials i.e. slogans, ads, logos etc creatively (Guadagno et al., 2013), and criticise corporate's decisions and by emphasizing conflicts between projected images and actions of corporate.

While news media presumes that authenticity and impartiality of content is important and their evaluations influence collective decisions (King and Soule, 2007), however not being neutral or false information does not affect influence or spread. On contrary, unrealistic accounts attract attention when they are expressed in a creative or humorous way (Heiress, van Neuen 2017) or mix emotions (Guadagno et al., 2013) reflect pre-existing opinion, spreading to a wide audience (Sunstein, 2017).

Some journalists in tradetional media make humor a trademark in their private columns and although these media often fall for satirical cartoons, traditional news media can sometimes become culture jamming too. In fact, these cartoons are also quite common in social media (Leskovec, Backstrom, and Kleinberg, 2009).

Humor can be used as a communication method in crisis management as well. For example, in February 2018, Kentucky Fried Chicken, England, due to change of their logistics company, when stock of chickens crisis arised due to chickens non delivery to KFC restaurants in UK apologized from their customers that crisis was a daily problem. Although the company has apologized when crisis was not solved and crises was worse, company hat to close majority of 900 restaurants throughout country. company, which had to organize a new website for announcement of few open restaurants, turned crisis into sympathy. Disappointed KFC customers flood social media with messages, rivals step in and crisis deepens, while KFC embraces instead of escaping crisis, responding to each criticism and apologizing by posting a full-page humorous advertisement a week later. By writing a sincere and clear apology "FCK, We're Sorry" by writing letters "FCK" instead of KFC on its logo, we thank its customers for their patience and their employees for their selfless work, and managed to manage crisis. According to published humorous apology text (Campaignlive.co, 2018) statistics, nearly 796.7 million people via social media.

Findus Horse Meat Case

When company Findus was found out that they used horse meat in their products (Dailymail, 2013), it triggered social media messages which used horse meat or meat products with horse figures, it does not matter whether there is a copyright or details, messages content were emotional and funny, and with quick spread of this content to digital networks, explained an organization's and industry's food safety problem to social media users. This ultimately urged organization to re-brand it costly, as it failed to regain its reputation three years later. As in example of Findus, usually in evaluation of product, content is shared with sarcasm and humor by social media users (Kumar and Combe, 2015).

Ethics and Corporate Reputation

Racial Bias and DoubleTree By Hilton Hotel Case

Bias based on race his increased lately in hotels (Glusac, 2018). Following crisis of a black customer forced to leave DoubleTree By Hilton Hotel in 2018, Triantafillidou and Yannas (2020) in their experimental research about a fictitious hotel of handling racious charged crisis for hotel's post-crisis reputation, with positive social media engagement and offline behavioral intentions, found that among interplays, Twitter was more effective compared to Instagram and Facebook.

Social Media and Politics

Mc Donald's Presidential's Election Case in US

Rim, Lee, and Yoo (2020), in their research about social-political advocacy corporates, found that brand boycotters were both in boycotting and advocators' networks, and were also in other brands boycotting networks which were both against Trump's and Republicans's policy.

Pınar DYO Case in Turkey

Selçuk Yaşar, CEO of Yaşar Holding, owner of Pınar Süt and other companies, sponsor of Karşıyaka Sport's Club has posted a political message after referendum and following post products of Pınar was boycotted (Kaya, 2019).

Corporate Reputation and Crisis Management

Scholars focused on corporate reputation in social media. Lallement et al., (2020), in their research of reputation about art events, found that online searching only affected who had either no opinion or positive opinion about event and that online search only amends of whom who have no prior opinion about show.

In a research about online reputation management in sport organizations, Kitchin et al., (2020) had a new case via one of supporter of an English football club and they found out that supporter's case was not correctly dealt by club and they suggest that for Online Reputation Management, sports organizations must implement specific reputation management practices.

Wang, Schuetz and Cai (2020) experimental research on choosing an ideal crisis strategy show that among three options as ignore, having noticed but stay silent and condemn company and share negative information, netizens conducted numeric simulations, company must decide either to react positively, in time, disclose fact, apologize/compensate or react negatively with denial or taking legal actions.

Zheng, Liu, and Lowry (2020) in their experimental research about secondary crisis communication on social media, found that consumer's reaction depends on response of firm, they want to believe that they are doing right i.e. in social conformance with others and scared of disliked by others if they buy from a company in crisis. Social conformance with negative word of mouth harm product in crises.

Jin, van der Meer, Lee, and Lu (2020), in their online experimential research found out that using factual elaboration and employee backup contributed to effective response in crises and quality of message affect corrective communication. Cheng, and Lee (2019), in their research of literature thematic review about post-truth online crises communication in China, found that unique crisis communication strategies are used in China influenced by political system, cultural values.

Javornik, Filieri, and Gumann (2020), in their experimental study about handling complaints with conversational human voice (CHV) had more positive perceptions compared to corporate voice and interactional justice affect process and satisfaction with handling complaints affect corporate image positively and indirectly Word of Mouth intentions. However procedural justice is negatively affected by conversational human voice.

With increase in digital usage in world data breaches has also increased social media scandals can increase negative effects about company, in their study, Confente et al. (2019) about how such events affected reputation of company and found that, before data breach users discussed perceived quality of company's offer after breaches they focused on corporate performance and customer orientation, and in case of intentional and internal breach of data, company's lack of investment in training was another point. Corporates who have strong corporate reputations, have a high appeal, which help companies increased customer satisfaction, trust, loyalty, attract top employees and during crises strong corporate reputation help (Wiedmann and Buxel, 2005).

Meng, Liang, and Yang (2011) cruise image affects positively and increases repurchasing intention. Ryschka et al. (2016) argued that crises management, using social media along with cultural values and band familiarity, speed in responding has affected corporate reputation perception in cruise line.

Social media platforms are where crises can start because offline (traditional) crisis communication where there is one-on-one relationship, but social media is the opposide and increases speed as reaches directly large audience (Coombs, 2014).

Crises is defined as a sudden, unexpected event (Coombs, 2007), corporate crises can be defined as unexpected negative events which threats brand's expected benefits (Dutta and Pullig, 2011). Crises are classified under different groups by researchers. Bernstein (2011) has grouped crises into three groups as creeping, slow-burn and sudden crises. Ulmer, Sellnow, and Seeger, (2011) classify it under two groups.

First group covers "crises caused by natural, uncontrollable factors" such as natural disasters or failure of products or crises arising from accidental events which can be caused intentionally by one employee within company or external (Coombs and Holladay, 2001).

Second group covers "intentionally caused crises" i.e. terrorism, sabotage etc. An important aspect of crises is data breaches, which are unpredictable, although not high probability but have an high impact, difficult to recover (Gaudenzi and Siciliano, 2017).

Sen and Borle, (2015) has also grouped data breach crises into three groups, as:

1. Intentional and internal (like stealing and sharing private customers' information knowingly),
2. Unintentional and internal as in accidental group above, (like security settings, exposing private data unintentionally)
3. External and intentional (like hacking software to access to private data etc.).

Intentional and internal cases however accidentally or by employees who are not competent may create crises, examples can be given as United Airlines and Mc Donalds cases. United Airlines and Mc Donalds cases can be given as an example of crises arising from accidental events within company.

United Airlines Case

For an example for a crisis arising within a company can be United Airlines case where management saw themselves as crisis managers and instead of apologizing sincerely, they have defined customer who has been deported out of aircraft by force as disruptive and belligerent within their company correspondence, which was shared by public and created more loss of reputation and reaction in social media against Airline (Brunner, 2019), (Bang, 2019).

Another example is McDonalds case where employee has posted asking McDonalds customers to share their experiences which created a crise in social media, even today accessible.

McDonalds case

New digital technologies, by enabling other online contents to have direct access via hyper text links make it easier to produce joint production process (Albu ve Etter, 2016). On contrary to news media before internet, hyper text interaction is created along with online links, they are created including news archive whit are related with non linear text knots (Manovich, 2002). As these links are non stop produced and change and as web sites enable unlimited additions from different sources, contents and configurations can progress unpredictively (Landow, 2006). For example, when McDonalds, started a campaign to create customers support accounts with #McDStories hashtag via Twitter in January 2012, many users all over world started, to share their negative unforgettable memories with hashtag of McDonalds open to public (Twitter.com, 2012). contents of tweets covered criticised flavour, unacceptable hygiene standards, chemical ingredients in products to accusing them causing obesity. Links to other social media sites, blogs, photos, videos and web sites and finally reaching to traditional newspapers and magazines (Hill, vd., 2012) and even years after first event, still accessable web site based event enriched story. McDonald's example, has created alternative channels where information is spread horizontally via social media, and allows social media users to question content of corporate communication and present alternative evaluations (Albu ve Etter, 2016).

Currently there are more two billion users are evaluating and discussing events, products and services via virtual social web sites like Facebook, Instagram, YouTube, blogs and evaluating sites like Tripadvisor and even via traditional news medias interactive comment applications. Although these platforms are used by organization as additional channels, they enable open access to public including consumers, politicians, citizens, activits, independent and alternative media and non-governmental organizations (Castells, 2011). These users, may present various evaluations from different information sources, their motivating instincts and their experienced restrictions.

McDonald has got another example in China, about food with expired date has created a crisis, a scandal which was discussed all over country in Chinese social media platform namely Sina Weibo, damaging sales and corporate image in 2014 (Forbes.com, 2014).

Intentional and Internal Crises Examples

Data breach cases are usually seen in finance/banking sector, as in HSBC and a Turkish Bank.

HSBC case

In 2017 HSBC employee, Herve Falciani had more than 300 thousand confidential data which were shared with international media (BBC.com, 2015).

In Turkey, bank employees, sold confidential private data to third parties are were filed lawsuit against them (Sabah, 2020).

CRISIS RESPONSE COMMUNICATION STRATEGIES

With social media increase it is more difficult to handle crises managements due to speedy widespread aspect of social media (Ramadan, 2017) due to empowerment of consumers' via social media to be able to disseminate their views immediately (Lowry et al., 2016). Scholars focused on how to overcome criseses (Coombs, 2014), (Utz, Schultz, Glocka, 2013).

Corporates who have a crisis management plan are fount to overcome crises more compared to others who do not have a plan (Fearn-Banks, 2010). Literature about crisis communication and corporate reputation have emphasized on how social media might create crises and affecting corporation reputation negatively (Ott and Theunissen, 2015).

There are researches showing how to involve social media in communication crises strategies (Hsu and Lawrence, 2016).

Researches about stakeholders roles in crises show that their recognition of responsibility (Coombs, 2004) and that they must be treated equally like any groups or individuals in crisis management (Fediuk, Coombs, and Botero, 2010).

Furthermore researchers suggest that social media to be used in crises communicating to deliver prompt and effective responses to stakeholders, customers, who are primary stakeholders, are critical for corporates (Rawlins, 2006) and relationship between stakeholders must be carefully monitored (Raithel and Schwaiger, 2015), especially during crises (Coombs et al., 2016).

Sturges (1994) has defined three types of communication strategy.

1. Instructing
2. Adjusting
3. Internalizing information

Other researchers focused on different aspects of crises communication, Cheng and Cameron, (2017) in their literature suggested that non-Western communication methods should be studied more. Rasmussen and Ihlen, (2017) argued that majority of social media users are not represented in research.

Austin, Fraustino, Jin, and Liu, (2017) in their Social Mediated Crisis Communication model proposed how to investigate social media crises before, after and during crises. Wherelse, Utz, Schultz and Glocka (2013) in their research, investigated how types of social media and messages affected publics in crisis communication (Utz, Schultz, and Glocka, 2013).

There are different reputation management models after a crisis like;

- Gillingham and Noizet's (2007) four-element model,
- Blanchard's (2011) seven element model,
- Utz, Schultz, and Glocka's (2013) networked crisis communication model,
- Coombs's (1998) seven crisis response model,
- Coombs and Holladay's (2009) tested two responses—sympathy and compassion,
- Siomkos's (1994) "corporate response continuum" of four corporate responses from "denial,", "involuntary product recall," "voluntary product recall," and "super effort",
- Coombs' (2014), Situational Crisis Communication Theory is based/focuses stakeholders' responsibility of crises evaluation, and their behavioral responses.

Situational Crisis Communication Theory (SCCT)

Coombs (1995), (2014) recommended response strategies during communication crises and suggested SCCT to be used in different types of crises, developed situation-oriented communication crises strategy (CCS) based on Weiner's (2006) attribution theory. There are four main crisis strategies in SCCT.

1. Diminishing aims to convince public that a crisis does not exist.
2. Denying aims to convince public that a crisis does not exist. Denial strategy is best strategy in case of misinformation crises, if corporate is accused, corporate must explain with evidences supporting actual situation.
3. Rebuilding aims to improve goodwill via offering compensation.
4. Bolstering aims to minimize offensiveness of crises via supporting company's existing goodwill.

Corporates while trying to protect their good reputation and their customers in market, usually apply a response strategy after a crisis (Coombs, 2010), wherelse other researchers do not agree with this (Dutta and Pullig, 2011). Some researchers argue that response strategies must be arranged according to crisis type (Singh, Crisafulli, and Quamina, 2019), where else others claim that this is argument is not valid with low involvement customers (Claeys and Cauberghe, 2014).

Image Repair Theory

Scholars argued that Benoit's (1997), 'Image Repair Theory' can be applied to crisis communication strategies Coombs, (2014).

Benoit has developed five strategies;

1. Denial
2. Evasion of Responsibility
3. Reducing Offensiveness
4. Correction Action and
5. Mortification

Image Repair Theory (IRT) which is based on 'apologia' and 'accounts', help corporates to handle offensive accusations and actions in 1995 (Benoit, 1997). His theory is applied in crisis communication literature and has been applied to descriptive rhetorical case studies as well (Kauffman, 2012).

United Airlines Case and Image Repair Theory

United Airlines crisis, has passed through two phases of crises communication, first started with defensive action followed with image repair strategy for correction action in 2017. United Airlines first avoided taking its responsibilities by differentiation and mortification strategies and CEO refused to apologize from their customers. However after crisis United Airlines consequently had to use corrective strategies to repair its image (Benoit, 2018). Poll argued that when airlines responses were widely spread in social media, customers/stakeholder become more outraged and they believed that company had bad or very bad reputation (Poll, 2017).

Secondary Crisis Communication on Social Media

Secondary Crisis Communication is like WOM (Word of Mouth) Communication (Brown et al, 2005), as it covers forwarding, sharing crisis messages, with negative comments on social media by consumers (Utz et al., 2013). It was used on dominant crisis communication, where consumers were passive receivers (Seeger, 2006), and where their dissemination of crisis information was defined as secondary crisis communication (SCC) (Zheng et al., 2018). However with social media, consumers sharing negative crisis communication via social media is shared with thousands, millions of consumers within hours. Shi et al, (2014) defines secondary crisis communication, as negative opinion broadcasting to consumers' followers via their homepages (Shi et al., 2014). Crisis managers must take into consideration Secondary Crisis Communication, increasing negative effects of product harm via social media which empowered consumers (Lyon and Montgomery, 2013). Furthermore, written comments on social media are permanent and more formal than face-to-face communication (Berger and Iyengar, 2013). It is very important prioritize consumer-centered communication over company-centered crisis communication considering destructive effect of Secondary Crisis Communication (Ki and Nekmat, 2014).

Social Media Crisis and Response Timing

Media communication during crisis requires careful attention for preparation and requires time for distribution to stakeholders, consumers and affects crisis response time (Prentice and Huffman, 2008) and involves legal involvement and resources of organization to be ready to take action and response timing is critical in a crisis. Post-crisis responses are also critical (Coombs, 2007), (Lukaszewski, 2013), Ulmer, Sellnow, and Seeger, 2007).

Crises are threatening because they can not be predicted or foreseen, however a quick timely and meaningful crisis response can prevent crisis getting being worse (Jin, 2010) and (Coombs, 2007).

Lukaszewski, argued that for crises management, the first one or two hours, named as golden hours, are very critical. Management must identify problems, manage victims, inform employees, contact the ones affected from crises, deal with stakeholders and media as without media communication during critical first few hours, then management has risk of speculations what went wrong, who is to blame and victims numbers (Lukaszewski, 2013).

Response Time and Corrective Action and DoubleTree By Hilton Hotel Case

When a black customer staying at Double Tree by Hilton Portland in United States was making a phone call, two employees of hotel called police, to remove guest from hotel, when guest shared it in his social media account, which went viral, and received a lot of angry messages from Twitter users. Due to three days holiday, it took three days for hotel management to be aware of crises. Management apologized from customer a few days later, taking corrective action by firing two employees, putting blame on them. For solution of social media crises, monitoring system, especially negative comments from users, etc. needs to be followed and resolved very well (KGW.com, 2018).

CONCLUSION

Social media communication is essential for all institutions, and it has radically changed and even transformed internal / external communication of all institutions. For this reason, institutions should focus on social media communication experts, managers, and giving special attention to communication with all participants through social media platforms. Organizations need to work with social media experts / communication experts and managers who know how to take precautions for possible social media communication risks. Social media platforms, which have turned into an open market for businesses, offer new business opportunities and find new customers as well as communication with their customers.

This open area, where consumers / customers are now focal point and determinant, is very important when faced with crises, as it is aimed at protecting corporate reputation as well as how crises can be managed. Unlike traditional media, it is even more important to intervene immediately and how to respond to crises that spread rapidly in social media. Through examples where social media crises could not be managed well, suggestions were made to managers / social media experts and practitioners on how to better manage them.

In social media crisis, accepting problem in order to reduce possible negative impact, sincerely apologize, correct mistake and take corrective action to prevent recurrence, act together with support of groups such as non-governmental organizations when necessary, pay attention to sensitivity of public, extraordinary attention to content of messages. showing, timing of messages is very important. After crisis, instead of accepting mistake and apologizing, instead of deleting relevant social media post, reacting instead of not entering into a discussion with followers, being late without intervening in time, ignoring sensitivities, can make crisis even worse.

In social media, different communication styles should be used by reacting immediately, using correct message contents and social media communication channels (Corciolani et al., 2016). During crisis, if there is an error, it should be accepted and apologized immediately, but necessary measures should be taken to prevent it from repeating, otherwise, if same error comes up again and again, apologizing every time may damage corporate reputation / trust.

Strategies may differ according to crisis, it might change according to culture as well, so International companies while dealing with social media crises which threaten their corporate reputation must take into consideration of population or country of which crises is to be handled as well.

REFERENCES

Ajzen, I., & Fishbein, M. (2005). *The influence of attitudes on behavior.* Academic Press.

Albu, O. B., & Etter, M. (2016). Hypertextuality and social media: A study of the constitutive and paradoxical implications of organizational Twitter use. *Management Communication Quarterly*, *30*(1), 5–31. doi:10.1177/0893318915601161

Austin, L., Fraustino, J. D., Jin, Y., & Liu, F. (2017). Crisis communication in a changing media environment: A review of the theoretical landscape in crisis communication and research gaps. *Social Media and Crisis Communication*, 423-448.

Bang, T. (2019). Defining the Concepts: What Are Ethics and Ethical Practice? *Public Relations Theory: Application and Understanding*, 63.

Barich, H., & Kotler, P. (1991). A framework for marketing image management. *MIT Sloan Management Review*, *32*(2), 94. PMID:10111301

Barnett, M. L., & Pollock, T. G. (Eds.). (2012). The Oxford handbook of corporate reputation. Oxford University Press.

BBC.com. (2015). *Profile: HSBC whistleblower Herve Falciani.* https://www.bbc.com/news/world-europe-31296007

BBC.com. (2017). *McDonald's deletes tweet attacking Donald Trump.* https://www.bbc.com/news/technology-39295504

Becker, K., & Lee, J. W. (2019). Organizational Usage of Social Media for Corporate Reputation Management. *Journal of Asian Finance, Economics and Business*, *6*(1), 231–240. doi:10.13106/jafeb.2019.vol6.no1.231

Bennett, W. L., & Segerberg, A. (2012). The logic of connective action: Digital media and the personalization of contentious politics. *Information Communication and Society*, *15*(5), 739–768. doi:10.1080/1369118X.2012.670661

Benoit, W. L. (1997). Image repair discourse and crisis communication. *Public Relations Review*, *23*(2), 177–186. doi:10.1016/S0363-8111(97)90023-0

Benoit, W. L. (2013). Image repair theory and corporate reputation. The handbook of communication and corporate reputation, 213-221.

Benoit, W. L. (2018). Crisis and image repair at United Airlines: Fly the unfriendly skies. *Journal of International Crisis and Risk Communication Research*, *1*(1), 2. doi:10.30658/jicrcr.1.1.2

Berger, J., & Iyengar, R. (2013). Communication channels and word of mouth: How the medium shapes the message. *The Journal of Consumer Research*, *40*(3), 567–579. doi:10.1086/671345

Bernstein, J. (2011). *Manager's guide to crisis management*. McGraw Hill Professional.

Bitektine, A. (2011). Toward a theory of social judgments of organizations: The case of legitimacy, reputation, and status. *Academy of Management Review*, *36*(1), 151–179. doi:10.5465/amr.2009.0382

Blanchard, H., Carvin, A., Whittaker, M. E., Fitzgerald, M., Harman, W., & Humphrey, B. (2010). *The case for integrating crisis response with social media*. White Paper. Washington, DC: American Red Cross.

Bloomberg. (2020). https://www.bloomberg.com/news/articles/2020-02-04/bp-is-still-paying-for-the-deepwater-horizon-spill

Brown, T. J., Barry, T. E., Dacin, P. A., & Gunst, R. F. (2005). Spreading the word: Investigating antecedents of consumers' positive word-of-mouth intentions and behaviors in a retailing context. *Journal of the Academy of Marketing Science*, *33*(2), 123–138. doi:10.1177/0092070304268417

Brunner, B. R. (Ed.). (2019). *Public relations theory: Application and understanding*. John Wiley & Sons.

Budd, J. F. Jr. (1994). How to manage corporate reputations. *Public Relations Quarterly*, *39*(4), 11.

Cameron, G., & Cheng, Y. (2017). The Status of Social-Mediated Crisis Communication (SMCC) Research: An Analysis of Published Articles in 2002–2014. In Social Media and Crisis Communication (pp. 29-40). Routledge.

Campa, D., & Zijlmans, E. W. A. (2019). Corporate social responsibility recognition and support for the arts: Evidence from European financial institutions. *European Management Journal*, *37*(6), 818–827. doi:10.1016/j.emj.2019.01.003

Campaignlive.co. (2018). *Plucky PR counters chicken FCK-up*. https://www.campaignlive.co.uk/article/plucky-pr-counters-chicken-fck-up/1485750

Casado, A. M., & Peláez, J. I. (2014). Intangible management monitors and tools: Reviews. *Expert Systems with Applications*, *41*(4), 1509–1529. doi:10.1016/j.eswa.2013.08.048

Castells, M. (2011). *The rise of the network society* (Vol. 12). John wiley & sons.

Cheng, Y., & Lee, C. J. (2019). Online crisis communication in a post-truth Chinese society: Evidence from interdisciplinary literature. *Public Relations Review*, *45*(4), 101826. doi:10.1016/j.pubrev.2019.101826

Cheng, Y., & Shen, H. (2020). United Airlines crisis from the stakeholder perspective: Exploring customers' ethical judgment, trust and distrust, and behavioral intentions. *Public Relations Review*, *46*(2), 101908. doi:10.1016/j.pubrev.2020.101908

Chun, R. (2005). Corporate reputation: Meaning and measurement. *International Journal of Management Reviews*, *7*(2), 91–109. doi:10.1111/j.1468-2370.2005.00109.x

Cian, L., & Cervai, S. (2014). Under the reputation umbrella. *Corporate Communications*, *19*(2), 182–199. doi:10.1108/CCIJ-10-2011-0055

Claeys, A. S., & Cauberghe, V. (2014). What makes crisis response strategies work? The impact of crisis involvement and message framing. *Journal of Business Research*, *67*(2), 182–189. doi:10.1016/j.jbusres.2012.10.005

Cone Communications. (2011). 2011 Online Influence Trend Tracker. Author.

Confente, I., Siciliano, G. G., Gaudenzi, B., & Eickhoff, M. (2019). Effects of data breaches from user-generated content: A corporate reputation analysis. *European Management Journal*, *37*(4), 492–504. doi:10.1016/j.emj.2019.01.007

Confetto, M. G., Conte, F., & Covucci, C. (2018). Empirical Evidence on CEO Reputation: Perspectives, Actions and Influence. *International Journal of Business and Management*, *13*(12).

Connelly, B. L., Certo, S. T., Ireland, R. D., & Reutzel, C. R. (2011). Signaling theory: A review and assessment. *Journal of Management*, *37*(1), 39–67. doi:10.1177/0149206310388419

Coombs, W. T. (1995). Choosing the right words: The development of guidelines for the selection of the "appropriate" crisis-response strategies. *Management Communication Quarterly*, *8*(4), 447–476. doi:10.1177/0893318995008004003

Coombs, W. T. (1998). An analytic framework for crisis situations: Better responses from a better understanding of the situation. *Journal of Public Relations Research*, *10*(3), 177–191. doi:10.12071532754xjprr1003_02

Coombs, W. T. (2004). Impact of past crises on current crisis communication: Insights from situational crisis communication theory. *The Journal of Business Communication, 41*(3), 265-289.

Coombs, W. T. (2007). Protecting organization reputations during a crisis: The development and application of situational crisis communication theory. *Corporate Reputation Review*, *10*(3), 163–176. doi:10.1057/palgrave.crr.1550049

Coombs, W. T. (2010). Parameters for crisis communication. The handbook of crisis communication, 17-53.

Coombs, W. T. (2014). *Ongoing crisis communication: Planning, managing, and responding*. Sage Publications.

Coombs, W. T., & Holladay, S. J. (2001). An extended examination of the crisis situations: A fusion of the relational management and symbolic approaches. *Journal of Public Relations Research*, *13*(4), 321–340. doi:10.1207/S1532754XJPRR1304_03

Coombs, W. T., & Holladay, S. J. (2009). Further explorations of post-crisis communication: Effects of media and response strategies on perceptions and intentions. *Public Relations Review*, *35*(1), 1–6. doi:10.1016/j.pubrev.2008.09.011

Coombs, W. T., Holladay, S. J., & Claeys, A. S. (2016). Debunking the myth of denial's effectiveness in crisis communication: Context matters. *Journal of Communication Management (London)*, *20*(4), 381–395. doi:10.1108/JCOM-06-2016-0042

Corciolani, M., Gistri, G., & Pace, S. (2016). *Exploring the palm oil crisis through the lens of different social media: an analysis of Facebook, YouTube and Twitter contents*. Mercati & Competitività.

Crisafulli, B., Singh, J., & Quamina, L. T. (2019). *Spreading of bad news online: how negative online word of mouth and crisis response influence consumer attitudes towards cause-brand alliances*. Academic Press.

Deephouse, D. L. (2000). Media reputation as a strategic resource: An integration of mass communication and resource-based theories. *Journal of Management*, *26*(6), 1091–1112. doi:10.1177/014920630002600602

Dobele, A., Lindgreen, A., Beverland, M., Vanhamme, J., & Van Wijk, R. (2007). Why pass on viral messages? Because they connect emotionally. *Business Horizons*, *50*(4), 291–304. doi:10.1016/j.bushor.2007.01.004

Dutta, S., & Pullig, C. (2011). Effectiveness of corporate responses to brand crises: The role of crisis type and response strategies. *Journal of Business Research*, *64*(12), 1281–1287. doi:10.1016/j.jbusres.2011.01.013

Dwivedi, Y. K., Kapoor, K. K., & Chen, H. (2015). Social media marketing and advertising. *The Marketing Review*, *15*(3), 289–309. doi:10.1362/146934715X14441363377999

Edmunds, J., & Turner, B. S. (2005). Global generations: Social change in the twentieth century. *The British Journal of Sociology*, *56*(4), 559–577. doi:10.1111/j.1468-4446.2005.00083.x PMID:16309436

Erel, I., Liao, R. C., & Weisbach, M. S. (2012). Determinants of cross-border mergers and acquisitions. *The Journal of Finance*, *67*(3), 1045–1082. doi:10.1111/j.1540-6261.2012.01741.x

Fearn-Banks, K. (2010). *Crisis Communications Student Workbook*. Routledge.

Ferreira, M., Zambaldi, F., & de Sousa Guerra, D. (2020). Consumer engagement in social media: Scale comparison analysis. *Journal of Product and Brand Management*, *29*(4), 491–503. doi:10.1108/JPBM-10-2018-2095

Fillis, I. (2003). Image, reputation and identity issues in the arts and crafts organization. *Corporate Reputation Review*, *6*(3), 239–251. doi:10.1057/palgrave.crr.1540203

Fombrun, C. J., Gardberg, N. A., & Sever, J. M. (2000). The Reputation Quotient SM: A multi-stakeholder measure of corporate reputation. *Journal of Brand Management*, *7*(4), 241–255. doi:10.1057/bm.2000.10

Fombrun, C. J., Ponzi, L. J., & Newburry, W. (2015). Stakeholder tracking and analysis: The RepTrak® system for measuring corporate reputation. *Corporate Reputation Review*, *18*(1), 3–24. doi:10.1057/crr.2014.21

Forbes.com. (2014). *McDonald's Faces Declining Sales In Asia After China Food Scandal.* Retrieved from https://www.forbes.com/sites/greatspeculations/2014/09/11/mcdonalds-faces-declining-sales-in-asia-after-china-food-scandal/?sh=58ab00426de1

Ford, S., Green, J., & Jenkins, H. (2013). *Spreadable media: I media tra condivisione, circolazione, partecipazione.* Maggioli Editore.

Gandini, A. (2016). Digital work: Self-branding and social capital in the freelance knowledge economy. *Marketing Theory, 16*(1), 123–141. doi:10.1177/1470593115607942

Gardberg, N. A. (2017). Corporate reputation: Fashion, fad, or phenomenon? *Corporate Reputation Review, 20*(3-4), 177–180. doi:10.105741299-017-0033-4

Gaudenzi, B., & Siciliano, G. (2017). Just do it: Managing IT and cyber risks to protect the value creation. *Journal of Promotion Management, 23*(3), 372–385. doi:10.1080/10496491.2017.1294875

Gillingham, D., & Noizet, J. (2007). A response model for the public relations management of a critical incident. *Disaster Prevention and Management: An International Journal.*

Glusac, E. (2018). Hotels grapple with racial bias. *The New York Times.* Accessed from www. nytimes. com/2018/08/01/travel/hotels-diversity-training. html

Gotsi, M., & Wilson, A. M. (2001). Corporate reputation: Seeking a definition. *Corporate Communications, 6*(1), 24–30. doi:10.1108/13563280110381189

Grover, P., Kar, A. K., & Ilavarasan, P. V. (2019). Impact of corporate social responsibility on reputation—Insights from tweets on sustainable development goals by CEOs. *International Journal of Information Management, 48*, 39–52. doi:10.1016/j.ijinfomgt.2019.01.009

Grützmacher, A. (2011). *Reputation 2.0: The role of social media in corporate reputation-Case Nokia.* Academic Press.

Guadagno, R. E., Okdie, B. M., & Muscanell, N. L. (2013). Have we all Just Become "Robo-Sapiens"? Reflections on social influence processes in the Internet age. *Psychological Inquiry, 24*(4), 301-309.

Harmeling, C. M., Moffett, J. W., Arnold, M. J., & Carlson, B. D. (2017). Toward a theory of customer engagement marketing. *Journal of the Academy of Marketing Science, 45*(3), 312–335. doi:10.100711747-016-0509-2

Harrigan, P., Miles, M. P., Fang, Y., & Roy, S. K. (2020). The role of social media in the engagement and information processes of social CRM. *International Journal of Information Management, 54*, 102151. doi:10.1016/j.ijinfomgt.2020.102151

Highhouse, S., Brooks, M. E., & Gregarus, G. (2009). An organizational impression management perspective on the formation of corporate reputations. *Journal of Management, 35*(6), 1481–1493. doi:10.1177/0149206309348788

Hill, S., Nalavade, A., & Benton, A. (2012, August). Social TV: Real-time social media response to TV advertising. In *Proceedings of the Sixth International Workshop on Data Mining for Online Advertising and Internet Economy* (pp. 1-9). 10.1145/2351356.2351360

Hootsuite, W. A. S. Y. (2020). *Digital 2020*. Global Digital Overview.

Hsu, L., & Lawrence, B. (2016). The role of social media and brand equity during a product recall crisis: A shareholder value perspective. *International Journal of Research in Marketing*, *33*(1), 59–77. doi:10.1016/j.ijresmar.2015.04.004

Huang, Y., & DiStaso, M. (2020). Responding to a Health Crisis on Facebook: The Effects of Response Timing and Message Appeal. *Public Relations Review*, *46*(3), 101909. doi:10.1016/j.pubrev.2020.101909

Javornik, A., Filieri, R., & Gumann, R. (2020). "Don't Forget that Others Are Watching, Too!" The Effect of Conversational Human Voice and Reply Length on Observers' Perceptions of Complaint Handling in Social Media. *Journal of Interactive Marketing*, *50*, 100–119. doi:10.1016/j.intmar.2020.02.002

Jenkins, H. (2006). *Confronting the challenges of participatory culture: Media education for the 21st century*. The MacArthur Foundation. Retrieved from http://digitallearning.macfound.org/atf/cf/%7B7E45C7E0-A3E0-4B89-AC9C-E807E1B0AE4E%7D/JENKINS_WHITE_PAPER.PDF

Jin, Y. (2010). Making sense sensibly in crisis communication: How publics' crisis appraisals influence their negative emotions, coping strategy preferences, and crisis response acceptance. *Communication Research*, *37*(4), 522–552. doi:10.1177/0093650210368256

Jin, Y., van der Meer, T. G., Lee, Y. I., & Lu, X. (2020). The Effects of Corrective Communication and Employee Backup on the Effectiveness of Fighting Crisis Misinformation. *Public Relations Review*, *46*(3), 101910. doi:10.1016/j.pubrev.2020.101910

Kauffman, J. (2012). Hooray for Hollywood? The 2011 Golden Globes and Ricky Gervais' image repair strategies. *Public Relations Review*, *38*(1), 46–50. doi:10.1016/j.pubrev.2011.09.003

Kaya, B. (2019). *Sosyal medya platformlarında ceo sözcülüğü ve kurumsal kriz iletişimi: Yaşar Holding Krizi'nin sosyal ceo'luk bağlamında incelenmesi* [Ceo spokesperson and corporate crisis communication on social media platforms: Examining the Yasar Holding Crisis in the context of social ceoship] (Doctoral dissertation). Kadir Has University.

KGW.com. (2018). *Portland DoubleTree apologizes to man who was 'calling his mother while black'*. https://www.kgw.com/article/news/local/portland-doubletree-takes-to-twitter-to-apologize-to-man-who-was-talking-on-the-phone-while-black/283-e6a15aeb-61fe-4ce1-a957-d4eab1beb8e0

Ki, E. J., & Nekmat, E. (2014). Situational crisis communication and interactivity: Usage and effectiveness of Facebook for crisis management by Fortune 500 companies. *Computers in Human Behavior*, *35*, 140–147. doi:10.1016/j.chb.2014.02.039

Kim, H. (2014). Enacted social support on social media and subjective well-being. *International Journal of Communication*, *8*, 21.

Kitchin, P. J., Paramio-Salcines, J. L., & Walters, G. (2020). Managing organizational reputation in response to a public shaming campaign. *Sport Management Review*, *23*(1), 66–80. doi:10.1016/j.smr.2019.03.009

Lai, I. K. W. (2019). Hotel image and reputation on building customer loyalty: An empirical study in Macau. *Journal of Hospitality and Tourism Management*, *38*, 111–121. doi:10.1016/j.jhtm.2019.01.003

Lallement, J., Dejean, S., Euzéby, F., & Martinez, C. (2020). The interaction between reputation and information search: Evidence of information avoidance and confirmation bias. *Journal of Retailing and Consumer Services*, *53*, 101787. doi:10.1016/j.jretconser.2019.03.014

Landow, G. P. (2006). *Hypertext 3.0: Critical theory and new media in an era of globalization*. JHU Press.

Lee, Y., & Kim, K. H. (2020). De-motivating employees' negative communication behaviors on anonymous social media: The role of public relations. *Public Relations Review*, *46*(4), 101955. doi:10.1016/j.pubrev.2020.101955

Lemon, K. N., & Verhoef, P. C. (2016). Understanding customer experience throughout the customer journey. *Journal of Marketing*, *80*(6), 69–96. doi:10.1509/jm.15.0420

Leskovec, J., Backstrom, L., & Kleinberg, J. (2009, June). Meme-tracking and the dynamics of the news cycle. In *Proceedings of the 15th ACM SIGKDD international conference on Knowledge discovery and data mining* (pp. 497-506). 10.1145/1557019.1557077

Logomyway. (2020). *Redesign the BP logo*. https://www.logomyway.com/1746/friends/BP_(Logo_Redesign_Contest).php.Access

Loureiro, S. M. C., & González, F. J. M. (2008). The importance of quality, satisfaction, trust, and image in relation to rural tourist loyalty. *Journal of Travel & Tourism Marketing*, *25*(2), 117–136. doi:10.1080/10548400802402321

Lowry, P. B., Zhang, J., Wang, C., & Siponen, M. (2016). Why do adults engage in cyberbullying on social media? An integration of online disinhibition and deindividuation effects with the social structure and social learning model. *Information Systems Research*, *27*(4), 962–986. doi:10.1287/isre.2016.0671

Lukaszewski, J. E. (2013). *Lukaszewski on crisis communication: What your CEO needs to know about reputation risk and crisis management*. Rothstein Publishing.

Lyon, T. P., & Montgomery, A. W. (2013). Tweetjacked: The impact of social media on corporate greenwash. *Journal of Business Ethics*, *118*(4), 747–757. doi:10.100710551-013-1958-x

Manovich, L. (2002). *The language of new media*. MIT Press.

Martynova, M., & Renneboog, L. (2008). A century of corporate takeovers: What have we learned and where do we stand? *Journal of Banking & Finance*, *32*(10), 2148–2177. doi:10.1016/j.jbankfin.2007.12.038

Marwick, A. E. (2013). *Status update: Celebrity, publicity, and branding in the social media age*. Yale University Press.

Maung, M., Wilson, C., & Yu, W. (2020). Does Reputation Risk Matter? Evidence from Cross-Border Mergers and Acquisitions. *Journal of International Financial Markets, Institutions and Money*, *66*, 101204. doi:10.1016/j.intfin.2020.101204

Meng, S. M., Liang, G. S., & Yang, S. H. (2011). The relationships of cruise image, perceived value, satisfaction, and post-purchase behavioral intention on Taiwanese tourists. *African Journal of Business Management*, *5*(1), 19–29.

Mikulaskova, J., Harsanyova, P., & Cambal, M. (2016). Internet Marketing as a Tool of Desirable Corporate Culture. *Proceedings of the European Conference on Intellectual Capital, İtalya.*

Moneycnn.com. (2017). *United loses $250 million of its market value*. https://money.cnn.com/2017/04/11/investing/united-airlines-stock-passenger-flight-video/

Nelson-Field, K., Riebe, E., & Newstead, K. (2013). The emotions that drive viral video. *Australasian Marketing Journal, 21*(4), 205–211. doi:10.1016/j.ausmj.2013.07.003

Osakwe, C. N., Ruiz, B., Amegbe, H., Chinje, N. B., Cheah, J. H., & Ramayah, T. (2020). A multi-country study of bank reputation among customers in Africa: Key antecedents and consequences. *Journal of Retailing and Consumer Services, 56*, 102182. doi:10.1016/j.jretconser.2020.102182

Ott, L., & Theunissen, P. (2015). Reputations at risk: Engagement during social media crises. *Public Relations Review, 41*(1), 97–102. doi:10.1016/j.pubrev.2014.10.015

Pace, K. M., Fediuk, T. A., & Botero, I. C. (2010). The acceptance of responsibility and expressions of regret in organizational apologies after a transgression. *Corporate Communications, 15*(4), 410–427. doi:10.1108/13563281011085510

Papacharissi, Z. (2012). Without you, I'm nothing: Performances of the self on Twitter. *International Journal of Communication, 6*, 18.

Petkova, A. P., Rindova, V. P., & Gupta, A. K. (2013). *No news is bad news: Sensegiving activities, media attention, and venture capital funding of new technology*. Academic Press.

Poll, H. (2017). *United Airlines' corporate reputation takes a nose dive: Negative perceptions of company's reputation jump 500 percent in April*. Academic Press.

Ponzi, L. J., Fombrun, C. J., & Gardberg, N. A. (2011). RepTrak™ pulse: Conceptualizing and validating a short-form measure of corporate reputation. *Corporate Reputation Review, 14*(1), 15–35. doi:10.1057/crr.2011.5

Portes, A., & Sensenbrenner, J. (1993). Embeddedness and immigration: Notes on the social determinants of economic action. *American Journal of Sociology, 98*(6), 1320–1350. doi:10.1086/230191

Prentice, S., & Huffman, E. (2008). Social medias new role in emergency management. Idaho National Laboratory, 2008, 1-5.

Raithel, S., & Schwaiger, M. (2015). The effects of corporate reputation perceptions of the general public on shareholder value. *Strategic Management Journal, 36*(6), 945–956. doi:10.1002mj.2248

Ramadan, Z. (2017). Examining the dilution of the consumer-brand relationship on Facebook: The saturation issue. *Qualitative Market Research, 20*(3), 335–353. doi:10.1108/QMR-07-2016-0064

Ramos, C. M., & Casado-Molina, A. M. (2020). Online corporate reputation: A panel data approach and a reputation index proposal applied to the banking sector. *Journal of Business Research, 122*, 121–130. doi:10.1016/j.jbusres.2020.08.061

Rani, N., Yadav, S. S., & Jain, P. K. (2014). Impact of domestic and cross-border acquisitions on acquirer shareholders' wealth: Empirical evidence from Indian corporate. *International Journal of Business and Management*, *9*(3), 88. doi:10.5539/ijbm.v9n3p88

Rasmussen, J., & Ihlen, Ø. (2017). Risk, crisis, and social media: A systematic review of seven years' research. *Nordicom Review*, *38*(2), 1–17. doi:10.1515/nor-2017-0393

Rawlins, B. L. (2006). *Prioritizing stakeholders for public relations.* Institute for Public Relations.

Reitz, A. (2012). Social Media's Function in Organizations: A Functional Analysis Approach. Global Media Journal: Canadian Edition, 5(2).

Rim, H., Lee, Y., & Yoo, S. (2020). Polarized public opinion responding to corporate social advocacy: Social network analysis of boycotters and advocators. *Public Relations Review*, *46*(2), 101869. doi:10.1016/j.pubrev.2019.101869

Rindova, V. P., Williamson, I. O., Petkova, A. P., & Sever, J. M. (2005). Being good or being known: An empirical examination of the dimensions, antecedents, and consequences of organizational reputation. *Academy of Management Journal*, *48*(6), 1033–1049. doi:10.5465/amj.2005.19573108

Rival, I. Q. (2020). *Social Media Industry Benchmark Report.* Academic Press.

Ryschka, A. M., Domke-Damonte, D. J., Keels, J. K., & Nagel, R. (2016). The effect of social media on reputation during a crisis event in the cruise line industry. *International Journal of Hospitality & Tourism Administration*, *17*(2), 198–221. doi:10.1080/15256480.2015.1130671

Ryu, K., Han, H., & Kim, T. H. (2008). The relationships among overall quick-casual restaurant image, perceived value, customer satisfaction, and behavioral intentions. *International Journal of Hospitality Management*, *27*(3), 459–469. doi:10.1016/j.ijhm.2007.11.001

Sabah Gazetesi. (2020). *Büyük bir bankanın 39 çalışanının müşterilerinin kredi kredi kayıt bilgilerini oto galerici, emlakçı gibi firma ve kişilere el altından para karşılığı sattığı ortaya çıktı* [It turns out that 39 employees of a major bank sell their customers' credit registration information to firms and individuals such as auto dealers and real estate agents for money under the table]. Retrieved from https://tr.sputniknews.com/turkiye/202009071042791613-39-banka-calisani-musteri-bilgilerini-para-karsiligi-oto-galerici-ve-emlakcilara-satmis/

Schaarschmidt, M., Walsh, G., & Evanschitzky, H. (2018). Customer interaction and innovation in hybrid offerings: Investigating moderation and mediation effects for goods and services innovation. *Journal of Service Research*, *21*(1), 119–134. doi:10.1177/1094670517711586

Scherer, K. R. (2005). What are emotions? And how can they be measured? *Social Sciences Information. Information Sur les Sciences Sociales*, *44*(4), 695–729. doi:10.1177/0539018405058216

Seeger, M. W. (2006). Best practices in crisis communication: An expert panel process. *Journal of Applied Communication Research*, *34*(3), 232–244. doi:10.1080/00909880600769944

Sen, R., & Borle, S. (2015). Estimating the contextual risk of data breach: An empirical approach. *Journal of Management Information Systems*, *32*(2), 314–341. doi:10.1080/07421222.2015.1063315

Shi, H., Wang, Y., Huisingh, D., & Wang, J. (2014). On moving towards an ecologically sound society: With special focus on preventing future smog crises in China and globally. *Journal of Cleaner Production, 64*, 9–12. doi:10.1016/j.jclepro.2013.07.024

Siomkos, G. J., & Kurzbard, G. (1994). The hidden crisis in product-harm crisis management. *European Journal of Marketing, 28*(2), 30–41. doi:10.1108/03090569410055265

Slate.com. (2020). *The Daily News Twitter account was tampered with after mass layoffs*. https://slate.com/technology/2018/07/the-daily-newss-twitter-account-was-tampered-with-after-mass-layoffs.html

Sofranec, D. (2016). 5 Tips for Handling Bad Online Reviews. *Pest Management Professional, 84*(11), 74.

Statista.com. (2020). *Share of U.S. adults who use social media 2019, by age*. https://www.statista.com/statistics/471370/us-adults-who-use-social-networks-age/

Sturges, D. L. (1994). Communicating through crisis: A strategy for organizational survival. *Management Communication Quarterly, 7*(3), 297–316. doi:10.1177/0893318994007003004

Sunstein, C. R. (2017). A prison of our own design: divided democracy in the age of social media. Academic Press.

Tansey, J., & O'riordan, T. (1999). Cultural theory and risk: A review. *Health Risk & Society, 1*(1), 71–90. doi:10.1080/13698579908407008

Thenextweb.com. (2012). *Starbucks apologizes to its Argentine customers on Twitter and Facebook, creates PR crisis*. https://thenextweb.com/la/2012/07/16/starbucks-apologizes-to-its-argentine-customers-on-twitter-and-facebook-creates-pr-crisis/

Triantafillidou, A., & Yannas, P. (2020). Social media crisis communication in racially charged crises: Exploring the effects of social media and image restoration strategies. *Computers in Human Behavior, 106*, 106269. doi:10.1016/j.chb.2020.106269

Twitter.com. (2012). https://twitter.com/search?q=%23McDStories%20&src=typed_query

Ulmer, R. R., Seeger, M. W., & Sellnow, T. L. (2007). Post-crisis communication and renewal: Expanding the parameters of post-crisis discourse. *Public Relations Review, 33*(2), 130–134. doi:10.1016/j.pubrev.2006.11.015

Ulmer, R. R., Sellnow, T. L., & Seeger, M. W. (2011). Defining crisis communication. *Effective Crisis Communication Moving From Crisis to Opportunity*, 2-24.

Unicef.org. (2020). *Keeping the world's children learning through COVID-19*. https://www.unicef.org/coronavirus/keeping-worlds-children-learning-through-covid-19

Untila Kaplan, O. (2019). *Media literacy in a changing process in Turkey. 11th International Conference on Electronics, Computers and Artificial Intelligence (ECAI)*, Pitesti, Romania. 10.1109/ECAI46879.2019.9042089

Utz, S., Schultz, F., & Glocka, S. (2013). Crisis communication online: How medium, crisis type and emotions affected public reactions in the Fukushima Daiichi nuclear disaster. *Public Relations Review, 39*(1), 40–46. doi:10.1016/j.pubrev.2012.09.010

Van Riel, C. B., & Fombrun, C. J. (2007). *Essentials of corporate communication: Implementing practices for effective reputation management*. Routledge. doi:10.4324/9780203390931

Villena, F., & Souto-Pérez, J. E. (2016). Sustainability, innovative orientation and export performance of manufacturing SMEs: An empirical analysis of the mediating role of corporate image. *Journal of Industrial Engineering and Management*, *9*(1), 35–58.

Walker, K. (2010). A systematic review of the corporate reputation literature: Definition, measurement, and theory. *Corporate Reputation Review*, *12*(4), 357–387. doi:10.1057/crr.2009.26

Walsh, G., & Beatty, S. E. (2007). Customer-based corporate reputation of a service firm: Scale development and validation. *Journal of the Academy of Marketing Science*, *35*(1), 127–143. doi:10.100711747-007-0015-7

Wang, L., Schuetz, C. G., & Cai, D. (2020). Choosing Response Strategies in Social Media Crisis Communication: An Evolutionary Game Theory Perspective. *Information & Management*, 103371.

Wang, Y., & Laufer, D. (2020). How does crisis management in China differ from the West?: A review of the literature and directions for future research. *Journal of International Management*, *26*(1), 100708. doi:10.1016/j.intman.2019.100708

Wei, Y. K. (2002). Corporate image as collective ethos: A poststructuralist approach. *Corporate Communications*, *7*(4), 269–276. doi:10.1108/13563280210449859

Weiner, B. (2010). Attribution theory. *The Corsini encyclopedia of psychology*, 1-2.

Wepener, M., & Boshoff, C. (2015). An instrument to measure the customer-based corporate reputation of large service organizations. *Journal of Services Marketing*, *29*(3), 163–172. doi:10.1108/JSM-01-2014-0026

Wiedmann, K. P., & Buxel, H. (2005). Corporate reputation management in Germany: Results of an empirical study. *Corporate Reputation Review*, *8*(2), 145–163. doi:10.1057/palgrave.crr.1540246

Yadav, R., Dokania, A. K., & Pathak, G. S. (2016). The influence of green marketing functions in building corporate image. *International Journal of Contemporary Hospitality Management*, *28*(10), 2178–2196. doi:10.1108/IJCHM-05-2015-0233

Zappavigna, M. (2012). *Discourse of Twitter and social media: How we use language to create affiliation on the web* (Vol. 6). A&C Black.

Zhang, Y., & Wiersema, M. F. (2009). Stock market reaction to CEO certification: The signaling role of CEO background. *Strategic Management Journal*, *30*(7), 693–710. doi:10.1002mj.772

Zheng, B., Bi, G., Liu, H., & Lowry, P. B. (2020). Corporate crisis management on social media: A morality violations perspective. *Heliyon*, *6*(7), e04435. doi:10.1016/j.heliyon.2020.e04435 PMID:32715127

Zheng, B., Liu, H., & Davison, R. M. (2018). Exploring the relationship between corporate reputation and the public's crisis communication on social media. *Public Relations Review*, *44*(1), 56–64. doi:10.1016/j.pubrev.2017.12.006

Compilation of References

Abbasi, N., & Huang, D. (2020). Digital Media Literacy: Social Media Use for News Consumption among Teenagers in Pakistan. *Global Media Journal*, *18*, 1–7.

Abdallah, S., & Jaleel, B. (2015). Website appeal: Development of an assessment tool and evaluation framework of e-marketing. *Journal of Theoretical and Applied Electronic Commerce Research*, *10*(3), 45–62. doi:10.4067/S0718-18762015000300005

Abidin, C. (2021, March) Digital influencers, internet celebrities and bloggers: an interview with Crystal Abidin. Interviewed by Issaaf Karhawi. *Intercom, Brazilian Journal of Communication Sciences, 44*(1). https://www.scielo.br/scielo.php?script=sci_arttext&pid=S1809-58442021000100289&lng=pt&nrm=iso&tlng=pt

Adler, P. S., & Kwon, S-W. (2002). *Social Capital: Prospects for a New Concept*. Retrieved from: https://bit.ly/32iacOi

Afonso, O. (2018). *Economia Social: conceito e características* [Social Economy: concept and characteristics]. Dinheiro Vivo.

Agariya, K., & Singh, D. (2011). What Really Defines Relationship Marketing? A Review of Definitions and General and Sector-Specific Defining Constructs. *Journal of Relationship Marketing*, *10*(4), 203–237. doi:10.1080/15332667.2011.624905

Ageeva, E. (2019). A Holistic Framework of Corporate Website Favourability. *Corporate Reputation Review*, *25*(5). https://www.researchgate.net/publication/335312535_A_Holistic_Framework_of_Corporate_Website_Favourability

Aggarwal, P., & McGill, A. L. (2007). Is That Car Smiling at Me? Schema Congruity as a Basis for Evaluating Anthropomorphized Products. *The Journal of Consumer Research*, *34*(4), 1–12. doi:10.1086/518544

Agrawal, A., Gams, J., & Goldfarb, A. (2018). *Prediction machines*. Harvard Business Review Press.

Ajzen, I. (1985). From Intentions to Actions: a Theory of Planned Behavior. In Action control (pp. 11-39). Springer Berlin Heidelberg. doi:10.1007/978-3-642-69746-3_2

Ajzen, I., & Fishbein, M. (2005). *The influence of attitudes on behavior*. Academic Press.

Akay, Ü., & Badlo, Y. (2021). Digital Marketing and Social Media: A Review. *International Conference on E-Business Technologies (EBT)*. Available at: https://ebt.rs/journals/index.php/conf-proc/article/view/83

Albu, O. B., & Etter, M. (2016). Hypertextuality and social media: A study of the constitutive and paradoxical implications of organizational Twitter use. *Management Communication Quarterly*, *30*(1), 5–31. doi:10.1177/0893318915601161

Al-Dmour, H., Masa'deh, R., Salman, A., Abuhashesh, M., & Al-Dmour, R. (2020). Influence of Social Media Platforms on Public Health Protection Against the COVID-19 Pandemic via the Mediating Effects of Public Health Awareness and Behavioral Changes: Integrated Model. *Journal of Medical Internet Research, 22*(8), e19996. doi:10.2196/19996 PMID:32750004

Algharabat, R., Rana, N. P., Dwivedi, Y. K., Alalwan, A. A., & Qasem, Z. (2018). The effect of telepresence, social presence and involvement on consumer brand engagement: An empirical study of non-profit organizations. *Journal of Retailing and Consumer Services, 40*, 139–149. doi:10.1016/j.jretconser.2017.09.011

Almeida, F., Santos, J., & Monteiro. (2020). *The Challenges and Opportunities in the Digitalization of Companies in a Post-COVID-19 World.* Retrieved from https://bit.ly/3AqBcqa

Álvarez-Nobell, A.; Molleda, J. C.; Moreno, A.; Athaydes, A.; Suárez-Monsalve, A. M. y Herrera, M. (2021). *Comunicación estratégica y relaciones públicas en América Latina: crisis del COVID-19 en la gestión de comunicación, ciberseguridad, situación de las mujeres, retos éticos y nuevas competencias. Resultados de una encuesta en 20 países* [Strategic communication and public relations in Latin America: crisis of COVID-19 in communication management, cybersecurity, situation of women, ethical issues and new competences. Results of a survey in 20 countries]. Bruselas: EUPRERA.

Amaral, F. (2016). *Introdução à ciência de dados* [Introduction to data science]. Editora Alta Books.

Amaro. (2021). *Hi, I am Mara.* https://amaro.com/br/pt/mara-influencer-virtual-3d

Amazon. (2021a). *Amazon Influencer Program.* Retrieved from https://www.amazon.com/shop/info

Amazon. (2021b). *Amazon Associates - Amazon's affiliate marketing program.* Retrieved from https://affiliate-program.amazon.com/

Amirova, D., & Zaporozhets, O. (2019). Social media marketing as an effective tool promotion. *The Eurasian Scientific Journal, 11*(2), 1–8.

Anderson, C. (2013, May). *Media Ecosystems: Some Notes Toward a Genealogy of the Term and an Application of it to Journalism Research.* Paper prepared for the "ESF Exploratory Workshop on Mapping the digital news ecosystem: Professional journalism, new producers and active audiences in the digital public sphere." Retrieved from: https://www.cwanderson.org/wp-content/uploads/2013/04/EcosystemGenealogy.pdf

Andrade, T. (2021). *Pepfluencer.* Instagram. Retrieved from https://www.instagram.com/p/COQnGerromM/

Andrade, M., & Franco, R. (2007). *Economia do conhecimento e organizações sem fins lucrativos Sociedade Portuguesa de Inovação* [Knowledge economy and non-profit organizations Portuguese Innovation Society]. Princípia Editora.

Anitta [@anitta]. (2021, September 30). *Skol Beats.* Instagram. Retrieved from https://www.instagram.com/p/B3DUl-DonudG/

Antoniadis, I., & Charmantzi, A. (2016). *Social network analysis and social capital in marketing: Theory and practical implementation.* Retrieved from: https://bit.ly/3nt0vVi

Antunes. J., & Paulo, R. (2008). O marketing relacional como novo paradigma [Relationship marketing as a new paradigm]. *Revista Portuguesa e Brasileira de Gestão*, 36-46.

Apostol, N. (2018). *Dimensiune de gen si munca in journalism* [Gender and work dimension of journalism]. Editura Universitatii din Bucuresti.

APR. (2020). *Annual bulletin of financial statements.* Available at: https://www.apr.gov.rs/upload/Portals/0/GFI_2021/Godisnji_bilten_2020/BiltenSI2020.pdf

Apuke, O. D. (2017). Quantitative Research Methods: A Synopsis Approach. *Arabian Journal of Business and Management Review*, *10*(6), 40–47.

Aral, S. (2020). *The Hype Machine*. Random House.

Araújo, C., & Sá, E. S. (2017). A importância do marketing social no turismo: Revisão da literatura [The importance of social marketing in tourism: a literature review]. *Revista Turismo & Desenvolvimento*, *1*(27/28), 713–731.

Argenti, P. (2006, July). How technology has influenced the field of corporate communication. *Journal of Business and Technical Communication*, *20*(3), 357-370. Retrieved 10 August, 2021, from https://web.archive.org/web/20200320012849id_/https://study.sagepub.com/sites/default/files/2%20Argenti%202006.pdf doi:10.1177/1050651906287260

Argenti, P. A. (2002, December). Crisis communication: Lessons from 9/11. *Harvard Business Review*. https://hbr.org/2002/12/crisis-communication-lessons-from-911

Aring, C. D. (1958). Sympathy and Empathy. *Journal of the American Medical Association*, *167*(4), 448–452. doi:10.1001/jama.1958.02990210034008 PMID:13538722

Aristóteles. (2003). Retórica das paixões [Rhetoric of Passions]. São Paulo: Martins Fontes.

Aronoff, C. (2012). *Acidente na Pennsylvania Road, 1908. In: Relações públicas: profissão e prática. 3a. edição* [Accident on Pennsylvania Road, 1908. In: Public relations: profession and practice. 3rd edition]. AMGH Editora. Retrieved 10 August, 2021, from https://books.google.com.br/books?id=h4OaAgAAQBAJ&pg=PA55&lpg=PA55&dq=lee+convidou+a+imprensa+para+visitar+local+do+acidente&source=bl&ots=i2KMrdE4rb&sig=ACfU3U1942C-BHra73fScSWrXSq40IHQBQ&hl=pt-BR&sa=X&ved=2ahUKEwiK1ZGm1rHzAhWZGLkGHYqFDuUQ6AF6BAgCEAM#v=onepage&q=lee%20convidou%20a%20imprensa%20para%20visitar%20local%20do%20acidente&f=false

Aronoff, C. (1975). Credibility of public relations for journalists. *Public Relations Review*, *1*(2), 45–56.

Ashley, C., & Tuten, T. (2015). Creative strategies in social media marketing: An exploratory study of branded social content and consumer engagement. *Psychology and Marketing*, *32*(1), 15–27. doi:10.1002/mar.20761

Atlas Brasil, I. D. H. M. (2021). *Atlas Brasil* [Atlas Brazil]. http://www.atlasbrasil.org.br/ranking

Augé, M. (2012). Não lugares [No places]. In Introdução a uma antropologia da supermodernidade. São Paulo: Papirus.

Austin, L., Fraustino, J. D., Jin, Y., & Liu, F. (2017). Crisis communication in a changing media environment: A review of the theoretical landscape in crisis communication and research gaps. *Social Media and Crisis Communication*, 423-448.

Avadani, I. (2017). Of Journalists and Money: The Employment of Journalists in Romania and its Influence on Media Freedom and Quality. *International Journal of Communication*, *11*, 1975–1997.

Avidar, R. (2017). Responsiveness and interactivity: Relational maintenance strategies in an online environment. In S. C. Duhe (Ed.), New media and public relations (pp. 229-238). Peter Lang Publishing Inc.

Ávila, R. C., & Campos, J. L. M. (2018). The social economy facing emerging economic concepts: Social innovation, social responsibility, collaborative economy, social enterprises, and solidary economy. *C.I.R.I.E.C. España*, *93*(93), 5–50.

Avison, D., Lau, F., Myers, M., & Nielsen, P. A. (1999). Action Research. *Communications of the ACM*, *42*(1), 94–97. doi:10.1145/291469.291479

Bach, C., & Enas, A. (2016). View of The Impact of Social Marketing on Public Behavior. *Journal of Engineering Research and Science*, *1*(5), 17–22.

Bahl, M. (2021). *Shopstreaming: The Future of Shopping*. Cognizant. Retrieved from https://cogniz.at/3oKF4jy

Baird, H. C., & Parasnis, G. (2011). From social media to social customer relationship management. *Strategy and Leadership*, *39*(5), 30–37. doi:10.1108/10878571111161507

Bakhtin, Ml. (2002). Marxismo e Filosofia da Linguagem [Marxism and Philosophy of Language] (10th ed.). São Paulo: Hucitec.

Bala, M., & Verma, D. (2018). A Critical Review of Digital Marketing. *International Journal of Management, IT & Engineering*, *8*(10), 321–339.

Baltatzis, G., Ormrod, D. G., & Grainger, N. (2008). *Social Networking Tools for Internal Communication in Large Organizations: Benefits and Barriers*. Paper presented at the 19th Australasian Conference on Software solutions, Australia.

Bambu, R. (2019, November 15). *Interviu Video. Campanie #Respectjurnaliştii. Cine a lansat-o şi ce-şi propune?* [Video Interview. #Respectjurnaliştii Campaign. Who launched it and what's the aim?]. https://www.paginademedia.ro/2019/11/interviu-video-campanie-respect-jurnalistii-cine-a-lansat-o-si-ce-si-propune/

Bandura, A. (1997). Self-efficacy: The Exercise of Control. *The Freeman*.

Bang, T. (2019). Defining the Concepts: What Are Ethics and Ethical Practice? *Public Relations Theory: Application and Understanding*, 63.

Barbosa, C. (2021). *Understanding how Generation Z perceives social media influencers and its impact on the adoption of COVID safe behaviours* [Master Dissertation]. Universidade Católica Portuguesa. Available at: https://repositorio.ucp.pt/bitstream/10400.14/35730/1/202781453.pdf

Barichello, E. M. M. R. (2014). Midiatização e cultura nas organizações da contemporaneidade: o processo de midiatização como matriz de práticas sociais [Mediatization and culture in contemporary organizations: The mediatization process as a matrix of social practices]. In M. Marchiori (Ed.), *Contexto organizacional midiatizado* (pp. 37–45). Difusão Editora.

Barichello, E. R., Scheid, D., & Moreira, E. H. (2017). Visibilidade e vigilância nas redes sociais digitais: oportunidade e desafio para as organizações [Visibility and surveillance in digital social networks: Opportunities and challenges for organizations]. In C. M. A. Scroferneker & L. R. Amorim (Eds.), *Re) leituras contemporâneas sobre comunicação organizacional e relações públicas* (pp. 175–189). EDIPUCRS. https://editora.pucrs.br/download/livros/1224.pdf

Barich, H., & Kotler, P. (1991). A framework for marketing image management. *MIT Sloan Management Review*, *32*(2), 94. PMID:10111301

Barnett, M. L., & Pollock, T. G. (Eds.). (2012). The Oxford handbook of corporate reputation. Oxford University Press.

Baron-Cohen, S. (2002). The extreme male brain theory of autism. *Trends in Cognitive Sciences*, *6*(6), 248–254. doi:10.1016/S1364-6613(02)01904-6 PMID:12039606

Baron-Cohen, S., & Wheelwright, S. (2004). The Empathy Quotient: An Investigation of Adults with Asperger Syndrome or High Functioning Autism, and Normal Sex Differences. *Journal of Autism and Developmental Disorders*, *34*(2), 163–175. doi:10.1023/B:JADD.0000022607.19833.00 PMID:15162935

Baron, R. J., & Adam, J. B. (2019). Mistrust in Science - A Threat to the Patient–Physician Relationship. *The New England Journal of Medicine*, *381*(2), 182–185. doi:10.1056/NEJMms1813043 PMID:31291524

Basil, D. Z., Diaz-Meneses, G., & Basil, M. D. (2019). Social Marketing in Action. Springer. doi:10.1007/978-3-030-13020-6

Baskerville, R. L. (1999). Investigating Software solutions with Action Research. *Communications of the Association for Software Solutions, 2,* 1-32. doi:10.17705/1CAIS.00219

Basu, T. (2021, January 25). The future of social networks might be audio. *MIT Technology Review*. Retrieved 10 August, 2021, from https://www.technologyreview.com/2021/01/25/1016723/the-future-of-social-networks-might-be-audio-clubhouse-twitter-spaces/

Batchelder, L., Brosnan, M., & Ashwin, C. (2017). The Development and Validation of the Empathy Components Questionnaire (ECQ). *PLoS One*, *12*(1), 1–34. doi:10.1371/journal.pone.0169185 PMID:28076406

Bateson, J., & Hoffman, D. (2016). *Princípios de Marketing de Serviços* [Services Marketing Principles]. Cengage Learning.

Bauman, Z. (2000). *Liquid Modernity*. Polity Press.

Baum, F., MacDougall, C., & Smith, D. (2006). Participatory action research. *Journal of Epidemiology and Community Health*, *60*(10), 854–857. doi:10.1136/jech.2004.028662 PMID:16973531

BBC.com. (2015). *Profile: HSBC whistleblower Herve Falciani*. https://www.bbc.com/news/world-europe-31296007

BBC.com. (2017). *McDonald's deletes tweet attacking Donald Trump*. https://www.bbc.com/news/technology-39295504

Becker, K., & Lee, J. W. (2019). Organizational Usage of Social Media for Corporate Reputation Management. *Journal of Asian Finance, Economics and Business*, *6*(1), 231–240. doi:10.13106/jafeb.2019.vol6.no1.231

Becker, M. H., Haefner, D. P., & Maiman, L. A. (1977). The health belief model in the prediction of dietary compliance: A field experiment. *Journal of Health and Social Behavior*, *18*(4), 348–366. doi:10.2307/2955344 PMID:617639

Bennett, W. L., & Segerberg, A. (2012). The logic of connective action: Digital media and the personalization of contentious politics. *Information Communication and Society*, *15*(5), 739–768. doi:10.1080/1369118X.2012.670661

Benoit, W. L. (2013). Image repair theory and corporate reputation. The handbook of communication and corporate reputation, 213-221.

Benoit, W. L. (1997). Image repair discourse and crisis communication. *Public Relations Review*, *23*(2), 177–186. doi:10.1016/S0363-8111(97)90023-0

Benoit, W. L. (2018). Crisis and image repair at United Airlines: Fly the unfriendly skies. *Journal of International Crisis and Risk Communication Research*, *1*(1), 2. doi:10.30658/jicrcr.1.1.2

Benveniste, É. (1989). *Problemas de linguística geral II* [Problems of general linguistics II]. Pontes.

Berger, J. (2014). *Contágio* [Contagion]. Texto Editores Ltda.

Berger, J., & Iyengar, R. (2013). Communication channels and word of mouth: How the medium shapes the message. *The Journal of Consumer Research*, *40*(3), 567–579. doi:10.1086/671345

Bernhardt, J. M., Mays, D., & Hall, A. K. (2012). Critical social marketing: Investigating alcohol marketing in the developing world. *Journal of Social Marketing*, *2*(2), 94–102.

Bernstein, J. (2011). *Manager's guide to crisis management*. McGraw Hill Professional.

Berry, L. L. (1995). Relationship Marketing of Services-Growing Interest, Emerging Perspectives. *Journal of the Academy of Marketing Science*, *23*(4), 236–245. doi:10.1177/009207039502300402

Berry, L. L., Carbone, L. P., & Haeckel, S. H. (2002). Managing the Total Customer Experience. *Sloan Management Review, 43*(3), 1–6.

Bitektine, A. (2011). Toward a theory of social judgments of organizations: The case of legitimacy, reputation, and status. *Academy of Management Review, 36*(1), 151–179. doi:10.5465/amr.2009.0382

Blanchard, H., Carvin, A., Whittaker, M. E., Fitzgerald, M., Harman, W., & Humphrey, B. (2010). *The case for integrating crisis response with social media*. White Paper. Washington, DC: American Red Cross.

Blessa, R. (2015). Merchandising no Ponto-de-Venda [Merchandising at Stores] (4th ed.). São Paulo: Atlas.

Bloomberg. (2020). https://www.bloomberg.com/news/articles/2020-02-04/bp-is-still-paying-for-the-deepwater-horizon-spill

Boarini, M. (2018). *Big data e inteligência artificial são a nova onda disruptiva a desafiar os profissionais* [Big data and artificial intelligence are the new disruptive wave to challenge professionals] [Paper presentation]. The meeting of Abrapcorp 2018, Goiânia-GO, Brazil. Retrieved 10 August, 2021, from https://abrapcorp.org.br/

Boarini, M. (2019). *Big data e inteligência artificial: aliados na detecção de oportunidades e crises* [Big data and artificial intelligence: allies in detecting opportunities and crises] [Paper presentation]. The meeting of Abrapcorp 2019, São Paulo-SP, Brazil. Retrieved 05 November, 2021, from https://abrapcorp.org.br/

Boarini, M. (2020). *A comunicação disruptiva do século XXI* [The disruptive communication of the 21st century XXI] (Unpublished Doctoral's thesis). Pontifícia Universidade Católica de São Paulo (PUC-SP), São Paulo-SP, Brasil.

Boarini, M. (2021). A audiência revelada: o big data acentua os desafios profissionais [The audience revealed: big data accentuates professional challenges]. In C. Terra, B. M. Dreyer, & J. F. Raposo (Eds.), *Comunicação organizacional: práticas, desafios e perspectivas digitais* (pp. 126–137). Summus Editorial.

Bogavac-Cvetković, N., Pavlović, R., & Cvetković, T. (2015). Strategic Importance of Innovation in Small and Medium Enterprises in the Era of Information Technology. In *Proceedings of the 3rd International Conference New Functional Materials and High Technology* (pp. 137-144). Tivat.

Bosch. (2017). *Guiding You Through Industrialization Projects Management: the workbook*. Bosch Car Multimedia.

Bourdieu, P. (1999). O Poder Simbólico [Symbolic Power] (2nd ed.). Rio de Janeiro: Bertrand Brasil.

Bove, L. L. (2019). Empathy for service: Benefits, unintended consequences, and future research agenda. *Journal of Services Marketing, 33*(1), 31–43. doi:10.1108/JSM-10-2018-0289

Boyd, D.M. & Ellison, N. (2007). Social Network Sites: Definition, History, and Scholarship. *Journal of Computer Mediated Communication, 13*(1), 210-230. doi:10.1111/j.1083-6101.2007.00393.x

Branco, J. (2021). *João Branco from Méqui*. LinkedIn. Retrieved from https://www.linkedin.com/in/falajoaobranco/

Brandão, E. (2012). Conceito de Comunicação Pública [Concept of Public Communication]. In *Comunicação Pública. Estado, mercado, sociedade e interesse público*. Atlas.

Brasil, L. U. G. (2021). *Who we are*. Retrieved from https://lugbrasil.com/quem-somos/

Braztoa, Associação Brasileira das Operadoras de Turismo. (2021). *Anuário* [Yearbook]. https://drive.google.com/file/d/15dqqAnlX1kROS3QVFG-BZxhAIBBa8qwW/view

Brick Fanatics. (2021). *About*. Retrieved from https://www.brickfanatics.com/about/

Brito, C., & Lencastre, P. (2014). *Novos Horizontes do Marketing* [New Horizons of Marketing]. Córdova: D. Quixote.

Brito, C. (2011). Relationship marketing: Old wine in a new bottle? *Journal Innovative Marketing*, *7*(1).

Brito, D. V., & Garcia, A. (2019). Posicionamento digital das Unidades de Saúde Pública em Portugal Continental em 2019 [Digital positioning of Public Health Units in Mainland Portugal in 2019]. *Comunicação Pública*, *15*(29), 1–12.

Brogan, C., & Smith, J. (2020). *Trust agents*. Wiley.

Broom, G., & Sha, B.-L. (2012). *Cutlip and Center's Effective Public Relations* (11th ed.). Pearson Education.

Brown, T. J., Barry, T. E., Dacin, P. A., & Gunst, R. F. (2005). Spreading the word: Investigating antecedents of consumers' positive word-of-mouth intentions and behaviors in a retailing context. *Journal of the Academy of Marketing Science*, *33*(2), 123–138. doi:10.1177/0092070304268417

Brunner, B. R. (Ed.). (2019). *Public relations theory: Application and understanding*. John Wiley & Sons.

Bruno, F. (2013). *Máquinas de ver, modos de ser: vigilância, tecnologia e subjetividade* [Seeing machines, ways of being: Surveillance, technology and subjectivity]. Sulina.

Budd, J. F. Jr. (1994). How to manage corporate reputations. *Public Relations Quarterly*, *39*(4), 11.

Cachich, D. (2021). *Daniela Cachich, Pepsico's CMO*. LinkedIn. Retrieved from https://www.linkedin.com/in/daniela-cachich/

Cacioppo, J., & Petty, R. (1984). The Elaboration Likelihood Model of Persuasion. In T. C. Kinnear (Ed.), *NA - Advances in Consumer Research* (Vol. 11, pp. 673–675). Association for Consumer Research. https://www.acrwebsite.org/volumes/6329/volumes/v11/NA%20-%2011

Caeiro, J. M. C. (2008). Economia social: Conceitos, fundamentos e tipologia [Social economy: concepts, foundations and typology]. *Revista Katálysis*, *11*(1), 61–72. doi:10.1590/S1414-49802008000100006

Cahyo, P. W., & Roostika, R. (2019). Building Positive Word-of-Mouth in the Shopping Tourism. *Review of Integrative Business and Economics Research*, *8*(s4), 372–386.

Calvino, Í. (1990). *As Cidades Invisíveis* [The Invisible Cities] (D. Mainardi, Trans.). Companhia das Letras.

Cameron, G., & Cheng, Y. (2017). The Status of Social-Mediated Crisis Communication (SMCC) Research: An Analysis of Published Articles in 2002–2014. In Social Media and Crisis Communication (pp. 29-40). Routledge.

Campa, D., & Zijlmans, E. W. A. (2019). Corporate social responsibility recognition and support for the arts: Evidence from European financial institutions. *European Management Journal*, *37*(6), 818–827. doi:10.1016/j.emj.2019.01.003

Campaignlive.co. (2018). *Plucky PR counters chicken FCK-up*. https://www.campaignlive.co.uk/article/plucky-pr-counters-chicken-fck-up/1485750

Canavilhas, J. (2011). El Nuevo Ecosistema Mediático [The New Media Ecosystem]. *Index - Comunicación*, *1*, 13-24. Retrieved from: https://journals.sfu.ca/indexcomunicacion/index.php/indexcomunicacion/article/view/4

Canclini, N. (1998). *Culturas híbridas* [Hybrid crops]. EDUSP.

Canclini, N. (2010). *Consumidores e cidadãos: conflitos multiculturais da globalização* [Consumers and citizens: multicultural conflicts of globalisation]. Ed. UFRJ.

Canon website. (2021). *Canon Connected*. Retrieved from https://www.canon-europe.com/pro/canon-connected/

Caprara, G. V., Barbaranelli, C., & Guido, G. (2001). Brand personality: How to make the metaphor fit? *Journal of Economic Psychology*, *22*(3), 377–395. doi:10.1016/S0167-4870(01)00039-3

Carceller-Maicas, N. (2016). Youth, health and social networks, Instagram as a research tool for health communication. *MÈTODE Science Studies Journal*, *6*, 227–233.

Cardoso, G. (2021). Confiança geral nas notícias aumenta bem como importância dos meios regionais [General confidence in the news increases as well as the importance of regional media]. *EJO – European Journalism Observatory*. Retrieved from: https://pt.ejo.ch/jornalismo/confianca-geral-nas-noticias-aumenta-bem-como-importancia-dos-meio-regionais

Cardoso, G. (2006). *Os Media na Sociedade em Rede* [The Media in the Network Society]. Fundação Calouste Gulbenkian.

Carré, A., D'Ambrosio, F., Bensalah, L., Stefaniak, N., & Besche-Richard, C. (2013). The Basic Empathy Scale in Adults (BES-A): Factor Structure of a Revised Form. *Psychological Assessment*, *25*(3), 679–691. doi:10.1037/a0032297 PMID:23815121

Carrefour Brasil. (2019, October 16). *Carina, elected Carrefour's new virtual assistant* [video]. Youtube. Retrieved from https://www.youtube.com/watch?v=0EC6WW9Pr_0

Casado, A. M., & Peláez, J. I. (2014). Intangible management monitors and tools: Reviews. *Expert Systems with Applications*, *41*(4), 1509–1529. doi:10.1016/j.eswa.2013.08.048

Casais, B., Fernandes, J., & Sarmento, M. (2019). Tourism innovation through relationship marketing and value co-creation: A study on peer-to-peer online platforms for sharing accommodation. *Journal of Hospitality and Tourism Management*, *42*(42), 51–57.

Cascais, F. (2001). *Dicionário de Jornalismo. As palavras dos media* [Journalism Dictionary. The words of the media]. Editorial Verbo.

Castells, M. (1998). *The Rise of the Network Society*. Blackwell Publishers.

Castells, M. (2003). *Sociedade em rede* [Networked Society]. Paz e Terra.

Castells, M. (2005). *The Network Society From Knowledge to Policy, The Network Society: From Knowledge to Policy Manuel Castells*. Center for Transatlantic Relations.

Castells, M. (2011). *The rise of the network society* (Vol. 12). John wiley & sons.

Castells, M. (2016). *A Sociedade em Rede. A Era da Informação: Economia, Sociedade e Cultura* [The Network Society - The Information Age: Economy, Society and Culture] (5th ed., Vol. 1). Fundação Calouste Gulbenkian.

CB [@casasbahia]. (2020, October 16). *Casas Bahia store*. Instagram. Retrieved from https://www.instagram.com/p/CGZ8MX3gG1X/

Cerezo, P. (2016). *Los Customer media - Medios líquidos para usuarios hiperconectados* [Customer media - Liquid media for hyperconnected users]. Evoca. Retrieved from: https://evocaimagen.com/dosieres/dosier-evoca-01-customer-media.pdf

CEVES. (2020). *Preduzeća u Srbiji i Agenda 2030* [Business in Serbia and Agenda 2030]. Available at: https://ceves.org.rs/wp-content/uploads/2021/04/Preduzeca-u-Srbiji-i-Agenda-2030-prioriteti-izazovi-i-kriza-COVID-19-1.pdf

Chaffey, D., Ellis-Chadwick, F., Mayer, R., & Johnston, K. (2009). *Internet Marketing: Strategy, Implementation and Practice*. Available at: https://books.mec.biz/tmp/books/5G7BGE3Z6KNWFOHBFCWN.pdf

Chaffey, D., & Chadwick, E. (2016). *Digital marketing: Strategy, implementation and practice*. Pearson.

Chandler, J., & Owen, M. (2002). *Developing Brands with Qualitative Market Research*. SAGE Publications. doi:10.4135/9781849208840

Charaudeau, P., & Maingueneau, D. (2004). *Dicionário de análise do discurso* [Dictionary of discourse analysis]. Contexto.

Cheng, Y., & Lee, C. J. (2019). Online crisis communication in a post-truth Chinese society: Evidence from interdisciplinary literature. *Public Relations Review*, *45*(4), 101826. doi:10.1016/j.pubrev.2019.101826

Cheng, Y., & Shen, H. (2020). United Airlines crisis from the stakeholder perspective: Exploring customers' ethical judgment, trust and distrust, and behavioral intentions. *Public Relations Review*, *46*(2), 101908. doi:10.1016/j.pubrev.2020.101908

Chen, K.-J. (2017). Humanizing Brands: An Examination of the Psychological Process of Anthropomorphism and its Effects on Consumer Responses. *Journal of Marketing Management*, *5*(2), 75–87.

Cheung, M., Pires, G., & Rosenberger, P. (2019). The Influence of Perceived Social Media Marketing Elements on Consumer-Brand Engagement and Brand Knowledge. *Asia Pacific Journal of Marketing and Logistics*, *32*(3), 695–720. doi:10.1108/APJML-04-2019-0262

Choedon, T., & Lee, Y. (2020). The Effect of Social Media Marketing Activities on Purchase Intention with Brand Equity and Social Brand Engagement: Empirical Evidence from Korean Cosmetic Firms. *The Knowledge Management Society of Korea*, *21*(3), 141–160.

Chou, W. Y. S., & Budenz, A. (2020). Considering emotion in COVID-19 vaccine communication: Addressing vaccine hesitancy and fostering vaccine confidence. *Health Communication*, *35*(14), 1718–1722. doi:10.1080/10410236.2020.1838096 PMID:33124475

Chun, R. (2005). Corporate reputation: Meaning and measurement. *International Journal of Management Reviews*, *7*(2), 91–109. doi:10.1111/j.1468-2370.2005.00109.x

Chu, S., & Sung, Y. (2015). Using a consumer socialization framework to understand electronic word-ofmouth (eWOM) group membership among brand followers on Twitter. *Electronic Commerce Research and Applications*, *14*(4), 251–260. doi:10.1016/j.elerap.2015.04.002

Cian, L., & Cervai, S. (2014). Under the reputation umbrella. *Corporate Communications*, *19*(2), 182–199. doi:10.1108/CCIJ-10-2011-0055

Cifra. (2021). *Evaluación de la Gestión de Ministros* [Evaluation of Ministers' Management]. https://www.cifra.com.uy/index.php/2021/08/10/evaluacion-de-la-gestion-de-ministros-3/

CJI (Centrul pentru Jurnalism Independent). (2015). *Starea sectorului mass-media din România în 2014 - Vulnerabilități și posibile soluții* [The status of the mass media sector in Romania in 2014 – Vulnerabilities and possible solutions]. CJI&Centras.

Claeys, A. S., & Cauberghe, V. (2014). What makes crisis response strategies work? The impact of crisis involvement and message framing. *Journal of Business Research*, *67*(2), 182–189. doi:10.1016/j.jbusres.2012.10.005

Coffman, J. (2002). *Public communication campaign evaluation: an environmental scan of challenges, criticisms, practice, and opportunities*. Communications Consortium Media Center. https://www.dors.it/documentazione/testo/200905/Public%20Communication%20Campaign%20Evaluation.pdf

Coghlan, D. (2019). *Doing action research in your own organization*. Sage.

Collinson, E., & Shaw, E. (2001). Entrepreneurial Marketing - a historical perspective on development and practice. *Management Decision*, *39*(4), 761–766. doi:10.1108/EUM0000000006221

Coman, C., Popica, M., & Rezeanu, C.I. (2020). The Adoption of Digital Marketing by SMEs Entrepreneurs. *International Conference on Digital Science 2018*. Available at: https://link.springer.com/chapter/10.1007/978-3-030-37737-3_37

Cone Communications. (2011). 2011 Online Influence Trend Tracker. Author.

Confente, I., Siciliano, G. G., Gaudenzi, B., & Eickhoff, M. (2019). Effects of data breaches from user-generated content: A corporate reputation analysis. *European Management Journal, 37*(4), 492–504. doi:10.1016/j.emj.2019.01.007

Confetto, M. G., Conte, F., & Covucci, C. (2018). Empirical Evidence on CEO Reputation: Perspectives, Actions and Influence. *International Journal of Business and Management, 13*(12).

Connelly, B. L., Certo, S. T., Ireland, R. D., & Reutzel, C. R. (2011). Signaling theory: A review and assessment. *Journal of Management, 37*(1), 39–67. doi:10.1177/0149206310388419

Coombs, W. T. (2004). Impact of past crises on current crisis communication: Insights from situational crisis communication theory. *The Journal of Business Communication, 41*(3), 265-289.

Coombs, W. T. (2010). Parameters for crisis communication. The handbook of crisis communication, 17-53.

Coombs, W. T. (1995). Choosing the right words: The development of guidelines for the selection of the "appropriate" crisis-response strategies. *Management Communication Quarterly, 8*(4), 447–476. doi:10.1177/0893318995008004003

Coombs, W. T. (1998). An analytic framework for crisis situations: Better responses from a better understanding of the situation. *Journal of Public Relations Research, 10*(3), 177–191. doi:10.12071532754xjprr1003_02

Coombs, W. T. (2007). Protecting organization reputations during a crisis: The development and application of situational crisis communication theory. *Corporate Reputation Review, 10*(3), 163–176. doi:10.1057/palgrave.crr.1550049

Coombs, W. T. (2014). *Ongoing crisis communication: Planning, managing, and responding*. Sage Publications.

Coombs, W. T., & Holladay, S. J. (2001). An extended examination of the crisis situations: A fusion of the relational management and symbolic approaches. *Journal of Public Relations Research, 13*(4), 321–340. doi:10.1207/S1532754XJPRR1304_03

Coombs, W. T., & Holladay, S. J. (2009). Further explorations of post-crisis communication: Effects of media and response strategies on perceptions and intentions. *Public Relations Review, 35*(1), 1–6. doi:10.1016/j.pubrev.2008.09.011

Coombs, W. T., Holladay, S. J., & Claeys, A. S. (2016). Debunking the myth of denial's effectiveness in crisis communication: Context matters. *Journal of Communication Management (London), 20*(4), 381–395. doi:10.1108/JCOM-06-2016-0042

Corciolani, M., Gistri, G., & Pace, S. (2016). *Exploring the palm oil crisis through the lens of different social media: an analysis of Facebook, YouTube and Twitter contents*. Mercati & Competitività.

Courchesne, A., Ravanas, P., & Pulido, C. (2019). Using Technology to Optimize Customer Relationship Management: The Case of Cirque du Soleil. *International Journal of Arts Management, 21*(2).

Crisafulli, B., Singh, J., & Quamina, L. T. (2019). *Spreading of bad news online: how negative online word of mouth and crisis response influence consumer attitudes towards cause-brand alliances*. Academic Press.

Cruz, I. (2017). Aplicación de la mercadotecnia relacional en una empresa de venta de café de Baja California [Application of relationship marketing in a coffee company in Baja California]. *Journal Región y Sociedad, 30*(71), 3–20.

Dakouan, C., Benabdelouahed, R., & Anabir, H. (2019). Inbound marketing vs. outbound marketing: Independent or complementary strategies. *Expert Journal of Marketing, 1*, 1–6.

Dançante, D. S. D. S. G. C. (2017). *O marketing social aplicado à saúde pública: as duas campanhas de sensibilização em Portugal* [Social marketing applied to public health: the two awareness campaigns in Portugal] (Master's thesis). Universidade de Évora, Portugal.

Datareportal. (2021). Available at: https://datareportal.com/reports/

Davenport, T. H. (2017). *Big data no trabalho* [Big Data at Work]. Editora Alta Books.

Davis, M. H. (1980). A Multidimensional Approach to Individual Differences in Empathy. *Journal of Personality and Social Psychology*, 1–19.

Davis, M. H. (1983). Measuring Individual Differences in Empathy: Evidence for a Multidimensional Approach. *Journal of Personality and Social Psychology*, *44*(1), 113–126. doi:10.1037/0022-3514.44.1.113

Deakins, D., & Freel, M. (2012). *Entrepreneurship and Small Firms*. The McGraw Hill Higher Education.

Deephouse, D. L. (2000). Media reputation as a strategic resource: An integration of mass communication and resource-based theories. *Journal of Management*, *26*(6), 1091–1112. doi:10.1177/014920630002600602

Delafrooz, N., Rahmati, Y., & Abdi, M. (2019). The influence of electronic word of mouth on Instagram users: An emphasis on consumer socialization framework. *Cogent Business & Management*, *6*(1), 1–14. doi:10.1080/23311975.2019.1606973

Deleuze, G. (2005). *Foucault* (C. S. Martins, Trans.). Brasiliense. (Original work published 1986)

Delgado-Ballester, E., Palazón, M., & Pelaez-Muñoz, J. (2017). This anthropomorphised brand is so loveable: The role of self-brand integration. *Spanish Journal of Marketing - ESIC, 21*, 89-101.

Dengkai, Tingxiu, & Raju. (2021). *Exploring the Factors that Influence Consumers Purchase Intentions in the Context of Live Streaming Commerce.* Retrieved from https://bit.ly/3oxFsSn

Denić, N., Petković, D., Vujović, V., Spasić, B., & Vujućić, I. (2018). *A survey of internet marketing by small and medium-sized enterprises for placing wine on the market*. Available at: https://www.sciencedirect.com/science/article/abs/pii/S0378437118305235

Dias, P. (2014). *Viver na Sociedade Digital. Tecnologias digitais, Novas Práticas e Mudanças Sociais* [Living in the Digital Society: Digital technologies, new practices and social change]. Princípia Editora.

Dickens, L., & Watkins, K. (1999). Action Research: Rethinking Lewin. *Management Learning*, *30*(2), 127–140. doi:10.1177/1350507699302002

Dinnie, K. (2008). *Nation Branding: concepts, issues, practices*. Elsevier.

Diyana, A., & Dolah, J. (2018). How Digital Marketing Affects Consumer Behavior. *Advances in Social Science, Education and Humanities Research Journal.* Available at:https://creativecommons.org/licenses/by-nc/4.0/

Dobele, A., Lindgreen, A., Beverland, M., Vanhamme, J., & Van Wijk, R. (2007). Why pass on viral messages? Because they connect emotionally. *Business Horizons*, *50*(4), 291–304. doi:10.1016/j.bushor.2007.01.004

Dolea, A. (2012). Institutionalizing government public relations in Romania after 1989. *Public Relations Review*, *38*(2), 354–366.

Domazet, I. (2018). Digital transformation of business portfolio through DCRM. In *Digital Transformation-New Challenges and Business Opportunities* (pp. 214–235). Silver and Smith Publishers.

Domazet, I. S., & Neogradi, S. (2019). Digital Marketing and Service Industry: Digital Marketing in the Banking Industry. In *Managing Diversity, Innovation, and Infrastructure in Digital Business* (pp. 20–40). IGI Global. doi:10.4018/978-1-5225-5993-1.ch002

Domazet, I., Đokić, O., & Milovanov, O. (2018). The Influence of Advertising Media on Brand Awareness. Management. *Journal of Sustainable Business and Management Solutions in Emerging Economies*, *23*(1), 13–22.

Domazet, I., Neogradi, S., & Simović, V. (2019). Značaj društvenih mreža kao digitalnih kanala komunikacije u srpskim bankama [The importance of social networks as digital communication channels in Serbian banks]. *Marketing.*, *50*(4), 289–297. doi:10.5937/markt1904289X

Duan, C., & Hill, C. E. (1996). The Current State of Empathy Research. *Journal of Counseling Psychology*, *43*(3), 261–274. doi:10.1037/0022-0167.43.3.261

Duarte, J. (2012) Instrumentos de comunicação pública [Public communication tools]. In Comunicação Pública. Estado, mercado, sociedade e interesse público. São Paulo: Atlas.

Duarte, J., & Barros, A. (Orgs.). (2009). Métodos e técnicas de pesquisa em comunicação [Research methods and techniques in communication]. São Paulo: Atlas.

Duarte, J., & Barros, A. (Eds.). (2005). *Métodos e técnicas de pesquisa em comunicação* [Research Methods and Techniques in Communication]. Atlas.

Duhé, S. (2012). *New media and Public Relations* (2nd ed.). Peter Lang.

Dutta, S., & Pullig, C. (2011). Effectiveness of corporate responses to brand crises: The role of crisis type and response strategies. *Journal of Business Research*, *64*(12), 1281–1287. doi:10.1016/j.jbusres.2011.01.013

Dwivedi, Y. K., Kapoor, K. K., & Chen, H. (2015). Social media marketing and advertising. *The Marketing Review*, *15*(3), 289–309. doi:10.1362/146934715X14441363377999

Edelman, D., & Singer, M. (2015). *The New Consumer Decision Journey*. McKinsey & Company. Retrieved from https://cutt.ly/EuGNIZP

Edelman. (2021) *Edelman Trust Barometer 2021*. Retrieved from https://www.edelman.com.br/sites/g/files/aatuss291/files/2021-03/2021%20Edelman%20Trust%20Barometer_Brazil%20%2B%20Global_POR_Imprensa_1.pdf

Edmunds, J., & Turner, B. S. (2005). Global generations: Social change in the twentieth century. *The British Journal of Sociology*, *56*(4), 559–577. doi:10.1111/j.1468-4446.2005.00083.x PMID:16309436

Eisenberg, N., Eggum, N. D., & Giunta, L. D. (2010). Empathy-Related Responding: Associations with Prosocial Behavior, Aggression, and Intergroup Relations. *Social Issues and Policy Review*, *4*(1), 143–180. doi:10.1111/j.1751-2409.2010.01020.x PMID:21221410

El 84% de la población aprueba la gestión de la pandemia realizada por Lacalle, según Factum [84% of the Population Approves Lacalle's Handling of the Pandemic, According to Factum]. (2021, October 13). *El Observador*. https://www.elobservador.com.uy/nota/el-84-de-la-poblacion-aprueba-la-gestion-de-la-pandemia-realizada-por-lacalle-segun-factum-2021101322377

El Qudsi, I. (2020, December 21). The state of influencer marketing: top insights for 2021. *Forbes*. https://www.forbes.com/sites/forbesagencycouncil/2020/12/21/the-state-of-influencer-marketing-top-insights-for-2021/?sh=6681a177ddcd

Elola, J. (2010). Entrevista: Rosental C. Alves (consultor Digital de Medios y Catedrático de Periodismo). O Futuro do Periodismo Digital - "Los medios deben aparcar su arrogancia" [Interview: Rosental C. Alves (Digital Media Consultant and Professor of Journalism). The future of Digital Journalism - "The media must park its arrogance"]. *Jornal El País*. Retrieved from: https://elpais.com/diario/2010/09/05/domingo/1283658757_850215.html

EMBRATUR. (2020). *Plano Aquarela 2020: marketing turístico internacional do Brasil* [Aquarela 2020 Plan: international tourism marketing of Brazil]. Disponível em: http://www.embratur.gov.br/lai_embratur_secom/export/sites/lai/galerias/download/Plano_Aquarela_2020.pdf

Enke, N., & Borchers, N. S. (2019). Social Media Influencers in Strategic Communication: A Conceptual Framework for Strategic Social Media Influencer Communication. *International Journal of Strategic Communication, 13*(4), 261–277. doi:10.1080/1553118X.2019.1620234

Epley, N., Waytz, A., & Cacioppo, J. T. (2007). On Seeing Human: A Three-Factor Theory of Anthropomorphism. *Psychological Review, 114*(4), 864–886. doi:10.1037/0033-295X.114.4.864 PMID:17907867

Erel, I., Liao, R. C., & Weisbach, M. S. (2012). Determinants of cross-border mergers and acquisitions. *The Journal of Finance, 67*(3), 1045–1082. doi:10.1111/j.1540-6261.2012.01741.x

Espanha, R., Mendes, R., & Fonseca, R. & Correia, T. (2013). O lugar e papel da internet na saúde: Contributos do caso português [The place and role of the internet in health: contributions from the Protuguese case]. *Portugal Saúde em Números, 1*, 41–49.

European Commission. (2021). 2021 *SME Country Fact Sheet*. Available at: https://ec.europa.eu/neighbourhood-enlargement/sites/default/files/serbia_-_sme_fact_sheet_2021.pdf

Eurostat. (2020). *Social media - statistics on the use by enterprises*. Available at: https://ec.europa.eu/eurostat/statistics-explained/index.php?title=Social_media_-_statistics_on_the_use_by_enterprises#Use_of_social_media_by_enterprises

Evans, T. (2010). We are all in PR now. *British Journalism Review, 21*(2), 31–36. doi:10.1177/0956474810374531

Ewing, M., Men, L. R., & O'Neill, J. (2019). Using social media to engage employees: Insights from internal communication managers. *International Journal of Strategic Communication, 13*(2), 532–550. doi:10.1080/1553118X.2019.1575830

Fairclough, N. (2001). *Discurso e mudança social* [Discourse and social change]. Editora Universidade de Brasília.

Farias, L. A. (2016). Opinião pública, mídias e organizações [Public opinion, media and organizations]. In M. K. Kunsch (Ed.), *Comunicação organizacional estratégica: aportes conceituais e aplicados* (pp. 241–254). Summus.

Fearn-Banks, K. (2010). *Crisis Communications Student Workbook*. Routledge.

Fernandes, G., Pessôa, C., Martins, A. R., Pinto, E. B., Ruão, T., Araújo, M., Pontes, J. P., & Machado, R. J. (2018). *A Conceptual Social Media Tool for Supporting Collaborative University-Industry R&D Programs*. Paper presented at the 2018 IEEE International Conference on Engineering, Technology and Innovation (ICE/ITMC), Stuttgart, Germany. 10.1109/ICE.2018.8436297

Ferrari, P. (2021). *Como sair das bolhas* [How to get out of bubbles] (2a. ed. rev.). Educ São Paulo.

Ferreira, J. (2021). *Como está a ser o seu confinamento? 56% dos portugueses dizem que "igual" ou "mais fácil" do que primeiro* [How is your confinement going? 56% of Portuguese say "equal" or "easier" than first]. Eco. Portal Sapo. Retrieved from: https://eco.sapo.pt/2021/03/18/como-esta-a-ser-o-seu-confinamento-56-dos-portugueses-dizem-que-igual-ou-mais-facil-do-que-primeiro/

Ferreira, V. (2019). *Portugal vai ser mais um caso de sucesso do Merco. Jornal Online Vida Económica* [Portugal will be another Merco success story. Online Journal Economic Life]. Retrieved from: https://www.vidaeconomica.pt/vida-economica-1/publicacoes/edicao-num-1793-do-vida-economica-de-12072019/negocios-e-empresas/portugal-vai-ser-mais-um-caso-de-sucesso-do-merco

Ferreira,G. (1997). *O posicionamento discursivo de "A Gazeta" e "A Tribuna" (Vitoria-ES / Brasil): uma explicação para entender a evolução de suas tiragens* [The discursive positioning of "A Gazeta" and "A Tribuna" (Vitoria-ES / Brazil): an explanation to understand the evolution of their circulation]. Academic Press.

Ferreira, G., Sampaio, A., & Fausto Neto, A. (2012). *Mídia, discurso e sentido* [Media, discourse and meaning]. Edufba.

Ferreira, M., Zambaldi, F., & de Sousa Guerra, D. (2020). Consumer engagement in social media: Scale comparison analysis. *Journal of Product and Brand Management*, *29*(4), 491–503. doi:10.1108/JPBM-10-2018-2095

Fields, S. K., Mahan, P., Tillman, P., Harris, J., Kaye, M., & Hojat, M. (2011). Measuring empathy in healthcare profession students using the Jefferson Scale of Physician Empathy: Health provider – student version. *Journal of Interprofessional Care*, *25*(4), 287–293. doi:10.3109/13561820.2011.566648 PMID:21554061

Figueroa, M. E., Kincaid, D. L., Rani, M., & Lewis, G. (2002). *Communication for social change: an integrated model for measuring the process and its outcomes*. Rockefeller Foundation and Johns Hopkins University Center for Communication Programs.

Filis, I., Johansson, U., & Wagner, B. (2003). A Conceptualisation of the Opportunities and Barriers to E-business Development in the Smaller Firm. *Journal of Small Business and Enterprise Development*, *10*(3), 336–344. doi:10.1108/14626000310489808

Fillis, I. (2003). Image, reputation and identity issues in the arts and crafts organization. *Corporate Reputation Review*, *6*(3), 239–251. doi:10.1057/palgrave.crr.1540203

Finset, A., Bosworth, H., Butow, P., Gulbrandsen, P., Hulsman, R., Pieterse, A., Street, R., Tschoetschel, R., & van Weert, J. (2020). Effective health communication – a key factor in fighting the COVID-19 pandemic. *Patient Education and Counseling*, *103*(5), 873–876. doi:10.1016/j.pec.2020.03.027 PMID:32336348

Firat, A., & Venkatesh, A. (1993). *Postmodernity*. The age of marketing. *International Journal of Research in Marketing*, *10*(3), 227–249. doi:10.1016/0167-8116(93)90009-N

Fitzgerald, M., Kruschwitz, N., Bonnet, D., & Welch, M. (2014). Embracing digital technology: A new strategic imperative. *MIT Sloan Management Review*, *55*, 1–12.

Flečer, K. (2003). *Upravljanje marketingom i informaciona tehnologija* [Marketing management and information technology]. Clio.

Floch, J. (1985). Le changement de formule d'un quotidien approche d'une double exigence: la modernité du discours et la fidélité du lectorat [The change of formula of a daily newspaper approaches a double requirement: the modernity of the discourse and the loyalty of the readership]. In Les Medias - Expériences recherches actuelles applications. Paris: IREP.

Floch, J. (1990). Sémiotique, marketing et communication [Semiotics, marketing and communication]. Paris: Presses Universitaires de France.

Floch, J. (1995). *Identités visuelles* [Visual identities]. Presses Universitaires de France.

Fombrun, C. J., Gardberg, N. A., & Sever, J. M. (2000). The Reputation Quotient SM: A multi-stakeholder measure of corporate reputation. *Journal of Brand Management*, *7*(4), 241–255. doi:10.1057/bm.2000.10

Fombrun, C. J., Ponzi, L. J., & Newburry, W. (2015). Stakeholder tracking and analysis: The RepTrak® system for measuring corporate reputation. *Corporate Reputation Review*, *18*(1), 3–24. doi:10.1057/crr.2014.21

Fonseca, M. J. (2012). *As campanhas de comunicação de marketing no âmbito da prevenção rodoviária portuguesa: um contributo para a análise da sua eficácia* [Portuguese road safety marketing communication campaigns: a contribution to the analysis of their effectiveness] (Doctoral dissertation). Universidade Fernando Pessoa, Porto, Portugal.

Fonseca, J. J. S. (2002). *Metodologia da pesquisa científica* [Scientific Research Methodology]. UEC Apostila.

Forbes.com. (2014). *McDonald's Faces Declining Sales In Asia After China Food Scandal.* Retrieved from https://www.forbes.com/sites/greatspeculations/2014/09/11/mcdonalds-faces-declining-sales-in-asia-after-china-food-scandal/?sh=58ab00426de1

Ford, S., Green, J., & Jenkins, H. (2013). *Spreadable media: I media tra condivisione, circolazione, partecipazione.* Maggioli Editore.

Foucault, M. (1985). *As palavras e as coisas. Uma arqueologia das ciências humanas* [Words and things. An archaeology of the human sciences.]. Martins Fontes.

Foucault, M. (2004). *A ordem do discurso* [The order of the discourse]. Loyola.

Foucault, M. (2012). *Arqueologia do Saber* [Archaeology of Knowledge]. Forense Universitária.

Foucault, M. (2014). *Vigiar e punir: nascimento da prisão* [Discipline and Punish: The Birth of the Prison] (42nd ed., R. Ramalhete, Trans.). Vozes. (Original work published 1975)

Fournier, S. (1998). Consumers and Their Brands: Developing Relationship Theory in Consumer Research. *The Journal of Consumer Research, 24*(4), 343–373. doi:10.1086/209515

FreeEx. (2014). *Harta politică a televiziunilor locale* [The Political Mapping of the Local TV stations]. FreeEx, Active Watch, Agenția de Monitorizare a Presei.

Freitas, R., & Porto, A. (2014). Nas ondas do Copacabana Palace: sobre a importância do Hotel na Constituição da Marca Rio [On the waves of Copacabana Palace: on the importance of the Hotel in the making of the Rio brand]. In *Congresso Brasileiro Científico de Comunicação Organizacional e de Relações Públicas.* Abrapcorp. Disponível: https://portal.abrapcorp.org.br/anais/

Fuchs, C. (2014). Social Media: A critical introduction. *Sage (Atlanta, Ga.).*

Furtado, C. (1974). *O mito do desenvolvimento econômico* [The myth of economic development]. Paz e Terra.

Gabriel, M. (2018). *Você, eu e os robôs* [You, me and the robots.]. Editora Atlas.

Galgali, P. (2017, December). *Digital Transformation and its Impact on Organizations' Human Resource Management.* IOR and Stakeholder Management, MCM, School of Communication and Information, Rutgers University. Retrieved from: https://www.academia.edu/35595152/Digital_Transformation_and_its_Impact_on_Organizations_Human_Resource_Management

Ganczarek, J., Hünefeldt, T., & Belardinelli, M. O. (2018). From "Einfühlung" to empathy: Exploring the relationship between aesthetic and interpersonal experience. *Cognitive Processing, 19*(2), 141–145. doi:10.100710339-018-0861-x PMID:29766344

Gandini, A. (2016). Digital work: Self-branding and social capital in the freelance knowledge economy. *Marketing Theory, 16*(1), 123–141. doi:10.1177/1470593115607942

Garcia, A., & Eiró-Gomes, M. (2020). O papel da comunicação: a utilização das redes sociais nos cuidados de saúde primários [The role of communication: the use of social media in primary health care]. Comunicação e Sociedade, 197-217.

Gardašević, J., Ćirić, M., & Carić, M. (2018). Razumevanje motiva koršćenja društvenih mreža u funkciji unapređenja komunikacije sa potrošačima [Understanding the motives for using social networks in the function of improving communication with consumers]. *Marketing*, *49*(4), 311–320.

Gardberg, N. A. (2017). Corporate reputation: Fashion, fad, or phenomenon? *Corporate Reputation Review*, *20*(3-4), 177–180. doi:10.105741299-017-0033-4

Gaudenzi, B., & Siciliano, G. (2017). Just do it: Managing IT and cyber risks to protect the value creation. *Journal of Promotion Management*, *23*(3), 372–385. doi:10.1080/10496491.2017.1294875

Gerdes, K. E., Segal, E. A., & Lietz, C. A. (2010). Conceptualizing and Measuring Empathy. *British Journal of Social Work*, *40*(7), 2326–2343. doi:10.1093/bjsw/bcq048

Ghinea, C., & Avadani, I. (2011, December). *Does media policy promote media freedom and independence? The case of Romania*. Hertie School of Governance (HERTIE).

Ghorbanzadeh, K. (2020). L'agence de communication, une rédaction comme une autre ? Interroger la frontière entre information et communication au prisme des routines de travail [The communication agency, a newsroom like any other? Questioning the boundary between information and communication through the lens of work routines]. *Questions de Communication*, *38*, 351-370.

Giddens, A. (1991). *As consequências da modernidade* [The consequences of modernity]. Editora Unesp.

Giddens, A. (1993). *A transformação da intimidade. Sexualidade, Amor e Erotismo nas Sociedades Modernas* [The Transformation of Intimacy. Sexuality, Love and Eroticism in Modern Societies]. Unesp.

Gillingham, D., & Noizet, J. (2007). A response model for the public relations management of a critical incident. *Disaster Prevention and Management: An International Journal*.

Giménez, M. P. (2017). *Aplicación de la Teoría de la Conducta Planificada en la Seguridad Vial: velocidad, alcohol y drogas* [Application of the Theory of Planned Behavior in Road Security: Speed, Alcohol and Drugs] (Doctoral dissertation). Universidad Católica San Antonio de Murcia. RIUCAM. http://hdl.handle.net/10952/2678

Glassdoor. (2021). *About us*. Retrieved from https://www.glassdoor.com/about-us/?_gl=1%2Ap63aiu%2A_ga%2AMTM5MzY3OTE2OC4xNjI0ODg5NjEw%2A_ga_RC95PMVB3H%2AMTYyNDg4OTYwOS4xLjAuMTYyNDg4OTYxNC41NQ

Glusac, E. (2018). Hotels grapple with racial bias. *The New York Times*. Accessed from www. nytimes. com/2018/08/01/travel/hotels-diversity-training. html

Gnoth, J. (2002). Leveraging export brands through a tourism destination brand. *Brand Management*, *9*(4-5), 262-280.

Gode, H. E., Johansen, W., & Thomsen, C. (2020). Employee engagement in generating ideas on internal social media: A matter of meaningfulness, safety and availability. *Corporate Communications*, *25*(2), 263–280. doi:10.1108/CCIJ-03-2019-0024

Godey, B., Manthiou, A., Pederzoli, D., Rokka, J., Aiello, J., Donvito, R., & Singh, R. (2016). Social media marketing efforts of luxury brands: Influence on brand equity and consumer behavior. *Journal of Business Research*, *69*(12), 5833–5841. doi:10.1016/j.jbusres.2016.04.181

Godin, S. (2019). *Isto é Marketing* [This is Marketing]. Ideias de Ler.

Goffman, E. (1988). Estigma. Notas sobre a manipulação da identidade deteriorada [Stigma. Notes on the manipulation of deteriorated identity] (4th ed.). São Paulo: LTC.

Golossenko, A., Pillai, K. G., & Aroean, L. (2020). Seeing brands as humans: Development and validation of a brand anthropomorphism scale. *International Journal of Research in Marketing*, *37*(4), 1–19. doi:10.1016/j.ijresmar.2020.02.007

Gomes, W. (2016). 20 anos de política, Estado e democracia digitais: uma “cartografia” do campo [20 years of digital politics, state and democracy: a “cartography” of the field]. In Democracia digital, comunicação política e redes. Teoria e prática. Rio de Janeiro: Folio Digital: Letra e Imagem.

González-Melado, F. J., & Di Pietro, M. L. (2020). La vacuna frente al Covid-19 y la confianza institucional [The Vaccine Against Covid-19 and Institutional Trust]. *Enfermedades Infecciosas y Microbiologia Clinica.* Advance online publication. doi:10.1016/j.eimc.2020.08.001 PMID:33069493

Goodman, N. (1978). *Ways of Worldmaking*. Hackett Publishing Company.

Goodyear, V., Armour, K., & Wood, H. (2019). Young people and their engagement with health-related social media: New perspectives. *Sport Education and Society*, *24*(7), 673–688. doi:10.1080/13573322.2017.1423464 PMID:31814804

GoPro. (2021). *The GoPro Awards recognizes you.* Retrieved from https://gopro.com/pt/br/awards

Gotsi, M., & Wilson, A. M. (2001). Corporate reputation: Seeking a definition. *Corporate Communications*, *6*(1), 24–30. doi:10.1108/13563280110381189

Grasu, N., Tasențe, T., & Sandu, M. (2014). Perception of Journalists on the Role of Public Relations. *Acta Universitatis Danubius*, *8*(2), 54–68.

Gregory, A. (2015). *Planning and managing public relations campaigns a strategic approach* (4th ed.). Kogan Page.

Greimas, A. (1976). *Semântica Estrutural* [Structural Semantics]. Cultrix.

Grover, P., Kar, A. K., & Ilavarasan, P. V. (2019). Impact of corporate social responsibility on reputation—Insights from tweets on sustainable development goals by CEOs. *International Journal of Information Management*, *48*, 39–52. doi:10.1016/j.ijinfomgt.2019.01.009

Grunig, J. E. (2009). Paradigms of global public relations in an age of digitalisation. *Prism*, *6*(2). http://praxis.massey.ac.nz/prism_on-line_journ.html

Grunig, J. E. (Ed.). (1992). *Excellence in public relations and communication management*. Lawrence Erlbaum Associates.

Grusin, R., & Bolter, D. J. (2000). *Remediation: Understanding new media*. The MIT Press.

Grützmacher, A. (2011). *Reputation 2.0: The role of social media in corporate reputation-Case Nokia*. Academic Press.

Guadagno, R. E., Okdie, B. M., & Muscanell, N. L. (2013). Have we all Just Become “Robo-Sapiens”? Reflections on social influence processes in the Internet age. *Psychological Inquiry, 24*(4), 301-309.

Guaraná Antartica. (2021). *Become a member of the 100 years.* Retrieved from https://www.guaranaantarctica.com.br/100anos/promocoes

Guido, G., & Peluso, A. M. (2015). Brand anthropomorphism: Conceptualization, measurement, and impact on brand personality and loyalty. *Journal of Brand Management*, *22*(1), 1–19. doi:10.1057/bm.2014.40

Gummesson, E., Mele, C., Polese, F., Gummesson, E., & Grönroos, C. (2012). The emergence of the new service marketing: Nordic School perspectives. *Journal of Service Management*, *23*(4), 479–497. doi:10.1108/09564231211260387

Gurau, C. (2008). Integrated online marketing communication: Implementation and management. *Journal of Communication Management (London)*, *12*(2), 169–184. doi:10.1108/13632540810881974

Guse, K., Levine, D., Martins, S., Lira, A., Gaardeb, J., Westmorlandc, W., & Gilliam, M. (2012). Interventions Using New Digital Media to Improve Adolescent Sexual Health: A Systematic Review. *The Journal of Adolescent Health*, *51*(6), 535–543. doi:10.1016/j.jadohealth.2012.03.014 PMID:23174462

Gutiérrez-García, E., Recalde, E., & Alfaro, J. (2020). Corporate communication in open innovation: A case-study of three multinationals. *Corporate Communications*, *26*(2), 348–364. Advance online publication. doi:10.1108/CCIJ-02-2020-0048

Hall, S. (2006). *A identidade cultural na pós-modernidade* [Cultural identity in post-modernity]. DP&A.

Hamdi, S., & Rajablu, M. (2012). Effect of Supervisor-Subordinate Communication and Leadership Style on Organizational Commitment of Nurses in Health Care Setting. *International Journal of Business and Management*, *7*(23), 7–18. doi:10.5539/ijbm.v7n23p7

Han, B.-C. (2017). *The burnout society*. Vozes Publishing House.

Han, B.-C. (2018). *In the Swarm: Digital Prospects*. Vozes Publishing House.

Hardy, J. (2022). *Branded content. The fateful merging of media and marketing*. Routledge.

Harmeling, C. M., Moffett, J. W., Arnold, M. J., & Carlson, B. D. (2017). Toward a theory of customer engagement marketing. *Journal of the Academy of Marketing Science*, *45*(3), 312–335. doi:10.100711747-016-0509-2

Harrigan, P., Miles, M. P., Fang, Y., & Roy, S. K. (2020). The role of social media in the engagement and information processes of social CRM. *International Journal of Information Management*, *54*, 102151. doi:10.1016/j.ijinfomgt.2020.102151

Harrison, K. (2020). *Make it easy for journalists to find information in your website*. Retrieved from: https://cuttingedgepr.com/make-easy-journalists-find-information-website/

Hartley, J. (2004). Case study research. In C. Cassell & G. Symon (Eds.), *Essential Guide to Qualitative Methods in Organizational Research* (pp. 323–333). Sage.

Harvey, D. (1989). From Managerialism to Entrepreneurialism. The Transformation in Urban Governance in Late Capitalism. *Geografiska Annaler. Series B, Human Geography*, *71*(1), 3–17.

Hassan, M., Belanche, D., & Casaló, L. V. (2019). *The Relevance of Empathy on Facebook Brand Communities*. Academic Press.

Heldman, A. B., Schindelar, J., & Weaver, J. B. III. (2013). Social media engagement and public health communication: Implications for public health organizations being truly "social". *Public Health Reviews*, *35*(1), 13. doi:10.1007/BF03391698

Henrique, A., & Miake, S. (2017). *Gestão do Conhecimento do Cliente (GCC): Proposta e Avaliação de um Modelo em um Grande Grupo Privado de Ensino Superior Brasileiro* [Customer Knowledge Management: Proposal and Evaluation of a Model in a Large Brazilian Private Higher Education Group]. Universidade Tecnológica Federal do Paraná.

Henriques, M. S., & Silva, D. R. (2021, July). *Indirect influence and strategy: notes on the inter-influence system and its possibilities for organizational communication* [Paper presentation]. 30th Annual Meeting of Compós 2021, São Paulo. https://proceedings.science/compos-2021/trabalhos/influencia-indireta-e-estrategia--notas-sobre-o-sistema-de-interinfluencias-e-suas-possibilidades-para-a-comunicacao-org

Hepp, A., & Hasebrink, U. (2013). *Human interaction and communicative figurations. The transformation of mediatized cultures and societies.* Communicative Figurations -Working Paper No. 2. Retrieved from: https://www.semanticscholar.org/paper/Human-interaction-and-communicative-figurations-.-Hepp-Hasebrink/7c092f9dcea75b5ce6aafbf5ab264261e4156e42

Hepp, A., & Hasebrink, U. (2013). *The communicative figurations of mediatized worlds: Mediatization research in times of the 'mediation of everything'*. Electronic Working Paper | No. 1. University of Bremen. Retrieved from: https://www.kommunikative-figurationen.de/fileadmin/user_upload/Arbeitspapiere/CoFi_EWP_No-1_Hepp.pdf

Hepp, A. (2014). As configurações comunicativas de mundos midiatizados: Pesquisa da midiatização na era da "mediação de tudo" [The communicative figurations of mediatized worlds: Mediatization research in times of the 'mediation of everything']. *MATRIZes*, *8*(1), 45–64. doi:10.11606/issn.1982-8160.v8i1p45-64

Hickin, R., & Bechtel, M. (2021, April). *Technology Futures: Projecting the Possible, Navigating What's Next. Insight Report.* World Economic Forum in collaboration with Deloitte. Retrieved from: https://www3.weforum.org/docs/WEF_Technology_Futures_GTGS_2021.pdf

Highhouse, S., Brooks, M. E., & Gregarus, G. (2009). An organizational impression management perspective on the formation of corporate reputations. *Journal of Management*, *35*(6), 1481–1493. doi:10.1177/0149206309348788

Hill, S., Nalavade, A., & Benton, A. (2012, August). Social TV: Real-time social media response to TV advertising. In *Proceedings of the Sixth International Workshop on Data Mining for Online Advertising and Internet Economy* (pp. 1-9). 10.1145/2351356.2351360

Hjarvard, S. (2012). Midiatização: Teorizando a mídia como agente de mudança social e cultural [Mediatization: Theorizing the media as an agent of social and cultural change]. *MATRIZes*, *5*(2), 53–91. doi:10.11606/issn.1982-8160.v5i2p53-91

Hjarvard, S. (2014). *A midiatização da cultura e da sociedade* [The Mediatization of Culture and Society] (A. G. Vieira, Trans.). Ed. UNISINOS. (Original work published 2013)

Hjarvard, S. (2019). The Janus face of digital connectivity: The transformation of social dependencies. In J. Ferreira, J. L. Braga, P. G. Gomes, A. F. Neto, & A. P. Rosa (Eds.), *Between what we say and what we think: Where is mediatization?* (pp. 241–264). FACOS-UFSM. https://repositorio.ufsm.br/bitstream/handle/1/19692/betweenwhatwesayandwhatwethink.pdf

Hobbs, B., Aubry, M., & Thuillier, D. (2008). The project management office as an organisational innovation. *International Journal of Project Management*, *26*(5), 547–555. doi:10.1016/j.ijproman.2008.05.008

Hoffman, M. L. (2000). Empathy, Its Arousal, and Prosocial Functioning. In Empathy and Moral Development: Implications for Caring and Justice (pp. 29-62). Cambridge University Press.

Hoffman, M. L. (2008). Empathy and Prosocial Behavior. In Handbook of Emotions (3rd ed., pp. 440-455). New York: The Guilford Press.

Hogan, R. (1969). Development of an Empathy Scale. *Journal of Consulting and Clinical Psychology*, *33*(3), 307–316. doi:10.1037/h0027580 PMID:4389335

Hojat, M., Gonnella, J. S., Nasca, T. J., Mangione, S., Vergare, M., & Magee, M. (2002). Physician Empathy: Definition, Components, Measurement, and Relationship to Gender and Specialty. *The American Journal of Psychiatry*, *159*(9), 1563–1569. doi:10.1176/appi.ajp.159.9.1563 PMID:12202278

Hojat, M., Mangione, S., Kane, G. C., & Gonnella, J. S. (2005). Relationships between scores of the Jefferson Scale of Physician Empathy. *Medical Teacher*, *27*(7), 625–628. doi:10.1080/01421590500069744 PMID:16332555

Hojat, M., Mangione, S., Nasca, T. S., Cohen, M. J., Gonnella, J. S., Erdmann, J. B., & Veloskyi, J. (2001). The Jefferson Scale of Pshysician Empathy: Development and Preliminary Psychometric Data. *Educational and Psychological Measurement*, *61*(2), 349–365. doi:10.1177/00131640121971158

Holladay, S. J., & Coombs, W. T. (2013). Public relations literacy: Developing critical consumers of public relations. *Public Relations Inquiry*, *2*(2), 125–146.

Holmes, D. (2009). New Media Theory. In Encyclopedia of Communication Theory. SAGE Publications.

Holmes, D. (2005). *Communication Theory: Media, Technology, Society*. Sage Publications.

Hootsuite & We Are Social. (2021). *Digital 2021: Global Overview Report*. https://datareportal.com/reports/digital-2021-global-overview-report

Hootsuite. (2021). *Digital 2021. Global Overview Report*. Available at: https://www.hootsuite.com/pt/pages/digital-trends-2021

Hootsuite. (2021). *Digital 2021: Global overview report*. Retrieved from https://bit.ly/3auhdwh

Hootsuite, W. A. S. Y. (2020). *Digital 2020*. Global Digital Overview.

Howard, C. (2004). Working With Reporters: Mastering The Fundamentals To Build Long-Term Relationships. Public Relations Quarterly, 49(1), 36-39.

Hsu, L., & Lawrence, B. (2016). The role of social media and brand equity during a product recall crisis: A shareholder value perspective. *International Journal of Research in Marketing*, *33*(1), 59–77. doi:10.1016/j.ijresmar.2015.04.004

Huang, R., Zhou, X., Ye, W., & Guo, S. (2020). Think versus feel: Two dimensions of brand anthropomorphism. *Journal of Product and Brand Management*, *29*(7), 1–15. doi:10.1108/JPBM-11-2018-2125

Huang, Y., & DiStaso, M. (2020). Responding to a Health Crisis on Facebook: The Effects of Response Timing and Message Appeal. *Public Relations Review*, *46*(3), 101909. doi:10.1016/j.pubrev.2020.101909

Huo, J., Desai, R., Hong, Y., Turner, K., Mainous, A. III, & Bian, J. (2019). Use of social media in health communication: Findings from the health information national trends survey 2013, 2014, and 2017. *Cancer Control*, *26*(1), 1–10. doi:10.1177/1073274819841442 PMID:30995864

IBGE. (2021). *O IBGE apoiando o combate à Covid*-19 [IBGE supporting the fight against Covid-19]. Disponível em: https://covid19.ibge.gov.br/pnad-covid/trabalho.php

IBGE. (2021). *População estimada* [Estimated population]. https://www.ibge.gov.br/pt/inicio.html

Idzikowski, A., Kuryło, P., Cyganiuk, J., & Ryczko, M. (2019). Customer Relationship Management (CRM)-philosophy and its significance for the enterprise. *System Safety: Human-Technical Facility-Environment, 1*(1).

Influencer Marketing Hub. (2022). *The State of Influencer Marketing 2022*: *Benchmark Report*. Retrieved from https://influencermarketinghub.com/influencer-marketing-benchmark-report/

Influencermh [@influencermh]. (2020, June 28). *What is an influencer.* Instagram. Retrieved from https://www.instagram.com/p/CCByOaRjijq/

Ingelmo Palomares, M., Navarro, C., & Sanz Lara, J. Á. (2018). Determining factors of success in internal communication management in Spanish companies: The influence of social media. *Corporate Communications*, *23*(3), 405–422. doi:10.1108/CCIJ-03-2017-0021

Internet 2020: cresce a liderança dos smartphone [Internet 2020: Smartphone leadership grows]. Retrieved from: https://www.marktest.com/wap/a/n/id~269e.aspx

IPSOS Srbija. (2021). *Mediji u Srbiji* [Media in Serbia]. Available at: http//www.ipsos.com/

iResearch Consulting Group. (2018). *China Live Webcast Marketing Market Research Report 2018.* Retrieved from https://bit.ly/3anpeD5

Irving, M. (2019). Para sustentabilizar o turismo na contemporaneidade. Ética e políticas públicas globais [To sustain tourism in contemporary times. Ethics and global public policies]. In Turismo: Ressignificando sustentabilidade. Rio de Janeiro: Folio Digital: Letra e Imagem.

Ishikawa, H., & Kiuchi, T. (2010). Health literacy and health communication. *BioPsychoSocial Medicine*, *4*(1), 1–5. doi:10.1186/1751-0759-4-18 PMID:21054840

Iturregui-Mardaras, L., Gutiérrez-Cuesta, J.-J., & Cantalapiedra-González, M.-J. (2020). Journalists and Public Relations professionals: From influence and dependence to journalistic disintermediation. *El Profesional de la Información*, *29*(3). https://doi.org/10.3145/epi.2020.may.20

Iwata, J. (2021). *Getting Started in CommTech: From Professional to Pathfinder.* Arthur W. Page Society. Retrieved from: https://commtechguide.page.org/getting-startedincommtech-from-professional-to-pathfinder/a-new-profession-emerges/

Janz, N. K., & Becker, M. H. (1984). The Health Belief Model: A decade later. *Health Education Quarterly*, *11*(1), 1–47. doi:10.1177/109019818401100101 PMID:6392204

Javornik, A., Filieri, R., & Gumann, R. (2020). "Don't Forget that Others Are Watching, Too!" The Effect of Conversational Human Voice and Reply Length on Observers' Perceptions of Complaint Handling in Social Media. *Journal of Interactive Marketing*, *50*, 100–119. doi:10.1016/j.intmar.2020.02.002

Jenkins, H. (2006). *Confronting the challenges of participatory culture: Media education for the 21st century*. The MacArthur Foundation. Retrieved from http://digitallearning.macfound.org/atf/cf/%7B7E45C7E0-A3E0-4B89-AC9C-E807E1B0AE4E%7D/JENKINS_WHITE_PAPER.PDF

Jenkins, H. (2006). *Cultura da Convergência* [Convergence Culture] (2nd ed.). *Aleph.*

Jenkins, H. (2015). *A cultura da convergência* [The culture of convergence]. Ed. Aleph.

Jenkins, H. (2016). *Convergence Culture - Where Old and New Media Collide*. University Press.

Jesus, A. (2019, March 21). A evolução da Plataforma Twitter em imagens e vídeos [The evolution of the Twitter Platform in images and videos]. *Techtudo*. Retrieved 05 November 2021, from https://www.techtudo.com.br/noticias/2012/03/evolucao-da-plataforma-do-twitter-em-imagens-e-videos.ghtml

Jewitt, C. (2009). *The Routledge Book of Multimodal Analysis*. Routledge.

Jin, Y. (2010). Making sense sensibly in crisis communication: How publics' crisis appraisals influence their negative emotions, coping strategy preferences, and crisis response acceptance. *Communication Research*, *37*(4), 522–552. doi:10.1177/0093650210368256

Jin, Y., van der Meer, T. G., Lee, Y. I., & Lu, X. (2020). The Effects of Corrective Communication and Employee Backup on the Effectiveness of Fighting Crisis Misinformation. *Public Relations Review*, *46*(3), 101910. doi:10.1016/j.pubrev.2020.101910

Jolliffe, D., & Farrington, D. P. (2006). Development and validation of the Basic Empathy Scale. *Journal of Adolescence*, *29*(4), 589–611. doi:10.1016/j.adolescence.2005.08.010 PMID:16198409

Jornal da Record [@jornaldarecord]. (2021). *Daily News from Record*. TikTok. Retrieved from https://www.tiktok.com/@jornaldarecord

Jost, F. (1997). La promesse des genres [The promise of genres]. Réseaux, 81.

Kamenković, S., & Lazarević-Moravčević, M. (2018). Ocena kvaliteta okruženja i njegov uticaj na poslovanje sektora MSPP u Srbiji [Assessment of the quality of the environment and its impact on the business of the SME sector in Serbia]. Institute of Economic Sciences.

Kapoor, K., Tamilmani, K., Nripendra, P., Pushp, P., Yogesh, K., & Sridha, R. (2018). *Advances in Social Media Research: Past, Present and Future*. Available at: https://link.springer.com/article/10.1007%2Fs10796-017-9810-y

Kapsali, M. (2011). Systems thinking in innovation project management: A match that works. *International Journal of Project Management*, *29*(4), 396–407. doi:10.1016/j.ijproman.2011.01.003

Karhawi, I. (2017, May). *Digital influencers: concepts and practices under discussion* [Paper presentation]. XI Brazilian Scientific Congress of Organizational Communication and Public Relations Researchers – Abrapcorp 2017, Belo Horizonte, Brazil. https://www.abrapcorp.org.br/portal/index.php/2011/10/anais-online/

Karhawi, I. (2021). Comunicação organizacional e influenciadores digitais: aproximações e conflitos [Organizational communication and digital influencers: approximations and conflicts]. In Comunicação organizacional: práticas, desafios e perspectivas digitais (pp. 141-153). Summus Editorial.

Karhawi, I. (2020). *From blogger to influencer: Stages of professionalization of the Brazilian fashion blogosphere*. Sulina Publishing House.

Karhawi, I., & Schmitz, D. (2021). Will there be a new post-pandemic digital influence? Four questions for debate. In R. C. Oliveira, D. Christino, & E. V. Machado Jr., (Eds.), *Covid -19 and the communication*. Cegraf UFG.

Kauffman, J. (2012). Hooray for Hollywood? The 2011 Golden Globes and Ricky Gervais' image repair strategies. *Public Relations Review*, *38*(1), 46–50. doi:10.1016/j.pubrev.2011.09.003

Kaufman, D. (2019). *A inteligência artificial irá suplantar a inteligência humana? (Coleção Interrogações)* [Will artificial intelligence supplant human intelligence? (Question Marks Collection)] (Locais do Kindle 178-181). Estação das Letras e Cores. Kindle.

Kaufmann, H. R., Filho, C. G., Silva, C. R., & Monteiro, P. R. (2019). Consumer-brand relationship development in the automotive market: An integrative model. *International Journal of Automotive Technology and Management*, *19*(3/4), 321–340. doi:10.1504/IJATM.2019.10022009

Kavaratzis, M. (2004). *From city marketing to city branding: Towards a theoretical framework for developing city brands. In Place Branding* (Vol. 1). Henry Stewart Publications.

Kaya, B. (2019). *Sosyal medya platformlarında ceo sözcülüğü ve kurumsal kriz iletişimi: Yaşar Holding Krizi'nin sosyal ceo'luk bağlamında incelenmesi* [Ceo spokesperson and corporate crisis communication on social media platforms: Examining the Yasar Holding Crisis in the context of social ceoship] (Doctoral dissertation). Kadir Has University.

Keller, K., & Machado, M. (2006). *Gestão estratégica de marcas* [Strategic brand management]. Person Prentice Hall.

KGW.com. (2018). *Portland DoubleTree apologizes to man who was 'calling his mother while black'*. https://www.kgw.com/article/news/local/portland-doubletree-takes-to-twitter-to-apologize-to-man-who-was-talking-on-the-phone-while-black/283-e6a15aeb-61fe-4ce1-a957-d4eab1beb8e0

Ki, E. J., & Nekmat, E. (2014). Situational crisis communication and interactivity: Usage and effectiveness of Facebook for crisis management by Fortune 500 companies. *Computers in Human Behavior*, *35*, 140–147. doi:10.1016/j.chb.2014.02.039

Kim, I., & Kuljis, J. (2010). Applying Content Analysis to Web based Content. *Proceedings of the ITI 2010 32nd International Conference on Information Technology Interfaces*. Retrieved from: https://www.researchgate.net/publication/220066206_Applying_Content_Analysis_to_Web-based_Content

Kim, A., & Ko, E. (2012). Do social media marketing activities enhance customer equity? An empirical study of luxury fashion brand. *Journal of Business Research*, *65*(10), 1480–1486. doi:10.1016/j.jbusres.2011.10.014

Kim, H. (2014). Enacted social support on social media and subjective well-being. *International Journal of Communication*, *8*, 21.

Kim, S., & Mcgill, A. L. (2011). Gaming with Mr. Slot or Gaming the Slot Machine? Power, Anthropomorphism, and Risk Perception. *The Journal of Consumer Research*, *38*(1), 1–15. doi:10.1086/658148

Kim, S., & Syn, S. (2016). Credibility and usefulness of health information on Facebook: A survey study with U.S. college students. *Information Research*, *21*(4), 1–32.

Kincaid, D. L. (1979). *The convergence Model of Communication*. EastWest Communication Institute.

Kiso, R. [@rkiso]. (2021, August 19). *What kind of content is most authentic?* Instagram. Retrieved from https://www.instagram.com/p/CSwMlSbrJhQ/?utm_medium=share_sheet

Kitchin, P. J., Paramio-Salcines, J. L., & Walters, G. (2020). Managing organizational reputation in response to a public shaming campaign. *Sport Management Review*, *23*(1), 66–80. doi:10.1016/j.smr.2019.03.009

Kite, J., McGill, B., Freeman, B., Vineburg, J., Li, V., Berton, N., & Grunseit, A. (2018). User Perceptions of the Make Healthy Normal campaign Facebook Page: A Mixed Methods Study. *Social Media + Society*, *4*(July-September), 1–17. doi:10.1177/2056305118794639

Kivimaki, M., Länsisalmi, H., Elovainio, M., Heikkilä, A., Lindström, K., Harisalo, R., Sipilä, K., & Puolimatka, L. (2000). Communication as a determinant of organizational innovation. *R & D Management*, *30*(1), 33–42. doi:10.1111/1467-9310.00155

KLM [@klm]. (2021, February 24). *Blue Crew* [video]. Instagram. Retrieved from https://www.instagram.com/p/CLq1fYpFz6g/

Kniazeva, M., & Belk, R. W. (2010). If This Brand Were a Person, or Anthropomorphism of Brands Through Packaging Stories. *Journal of the Academy of Marketing Science*, *20*(3), 231–238.

Koch, T., Obermaier, M., & Riesmeyer, C. (2017). Powered by public relations? Mutual perceptions of PR practitioners' bases of power over journalism. *Journalism*, 1–17. doi:10.1177/1464884917726421

Koch, T., Viererbl, B., & Schulz-Knappe, C. (2021). How much journalism is in brand journalism? How brand journalists perceive their roles and blur the boundaries between journalism and strategic communication. *Journalism*. Advance online publication. doi:10.1177/14648849211029802

Kotler, P., & Keller, K. (2006). Marketing de lugares [Seat Marketing]. In Como conquistar crescimento de longo prazo na América Latina e no Caribe. São Paulo: Prentice Hall.

Kotler, P. (2000). *Marketing Management, Millenium Edition*. Pearson Custom Publishing.

Kotler, P., Hermawan, K., & Setiawan, I. (2016). *Marketing 4.0: Moving from Traditional to Digital*. Wiley.

Kotler, P., Kartajaya, H., & Setiawan, I. (2016). *Marketing 3.0: Do produto e do consumidor até ao espírito humano* [Marketing 3.0: From product and consumer to the human spirit]. Actual.

Kotler, P., Kartajaya, H., & Setiawan, I. (2017). *Marketing 4.0: Do tradicional ao Digital* [Marketing 4.0: From traditional to digital]. Sextante Editora.

Kotler, P., Kartajaya, H., & Setiawan, I. (2017). *Marketing 4.0: Mudança do Tradicional para o Digital* [Marketing 4.0: Moving from Traditional to Digital]. Conjuntura Actual Editora.

Kotler, P., & Keller, K. L. (2012). *Administração de Marketing* (14th ed.). Pearson Education.

Kotler, P., & Lee, N. R. (2011). *Social Marketing: Changing Behaviors for Good.* SAGE Publications.

Kowal, E. (2021). What Is an Online Newsroom & Why Do You Need One*? Prowly Magazine*. Retrieved from: https://prowly.com/magazine/need-online-newsroom/

Kramp. (2015). *Journalism, representation and the Public Sphere*. Bremen: Edition lumière.

Kreps, G. (2012a). Translating health communication research into practice: The importance of implementing and sustaining evidence-based health communication interventions. *Atlantic Journal of Communication*, *20*(1), 5–15. doi:10.1080/15456870.2012.637024

Kreps, G. (2012b). The maturation of health communication inquiry: Directions for future development and growth. *Journal of Health Communication*, *17*(5), 495–497. doi:10.1080/10810730.2012.685802 PMID:22571837

Kreps, G. (2017). The relevance of health literacy to mHealth. *Information Services & Use*, *37*(2), 123–130. doi:10.3233/ISU-170828 PMID:28972527

Krippendorff, K. (2013). *Content Analysis. An Introduction to its Methodology*. Sage.

Kristoffersen, L., & Singh, S. (2004). Successful application of a customer relationship management program in a nonprofit organization. *Journal of Marketing Theory and Practice*, *12*(2), 28–42. doi:10.1080/10696679.2004.11658517

Krstić, A., & Đurđević, B. (2017). Marketing na društvenim mrežama [Social media marketing]. *Marketing*, *48*(4), 254–260.

Krums, J. (2001, September 11). *Post on TwitPic*. Retrieved 10 August, 2021, from https://twitpic.com/135xa

Kullin, H. (2009, January 16). *Social media in the Hudson River plane crash.* Retrieved 10 August, 2021, from https://www.socialmediatoday.com/content/social-media-hudson-river-plane-crash

Kumari, K. (2021). Impact of digital marketing during pandemic period with special reference to north Chennai city. *Turkish Journal of Physiotherapy and Rehabilitation*, *32*(3), 17357-17368.

Kunsch, M. (2018). A comunicação estratégica nas organizações contemporâneas [Strategic communication in contemporary organisations]. Media & Jornalismo, 33, 13-24. doi:10.14195/2183-5462_33_1

Kunsch, M., & Krohling, M. (Org.). (2009). Comunicação organizacional [Organisational communication] (vol. 2). São Paulo: Editora Saraiva.

Kunsch, M. M. K. (2003). *Public relations planning in integrated communications*. Summus Publishing House.

Kunsch, M. M. K. (2016). Prefácio. In M. M. K. Kunsch (Ed.), *Comunicação organizacional estratégica: aportes, conceitos e aplicados* [Strategic organizational communication: contributions, concepts and applied] (pp. 9–13). Summus Editorial.

Kunsch, M. M. K. (2016). *Strategic organizational communication: conceptual and applied contributions*. Summus Publishing House.

L'Etang, J. (2008). Public Relations – Concepts, Practice and Critique. *Sage (Atlanta, Ga.)*.

La Nación [@lanacioncom]. (2021). *La Nación*. TikTok. Retrieved from https://www.tiktok.com/@lanacioncom?lang=pt-BR

Lai, I. K. W. (2019). Hotel image and reputation on building customer loyalty: An empirical study in Macau. *Journal of Hospitality and Tourism Management*, *38*, 111–121. doi:10.1016/j.jhtm.2019.01.003

Lallement, J., Dejean, S., Euzéby, F., & Martinez, C. (2020). The interaction between reputation and information search: Evidence of information avoidance and confirmation bias. *Journal of Retailing and Consumer Services*, *53*, 101787. doi:10.1016/j.jretconser.2019.03.014

Landow, G. P. (2006). *Hypertext 3.0: Critical theory and new media in an era of globalization*. JHU Press.

Langer, E. (2014, January 15). *The five-year anniversary of Twitter's defining moment.* CNBC. Retrieved 10 August, 2021, from https://www.cnbc.com/2014/01/15/the-five-year-anniversary-of-twitters-defining-moment.html

Latour, B. (2012). *Reagregando o social. Uma introdução à teoria do ator-rede* [Reaggregating the social. An introduction to actor-network theory]. Edufba.

Lauro, S., Tursunbayeva, A., & Antonelli, G. (2019). How Nonprofit Organizations Use Social Media for Fundraising: A Systematic Literature Review. *International Journal of Business and Management*, *14*(7), 1–22. doi:10.5539/ijbm.v14n7p1

Lazarević-Moravčević, E. D., & Kamenković, S. (2018). Uticaj poslovnog okruženja na performanse sektora MSPP u Srbiji [The impact of the business environment on the performance of the SME sector in Serbia]. *Business Economics (Cleveland, Ohio)*, *12*(1), 33–53.

Lazarević-Moravčević, M., Lazić, M., & Kaličanin, T. (2019). Primena marketing koncepta u malim preduzećima [Application of marketing concept in small businesses]. *International Scientific Conference: Challenges of modern marketing*, 242-249.

Lazarević-Moravčević, M. (2019). Characteristics of marketing communication strategy of a small enterprise. *Economic Analysis*, *2*, 104–112.

Lazarević-Moravčević, M., Domazet, I., & Lazić, M. (2021). Characteristics of Market Communication in Modern Business. *Proceedings of the 26th International Scientific Conference Strategic Management and Decision Support Systems in Strategic Management*, 142-149. 10.46541/978-86-7233-397-8_134

Lazarus, J. V., Ratzan, S. C., Palayew, A., Gostin, L. O., Larson, H. J., Rabin, K., & El-Mohandes, A. (2021). A global survey of potential acceptance of a COVID-19 vaccine. *Nature Medicine*, *27*(2), 225–228. doi:10.103841591-020-1124-9 PMID:33082575

Le Monde [@lemondefr]. (2021). *Le Monde*. TikTok. Retrieved from https://www.tiktok.com/@lemondefr?lang=pt-BR

Lee, E.-J. (2016). Empathy can increase customer equity related to pro-social brands. *Journal of Business Research*, *69*(9), 3748–3754. doi:10.1016/j.jbusres.2015.05.018

Lee, Y., & Kim, K. H. (2020). De-motivating employees' negative communication behaviors on anonymous social media: The role of public relations. *Public Relations Review*, *46*(4), 101955. doi:10.1016/j.pubrev.2020.101955

Lefebvre, C. (2011). An integrative model for social marketing. *Journal of Social Marketing*, *1*(1), 54–72. doi:10.1108/20426761111104437

Lefebvre, C. (2012). Transformative social marketing: Co-creating the social marketing discipline and brand. *Journal of Social Marketing*, *2*(2), 118–129. doi:10.1108/20426761211243955

LegoMBrinq. (2021). *Fãs da marca Lego* Retrieved from https://www.legombrinq.com.br/fas

Lemon, K. N., & Verhoef, P. C. (2016). Understanding customer experience throughout the customer journey. *Journal of Marketing*, *80*(6), 69–96. doi:10.1509/jm.15.0420

Lemos, A. (2013). *A comunicação das coisas. Teoria ator-rede e cibercultura* [The communication of things. Actor-network theory and cyberculture]. Annablume.

Lemos, A. (2021). *A tecnologia é um virus* [Technology is a Virus]. Editora Sulina.

Leskovec, J., Backstrom, L., & Kleinberg, J. (2009, June). Meme-tracking and the dynamics of the news cycle. In *Proceedings of the 15th ACM SIGKDD international conference on Knowledge discovery and data mining* (pp. 497-506). 10.1145/1557019.1557077

Levinson, J. C. (2009). *Gerila Marketing – jednostavne i jeftine strategije za ostvarivanje velikog profita od vašeg malog biznisa* [Guerrilla Marketing - Simple And Cheap Strategies To Make Big Profits From Your Small Business]. IPS Media.

Lévy, P. (2019). Collective Intelligence, the Future of Internet and the IEML. *Humanist Studies & the Digital Age*, *6*(1), 6-31. Available at: http://journals.oregondigital.org/index.php/hsda/article/view/4620/4513

Lévy, P. (1990). *As Tecnologias da Inteligência - O Futuro do Pensamento na Era da Informática* [Intelligence Technologies - The Future of Thinking in the Information Age]. Instituto Piaget.

Lezotte, C. (2014). Automotive knowledge, auto activism, and women's online car advice. *Feminist Media Studies*, 691–706.

Li, C. (2019). *The Disruption Mindset: Why Some Organizations Transform While Others Fail Hardcover*. Ideapress Publishing.

Lil Miquela [@lilmiquela]. (2021, October 9). *Instagram*. Retrieved 09 October, 2021, from https://www.instagram.com/lilmiquela/?hl=pt-br

Lindon, D., Lendrevie, J., Lévy, J., Dionísio, P., & Rodrigues, J. V. (2004). *Mercator XXI: Teoria e Prática do Marketing* (10th ed.). Dom Quixote.

Lindon, D., Lendrevie, J., Lévy, J., Dionísio, P., & Rodrigues, V. (2018). *Teoria e Prática do Marketing*. Lisboa: D. Quixote.

Linke, A., & Zerfass, A. (2011). Internal communication and innovation culture: Developing a change framework. *Journal of Communication Management (London)*, *15*(4), 332–348. doi:10.1108/13632541111183361

Lipäinen, H. S. M., Karjaluoto, H. E., & Nevalainen, M. (2014). Digital channels in the internal communication of a multinational corporation. *Corporate Communications: An International Journal of Business and Management*, *19*(3), 275–286. doi:10.1108/CCIJ-07-2012-0050

Lister, M. (2009). *New Media: a critical introduction* (2nd ed.). Routledge.

Lloyd, J., & Toogood, L. (2015). *Journalism and PR. News media and public relations in the digital age. Reuters Institute for the Study of Journalism*. Oxford University.

Logomyway. (2020). *Redesign the BP logo*. https://www.logomyway.com/1746/friends/BP_(Logo_Redesign_Contest).php.Access

Lopes, M. (2004). *As fronteiras entre as ciências sociais vistas da comunicação. Uma aproximação aos estudos sociais das ciências* [The boundaries between the social sciences as seen from communication. An approach to social science studies]. http://www.compos.org.br/e-compos

Loureiro, S. M. C., & González, F. J. M. (2008). The importance of quality, satisfaction, trust, and image in relation to rural tourist loyalty. *Journal of Travel & Tourism Marketing*, *25*(2), 117–136. doi:10.1080/10548400802402321

Loureiro, S. M., & Lopes, R. (2012). Brand Credibility And Self-Brand Connection As Drivers To Cool Brands. *Global Marketing Conference*, (pp. 1551-1569). Academic Press.

Lovelock, C., & Jochen, W. (2011). *Understanding Digital Marketing*. Kogan Page Limited.

Lovelock, C., & Wirtz, J. (2009). *Service Marketing: people, technology, and strategy*. Pearson.

Lowry, P. B., Zhang, J., Wang, C., & Siponen, M. (2016). Why do adults engage in cyberbullying on social media? An integration of online disinhibition and deindividuation effects with the social structure and social learning model. *Information Systems Research*, *27*(4), 962–986. doi:10.1287/isre.2016.0671

Lukaszewski, J. E. (2013). *Lukaszewski on crisis communication: What your CEO needs to know about reputation risk and crisis management*. Rothstein Publishing.

Lupu, C. (2021). *Journalism: An obstacle race, with fewer and fewer winners*. Center for Independent Journalism.

Lyon, T. P., & Montgomery, A. W. (2013). Tweetjacked: The impact of social media on corporate greenwash. *Journal of Business Ethics*, *118*(4), 747–757. doi:10.100710551-013-1958-x

Lywood, J., Stone, M., & Ekinci, Y. (2009). Customer experience and profitability: An application of the empathy rating index (ERIC) in UK call centres. *Database Marketing & Customer Strategy Management*, *16*(3), 207–214. doi:10.1057/dbm.2009.24

Machado, A. T., Antunes, A. C., & Miranda, S. (2016). *Marketing social através de campanhas de comunicação: o caso da Associação Portuguesa de Apoio à Vítima (APAV)* [Social marketing through communication campaigns: the case of the Portuguese Association for Victim Support]. Revista Portuguesa de Marketing.

MacInnis, D. J., & Folkes, V. S. (2017). Humanizing brands: When brands seem to be like me, part of me, and in a relationship with me. *Journal of Consumer Psychology*, *27*(3), 355–374. doi:10.1016/j.jcps.2016.12.003

Macnamara, J. (2016). The Continuing Convergence of Journalism and PR: New Insights for Ethical Practice from a Three-Country Study of Senior Practitioners. *Journalism & Mass Communication Quarterly*, *93*(1), 118–141.

Macnamara, J. (2020). Journalism, Public Relations and Spin. In K. Wahl-Jorgensen & T. Hanitzsch (Eds.), *The Handbook of Journalism Studies* (2nd ed., pp. 341–355). Routledge.

Macy's. (2021). *Macy's Style Crew*. Retrieved from https://www.macys.com/style-crew/

Magazine Luiza [@magazineluiza]. (2021). *Magazine Luiza Store*. Instagram. Retrieved from https://www.instagram.com/magazineluiza/

Magrani, E. (2019). *Entre dados e robôs* [Between data and robots]. Arquipelago Editorial Ltda.

Maia, B. (2021, June 9). A importância do analytics na crise da Covid-19. [The importance of analytics in the Covid-19 crisis]. *MIT Sloan Management Review*. Retrieved 10 August, 2021, from https://www.mitsloanreview.com.br/post/a-importancia-do-analytics-na-crise-da-covid-19

Maia, R. C. M. (2003). Dos dilemas da visibilidade midiática para a deliberação política [From the dilemmas of media visibility to political deliberation]. In *Anais da XII Reunião Anual da Associação de Pós-graduação em comunicação – Compós* (v. 1, pp. 1-22). http://www.compos.org.br/data/biblioteca_937.pdf

Mainguenau, D. (2001). *Análise de textos de comunicação* [Analysis of communication texts.]. Cortez.

Malte, A. (2013). The communication of innovation: an empirical analysis of the advancement of innovation. *Discussion Papers on Strategy and Innovation*, 1-29.

Manovich, L. (2002). *The language of new media*. MIT Press.

Marangoni, S. M. (2015). *Marketing de Serviços* [Services Marketing]. Estácio.

Marketing Mreža. (2017). Available at: https://marketingmreza.rs/svega-25-srednjih-malih-preduzeca-ima-osobu-zaduzenu-samo-za-marketing/

Marktest. (2019). *Redes sociais: números e tendências* [Social networks: numbers and trends]. Available at: https://www.marktest.com/wap/a/n/id~25a8.aspx

Martínez, A. M., Monserrat, J. M., & Campillo, A. C. (2017). El paradigma relacional en las estrategias de las organizaciones de marketing de destinos: Interactividad y función social en las webs turísticas oficiales. *Revista Latina de Comunicación Social*, *4*(72), 374–396.

Martins, O., Dourado, M., Paço, A., Mainardes, E. W., & Rodrigues, R. G. (2014). O marketing social e a promoção de mudanças estruturais no aleitamento materno [Social marketing and the promotion of structural changes in breastfeeding]. *Revista de Administração de Empresas*, *54*(4), 370–380. doi:10.1590/S0034-759020140403

Martynova, M., & Renneboog, L. (2008). A century of corporate takeovers: What have we learned and where do we stand? *Journal of Banking & Finance*, *32*(10), 2148–2177. doi:10.1016/j.jbankfin.2007.12.038

Marwick, A. E. (2013). *Status update: Celebrity, publicity, and branding in the social media age*. Yale University Press.

Maung, M., Wilson, C., & Yu, W. (2020). Does Reputation Risk Matter? Evidence from Cross-Border Mergers and Acquisitions. *Journal of International Financial Markets, Institutions and Money*, *66*, 101204. doi:10.1016/j.intfin.2020.101204

Mayer-Schoenberger, V., & Cukier, K. (2013). *Big data.* Campus Publishing House.

Mayer-Schoenberger, V., & Cukier, K. (2013). *Big data: como extrair volume, variedade, velocidade e valor da avalanche da informação cotidiana* [Big data: how to extract volume, variety, speed and value from the avalanche of everyday information]. Editora Campus.

McCartney, W. W., & Campbell, C. R. (2006). Leadership, management, and derailment. *Leadership and Organization Development Journal*, *27*(3), 190–202. doi:10.1108/01437730610657712

Mehrabian, A., & Epstein, N. (1972). A measure of emotional empathy. *Journal of Personality*, *40*(4), 525–543. doi:10.1111/j.1467-6494.1972.tb00078.x PMID:4642390

Meira, P., & Santos, C. (2012). Programas de marketing social: Proposição e exame de uma estrutura conceitual de avaliação de resultados [Social marketing programmes: proposing and examining a conceptual framework for outcome evaluation]. *Revista de Administração Pública*, *46*(2), 493–522. doi:10.1590/S0034-76122012000200008

Melo, F., Gotardo, A., & Freitas, R. (2019). A (re)construção da Marca Rio e seus discursos: medo, comunicação e megaeventos [The (re)construction of the Rio Brand and its discourses: fear, communication and mega events]. In *Congresso Brasileiro Científico de Comunicação Organizacional e de Relações Públicas*. Abrapcorp. Disponível: https://portal.abrapcorp.org.br/anais-abrapcorp/2019/

Meng, S. M., Liang, G. S., & Yang, S. H. (2011). The relationships of cruise image, perceived value, satisfaction, and post-purchase behavioral intention on Taiwanese tourists. *African Journal of Business Management*, *5*(1), 19–29.

Men, L. R. (2014). Strategic Internal Communication: Transformational Leadership, Communication Channels, and Employee Satisfaction. *Management Communication Quarterly*, *28*(2), 264–284. doi:10.1177/0893318914524536

Men, L. R. (2015). The internal communication role of the chief executive officer: Communication channels, style, and effectiveness. *Public Relations Review*, *41*(4), 461–471. doi:10.1016/j.pubrev.2015.06.021

Men, L. R., & Bowen, S. A. (2017). *Excellence in internal communication management.* Business Expert Press.

Mercer, S. W., & Reynolds, W. J. (2002). Empathy and quality of care. *The British Journal of General Practice, 52,* S9–S12. PMID:12389763

Mesquita, K., Ruão, T., & Andrade, J. G. (2020, December). Transformações da comunicação organizacional: novas práticas e desafios nas mídias sociais. Dinâmicas comunicativas e transformações sociais [Transformations of organizational communication: new practices and challenges in social media. Communicative dynamics and social transformations]. In *Atas das VII Jornadas Doutorais em Comunicação & Estudos Culturais.* CECS – Centro de Estudos de Comunicação e Sociedade Universidade do Minho Braga. Retrieved 10 August, 2021, from http://www.lasics.uminho.pt/ojs/index.php/cecs_ebooks/article/view/3301/3190

Michaelson, D., & Stacks, D. (2010). *A Professional and Practitioner's Guide to Public Relations Research, Measurement, and Evaluation.* New York: Business Expert Press.

Middleberg, D. (2001). *Winning PR in the Wired World.* New York: McGraw-Hill.

Mihăilă, V. (2017). The changing nature of innovation-based social marketing programs: The case of health promotion programs. *Manager Journal, 25*(1), 176–184.

Mikulaskova, J., Harsanyova, P., & Cambal, M. (2016). Internet Marketing as a Tool of Desirable Corporate Culture. *Proceedings of the European Conference on Intellectual Capital, İtalya.*

Ministerio de Salud Pública – Uruguay [@MSPURUGUAY]. (2021g, January 5). *En comparencia ante la Comisión de Salud Pública del @SenadoUy, el ministro @DrDanielSalinas explicó el trabajo realizado desde marzo hasta la fecha* [In appearance before the Public Health Commission of the @SenadoUy, the Minister @DrDanielSalinas explained the work carried out from March to date] [Image attached] [Tweet]. Twitter. https://twitter.com/MSPUruguay/status/1346539663104888833

Ministerio de Salud Pública - Uruguay [@MSPURUGUAY]. (2021h, February 25). *A las 23:07 hs arribaron las primeras dosis de vacunas del Laboratorio Sinovac. Funcionarios del MSP y del Laboratorio Calmette...* [At 11:07 p.m. the first doses of vaccines arrived from the Sinovac Laboratory. Officials of the MSP and the Calmette Laboratory...] [Image attached] [Tweet]. Twitter. https://twitter.com/MSPUruguay/status/1365132134697082880

Ministerio de Salud Pública - Uruguay. (2021a). *Plan de Vacunación Covid-19* [Covid-19 Vaccination Plan]. https://www.gub.uy/uruguaysevacuna

Ministerio de Salud Pública - Uruguay. (2021b, March 1). *Plan de vacunación contra COVID-19: Responsabilidad cívica y solidaria* [Vaccination Plan Against Covid-19: Civil Responsibility and Solidarity]. https://www.gub.uy/ministerio-salud-publica/comunicacion/noticias/plan-vacunacion-contra-covid-19-responsabilidad-civica-solidaria

Ministerio de Salud Pública - Uruguay. (2021c, May 27). *Estudio sobre efectividad vacunal* [Study of Vaccine Effectiveness]. https://www.gub.uy/ministerio-salud-publica/comunicacion/noticias/estan-disponibles-datos-preliminares-del-estudio-efectividad-vacunal

Ministerio de Salud Pública - Uruguay. (2021d, July 12). *Ciencia en clave de fútbol* [Science in football key]. https://www.gub.uy/ministerio-salud-publica/comunicacion/noticias/campana-efectividad-vacunal-ciencia-clave-futbol

Ministerio de Salud Pública - Uruguay. (2021e, October 25). *Informe epidemiológico COVID-19 Actualización al 25 de octubre de 2021* [COVID-19 Epidemiological Report Update as of October 25, 2021]. https://www.gub.uy/ministerio-salud-publica/comunicacion/noticias/informe-epidemiologico-covid-19-actualizado-18-enero-2021

Ministerio de Salud Pública - Uruguay. (2021f, November 1). *Monitor de datos de vacunación Covid-19* [Covid-19 Vaccination Data Monitor]. https://monitor.uruguaysevacuna.gub.uy/

Ministerio de Salud Pública - Uruguay. (2021i, February 26). *Campaña de vacunación COVID-19* [Covid-19 Vaccination Campaign] #UruguaySeVacuna. [Videos]. YouTube. https://www.youtube.com/playlist?list=PL4O9exeLSKwyeofFVi_3x3Vqcl1gZ-6Qa

Ministry of Economy. (2020). *Report on small and medium enterprises and entrepreneurs.* Available at: https://privreda.gov.rs/wp-content/uploads/2021/05/Izvestaj-MSPP-2018_FIN.pdf

Miquel-Romero, M. J., Caplliure-Giner, E. M., & Adame-Sánchez, C. (2014). Relationship marketing management: Its importance in private label extension. *Journal of Business Research, 67*(5), 667–672. doi:10.1016/j.jbusres.2013.11.025

Miranda criticó la lentitud del gobierno y dijo que es necesario tomar medidas urgentes. El presidente del Frente Amplio dijo además que el partido tiene numerosos vínculos para acelerar la llegada de la vacuna si es necesario [Miranda criticized the government's slowness and said urgent action is needed. The president of the Frente Amplio also said that the party has numerous links to accelerate the arrival of the vaccine if necessary]. (2021, December 14). *El País.* https://www.elpais.com.uy/informacion/politica/miranda-critico-lentitud-gobierno-dijo-necesario-tomar-medidas-urgentes.html

Moloney, K. (2000). *Rethinking Public Relations: The Spin and the Substance*. Routledge.

Moneycnn.com. (2017). *United loses $250 million of its market value.* https://money.cnn.com/2017/04/11/investing/united-airlines-stock-passenger-flight-video/

Monllos, K. (2019, August 5). 1 year in, IPG attributes growth and new business wins to Acxiom acquisition. *Digiday.* Retrieved 05 November 2021, from https://digiday.com/marketing/one-year-ipg-attributes-growth-new-business-wins-acxiom-acquisition/

Montagni, I., Ouazzani-Touhami, K., Mebarki, A., Texier, N., Schück, S., & Tzourio, C. (2021). Acceptance of a Covid-19 vaccine is associated with ability to detect fake news and health literacy. Journal of Public Health. *Journal of Public Health, 43*(4), 695–702. Advance online publication. doi:10.1093/pubmed/fdab028 PMID:33693905

Mooradian, T. A., Matzler, K., & Szykman, L. (2008). Empathetic responses to advertising: Testing a network of antecedents and consequences. *Marketing Letters, 19*(2), 79–92. doi:10.100711002-008-9032-7

Moravcikova, D., & Kliestikova, J. (2017). *Brand Building with Using Phygital Marketing Communication.* Retrieved from https://bit.ly/2pcQgJ3

Moreira, A. (2020). Rio Media Center: comunicação e produção de sentidos sobre a Cidade Olímpica [Rio Media Center: communication and production of meaning about the Olympic City]. In *Congresso Brasileiro Científico de Comunicação Organizacional e de Relações Públicas.* Abrapcorp. Disponível: http://portal.abrapcorp2.org.br/anais-abrapcorp/2020/gts.php/

Moreira, S. (2009). Análise documental como método e como técnica [Documentary analysis as method and as technique]. In *Métodos e técnicas de pesquisa em comunicação.* Atlas.

Moreno, A. R., & Peres, F. (2020). Comunicación de riesgos ante el Coronavirus [Communication risks in the face of the Coronavirus]. *Boletín sobre COVID-19, 1*(4), 7-9.

Morin, C. (2011). Neuromarketing: The New Science of Consumer Behavior. *Society, 48*(2), 131–135. doi:10.100712115-010-9408-1

Morris, T., & Goldsworthy, S. (2012). *PR Today – the authoritative guide to public relations.* Palgrave Macmillan.

Moya, M. (2000). Persuasión y cambio de actitudes [Persuasion and change of attitudes]. *Psicologia e Sociedade*, 153–170.

Munns, A. K., & Bjeirmi, B. F. (1996). The role of project management in achieving project success. *International Journal of Project Management, 14*(2), 81–88. doi:10.1016/0263-7863(95)00057-7

Nancy, R., Michael, L., & William, S. (2011). *A Declaration of Social Marketing*. Sage Publications.

Nawi, N., Ghani, N., Abdullah, A., Alareeni, B., & Deraman, N., Hasan, M., & Zaato, S. (2021). Social Media Marketing to Enhance Customer Equity on Fashion Apparel Brand among University Students. *Journal of Information Technology Management, 13*(2), 75–92.

Nelson-Field, K., Riebe, E., & Newstead, K. (2013). The emotions that drive viral video. *Australasian Marketing Journal, 21*(4), 205–211. doi:10.1016/j.ausmj.2013.07.003

Neri, A. (2021, June). *Digital Culture Guidebook*. World Economic Forum. Retrieved from: https://www3.weforum.org/docs/WEF_Digital_Culture_Guidebook_2021.pdf

Nespereira, J. (2014). *Estrategias discursivas en la comunicación de crisis sanitarias (retórica y teoría de la argumentación): el caso de la gripe A en 2009* [Discursive strategies in the communication of health crises (rhetoric and theory of argumentation): the case of influenza A in 2009]. (Doctoral dissertation, Universidad de Valladolid). Teseo. https://www.educacion.gob.es/teseo/mostrarSeleccion.do

Neto, B. (2019). Newsroom 3.0: Managing Technological and Media Convergence in Contemporary Newsrooms. *Proceedings of the 52nd Hawaii International Conference on System Sciences*. Retrieved from: https://www.researchgate.net/publication/330467967_Newsroom_30_Managing_Technological_and_Media_Convergence_in_Contemporary_Newsrooms

Neumann, D. L., Chan, R. C., Boyle, G. J., Wang, Y., & Westbury, H. R. (2015). Measures of Empathy: Self-Report, Behavioral, and Neuroscientific Approaches. In Measures of Personality and Social Psychological Constructs (pp. 257-289). Academic Press.

Newman, D. (2017, June 6). How Shifting Communication Trends Are Impacting Digital Transformation. *Forbes*. Retrieved from: https://www.forbes.com/sites/danielnewman/2017/06/06/how-shifting-communication-trends-are-impacting-digital-transformation/#12a070b3408f

Nielsen, R., & Selva, M. (2019). *More Important, But Less Robust? Five Things Everybody Needs to Know about the Future of Journalism*. Reuters Institute Report. Retrieved from: https://reutersinstitute.politics.ox.ac.uk/our-research/more-important-less-robust-five-things-everybody-needs-know-about-future-journalism

Ningrum, K., & Roostika, R. (2021). The influence of social media marketing activities on consumer engagement and brand knowledge in the culinary business in Indonesia. *International Journal of Research in Business and Social Science, 10*(5), 34–45. doi:10.20525/ijrbs.v10i5.1314

Noonoouri [@noonoouri]. (2021, October 9). *Instagram*. https://www.instagram.com/noonoouri/?hl=pt-br

Novelli, A. (2006). O papel institucional da Comunicação Pública para o sucesso da governança [The institutional role of Public Communication for successful governance]. *Organicom,* 4.

Nutbeam, D. (2000). Health literacy as a public health goal: A challenge for contemporary health education and communication strategies into the 21st century. *Health Promotion International, 15*(3), 259–267. doi:10.1093/heapro/15.3.259

Obradović, M., Alčaković, S., & Pavlović, O. (2018). Effective Use of E-Mail Marketing on Example of Small and Medium-Sized Enterprises in Serbia. *Proceedings of the International Scientific Conference on Information Technology and Data Related Research – SINTEZA 2018*, 79-84. 10.15308/Sinteza-2018-79-84

Ognjanov, G. (2013). Integrisane marketinške komunikacije [Integrated marketing communications]. Faculty of Economics.

Oliveira, I. L., & Paula, M. A. (2007). *O que é comunicação estratégica nas organizações* [What is strategic communication in organizations]. Paulus.

Oliveira, T. M. V. (2001). Amostragem não Probabilística: Adequação de Situações para uso e Limitações de amostras por Conveniência, Julgamento e Quotas [Non-Probability Sampling: Suitability of Contexts for Use and Limitations of Convenience, Judgmental and Quota Sampling]. *Administração Online*, *2*(3), 1–7.

Oprena, A., & Vinerean, S. (2015). A New Development in Online Marketing: Introducing Digital Inbound Marketing. *Expert Journal of Marketing*, *3*(1), 29–34.

Oreo Academy. (2021). *What is the Oreo Academy?* Retrieved from https://www.oreoacademy.es/oreo-academy.php

Osakwe, C. N., Ruiz, B., Amegbe, H., Chinje, N. B., Cheah, J. H., & Ramayah, T. (2020). A multi-country study of bank reputation among customers in Africa: Key antecedents and consequences. *Journal of Retailing and Consumer Services*, *56*, 102182. doi:10.1016/j.jretconser.2020.102182

Ott, L., & Theunissen, P. (2015). Reputations at risk: Engagement during social media crises. *Public Relations Review*, *41*(1), 97–102. doi:10.1016/j.pubrev.2014.10.015

Ozaeta, D. E. L., & An, I. L. (2014). Use of Internal Communication Tools among AG&P Employees. *Journal of Education and Literature*, *1*(1), 20–30.

Pace, K. M., Fediuk, T. A., & Botero, I. C. (2010). The acceptance of responsibility and expressions of regret in organizational apologies after a transgression. *Corporate Communications*, *15*(4), 410–427. doi:10.1108/13563281011085510

Palmatier, R. W., Dant, R. P., Grewal, D., & Evans, K. R. (2006). Factors influencing the effectiveness of relationship marketing: A meta-analysis. *Journal of Marketing*, *70*(4), 136–153. doi:10.1509/jmkg.70.4.136

Pan American Health Organization. (2021). *Guía para elaborar una estrategia de comunicación de riesgos sobre las vacunas contra la COVID-19* [Guide to developing a risk communication strategy on COVID-19 vaccines]. https://iris.paho.org/handle/10665.2/53259

Papacharissi, Z. (2012). Without you, I'm nothing: Performances of the self on Twitter. *International Journal of Communication*, *6*, 18.

Parasuraman, A., & Grewal, D. (2000). The Impact of Technology on the Quality-Value-Loyalty Chain: A Research Agenda. *Journal of the Academy of Marketing Science*, *28*(1), 168–174. doi:10.1177/0092070300281015

Pardes, A. (2020, December 16). The future of social media is all talk. *Wired*. Retrieved 10 August, 2021, from https://www.wired.com/story/the-future-of-social-media-is-all-talk/

Pariser, E. (2011). *O filtro invisível* [The invisible filter]. Jorge Zahar Editor. Kindle.

Parker, R., & Ratzan, S. C. (2010). Health literacy: A second decade of distinction for Americans. *Journal of Health Communication*, *15*(sup2, S2), 20–33. doi:10.1080/10810730.2010.501094 PMID:20845190

Parvatiyar, A., & Sheth, J. (2001). Customer relationship management: Emerging practice, process, and discipline. *Journal of Economic and Social Research*, *3*(2), 1–34.

Paul, A. (2016). *Forța economică a femeilor* [The economic force of women]. Polirom.

Payot. (2021). *Boca Rosa by Payot*. Retrieved from https://www.lojapayot.com.br/bia%20todo%20dia?utm_source=Google&utm_medium=cpc&utm_campaign=lancamento-bia-todo-dia

Peattie, K., & Peattie, S. (2009). Social marketing: A pathway to consumption reduction. *Journal of Business Research*, *62*(2), 260–268. doi:10.1016/j.jbusres.2008.01.033

Peiser, J. (2019, February 5). The rise of the robot reporter. *The New York Times*. Retrieved 10 August, 2021, from https://www.nytimes.com/2019/02/05/business/media/artificial-intelligence-journalism-robots.html

Péninou, G. (1976). *Semiótica de la publicidade* [Semiotics of advertising]. Editorial Gustavo Gili.

Pennycook, G., & Rand, D. G. (2021, May). The Psychology of Fake News. *Trends in Cognitive Sciences*, *25*(5), 388–402. doi:10.1016/j.tics.2021.02.007 PMID:33736957

Peruzzo, C. (2012). Comunicação e terceiro setor [Communication and the third sector]. IN Comunicação Pública. Estado, mercado, sociedade e interesse público. São Paulo: Atlas.

Peterson, R. A., Balasubramanian, S., & Bronnenberg, B. (1997). Exploring the implications of the internet for consumer marketing. *Journal of the Academy of Marketing*, *25*(4), 329–346. doi:10.1177/0092070397254005

Petkova, A. P., Rindova, V. P., & Gupta, A. K. (2013). *No news is bad news: Sensegiving activities, media attention, and venture capital funding of new technology*. Academic Press.

Petty, R. E., & Cacioppo, J. T. (1986). The Elaboration Likelihood Model of Persuasion. In *Communication and persuasión: central and peripheral routes to attitude change* (pp. 1–24). Springer.

Phillips, D., & Young, P. (2009). *Online Public Relations - A Practical Guide to Developing an Online Strategy in the World of Social Media*. Kogan Page.

Phills, J., Deiglmeier, K., & Miller, D. (2008). Rediscovering Social Innovation. *Stanford Social Innovation Review*, *6*(4), 36–42.

PIAUÍ. (2021). https://www.pi.gov.br/noticias/wellington-dias-firma-parceria-com-a-franca-em-evento-de-turismo-sustentavel-pos-covid-19/

Piculell, E., Skär, L., Sanmartin, J., Anderberg, P., & Bohman, D. (2021). A concept analysis of health communication in a home environment: Perspectives of older persons and their informal caregivers. *Scandinavian Journal of Caring Sciences*, *35*(3), 1006–1024. doi:10.1111cs.12928 PMID:33145836

Pinheiro, J. (2009). Semantic Web: A Network of Concepts. *Cadernos UniFOA, 9*, 23-27. Retrieved from: https://revistas.unifoa.edu.br/index.php/cadernos/article/download/930/854

Pinto, P., Brasileiro, F., Antunes, M., & Almeida, A. (2020). COVID-19 no Instagram: Prácticas de comunicação estratégica das autoridades de saúde durante a Pandemia [COVID-19 on Instagram: health authorities' strategic communication practices during the Pandemic]. *Comunicação Pública*, *15*(29), 1–18. doi:10.4000/cp.11288

Pioniri. (2021). *Stanje društvenih medija u Srbiji* [The state of social media in Serbia]. Available at https: //pioniri.com/sr/socialserbia2020/

Plaisime, M., Robertson-James, C., Mejia, L., Núñez, A., Wolf, J., & Reels, S. (2020). Social Media and Teens: A Needs Assessment Exploring the Potential Role of Social Media in Promoting Health. *Social Media + Society*, *6*(January-March), 1–11. doi:10.1177/2056305119886025

PMI. (2017). *A guide to the project management body of knowledge: (PMBOK® guide)*. Project Management Institute.

Poll, H. (2017). *United Airlines' corporate reputation takes a nose dive: Negative perceptions of company's reputation jump 500 percent in April*. Academic Press.

Ponzi, L. J., Fombrun, C. J., & Gardberg, N. A. (2011). RepTrak™ pulse: Conceptualizing and validating a short-form measure of corporate reputation. *Corporate Reputation Review*, *14*(1), 15–35. doi:10.1057/crr.2011.5

Popescu, M., Bodea, R., & Toma, R. (2021). Monitoring Media Pluralism in the Digital Era. Application of the Media Pluralism Monitor in the European Union, Albania, Montenegro, The Republic of North Macedonia, Serbia & Turkey in the year 2020. Country report: Romania. Center for Independent Journalism.

Portal, S., Abratt, R., & Bendixen, M. (2018). Building a human brand: Brand anthropomorphism unravelled. *Business Horizons*, *61*(3), 367–374. doi:10.1016/j.bushor.2018.01.003

Porter, M. (2018). *The second Media Age*. John Wiley & Sons.

Portes, A., & Sensenbrenner, J. (1993). Embeddedness and immigration: Notes on the social determinants of economic action. *American Journal of Sociology*, *98*(6), 1320–1350. doi:10.1086/230191

Porto, A., & Santos, M. (2015). Rio 450 anos: a celebração como estratégia da campanha comemorativa em homenagem à Cidade Maravilhosa [Rio 450 years: the celebration as strategy of the commemorative campaign in honor of the Marvelous City]. In *Congresso Brasileiro Científico de Comunicação Organizacional e de Relações Públicas*. Abrapcorp. Disponível: https://ebooks.pucrs.br/Ebooks/Pdf/978-85-397-0751-5.pdf

Prentice, S., & Huffman, E. (2008). Social medias new role in emergency management. Idaho National Laboratory, 2008, 1-5.

Puzakova, M., Kwak, H., & Rocereto, J. (2009). Pushing the Envelope of Brand and Personality: Antecedents and Moderators of Anthropomorphized Brands. *Advances in Consumer Research. Association for Consumer Research (U. S.)*, *36*, 413–420.

Quéré, L. (2005). "Dispositifs de confiance" dans l'espace public [Confidence-building devices in the public space]. Reseaux, 132.

Qusef, A., & Ismail, K. (2016). *Social Media in Project Communications Management.* Paper presented at the 7th International Conference on Computer Science and Information Technology (CSTT), Amman, Jordan.

Rabahy, W. (2006). Aspectos do turismo mundial, situação e perspectivas desta atividade no Brasil [Aspects of world tourism, situation and perspectives of this activity in Brazil]. *Observatório de Inovação do turismo – Revista Acadêmica, 1*(1).

Rafiqi, H. (2021). *Recreating Marketing Strategies Post Covid-19: The Marketing Word of "New Normal"*. Retrieved from https://bit.ly/3BttdtT <https://bit.ly/3BttdtT>

Rahimi, R., & Kozak, M. (2017). Impact of Customer Relationship Management on Customer Satisfaction: The Case of a Budget Hotel Chain. *Journal of Travel & Tourism Marketing*, *34*(1), 40–51. doi:10.1080/10548408.2015.1130108

Raithel, S., & Schwaiger, M. (2015). The effects of corporate reputation perceptions of the general public on shareholder value. *Strategic Management Journal*, *36*(6), 945–956. doi:10.1002mj.2248

Ramadan, Z. (2017). Examining the dilution of the consumer-brand relationship on Facebook: The saturation issue. *Qualitative Market Research*, *20*(3), 335–353. doi:10.1108/QMR-07-2016-0064

Ramons, C., & Jerónimo, P. (2021). Conferências de Imprensa da Direção Geral de Saúde no Fcaebook: uma análise à interatividade durante a pandemia. [Directorate-General of Health Press conferences on Facebook: an analysis of interactivity during the pandemic]. In F. R. Cádima & I. Ferreira (Coords.), *Perspetivas multidisciplinares da Comunicação em context de Pandemia* (Vol. 1, pp. 126-143). Coleção ICNOVA.

Ramos, C. M., & Casado-Molina, A. M. (2020). Online corporate reputation: A panel data approach and a reputation index proposal applied to the banking sector. *Journal of Business Research*, *122*, 121–130. doi:10.1016/j.jbusres.2020.08.061

Rani, N., Yadav, S. S., & Jain, P. K. (2014). Impact of domestic and cross-border acquisitions on acquirer shareholders' wealth: Empirical evidence from Indian corporate. *International Journal of Business and Management*, *9*(3), 88. doi:10.5539/ijbm.v9n3p88

Rani, S. (2019). Digital marketing and social media – a step to thrive in business, *International Journal of Management, IT & Engineering*, *9*(3), 394–415.

Raposo, J. F. (2020). Comunicação, visibilidade e organizações: reflexões e apontamentos sobre a comunicação organizacional de dados [Communication, visibility and organizations: Reflections and notes on organizational data communication]. In E. Saad (Ed.), *Caminhos da Comunicação: Tendências e Reflexões sobre o Digital* (pp. 83–96). Editora Appris.

Rasmussen, J., & Ihlen, Ø. (2017). Risk, crisis, and social media: A systematic review of seven years' research. *Nordicom Review*, *38*(2), 1–17. doi:10.1515/nor-2017-0393

Ratzan, S. C., & Parker, R. M. (2006). Health literacy—Identification and response. *Journal of Health Communication*, *11*(8), 713–715. doi:10.1080/10810730601031090 PMID:17190778

Rauschnabel, P. A., & Ahuvia, A. C. (2014). You're so lovable: Anthropomorphism and Brand Love. *Journal of Brand Management*, *21*(5), 372–395. doi:10.1057/bm.2014.14

Rawlins, B. L. (2006). *Prioritizing stakeholders for public relations*. Institute for Public Relations.

Ray, A. (2012). *The Methodology of Sampling and Purposive Sampling*. Grin Verlag.

Reardon, M. (2011, September 7). Post 9/11: Can we count on cell networks. *CBS News*. Retrieved 10 August, 2021, from https://www.cbsnews.com/news/post-9-11-can-we-count-on-cell-networks/

Redação Nubank. (2021, June 21). *Anitta is the new board member*. Retrieved from https://blog.nubank.com.br/anitta-nubank-membro-conselho/

Reeder, L., Temple, E., Petheram, L., Marks, K., & Stephens, L. (2016). *Empathy Conversations-Testing their effectiveness as a policy-making instrument: A Pilot Study*. Academic Press.

Reid, C., Davis, H., Horlin, C., Anderson, M., Baughman, N., & Campbell, C. (2013). The Kids' Empathic Development Scale (KEDS): A multi-dimensional measure of empathy in primary school-aged children. *British Journal of Developmental Psychology*, *31*(2), 231–256. doi:10.1111/bjdp.12002 PMID:23659893

Reitz, A. (2012). Social Media's Function in Organizations: A Functional Analysis Approach. Global Media Journal: Canadian Edition, 5(2).

Remidez, H., & Jones, N. B. (2012). Developing a Model for Social Media in Project Management Communications. *International Journal of Business and Social Science*, *3*(3), 33–36.

Reniers, R. L., Corcoran, R., Drake, R., Shryane, N. M., & Völlm, B. (2011). The QCAE: A Questionnaire of Cognitive and Affective Empathy. *Journal of Personality Assessment*, *93*(1), 84–95. doi:10.1080/00223891.2010.528484 PMID:21184334

Renner. (2021). *Meet Rennata*. Retrieved from https://www.lojasrenner.com.br/lp/conheca-rennata

Republički zavod za statistiku [Republican Bureau of Statistics]. (2020). *ICT in Serbia*. Available at: https://www.stat.gov.rs/sr-latn/vesti/20200922-godisnje-istrazivanje-o-ikt/?a=27&s=0

ResearchLive. (2020, October 21). *Edelman relaunches intelligence unit.* Retrieved 05 November, 2021, from https://www.research-live.com/article/news/edelman-relaunches-intelligence-unit/id/5075542

Rexona Brasil [@rexonabrasil]. (2021, March 22). *Should I turn off the faucet when soaping my hands?* Instagram. Retrieved from https://www.instagram.com/p/CMvCXs9jViS/

Ricouer, P. (1994). Tempo e Narrativa [Time and Narrative]. Campinas: Papirus.

Ricouer, P. (2007). Les références du langage [The language references]. Seuil.

Riel, C. B. N. (2014). *Reputação* [Reputation]. Editora Campus.

Ries, L., & Ries, A. (2008). *A queda da Publicidade e a ascensão das Relações-Públicas* [The Fall of Advertising and the Rise of PR] (2ª ed.). Lisboa: Notícias Editorial.

Riess, H. (2017). The Science of Empathy. *Journal of Patient Experience*, *4*(2), 74–77. doi:10.1177/2374373517699267 PMID:28725865

Rim, H., Lee, Y., & Yoo, S. (2020). Polarized public opinion responding to corporate social advocacy: Social network analysis of boycotters and advocators. *Public Relations Review*, *46*(2), 101869. doi:10.1016/j.pubrev.2019.101869

Rindova, V. P., Williamson, I. O., Petkova, A. P., & Sever, J. M. (2005). Being good or being known: An empirical examination of the dimensions, antecedents, and consequences of organizational reputation. *Academy of Management Journal*, *48*(6), 1033–1049. doi:10.5465/amj.2005.19573108

Rival, I. Q. (2020). *Social Media Industry Benchmark Report.* Academic Press.

Rodrigues, W. (2021). *A importância do E-Commerce e das Plataformas Digitais para as PMEs: Uma reflexão à luz do contexto do COVID-19* [The importance of e-commerce and digital platforms for SMEs: A reflection on the light of Covid-19]. Retrieved from https://bit.ly/3lpSX4L <https://bit.ly/3lpSX4L>

Rogers, E. M. (1995). *Diffusion of Innovations* (4th ed.). Free Press.

Rogers, E. M., & Kincaid, D. L. (1981). *Communication Networks: Towards a New Paradigm for Research.* Free Press.

Roozenbeek, J., Schneider, C. R., Dryhurst, S., Kerr, J., Freeman, A. L., Recchia, G., van der Bles, A. M., & van der Linden, S. (2020). Susceptibility to misinformation about COVID-19 around the world. *Royal Society Open Science*, *7*(10), 201199. doi:10.1098/rsos.201199 PMID:33204475

Rosa, K. C. (2020). As experiências sensoriais dos shoppers nas compras virtuais: um estudo sobre o shopstreaming da Dengo Chocolates durante a pandemia de coronavírus [The sensorial experiences of shoppers in virtual shopping: A study about shopstreaming focusing Dengo Chocolats during de Coronavirus pandemic]. Retrieved from: https://bit.ly/3kWdo8F

Rose, S. (2016). *12 Features of a Great Site Search Function.* SilverDisc. Retrieved from: https://www.silverdisc.co.uk/blog/2016/02/19/12-features-great-site-search-function

Rosenstock, I. M., Strecher, V. J., & Becker, M. H. (1988). Social Learning Theory and the Health Belief Model. *Health Education Quarterly*, *15*(2), 175–183. doi:10.1177/109019818801500203 PMID:3378902

Ruão, T., Fernández-Souto, A. B., (2020). Advanced public relations: enhancing a reflexive and educational approach. *Comunicação e Sociedade*, 9-15.

Ruão, T., Marinho, S. & Silva, S. (2020). Scientific report E1.2.1 Software solution requirements for supporting project management processes. *Factory of Future Project.*

Rução, T., Lopes, A., & Pessôa, C. (2018). Gerir identidades e culturas em organizações temporárias: o papel da comunicação [Managing identities and cultures in temporary organizations: the role of communication]. In J. Ferreira & A. T. Peixinho (Eds.), *Narrativas mediáticas e comunicação: construção da memória como processo de identidade organizacional* (pp. 1–19). Imprensa da Universidade de Coimbra.

Rubim, A., Barbalho, A., & Calabre, L. (Org.). (2015). Políticas culturais no governo Dilma [Cultural policies in Dilma's government]. Salvador: Edufba.

Rus, H., & Cameron, L. (2016). Health communication in social media: Message features predicting user engagement on diabetes-related Facebook pages. *Annals of Behavioral Medicine*, *50*(5), 678–689. doi:10.100712160-016-9793-9 PMID:27059761

Rutten, R. (2016). Knowledge Creation in Temporary Organizations. In M. Peris-Ortiz & J. Ferreira (Eds.), *Cooperative and Networking Strategies in Small Business, Innovation, Technology and Knowledge Management*. Springer International Publishing.

Ryan, M., & Martinson, D. L. (1988). Journalists and Public Relations Practitioners: Why the Antagonism? *The Journalism Quarterly*, *65*(1), 131–140.

Ryschka, A. M., Domke-Damonte, D. J., Keels, J. K., & Nagel, R. (2016). The effect of social media on reputation during a crisis event in the cruise line industry. *International Journal of Hospitality & Tourism Administration*, *17*(2), 198–221. doi:10.1080/15256480.2015.1130671

Ryu, K., Han, H., & Kim, T. H. (2008). The relationships among overall quick-casual restaurant image, perceived value, customer satisfaction, and behavioral intentions. *International Journal of Hospitality Management*, *27*(3), 459–469. doi:10.1016/j.ijhm.2007.11.001

Rzymski, P., Borkowski, L., Drąg, M., Flisiak, R., Jemielity, J., Krajewski, J., Mastalerz-Migas, A., Mastalerz-Migas, A., Matyja, A., Pyrc, K., Simon, K., Sutkowski, M., Wysocki, J., Zajkowska, J., & Fal, A. (2021). The strategies to support the COVID-19 vaccination with evidence-based communication and tackling misinformation. *Vaccines*, *9*(2), 109. doi:10.3390/vaccines9020109 PMID:33535716

Sabah Gazetesi. (2020). *Büyük bir bankanın 39 çalışanının müşterilerinin kredi kredi kayıt bilgilerini oto galerici, emlakçı gibi firma ve kişilere el altından para karşılığı sattığı ortaya çıktı* [It turns out that 39 employees of a major bank sell their customers' credit registration information to firms and individuals such as auto dealers and real estate agents for money under the table]. Retrieved from https://tr.sputniknews.com/turkiye/202009071042791613-39-banka-calisani-musteri-bilgilerini-para-karsiligi-oto-galerici-ve-emlakcilara-satmis/

Saboor, F., Jan, M. A., Raheem, T., & Rizwan, M. (2011). Impact of Teenagers on Family Purchase Decisions: Considering the role of Internet. *Journal of Business and Management*, •••, 101–105.

Salaverría, R. (2005). An immature medium. *Gazette The International Journal for Communication Studies*, *67*(1), 69–86. Retrieved 10 August, 2021, from https://dadun.unav.edu/bitstream/10171/5076/1/gazette67_salaverria.pdf doi:10.1177/0016549205049179

Sampaio, A. (2020). Comunicação social em territórios [Social communication in territories]. Salvador: UFBA, Escola de Administração; Superintendência de Educação a Distância.

Sampaio, A. (2012). A marca em produtos midiáticos: o estudo do posicionamento discursivo aplicado ao telejornalismo [The brand in media products: the study of discursive positioning applied to telejournalism]. In *Mídia, discurso e sentido* (pp. 217–236). Edufba.

Sampaio, A., & Caliman, L. (2015). Brasil, "o mundo se encontra aqui": manifestações discursivas da marca país rumo à copa de 2014 [Brazil, "the world meets here": discursive manifestations of the country brand towards the 2014 World Cup]. In *Temas Contemporâneos*. Edufba.

Sampaio, A., & Oliveira, J. (2020). Posicionamento da marca Barcelona. Uma disputa de sentidos entre as nacionalidades espanhola e catalã [Positioning the Barcelona brand. A dispute of senses between the Spanish and Catalan nationalities]. *Organicom*, *17*(32), 2020.

Sanches, R., & Sekles, F. (2008). From country-of-origin and national identity to nation branding - Country Case Insight – Brazil. In *Nation Branding: concepts, issues, practices* (pp. 131–160). Elsevier.

Santaella, L. (2013). *Comunicação ubíqua* [Ubiquitous Communication]. Editora Paulus.

Santora, J. (2021). *13 Influencer Marketing Trends to Watch in 2021*. Influencer Marketing Hub. Retrieved from https://influencermarketinghub.com/influencer-marketing-trends/

Santos, F. de A. O. G. dos. (2018). A *comunicação estratégica em organizações sem fins lucrativos: A Liga Portuguesa Contra o Cancro como estudo de caso* [Strategic communication in non-profit organizations: The Portuguese League Against Cancer as a case study] (Master's thesis). Universidade Nova, Lisboa, Portugal.

Santos, M. (2003). Por uma outra globalização. Do pensamento único à consciência universal [For another globalisation. From the single thought to universal consciousness]. *Record*.

Santos, M. (2009). *Metrópole corporativa fragmentada: o caso de São Paulo* [Fragmented corporate metropolis: the case of São Paulo]. Edusp.

Santos, M. (2014). *O espaço do cidadão* [The citizen's space]. Edusp.

Schaarschmidt, M., Walsh, G., & Evanschitzky, H. (2018). Customer interaction and innovation in hybrid offerings: Investigating moderation and mediation effects for goods and services innovation. *Journal of Service Research*, *21*(1), 119–134. doi:10.1177/1094670517711586

Scheer, L. K., Miao, C. F., & Palmatier, R. W. (2014). Dependence and interdependence in marketing relationships: Meta analytic insights. *Journal of the Academy of Marketing Science*, *43*(6), 694–712. doi:10.100711747-014-0418-1

Scheid, D., Machado, J., & Pérsigo, P. M. (Eds.). (2018). *Estrato de verbetes: dicionário de comunicação organizacional* [Strata of entries: An organizational communication dictionary]. FACOS – UFSM. https://www.ufsm.br/grupos/estrato/publicacoes

Scherer, K. R. (2005). What are emotions? And how can they be measured? *Social Sciences Information. Information Sur les Sciences Sociales*, *44*(4), 695–729. doi:10.1177/0539018405058216

Schiavo, R. (2013). Health Communication. *Theory into Practice*, *217*.

Schiavo, R. (2013). *Health communication: From theory to practice* (Vol. 217). John Wiley & Sons.

Schivinski, B., Christodoulides, G., & Dabrowski, D. (2016). Measuring Consumers' Engagement with Brand-Related Social-Media Content - Development and Validation of a Scale That Identifies Levels of Social-Media Engagement With Brands. *Journal of Advertising Research*, *56*(1), 1–18. doi:10.2501/JAR-2016-004

Schleyer, T. K., & Forrest, J. L. (2000). Methods for the Design and Administration of Web- based Surveys. *Journal of the American Medical Informatics Association: JAMIA*, *7*(4), 416–425. doi:10.1136/jamia.2000.0070416 PMID:10887169

Schreiber, M. (2020). *30 anos da Constituição: a Carta Magna brasileira é generosa demais?* [30 years of the Constitution: is the Brazilian Magna Carta too generous?]. https://www.bbc.com/portuguese/brasil-45754119

Schroeder, P., & Amadeo, B. (2021). Communication Strategy for COVID-19 in Uruguay. In Strategic Communication in Context: Theoretical Debates and Applied Research (pp. 295-322). UMinho Editora. doi:10.21814/uminho.ed.46.13

Schudson, M. (1978). *Discovering the News: a social history of American newspapers*. Basic Books.

Schultz, É., & Ward, J. K. (2021). Public Perceptions of Scientific Advice: Towards a Science Savy Public Culture? *Public Health, 194*, 86–88. doi:10.1016/j.puhe.2021.02.007 PMID:33866149

Schwab, K. (2016). *A quarta revolução industrial* [The fourth industrial revolution]. Edipro.

Schwarzinger, M., & Luchini, S. (2021). Addressing COVID-19 vaccine hesitancy: Is official communication the key? *The Lancet. Public Health, 6*(6), e353–e354. doi:10.1016/S2468-2667(21)00108-0 PMID:33991483

Schwarzl, S., & Grabowska, M. (2015). Online marketing strategies: The future is here. *Journal of International Students, 2*(2), 187–196. doi:10.14254/2071-8330.2015/8-2/16

Schwarzmüller, T. (2018). How Does the Digital Transformation Affect Organizations? Key Themes of Change in Work Design and Leadership. *Management Revue - Socio-Economic Studies, 29*(2), 114-138.

Scolari, C. A. (2013). Más allá de McLuhan: Hacia una ecología de los medios [Beyond McLuhan: Toward a Media Ecology]. In A. Rublescki & E. M. R. Barichello (Eds.), *Ecologia da Mídia* (pp. 33–39). FACOS-UFSM.

Scott, D. M. (2017). The new rules of marketing and PR (6a. ed.). Wiley. Kindle.

Scott, T., Scott, P., Stokes, P., Moore, N., Smith, S. M., & Ward, T. (2015). *Reconceptualising the Consumer Journey in the Digital Age – An Exploratory Study of the United Kingdom Retail Sector.* Retrieved from: https://bit.ly/3HzxQ95

Seeger, M. W. (2006). Best practices in crisis communication: An expert panel process. *Journal of Applied Communication Research, 34*(3), 232–244. doi:10.1080/00909880600769944

Semprini, A. (1992). El marketing de la marca [The marketing of a brand]. In Una aproximación semiótica. Barcelona: Paidós.

Semprini, A. (1996). Analyser la communication [Analysing communication]. In Comment analyser les images, les médias, la publicité. Paris: L'Harmattan.

Semprini, A. (2005). La marque [The mark]. In Une puissance fragile. Paris: Vuibert.

Semprini, A. (2006). A marca pós-moderna. Poder e fragilidade da marca na sociedade contemporânea [The postmodern brand. Power and fragility of the brand in contemporary society]. São Paulo: Estação das Letras.

Semprini, A. (2000). *CNN et la mondialisation de l'imaginaire* [CNN and the globalisation of the imagination]. CNRS.

Sen, R., & Borle, S. (2015). Estimating the contextual risk of data breach: An empirical approach. *Journal of Management Information Systems, 32*(2), 314–341. doi:10.1080/07421222.2015.1063315

Seo, E., & Park, J. (2018). A study on the effects of social media marketing activities on brand equity and customer response in the airline industry. *Journal of Air Transport Management, 66*, 36–41. doi:10.1016/j.jairtraman.2017.09.014

Serrat, O. (2017). The Future of Social Marketing. Springer. doi:10.1007/978-981-10-0983-9_17

Sharma, S., Singh, S., Kujur, F., & Das, G. (2021). Social Media Activities and Its Influence on Customer-Brand Relationship: An Empirical Study of Apparel Retailers' Activity in India. *Journal of Theoretical and Applied Electronic Commerce Research, 16*(4), 602–617. doi:10.3390/jtaer16040036

Shedden, D. (2015, January 15). *Today in media history: 2009 Hudson River crash-landing photo sent with Twitter.* Poynter Institute. Retrieved 10 August, 2021, from https://www.poynter.org/reporting-editing/2015/today-in-media-history-2009-hudson-river-crash-landing-photo-sent-with-twitter/

Shenhar, A. J., & Dvir, D. (1996). Toward a typological theory of project management. *Research Policy*, *25*(4), 607–632. doi:10.1016/0048-7333(95)00877-2

Shi, H., Wang, Y., Huisingh, D., & Wang, J. (2014). On moving towards an ecologically sound society: With special focus on preventing future smog crises in China and globally. *Journal of Cleaner Production*, *64*, 9–12. doi:10.1016/j.jclepro.2013.07.024

Shirbagi, N. (2007). Exploring Organizational Commitment and Leadership Frames within Indian and Iranian Higher Education Institutions. *Bulletin of Education & Research*, *29*(1), 17–32.

Shirky, C. (2011). *The political power of social media: Technology, the public sphere, and political change. Foreign affairs.* Available at: http://sites.asiasociety.org/womenleaders/wp-content/uploads/2010/05/The-Political-Power-of-Social-Media-Foreign-Affairs2.pdf

Siegel, E. (2017). *Análise preditiva* [Predictive analysis]. Editora Alta Books.

Silva, D. W., & Baldissera, R. (2019). Comunicação organizacional e as estratégias de invisibilidade e de redução/direcionamento da visibilidade nas mídias sociais [Organizational communication and the strategies for invisibility and reduction/guidance of visibility in social media]. *Organicom, 16*, 15-26. https://www.revistas.usp.br/organicom/article/view/163239

Silva, D. W., & Baldissera, R. (2020). Comunicação organizacional e estratégias de direcionamento da visibilidade nas mídias sociais [Organizational communication and visibility targeting strategies on social media]. *ECCOM*, 11(22), 187 – 199. http://unifatea.com.br/seer3/index.php/ECCOM/article/view/1123

Silva, S. T. M. (2010). *Relações públicas: história e contextualizações* [Public relations: history and contextualizations]. Interprogramas de Mestrado das Faculdades Cásper Líbero. Retrieved 10 August, 2021, from https://casperlibero.edu.br/wp-content/uploads/2014/04/Sandro-Takeshi-Munakata-da-Silva.pdf

Silveirinha, M. J. (2002). *Novos Media, Velhas Questões* [New Media, Old Issues]. BOCC - Biblioteca Online de Ciências da Comunicação. Retrieved from: http://bocc.ufp.pt/pag/silveirinha-maria-joao-novos-media-velhas-questoes.pdf

Silvius, G. (2016). Social Project Management? In G. Silvius (Ed.), *Strategic Integration of Social Media into Project Management Practice* (pp. 207–293). IGI Global. doi:10.4018/978-1-4666-9867-3.ch017

Siomkos, G. J., & Kurzbard, G. (1994). The hidden crisis in product-harm crisis management. *European Journal of Marketing*, *28*(2), 30–41. doi:10.1108/03090569410055265

Slade-Brooking, C. (2016). *Creating a Brand Identity- A Guide for Designers.* Laurence King Publishing Ltd.

Slate.com. (2020). *The Daily News Twitter account was tampered with after mass layoffs.* https://slate.com/technology/2018/07/the-daily-newss-twitter-account-was-tampered-with-after-mass-layoffs.html

Sleeping Giants Brasil. (2021, June 28). *#desmonetizasikera*. Twitter. Retrieved from https://twitter.com/slpng_giants_pt/status/1409529130195038209

Sneader, K., & Singhal, S. (2020). *Além do coronavírus: o caminho para o próximo normal* [Beyond coronavirus: The path to the new normal]. Retrieved from https://mck.co/3cz9fUi

Sneader, K., & Singhal, S. (2021). *O novo normal chegou: tendências que definirão 2021 - e o futuro* [The new normal is here: trends that will define 2021 - and the future]. Retrieved from https://mck.co/3mGVoiM

Soares, T. (2005). Os Meios de Comunicação Social na Internet: Contributos para a Análise Sociológica dos Cibermedia [The Means of Social Communication on the Internet: Contributions to the Sociological Analysis of Cybermedia]. *Livro de actas - 4º SOPCOM*, 1485-1494. Retrieved from: http://www.bocc.ubi.pt/pag/soares-tania-meios-comunicacao-social-internet.pdf

Socialbakers. (2020). *State of Social Media Report: The Impact of COVID-19*. Retrieved from https://bit.ly/3qQhQHV

Sodré, M. (2002). *Antropológica do Espelho - Uma Teoria da Comunicação Linear e em Rede* [Mirror Anthropology - A Theory of Linear and Networked Communication]. Editora Vozes.

Sodré, M. (2013). *Antropológica do espelho: uma teoria da comunicação linear e em rede* [Anthropology of the mirror: A linear network theory of communication] (8th ed.). Vozes.

Sodré, M. (2019). Between institution and organization. In J. Ferreira, J. L. Braga, P. G. Gomes, A. F. Neto, & A. P. Rosa (Eds.), *Between what we say and what we think: Where is mediatization?* (pp. 265–274). FACOS-UFSM. https://repositorio.ufsm.br/bitstream/handle/1/19692/betweenwhatwesayandwhatwethink.pdf

Sofranec, D. (2016). 5 Tips for Handling Bad Online Reviews. *Pest Management Professional*, *84*(11), 74.

Souza, S., Pitombo, T., Zaccaria, R., & Monteiro, T. (2018). Social Responsibility and Social Marketing at Monsanto. *Responsabilidade Social e Marketing Social na Monsanto.*, *8*(2), 6–20.

Stacks, D., & Bowen, S. (2013). *Dictionary of Public Relations Measurement and Research.* IPR Measurement Commission. Institute for Public Relations.

Stanković, U., Ćurčić, N., & Dragićević, V. (2010). On-line promotivne tehnike kao faktor unapređenja promotivnih mogućnosti veb sajtova [Online promotional techniques as a factor in improving the promotional capabilities of websites]. *Ekonomske teme, 3,* 421-435.

Statista Global Consumer Survey. (2021). *The influence of influencers*. Instagram. Retrieved from https://www.instagram.com/p/CPa8AahLuJV/

Statista. (2021). *Global digital population as of January 2021*. Available at: https://www.statista.com/statistics/617136/digital-population-worldwide/

Statista. (2021, September 24). *Forecast number of mobile devices worldwide from to 2020 to 2025*. Retrieved 05 November, 2021, from https://www.statista.com/statistics/245501/multiple-mobile-device-ownership-worldwide/#:~:text=In%20 2021%2C%20the%20number%20of,devices%20compared%20to%202020%20levels

Statista.com. (2020). *Share of U.S. adults who use social media 2019, by age*. https://www.statista.com/statistics/471370/us-adults-who-use-social-networks-age/

Stepien, K. A., & Baernstein, A. (2006). Education for Empathy: A Review. *Journal of General Internal Medicine*, *21*(5), 524–530. doi:10.1111/j.1525-1497.2006.00443.x PMID:16704404

Stockdale, R., & Standing, C. (2004, August). Benefits and barriers of electronic marketplace participation: An SME perspective. *Journal of Enterprise Information Management*, *17*(4), 301–311. Advance online publication. doi:10.1108/17410390410548715

Storlie, C. B., Pollock, B. D., Rojas, R. L., Demuth, G. O., Johnson, P. W., Wilson, P. M., Heinzen, E. P., Liu, H., Carter, R. E., Habermann, E. B., Kor, D. J., Neville, M. R., Limper, A. H., Noe, K. H., Bydon, M., Franco, P. M., Sampathkumar, P., Shah, N. D., Dunlay, S. M., & Dowdy, S. C. (2021). Quantifying the Importance of COVID-19 Vaccination to Our Future Outlook. *Mayo Clinic Proceedings*, *96*(7), 1890–1895. doi:10.1016/j.mayocp.2021.04.012 PMID:34218862

Strähle, J., & Gräff, C. (2017). The Role of Social Media for a Sustainable Consumption. In Green Fashion Retail. Springer.

Strecher, V. J., McEvoy DeVellis, B., Becker, M. H., & Rosenstock, I. M. (1986). The role of self-efficacy in achieving health behavior change. *Health Education Quarterly*, *13*(1), 73–92. doi:10.1177/109019818601300108 PMID:3957687

Strecher, V. J., & Rosenstock, I. M. (1997). *The Health Belief Model*. Jossey-Bass.

Sturges, D. L. (1994). Communicating through crisis: A strategy for organizational survival. *Management Communication Quarterly*, *7*(3), 297–316. doi:10.1177/0893318994007003004

Sunstein, C. R. (2017). A prison of our own design: divided democracy in the age of social media. Academic Press.

Surugiu, R. (2016). The Fragile Professional Identities of Digital Journalists in Romania. In J. Webster & K. Randle (Eds.), *Virtual Workers and the Global Labour Market* (pp. 179–198). Palgrave Macmillan.

Syed-Abdul, S., Fernandez-Luque, L., Jian, W., Li, Y., Crain, S., Hsu, M., Wang, Y., Khandregzen, D., Chuluunbaatar, E., Nguyen, P. A., & Liou, D. M. (2013). Misleading health-related information promoted through video-based social media: Anorexia on YouTube. *Journal of Medical Internet Research*, *15*(2), 30. doi:10.2196/jmir.2237 PMID:23406655

Taber, K. (2017). The Use of Cronbach's Alpha When Developing and Reporting Research Instruments in Science Education. *Research in Science Education*, *48*(6), 1273–1296. doi:10.100711165-016-9602-2

Tansey, J., & O'riordan, T. (1999). Cultural theory and risk: A review. *Health Risk & Society*, *1*(1), 71–90. doi:10.1080/13698579908407008

Tansley, A. G. (1935). The use and abuse of vegetational concepts and terms. *Ecology*, *16*, 284–307.

Tench, R., & Bridge, G. (2021). Developing effective Health Communication Campaigns. In Strategic Communication in Context: Theoretical Debates and Applied Research (pp. 69-86). UMinho Editora. doi:10.21814/uminho.ed.46.4

Terra, C. F. (2009, September 4-7). A comunicação organizacional em tempos de redes sociais on-line e de usuários-mídia [Organizational communication in times of online social networks and users-media]. *Intercom IX Encontro dos Grupos/Núcleos de Pesquisa em Comunicação, evento componente do XXXII Congresso Brasileiro de Ciências da Comunicação.* Retrieved 10 August, 2021, from http://www.carolterra.com.br/wp-content/uploads/2015/06/Artigo_Intercom2009.pdf

Terra, C. F. (2011). *Mídias sociais...e agora?* [Social media... now what?]. Difusão Editora.

Terra, C. F. (2011). *O que as organizações precisam fazer para serem bem vistas nas mídias sociais sob a ótica da Comunicação Organizacional e das Relações Públicas* [What organizations need to do to be well-viewed on social media from the perspective of Organizational Communication and Public Relations]. The meeting of Abrapcorp 2011, Brazil. Retrieved 10 August, 2021, from http://www.carolterra.com.br/wp-content/uploads/2015/06/Abrapcorp-2011.pdf

Terra, C. F. (2017). From broadcast to socialcast: notes on the long tail of digital influence. Communicare Magazine, 17, 80-95.

Terra, C. F. (2011). *Social Media...Now What? What you need to know to implement a social media project*. Difusão Publishing House.

Terra, C. F. (2018). Content producer user. In D. Scheid, J. Machado, & P. M. Pérsigo (Eds.), *Strata of entries: dictionary of organizational communication* (p. 128). FACOS-UFSM.

Terra, C. F. (2019). Influência digital: oportunidade para a comunicação organizacional [Digital influence: An opportunity for organizational communication]. In D. Scheid, J. Machado, & P. M. Pérsigo (Eds.), *Tendências em comunicação organizacional: Temas emergentes no contexto das organizações* (pp. 22–37). FACOS – UFSM. https://www.ufsm.br/grupos/estrato/publicacoes

Terra, C. F. (2020). Publishers de conteúdo no ambiente digital: as marcas no papel de influenciadoras digitais [Content publishers in the digital environment: Brands in the role of digital influencers]. In E. Saad (Ed.), *Caminhos da Comunicação: Tendências e Reflexões sobre o Digital* (pp. 97–112). Editora Appris.

Terra, C. F. (2021). *Digital influencer brands: How to transform organizations into digital content producers*. Difusão Publishing House.

The Online Newsroom Survey Report. (2012). *TekGroup*. Retrieved from: https://www.tekgroup.com/online-newsroom/list-of-things-journalists-expect-in-online-newsroom.htm

Thelwall, M. (2000). Effective Websites for Small and Medium-Sized Enterprises. *Journal of Small Business and Enterprise Development*, *7*(2), 149–159. doi:10.1108/EUM0000000006836

Thenextweb.com. (2012). *Starbucks apologizes to its Argentine customers on Twitter and Facebook, creates PR crisis.* https://thenextweb.com/la/2012/07/16/starbucks-apologizes-to-its-argentine-customers-on-twitter-and-facebook-creates-pr-crisis/

Thompson, J. B. (2008a). *A mídia e a modernidade. Uma teoria social da mídia* [The Media and Modernity. A Social Theory of the Media] (10th ed.). Vozes.

Thompson, J. B. (2008b). A nova visibilidade [The new visibility]. *MATRIZes*, *1*(2), 15–38. doi:10.11606/issn.1982-8160.v1i2p15-38

Thompson, J. B. (2020). Mediated Interaction in the Digital Age. *Theory, Culture & Society*, *37*(1), 3–28. doi:10.1177/0263276418808592

Tironi, E., & Cavallo, A. (2006). *Comunicación Estratégica: Vivir em um mundo de señales* [Strategic Communication: Living in a world of signs]. Taurus.

Toffler, A. (2014). *A terceira onda* [The third wave]. Editora Record.

Tormo, M. J., & Banegas, J. R. (2001). Mejorar la comunicación de riesgos en Salud Pública: sin tiempo para demoras [Improve risk communication in Public Health: no time for delays]. *Revista Española de Salud Pública, 75*(1). http://scielo.isciii.es/scielo.php?script=sci_arttext&pid=S1135-57272001000100001&lng=es&tlng=es

Tow, W., Dell, P., & Venable, J. (2010). Understanding information disclosure behavior in Australian Facebook users. *Journal of Information Technology*, *25*(2), 126–136. doi:10.1057/jit.2010.18

Triantafillidou, A., & Yannas, P. (2020). Social media crisis communication in racially charged crises: Exploring the effects of social media and image restoration strategies. *Computers in Human Behavior*, *106*, 106269. doi:10.1016/j.chb.2020.106269

Tripp, D. (2005). Pesquisa-ação: Uma introdução metodológica [Action research: a methodological introduction]. *Educação e Pesquisa*, *31*(3), 443–466. doi:10.1590/S1517-97022005000300009

Trivinho, E. R. (2011). Visibilidade mediática, melancolia do único e violência invisível na cibercultura [Media visibility, melancholy of the unique and invisible violence in cyberculture]. *MATRIZes*, *4*(2), 111–125. doi:10.11606/issn.1982-8160.v4i2p111-125

Tugrul, T. (2014). Brand experience effects on consumer social media marketing perceptions and brand value. *Journal of Global Strategic Management*, *8*(2), 39–47.

Túñez-López, M., Costa-Sánchez, C., & Valdiviezo, C. (Eds.). (2018). *Comunicación Organizacional en entornos online: gestión, actores y recursos* [Organizational Communication in Online Enviroments: Management, Actors and Resources]. Sociedad Latina de Comunicación Social. http://www.cuadernosartesanos.org/2018/cac149.pdf

Tunstall, J. (1971). *Journalists at Work: specialist correspondents: their news organizations, news sources, and competitor-colleagues*. Constable London.

Turner, J. R., & Müller, R. (2003). On the nature of the project as a temporary organization. *International Journal of Project Management*, *21*(1), 1–8. doi:10.1016/S0263-7863(02)00020-0

Tuten, T. L., & Solomon, M. (2012). *Social Media Marketing*. Sage.

Twitter.com. (2012). https://twitter.com/search?q=%23McDStories%20&src=typed_query

Ulmer, R. R., Sellnow, T. L., & Seeger, M. W. (2011). Defining crisis communication. *Effective Crisis Communication Moving From Crisis to Opportunity*, 2-24.

Ulmer, R. R., Seeger, M. W., & Sellnow, T. L. (2007). Post-crisis communication and renewal: Expanding the parameters of post-crisis discourse. *Public Relations Review*, *33*(2), 130–134. doi:10.1016/j.pubrev.2006.11.015

Unicef.org. (2020). *Keeping the world's children learning through COVID-19*. https://www.unicef.org/coronavirus/keeping-worlds-children-learning-through-covid-19

Untila Kaplan, O. (2019). *Media literacy in a changing process in Turkey. 11th International Conference on Electronics, Computers and Artificial Intelligence (ECAI)*, Pitesti, Romania. 10.1109/ECAI46879.2019.9042089

Uruguay Presidencia. (2021, January 23). *Gobierno adquirió 3,75 millones de vacunas contra la COVID-19 y aspira a inocular a 2,8 millones de personas* [The Goverment acquired 3.75 millon vaccines against Covid-19 and aims to inoculate 2.8 milion people]. https://www.gub.uy/presidencia/comunicacion/noticias/gobierno-adquirio-375-millones-vacunas-contra-covid-19-aspira-inocular-28

USAID. (2020). *Anketa "1000 preduzeća"* [Survey "1000 companies"]. Available at: https://saradnja.rs/wp-content/uploads/2020/11/Anketa-1000-preduze%C4%87a-2020.pdf

Utz, S., Schultz, F., & Glocka, S. (2013). Crisis communication online: How medium, crisis type and emotions affected public reactions in the Fukushima Daiichi nuclear disaster. *Public Relations Review*, *39*(1), 40–46. doi:10.1016/j.pubrev.2012.09.010

Vacunas: el FA suma presión al gobierno con nuevas críticas por falta de transparencia [Vaccines: the FA adds pressure to the government with new criticism for lack of transparency]. (2021, February 19). *El Observador*. https://www.elobservador.com.uy/nota/frente-amplio-vuelve-a-la-carga-por-las-vacunas-y-reclama-por-su-llegada-202121817480

Van Dalen, A. (2020). Journalism, Trust, and Credibility. In K. Wahl-Jorgensen & T. Hanitzsch (Eds.), *The Handbook of Journalism Studies* (2nd ed., pp. 356–371). Routledge.

Van Djick, J. (2013). Facebook and the engineering of connectivity: a multi-layered approach to social media platforms. *Convergence: The International Journal of Research into New Media Technologies*. https://journals.sagepub.com/doi/abs/10.1177/1354856512457548

Van Djick, J. (2019). *The platform society: An interview with José van Dijck*. DigiLabour Research Group. https://digilabour.com.br/2019/03/06/a-sociedade-da-plataforma-entrevista-com-jose-van-dijck/

Van Riel, C. B., & Fombrun, C. J. (2007). *Essentials of corporate communication: Implementing practices for effective reputation management*. Routledge. doi:10.4324/9780203390931

Velasquez, A. (2018). From the mass media to social media: reflections on the new media ecology. *Revista Latina de Comunicación Social*, *73*, 583-594. Retrieved from: http://www.revistalatinacs.org/073paper/1270/29en.html

Verčič, A. T., Verčič, D., & Sriramesh, K. (2012). Internal communication: Definition, parameters, and the future. *Public Relations Review*, *38*(2), 223–230. doi:10.1016/j.pubrev.2011.12.019

Verón, E. (2013). La semiosis social, 2. Ideas, momentos, interpretantes [Social Semiosis, 2. Ideas, Moments, Interpreters]. Buenos Aires: Paidós Planeta.

Verón, E. (1983). *Il est là, je le vois, il me parle. Communications* [He is there, I see him, he speaks to me. Communications]. Academic Press.

Verón, E. (1985). *L'analyse du "contrat de lecture": une nouvele methode pour les etudes de positionnement des supports presse* [The "reading contract" analysis: a new method for media positioning studies]. IREP.

Verón, E. (1997). Esquema para el análisis de la mediatización [An approach to analysing mediatization]. *Revista Diálogos de la Comunicacion*, *48*, 9–16.

Victoria's Secret [@victoriassecret]. (2021, June 16). *VS Collective*. Instagram. Retrieved from https://www.instagram.com/p/CQMruB5n9jx/

Vidas-Bubanja, M. (2021). Uticaj pandemije COVID -19 na digitalnu transformaciju privrede Srbije [The impact of the COVID-19 pandemic on the digital transformation of the Serbian economy]. *Ekonomski vidici, 1-2*, 47-62.

Vidas-Bubanja, M., & Madžar, L. (2019). Importance of Innovation and Knowledge for Economic Development of the Country and the Competitive Business of Company. *Journal of Social Sciences*, *11*(11), 157–173.

Villena, F., & Souto-Pérez, J. E. (2016). Sustainability, innovative orientation and export performance of manufacturing SMEs: An empirical analysis of the mediating role of corporate image. *Journal of Industrial Engineering and Management*, *9*(1), 35–58.

Vizer, E., & Carvalho, H. (2013). La metáfora ecológica em la era de la mediatizacion [The ecological metaphor in the era of mediatization]. In A. Rublescki & E. M. R. Barichello (Eds.), *Ecologia da Mídia* (pp. 41–58). FACOS-UFSM.

Vries, R. E., Bakker-Pieper, A., & Ostenveld, W. (2010). Leadership = Communication? The Relations of Leaders' Communication Styles with Leadership Styles, Knowledge Sharing and Leadership Outcomes. *Journal of Business and Psychology*, *25*(3), 367–380. doi:10.100710869-009-9140-2 PMID:20700375

Vries, R. E., Bakker-Pieper, A., Siberg, R. A., Gameren, K., & Vlug, M. (2009). The Content and Dimensionality of Communication Styles. *Communication Research*, *36*(2), 178–206. doi:10.1177/0093650208330250

Vukmirović, V., Domazet, I., & Kostić-Stanković, M. (2020). Personalized Social Media Communication based on Millennials' Attitudes. *Conference Proceedings - International Scientific Conference Strategic Management and Decision Support Systems in Strategic Management*, 97-103. 10.46541/978-86-7233-386-2_13

Vuuren, M., Jong, M., & Seydel, E. R. (2006). Direct and indirect effects of supervisor communication on organizational commitment. *Corporate Communications: An International Journal of Business and Management*, *12*(2), 116–128. doi:10.1108/13563280710744801

Waddington, S. (2012). *Share This - The Social Media Handbook for PR Professionals*. Wiley. doi:10.1002/9781119207856

Walker, K. (2010). A systematic review of the corporate reputation literature: Definition, measurement, and theory. *Corporate Reputation Review*, *12*(4), 357–387. doi:10.1057/crr.2009.26

Walsh, G., & Beatty, S. E. (2007). Customer-based corporate reputation of a service firm: Scale development and validation. *Journal of the Academy of Marketing Science*, *35*(1), 127–143. doi:10.100711747-007-0015-7

Wang, C. S., Lin, S. L., Chou, T. H., & Li, B. Y. (2019). An integrated data analytics process to optimize data governance of non-profit organization. *Computers in Human Behavior*, *101*, 495–505. doi:10.1016/j.chb.2018.10.015

Wang, L., Schuetz, C. G., & Cai, D. (2020). Choosing Response Strategies in Social Media Crisis Communication: An Evolutionary Game Theory Perspective. *Information & Management*, 103371.

Wang, Y., & Laufer, D. (2020). How does crisis management in China differ from the West?: A review of the literature and directions for future research. *Journal of International Management*, *26*(1), 100708. doi:10.1016/j.intman.2019.100708

Wardle, C. (2019, October 21). Information disorder: "The techniques we saw in 2016 have evolved". *First Draft*. Retrieved 10 August, 2021, from https://firstdraftnews.org/articles/information-disorder-the-techniques-we-saw-in-2016-have-evolved/

Waszak, P., Kasprzycka-Waszak, W., & Kubanek, A. (2018). The spread of medical fake news in social media–the pilot quantitative study. *Health Policy and Technology*, *7*(2), 115–118. doi:10.1016/j.hlpt.2018.03.002

Waters, R., Tindall, N., & Morton, T. (2010). Media Catching and the Journalist–Public Relations Practitioner Relationship: How Social Media are Changing the Practice of Media Relations. *Journal of Public Relations Research*, *22*(3), 241–264. doi:10.1080/10627261003799202

Waytz, A., Cacioppo, J., & Epley, N. (2010). Who Sees Human? The Stability and Importance of Individual Differences in Anthropomorphism. *Perspectives on Psychological Science*, *5*(3), 219–232. doi:10.1177/1745691610369336 PMID:24839457

We are social. (2021). *Digital 2021 Global overview report*. Retrieved 10 August, 2021, from https://wearesocial-cn.s3.cn-north-1.amazonaws.com.cn/common/digital2021/digital-2021-global.pdf

Webb, A. (2019). *The big nine*. Hachette Book Group.

Weick, K. E. (1979). *The Social Psychology of Organizing*. Random House.

Weiner, B. (2010). Attribution theory. *The Corsini encyclopedia of psychology*, 1-2.

Weiner, M. (2021). *PR Technology, Data and Insights - Igniting a Positive return on Your Communications Investment*. Kogan Page.

Wei, Y. K. (2002). Corporate image as collective ethos: A poststructuralist approach. *Corporate Communications*, *7*(4), 269–276. doi:10.1108/13563280210449859

Wepener, M., & Boshoff, C. (2015). An instrument to measure the customer-based corporate reputation of large service organizations. *Journal of Services Marketing*, *29*(3), 163–172. doi:10.1108/JSM-01-2014-0026

What's The Story? (n.d.). *The 2013 Newsroom Report: how the world's top 100 brands are using online newsrooms to tell their stories*. MyNewsdesk. Retrieved from: https://pages.mynewsdesk.com/rs/mynewsdesk/images/The%202013%20Newsroom%20Report%20by%20Mynewsdesk.pdf

Whatmough, D. (2019). *Digital PR. PRCA practice guides*. Emerald Publishing Limited.

Wiard, V. (2019). *News Ecology and News Ecosystems. In Oxford Research Encyclopedia of Communication*. Oxford University Press.

Wiedmann, K. P., & Buxel, H. (2005). Corporate reputation management in Germany: Results of an empirical study. *Corporate Reputation Review*, *8*(2), 145–163. doi:10.1057/palgrave.crr.1540246

Wiencierz, C., & Roetgger, U. (2019, May). Big data in Public Relations: A Conceptual Framework. *The Public Relations Journal*, *12*(3). Retrieved August 10, 2021, from https://prjournal.instituteforpr.org/wp-content/uploads/Wiencierz-Roettger_Big-Data-in-Public-Relations-A-Conceptual-Framework_PR-Journal.pdf

Wieseke, J., Geigenmüller, A., & Kraus, F. (2012). On the role of empathy in customer-employee interactions. *Journal of Service Research*, *15*(3), 316–331. doi:10.1177/1094670512439743

Wispé, L. (1986). The distinction between sympathy and empathy: To call forth a concept, a word is needed. *Journal of Personality and Social Psychology*, *50*(2), 314–321. doi:10.1037/0022-3514.50.2.314

Wong, C., Merchant, R., & Moreno, M. (2014). Using social media to engage adolescents and young adults with their health. *Health Care*, *2*(4), 220–224. PMID:25984444

World Economic Forum. (2019). *The Global Competitiveness Report 2019*. Available at:https://www.weforum.org/reports/how-to-end-a-decade-of-lost-productivity-growth

WTTC. (2021). *Economic impact reports*. Disponível em: https://wttc.org/Research/Economic-Impact

Wu, S. I., & Hung, J. M. (2008). A performance evaluation model of CRM on non-profit organizations. *Total Quality Management*, *19*(4), 321–342. doi:10.1080/14783360701591978

Yadav, M., & Rahman, Z. (2017). Measuring consumer perception of social media marketing activities in e-commerce industry: Scale development & validation. *Telematics and Informatics*, *34*(7), 1294–1307. doi:10.1016/j.tele.2017.06.001

Yadav, R., Dokania, A. K., & Pathak, G. S. (2016). The influence of green marketing functions in building corporate image. *International Journal of Contemporary Hospitality Management*, *28*(10), 2178–2196. doi:10.1108/IJCHM-05-2015-0233

Yang, L. W., Aggarwal, P., & McGill, A. L. (2019). The 3 C's of anthropomorphism: Connection, comprehension, and competition. *Counselling Psychology Review*, *3*(1), 3–19.

Yim, F. H. K., Anderson, R. E., & Swaminathan, S. (2004). Customer relationship management: Its dimensions and effect on customer outcomes. *Journal of Personal Selling & Sales Management*, *24*(4), 263–278.

Yin, R. (2001). *Estudo de caso: planejamento e métodos* [Case Studies: Planning and methods]. 2nd ed.). Bookman.

Yin, R. K. (2009). *Case Study Research. Design and Methods* (4th ed.). Sage.

Youpix. (2021). *ROI and Influence 2021*. Retrieved from https://drive.google.com/file/d/1qbOuD6mJvBhPoFDv0LyNnDYUpPBwP8ko/view

Zappavigna, M. (2012). *Discourse of Twitter and social media: How we use language to create affiliation on the web* (Vol. 6). A&C Black.

Zeithaml, A., Dwayne, G., & Bitner, M. (2014). *Os Fundamentos do Marketing de Serviços* [The Fundamentals of Services Marketing]. McGraw-Hill.

Zerfass, A. (2021). *ECM - The European Communication Monitor 2021*. Retrieved from: https://www.communication-monitor.eu/2021/05/21/ecm-european-communication-monitor-2021/

Zerfass, A., & Huck, S. (2007). Innovation, Communication, and Leadership: New Developments in Strategic Communication. *International Journal of Strategic Communication*, *1*(2), 107–122. doi:10.1080/15531180701298908

Zhang, Y., & Wiersema, M. F. (2009). Stock market reaction to CEO certification: The signaling role of CEO background. *Strategic Management Journal*, *30*(7), 693–710. doi:10.1002mj.772

Zheng, B., Bi, G., Liu, H., & Lowry, P. B. (2020). Corporate crisis management on social media: A morality violations perspective. *Heliyon*, *6*(7), e04435. doi:10.1016/j.heliyon.2020.e04435 PMID:32715127

Zheng, B., Liu, H., & Davison, R. M. (2018). Exploring the relationship between corporate reputation and the public's crisis communication on social media. *Public Relations Review*, *44*(1), 56–64. doi:10.1016/j.pubrev.2017.12.006

Zhou, Q., Valiente, C., & Eisenberg, N. (2003). Empathy and Its Measurement. In S. J. Lopez & C. R. Snyder (Eds.), *Positive psychological assessment: A handbook of models and measures* (pp. 269–284). American Psychological Association. doi:10.1037/10612-017

Zhu, C., Xu, X., Zhang, W., Chen, J., & Evans, R. (2020). How health communication via Tik Tok makes a difference: A content analysis of Tik Tok accounts run by Chinese Provincial Health Committees. *International Journal of Environmental Research and Public Health*, *17*(1), 192. doi:10.3390/ijerph17010192 PMID:31892122

Živadinović, V., & Zelić, M. (2014*). Uticaj online-tržišta i digitalnih tehnologija na reputaciju preduzeća* [The impact of online markets and digital technologies on a company's reputation]. Infoteh-Jahorina. Available at: https://infoteh.etf.ues.rs.ba/zbornik/2014/radovi/RSS-3/RSS-3-4.pdf

Zuboff, S. (2019). *The age of surveillance capitalism*. PublicAffairs Hachette Book Group.

Zuckoff, M. (2019). *Fall and rise: The story of 9/11*. Harper.

Zyl, A. S. (2009). The impact of Social Networking 2.0 on organisations. *The Electronic Library*, *27*(6), 906–918. doi:10.1108/02640470911004020

About the Contributors

José Gabriel Andrade is a researcher and professor on media, marketing and communication at the University of Minho. José holds a European PhD in Communication Sciences from the Catholic University of Portugal with the support of the Portuguese Foundation for Science and Technology, Fundação para a Ciência e a Tecnologia (FCT) and a Master in Communication Sciences: Communication, Organisation and New Technologies from the Portuguese Catholic University, Universidade Católica Portuguesa - UCP, with the support of the high level scholarship Program of the European Union for Latin America (Alban). He coordinated the master's degree on Digital Communication and integrated the structure responsible for quality management, internships, communication and interface with the community at the University, actively participating in the professional and personal development of the students.

Teresa Ruão is senior lecturer in the Communication Sciences Department at the University of Minho and Pro-Rector for Institutional Communication, since 2021. She has held several positions within the University of Minho over the years. Notably, she served as Vice-President of the Institute of Social Sciences and President of the Pedagogical Council between 2010 and 2019; and was Vice-Head of the Communication and Society Research Centre from 2019 to 2021. Within the university context, she was also a member of the Academic Senate, the QMS Monitoring Committee and the Alumni Council. She has a PhD in Communication Sciences (2008) from the University of Minho and researches on Organizational and Strategic Communication. Develops teaching activities in the field of Organizational Communication and Public Relations. She is a member of the Portuguese Communication Sciences Association (Sopcom) and was a board member of its Organizational Communication Work Group for 10 years. She is also a member of ECREA, IAMCR, and a regular reviewer for ICA, the most important international associations in her field of investigation. She has been an evaluator for the Portuguese Foundation for Science and Technology, since 2017, and for the Portuguese Agency for Assessment and Accreditation of Higher Education, since 2018. As a researcher, she has been a member of several research projects, has published numerous books, papers, scientific reports and was a speaker in several national and international congresses.

* * *

Paulo Cardoso is a PhD in Advertising and Public Relations from the Autonomous University of Barcelona. Assistant Professor at the Lusíada University of Porto and Associate Professor at Fernando Pessoa University, he teaches in the areas of Marketing and Communication. He is a researcher at COMEGI (Center for Research in Organizations, Markets and Industrial Management).

Patricia Dias is a PhD in Communication Sciences by Universidade Católica Portuguesa, Patrícia Dias coordinates the post-graduate course Social Brands - Communication and Marketing in the Digital Environment. In 2019, she was a visiting researcher at the Arctic University of Norway. Researcher at CECC and CRC-W, she currently coordinates the project "0-3 DigiKids - Use of Touchscreen Devices by Children up to 3 years old" and leads the Portuguese team of the project "Use of Digital Technologies by Children and Teenagers during the COVID-19 Pandemic in Europe", coordinated by the JRC-European Commission. Her main research interests are the use of digital media by children and also within organizational communication, marketing and branding. She is the author of several publications about the social impact of digital media and the use of smartphones.

Ivana Domazet is a Principal Research Fellow at the Institute of Economic Sciences and Professor at the Faculty for Banking, Insurance and Finance, Union University. She teaches courses on Marketing Management, Market Research and Competitiveness Enhancement (postgraduate studies). Her scientific interest refers to: Improving Competitiveness, National Branding, Marketing Research and Strategy, CRM and Strategic Management. She published a numerous papers related to foregoing topics. She is President of Scientific Council at the Institute of Economic Sciences, Vice-president of Board member of the Institute of Economics Sciences, Board member of the Institute of Social Science, member of Serbian Scientific Association of Economists and Serbian Marketing Association.

Alexandre Duarte, with a PhD in Communication Sciences from University of Minho, a Master degree in Communication & Image and a Bachelor in Marketing & Advertising by IADE, is the Ruler of several classes in Universidade Católica Portuguesa and in IADE/Universidade Europeia, visiting Professor in other Universities, researcher of the R&D Unit CECS from Universidade do Minho, and Course Coordinator of OFICINA de PORTFOLIO™. Throughout his career, Alexandre had the opportunity to work for several multinational advertising agencies, in Portugal and Brazil, such as TBWA, Saatchi & Saatchi, Ogilvy, W/Portugal, W/Brazil, Lowe&Partners, or BrandiaCentral as a Senior Creative Copywriter. Author of many seminars on communication, regularly participates in different conferences and lectures in both business and academic contexts. It is the former Communications Director of the Portuguese Federation of Krav Maga, Text Editor of the Surf Magazine SOUP and occasionally collaborates with many other academic and professional media. Between 2012 and 2014, was the Tutor of the EUROBEST Young Marketers Academy and in the beginning of 2014, was appointed CEO of RESTART, an Institute of Creativity, Arts and New Technologies. In 2018 was invited to teach in the Communication Sciences Master of Universidade Católica Portuguesa, where now Coordinates the Post-Graduation Courses in Advertising&Creativity and Service Design and, in 2019 was re-elected member of the Directors Board of EDCOM - European Institute for Commercial Communications Education.

Manuel José Fonseca, PhD in Information Sciences, was born in Lisbon in 1971. He played professional activities such as marketing communications technician and professor of higher education. He is currently adjunct Professor at the Polytechnic Institute of Viana do Castelo (Portugal) and Coordinator of the Marketing Master's degree at its Business School (ESCE-IPVC). He is a researcher at UNIAG (Applied Management Research Unit, since 2014).

Priscila Krolow is co-founder and manager of Tr3s Comunicação. She has been working with advertising for over 10 years in Brazil and Portugal. Master in Digital Communication at Catholic University of Portugal (UCP), PhD student in Communication Sciences at Catholic University of Portugal (UCP). Her research interests are digital marketing and communication strategies, social media marketing, digital influencers.

Marija Lazarević-Moravčević is a Research Associate at the Institute of Economic Sciences in Belgrade and an associate professor at the Faculty for Banking, Insurance and Finance, Union University, Belgrade. At the faculty, she is engaged in courses in the field of Business Economics and Management: Strategic Management, Marketing Principles, Integrated Marketing Communications and Sales Management. Her scientific interest refers to: strategic management, management of small and medium enterprises and market communication. She is the author and co-author of several scientific and professional papers published in domestic and international publications. She has participated in the realization of a significant number of scientific studies and research projects.

Sandra Marinho is a Lecturer in the Communication Sciences Department at the University of Minho and Vice-Head of the Communication and Society Research Centre (CECS). She has a PhD in Communication Sciences (2012) from the University of Minho, where she teaches Research Methods and Communication Theories. Her main research area is Journalism Education.

Kevser Meral is a PhD candidate in Advertising and Public Relations in Bahçeşehir University, Istanbul, expected to graduate in 2020. She has completed her BA in Boğaziçi University in Philosphy and completed her master degree in Boğaziçi University, Master of Arts Program in International Relations: Turkey, Europe, and the Middle East. She speaks English, French (graduated from Notre Dame de Sion French High School) and German.

Sara Oliveira is a twenty-two-year-old university student. In 2020 she graduated in Marketing at the University of Minho and then, in that same year, entered a Master's Degree in Digital Communication at the Portuguese Catholic University. In 2021, she collaborated with the School of Economics and Management of the University of Minho in a digital project for the dynamization of the communication network and the consequent management of their social media, for a period of six months. Finally, as part of a curricular internship, she collaborates with Juventude Cruz Vermelha where she is studying the brand's communication strategies.

Sandra Pereira is Lecturer and Coordinator of the Master in Strategic Management of Public Relations at ESCS.

Daiane Scheid has been a Professor of Communication (especially in the Public Relations area) for over 10 years. She has worked at the University of Caxias do Sul, Brazil and currently works in the Department of Communication Sciences at the Federal University of Santa Maria (UFSM), on the campus of Frederico Westphalen/RS, Brazil. She holds a Ph.D. degree in Communication from UFSM, and has recently completed her Postdoctoral Studies at the Center for Communication and Society Studies at the University of Minho, Portugal. She is a researcher at EstratO (Organizational Media Strategies), a Research Group that has been developing studies to contribute to the Organizational Communication Area. She works mainly on the following topics: Organizational and Strategic Communication, Visibility and Media, and Public Relations.

Patricia Schroeder is a Professor of Strategic Communication and Crisis Communication at the University of Montevideo and guest lecturer at universities in Portugal, Peru, Paraguay, Ecuador, Colombia and Chile. Director of the Master in Communication Management. Specialised in communication with a strategic and global focus, covering analysis and development in public affairs, internal communication and marketing communication. Communication consultant in the area of health, international organisations, educational institutions, NGOs and service companies in general. Currently communication advisor at the Ministry of Public Health. Currently pursuing a doctoral programme (Faculty of Communication, Austral University). Research on communication in complex medical procedures at the third level of care. Master in Communication Management in Organisations (Austral University). Strategic Management and Trade Planning (School of Business, Georgetown University). Research on communication and health: communication in complex medical procedures at the third level of care, communication management of the Covid-19 pandemic.

Sonia Silva is a Lecturer at UTAD and member of the Communication and Society Research Centre (CECS). She has a PhD thesis in Communication Sciences (2020) from the University of Minho and teaches and researches mainly in the area of Strategic Communication.

Romina Surugiu is Associate Professor of Journalism and Media Studies, and Vice Dean of the Faculty of Journalism and Communication Studies, University of Bucharest. She holds a PhD in Philosophy from the University of Bucharest (2006), and worked as a postdoctoral researcher in Communication Studies at the University of Bucharest (2010-2013), and at the Uppsala University (2012). She has published/coordinated research on journalism practice and specialised journalism, on the dynamics of work and gender in the media, and on the history of the European television. She served as a board member of Romanian Public Television. She was a management committee member of the EU COST Action on the Dynamics of Virtual Work IS 1202 (2012-2016, chair: Professor Ursula Huws). She is active member of the Board of RN 18 Sociology of Communications and Media Research, European Sociological Association.

Carolina Terra has a postdoctoral degree, is a doctor, master and specialist from University of São Paulo (USP); Public relations majored in Stadual University of São Paulo. Leader of the Influcom research group, at Cásper Líbero University, and part of Com+, another research group USP. She has worked for companies such as FIAT, Vivo, MercadoLivre, Agência Ideal, Garoto and Nestlé. Currently, she is a researcher, consultant and professor. She is also editor of the RPalavreando Blog (http://rpalavreando.com.br).

Index

H

I

J

L

M

N

O

P

R

S

T

V

W

www.ingramcontent.com/pod-product-compliance
Lightning Source LLC
LaVergne TN
LVHW081251011026
849162LV00006BA/1481

9781799897903